MEDIATRIX

MEDIATRIX

Mediatrix

Women, Politics, and Literary Production in Early Modern England

JULIE CRAWFORD

OXFORD
UNIVERSITY PRESS

OXFORD

UNIVERSITY PRESS

Great Clarendon Street, Oxford, OX2 6DP,
United Kingdom

Oxford University Press is a department of the University of Oxford.
It furthers the University's objective of excellence in research, scholarship,
and education by publishing worldwide. Oxford is a registered trade mark of
Oxford University Press in the UK and in certain other countries

First Edition published in 2014

Impression: 1

Published in the United States of America by Oxford University Press
198 Madison Avenue, New York, NY 10016, United States of America

British Library Cataloguing in Publication Data
Data available

Library of Congress Control Number: 2014936274

ISBN 978–0–19–871261–9

Printed and bound by
CPI Group (UK) Ltd, Croydon, CR0 4YY

Acknowledgements

There are many people to whom I owe thanks. I hope my deep indebtedness to the feminist scholars who first took early modern women as their subject are apparent both in the book itself and in its notes. In particular, *Mediatrix* would not exist if it were not for the groundbreaking work of Margaret P. Hannay, Mary Ellen Lamb, Linda Levy Peck, Barbara Lewalski, David Norbrook, and Josephine A. Roberts, only one of whom I am lucky enough to know. Two universities provided the means and support for much of the work in this book, Simon Fraser University, where I taught for two years, and Columbia University. I owe special thanks to the chairs at both the institutions, Betty Schellenberg and Tom Grieve at SFU, and David Scott Kastan and Jean Howard at Columbia. I am also grateful to SSHRC (under the aegis of SFU) and to the Lenfest family, both of which provided me with much-appreciated recognition and much-needed funds. Thanks also to the research assistants who helped with this project, including Frederick Bengtsson, Bryan Lowrance, Ivan Lupic, Alexander Lash, and, especially, Emily Madison. Above all, my thanks to the people at Oxford University Press, particularly Jacqueline Baker, Rachel Platt, Saipriya Kannan, and the excellent copy editor Jane Robson. I am also enormously grateful to my students, both graduate and undergraduate, majors and non. Jean Howard has been a huge supporter of me and my work for many years now and I wish I had words to register how grateful I am for her support, example, and collegiality. Special thanks also go to Alan Stewart and Molly Murray; I cannot imagine better early modern colleagues. Molly's own work on Donne, and her scrupulous editing of mine, made a huge impact on Chapter 3. I also offer thanks to other Columbia/Barnard colleagues, particularly Lila Abu Lughod, Rachel Adams, Katherine Biers, Yvette Christiansë, Sarah Cole, Susan Crane, Nick Dames, Jenny Davidson, Brent Hayes Edwards, Katherine Franke, Achsah Guibbory, Saidiya Hartman, Marianne Hirsch, Eleanor Johnson, Sharon Marcus, Edward Mendelson, Christia Mercer, Roz Morris, Bruce Robbins, Paul Strohm, and Colm Tóibín (who came up with the title for my book). Many fellow scholars in the field have supported my work, both directly and indirectly. While I wish I could thank them all, and feel crushed at the prospect of leaving some unnamed— particularly those who wrote tenure letters for me and have not yet identified themselves—I want to thank: Margreta De Grazia, Fran Dolan, Margie Ferguson, Gil Harris, Hilary Hinds, Mary Ellen Lamb, Christina

Luckyj, Thomas Luxon, Arthur Marotti, Jeff Masten, Madhavi Menon, Maureen Quilligan, Phyllis Rackin, Bill Sherman, Kathryn Schwarz, Laurie Shannon, Peter Stallybrass, Valerie Traub, Micheline White, and Susan Wiseman. The scholars to whom I owe the greatest debt, however, are the members of my two writing groups: Mary Bly, Mario DiGangi, Will Fisher, and Natasha Korda; and Pamela Brown, Bianca Calabresi, Natasha Korda (again), Bella Mirabella, Tanya Pollard, Nancy Selleck, and, for a time we all now look upon as a great gift, Sasha Roberts. Their generous and exacting work made mine better. Pam and Bianca, in particular, were tireless supporters of this book. If one could dedicate a chapter of a book to someone without looking cheap, I would dedicate Chapter 1 to Bianca; it wouldn't be what it is without her. I also want to thank my family. Each of my mother's sisters and her brother, who not only read the first book but had interesting things to say about it, has expressed ongoing interest in my work. My parents have provided more forms of support than I could name, not least the confidence (sometimes merited) that good parenting provides. I am also grateful for the support of my siblings and their families, particularly my brother Patrick who is either genuinely interested in my work or fakes it really well. My final thanks go to my chosen people, particularly Giselle Anatol, Christina Antonick, Sara Beam, Valerie Berlin, Mary Bly, Andrew Botterell, Juliette Cherbuliez, Álvaro Enrigue, Rhonda Frederick, Jen Harvie, Hilary Hinds, Jane Hunter, Dee Hurt, Nora Jaffary, Phil Joseph, Rayna Kalas, Deb Kilbride, Rue Landau, Valeria Luiselli, Vanessa Martin, Bill Mathews, Ann McDermott, Cynthia Miller, Inez Murray, Molly Murray, Amy Rutkin, Gillian Silverman, Kerry Smith, Jackie Stacey, Aoibheann Sweeney (twice), Alessandro Vettori, and, for hours of running and intellectual exchange, Molly Tambor. I am, in the end, most grateful to those who live with me—and thus with my projects. Liza has read my work on what she calls "The Cow's Arcadia" for many years now. Her labor—both in reading my work and, as crucially, in providing the circumstances that enabled me to write it—is a gift second in greatness only to her character. Jonas prefers Milton to the authors I write about here, but he likes seeing my name in print regardless. I am grateful that he thinks writing books is a good way to spend time. During (what should have been) the final stages of writing this book, Maeve was born, and she is wonderful in every way. She is also four years old. This book is dedicated, accordingly, to all working mothers, but chief among them, because I love her best, Elizabeth Anne Yukins. As John Donne wrote to Lucy Harington Russell, "to admit / No knowledge of your worth, is some of it."

Contents

List of Illustrations

Introduction

In a letter John Donne wrote to Sir Henry Goodere in the early years of his courtship of Lucy Harington Russell, Countess of Bedford, as his patron, he pondered whether she was the "proper Mediatrix" to present his case to the necessary people.[1] His term evoked Bedford's status as an influential go-between in early Jacobean political and literary circles, and thus her ability to serve as an intermediary on his behalf ("mediatrix," *OED*).[2] But "Mediatrix" was also the term the catechism of the Catholic Church used for the Virgin Mary, the preeminent mediator between God and humankind.[3] To some extent such language of intercession was normative at the time; James I's investment in the divine right of kings helped to produce a corollary set of courtier "saints" or intermediaries who promised would-be acolytes that they would intervene on their behalf with their God-like king.[4]

---

[1] Donne, *Letters to Several Persons of Honor*, 193.

[2] Other terms used for the women who served in such semi-official political capacities in early modern England included "go-betweens" (Peck) and "almoners of ways" (Stone). Donne's term, however, captures the textual aspect of the work of such mediators. For other uses of the term "mediatrix," see the English translation of the letter by Jean-Louis Guez, seigneur de Balzac, "To Madam DESLOGES" (*A Collection of Some Modern Epistles of Monsieur de Balzac: Carefully Translated Out of French* (1639), 152); and the first volume of Holinshed's *Chronicles*, which refers to multiple women as "Mediatrix" (*The firste [laste] volume of the chronicles of England* (1577), 875, 912, 1701). In Bartholomew Yong's translation of Montemayor's *Diana*, Felicia, the "seruant and minister in the Temple of chaste Diana," also refers to herself as a "mediatrix," telling the "noble Disteus" that the Gods "haue deyned to humble themselues without any merit of mine, to make a mediatrix for thee." *Diana of George of Montemayor: Translated Out of Spanish into English by Bartholomew Yong of the Middle Temple* (London, 1598), 312. The term also appears frequently in romances. In Charles Sorel's *The extravagant shepherd, the anti-romance, or, The history of the shepherd Lysis translated out of French* (1653), "Amaryllis" serves as a "mediatrix" in defense of romances ("The Oration of AMARYLLIS, mediating for Romances," 77–8).

[3] See e.g. A.G., *The vviddoues mite cast into the treasure-house of the prerogatiues, and prayses of our B. Lady, the immaculate, and most glorious Virgin Mary, the Mother of God* (Saint-Omer: English College Press, 1619): "By him we beg of thee, that thou wilt intercede for vs to him, that we may liue in his feare, and dye in his fauour: and that as heere we haue the comfort to enioy thee, as our chiefe Mediatrix of Intercession towards him; so with thee & at thy feet, we may prayse, and glorify him in al eternity, as our only Mediatour of Redemption" (165).

[4] See Linda Levy Peck, "Benefits, Brokers and Beneficiaries." I discuss this argument further in Ch. 3.

Yet Donne's use of a term as charged with Mariolatry as "Mediatrix" also alluded, with characteristic irony, to his own well-known Catholic origins, and, in a slightly more confrontational way, to Bedford's reputation as a particularly godly, even puritan, Protestant. Donne's use of "Mediatrix" was thus both honorific—an acknowledgement of Bedford's cultural and political influence—and provocative, configuring a bond between them that was at once material (he wanted her financial support) and dialogic. It was also necessarily and acutely conscious of the other activities in which Bedford was involved, and the other media in which she worked. Each of the women discussed in this book can be characterized as a "Mediatrix" in much the same way as Donne characterized Bedford: politically and culturally powerful, but with an edge of oppositionism; at once a patron to be honored and a force to be reckoned with; a maker of texts and a maker of careers.

Mediatrix is predicated on a now decades-long history of scholarship on early modern women writers. This history is characterized by books whose titles blazon their authors' and editors' politics and intentions, including *The Paradise of Women* (1981), *Reason's Disciples* (1982), *First Feminists* (1985), *Redeeming Eve* (1987), *Oppositional Voices* (1992), and *Writing Women* (1993).[5] Many feminist scholars of the 1980s and 1990s put the work of women writers in dialogue with what they saw as the pervasive patriarchal and misogynist discourse of the time; as Elaine V. Beilin put it, "The nature of woman, her duties, and her limitations, were topics constantly in the air" (*Redeeming Eve*, p. xviii). Yet in arguing that women's writing served as an (often) effective form of political resistance to what were undoubtedly powerful discourses, these critics often gave those discourses too much credit. As Phyllis Rackin has argued, to claim that misogyny was "everywhere" in the period serves, in unintended ways, to encourage us to find it everywhere.[6] Such arguments also placed women's writing, seemingly incontrovertibly, in dialogue with debates and discourses about "women's nature" and "women's authorship," assumptions that pardoxically delimited its scope.[7]

[5] *The Paradise of Women* was edited by Betty Travitsky; *First Feminists* by Moira Ferguson; and *The Renaissance Englishwoman in Print* by Anne M. Haselkorn and Betty S. Travitsky. Elaine V. Beilin wrote *Redeeming Eve*; Tina Krontiris *Oppositional Voices*; and Barbara Lewalski *Writing Women in Jacobean England*. Louise Schleiner wrote *Tudor and Stuart Women Writers* in 1994. Many of these scholars rightly give due to earlier projects of feminist reclamation, notably the work of Ruth Hughey, "Cultural Interests of Women in England from 1524–1640: Indicated in the Writings of the Women" (1932); and Charlotte Kohler, "The Elizabethan Woman of Letters" (1936). While I am indebted to all of these authors, *Mediatrix* could not have been written without the work of Margaret P. Hannay, whose work on Mary Sidney Herbert and Mary Sidney Wroth informs the arguments in Chs 1 and 4.

[6] See Phyllis Rackin, "Misogyny is Everywhere." "Reminders that women were expected to be chaste, silent, and obedient," Rackin argues, "probably occur more frequently in recent scholarship than they did in the literature of Shakespeare's time" (44).

[7] Wendy Wall has also questioned the naturalness of creating a category of "women writers." "Do a 1630s petitioner to Parliament, a 1590s queen, and an urban Tudor

Yet the women who produced literary texts in the early modern period did not do so primarily in order to "find a voice" in print, nor to make cultural space for such a phenomenon as "the woman writer." Their motivations for writing and publishing literary texts were as varied as those of men: they wrote for literary experimentation and pleasure; for fame, or its mitigation; for economic survival and socioeconomic ambition; for friends, supporters, and communities; for purposes of criticism and advice. The same can be said, moreover, of the women who supported writers, and those who were their readers. Margaret J. M. Ezell pointed out years ago that printed texts represent only a fraction of the ways in which women participated in literary culture, and subsequent work on coterie and communal manuscript literary production has revealed the startling range of women's literary practices.[8] I want to suggest here that we can see this work in acts of patronage and literary dedications as well.

In the preface to her translation of Diego Ortúñez de Calahorra's Spanish romance, *The Mirrour of Princely deedes and Knighthood* (1578), Margaret Tyler defends her act of translating a secular romance with the claim "that it is all one for a woman to pen a story, as for a man to address his story to a woman."[9] Feminist scholars have focused on Tyler's preface, particularly this line, as the earliest feminist defense of women's writing.[10] Yet in the excitement of finding an early modern woman defending women's use of the pen, scholars ignored the hinge clause of Tyler's claim. The parallel that

serving woman have enough in common to allow us to generalize about them?" she asks ("Circulating Texts in Early Modern England," 49). As Wall points out, if we question this category, and the idea that all women writers were proto-feminists (in our own model), "Women writers may no longer fit the pattern of heroic liberal subjects valiantly fighting patriarchy." But, she adds, the "trade-off is that their work allows for a more historically accurate picture of the circumstances in which gender functions as a social force" (50).

[8] Ezell, "'To Be Your Daughter in Your Pen': The Social Functions of Literature in the Writings of Lady Elizabeth Brackley and Lady Jane Cavendish." For recent work on women's activities as authors and co-authors, manuscript compilers, verse collectors, and keepers of commonplace books, see *The Verse Miscellany of Constance Aston Fowler*; *The Southwell-Sibthorpe Commonplace Book*; and *English Manuscript Studies 1100–1700*, ix. *Writings by Early Modern Women*. Many of these activities took place in family circles and homes: Sir John Harington's daughters, Frances and Ellina, transcribed poems in one manuscript, and William Cavendish's daughters co-authored a manuscript collection of verses and plays. On the Harington family, see Arthur F. Marotti, *Manuscript, Print and the English Renaissance Lyric*, 26; and on the Cavendish family, Ezell, "'To Be Your Daughter in Your Pen.'"

[9] *The Mirroir of Princely deedes and Knighthood*, A4ᵛ.

[10] Moira Ferguson calls the preface "the first explicitly feminist argument published by a woman...in English," and Tina Krontiris discusses it as a radical empowerment of the woman writer (*First Feminists*, 52; *Oppositional Voices*, 44–9). Mary Ellen Lamb argues that Tyler's claim foregrounds "the significance of women's reading as a condition of their writing," acknowledging the importance of women's reading even as she subordinates it to writing, but goes on to argue that most early modern constructions of women readers "were designed to deny women the independent subjectivity that lies at the core of authorship" ("Constructions of Women Readers," 24).

Tyler draws between a man addressing a story to a woman and a woman penning a story is predicated on the idea that texts and textual meanings are produced by both writers and their addressees, and in moments of consumption as well as creation. Her subsequent observation that women have a particular relationship to "such workes, as appeare in their name" indicates how seriously such dedications were taken in the period, and hints at the collaborative nature of literary production more generally.[11] Many early modern authors characterized their patrons and dedicatees as co-authors of their work. In one of his many dedications to Mary Sidney Herbert, for example, Samuel Daniel claimed that his "Rhymes" were a joint project, "Begotten by [her] hand, and [his] desire."[12] Rather than mere hyperbole, claims like Daniel's tell us something crucial about a mode of literary production in which the productive (and contentious) collusion of supporting, creating, transcribing, and reading literary texts lay at the core of authorship. The women identified in the titles of and epistolary dedications to texts such as *The Countess of Pembroke's Arcadia* were thus neither merely titular nor ornamental. Nor, for that matter, were they necessarily subordinate to other more important concerns, such as the author's seeking of recognition or preference from sources far more powerful (and presumptively male) than the dedicatee herself.[13] More than mere flattery, authors' solicitation and interpellation of women patrons and readers was often part of an ongoing engagement with the causes in which those women were actively and vitally involved. Indeed in many cases, the production of literature was itself a form of activism.

[11] In their dedications to women, Tyler suggests, male authors "minde not onely to borrowe names of worthie personages, but the testimonies also for their further credite, which neither the one may demaund without ambition, nor the other graunt with out ouerlightnesse" (A4ʳ). It is, in other words, both a serious, and a reciprocal, business. "If women be excluded from the viewe of such workes, as appeare in their name," she goes on to ask, "or if glorie onely be sought in our common inscriptions, it mattereth not whether the partyes be men or women, whether aliue or dead." Like writing, in other words, reading is a vital ("aliue") part of of literary production.

[12] Samuel Daniel, "To the Right Honorable, the Lady Mary, Countesse of Pembrooke," prefatory sonnet to the 1594 edn of *Delia*, cited in Hannay, *Philip's Phoenix*, 118:

> Great Patrones of these my humble Rymes
> Which thou from out thy greatnes doost inspire:
> Sith onely thou hast deign'd to rayse them higher,
> Vouchsafe now to accept them as thine owne,
> Begotten by thy hand, and my desire. (sig. A2)

Mary Sidney Herbert presented the psalms she and her brother translated to the Queen in "both our names" (Hannay, *Philip's Phoenix*, 91).

[13] As Juliet Fleming has argued, texts, even when addressed to women, could be part of a homosocial agenda—men promoting the interests of men—and indifferent to or critical of the women they ostensibly addressed. "The Ladies' Man and the Age of Elizabeth." See also Patricia Parker's discussion of the forms of triangulation in which a woman becomes "the enabling matter of male discourse" (*Literary Fat Ladies*, 132).

The four chapters in *Mediatrix* are devoted to four interrelated communities in which noted mediatrixes played central roles, and to the texts they produced. The first centers on Mary Sidney Herbert, the Sidney alliance, and *The Countess of Pembroke's Arcadia*; the second on Margaret Hoby's community of readers in recusant Yorkshire and the godly texts her reading kept alive; the third on the circle surrounding Lucy Harington Russell, Countess of Bedford, and John Donne's verse letters and occasional poems; and the last on Mary Wroth, the Sidney-Herbert alliance, and *The Countess of Montgomery's Urania*. While many of the women who appear in the pages of the book are familiar figures in feminist literary history, I look at their contributions to early modern culture less in terms of their gender or their seemingly discrete roles as writers, patrons, or readers, than in terms of their religious and political affiliations and commitments. The four communities I discuss were related to each other not only by birth and marriage, but by their engagement with the cause loosely identified as militant Protestantism, represented in the late sixteenth and early seventeenth centuries primarily by the Sidney and Herbert families and their allies, and advanced in no small part by the production and circulation of literary texts.[14] By looking at the work these communities produced, as well as the places in and the means by which they did so, I argue not only that women played a central role in the production of some of England's most important literary texts, but that the work they produced was an essential part of the political, as well as the literary, culture of early modern England.

I. COMMUNITIES, COTERIES, AND ALLIANCES

Society must always consist among two or more.

(T.E., *The Lawes Resolutions of Women's Rights*, 1632)

In proposing the mediatrix as indispensible to the political world of early modern England, I am also proposing a particular view of social and political life, one centered on structures that scholars alternately term "communities,"

---

[14] These relations are complex. Margaret Hoby had been married to a Devereux and a Sidney before she married Sir Thomas Posthumous Hoby, and was related by marriage to Lucy Harington Russell; Harington Russell, in turn, was related to the Sidneys (her paternal grandmother was Lucy Sidney, the aunt of Sir Philip Sidney and Mary Sidney Herbert), and was allied in court and parliament with William Herbert, Mary Sidney Herbert's son and Mary Wroth's cousin and lover. Harington Russell was also Mary Wroth's godmother, and Dorothy Percy, Dorothy Devereux's daughter, married Wroth's brother Robert Sidney. While the nexus of familial, marital, and dynastic relationships is a tight one, this book is more concerned with the religious, political, and intellectual interests and causes shared by these communities, despite their regional and, to a lesser extent, temporal distance from one another.

"coteries," and "alliances." Larger than the "little commonwealth" of marriage, and smaller than the body politic of the nation, these structures of affiliation were at once heuristics of interpretation, and materially real; indeed it is precisely this duality that makes them such interesting subjects of study.[15] In revisiting the claim that the restricted, patriarchal, nuclear family was the primary basis of social organization in the period, scholars have turned their attention to the extended household and to wider kinship and affinity networks: communities that cohered around shared familial, regional, socioeconomic, religious, and political interests.[16] Frequently, the production of literature was both an expression of a given community's interests and a means of promoting them.[17] Among other things, the production of literature helped to create and sustain exclusive societies: what Earl Miner calls "the little society of the good few."[18] Philip Sidney's dedication of the *Arcadia* to his sister, as well as his frequent appeals to women readers throughout the text itself, suggest that his romance was intended to affirm, entertain, and solicit the interpretive attention of a community of readers. Literary production also helped to shore up or confirm threatened or minority values. Margaret

---

[15] Many scholars question the usefulness of the concept of "community" altogether. Alan Macfarlane claims that community is a "heuristic concept," and Judith Scherer Herz points out that coteries and communities can be no more than the function of a critic's desire or imagination, "less found objects than artifacts of the discovery process, constructed to serve varied critical, theoretical and historical ends" (*Reconstructing Historical Communities*, 4; "Of Circles, Friendship, and the Imperatives of Literary History," 15). In "Literary Circles and Communities," I argue that, whether or not a given circle existed (in a particular form), contemporaries nonetheless conceived of it as such, imagining it into a kind of textual, and thus cultural, existence.

[16] For the "restricted patriarchal nuclear family," see Lawrence Stone, *The Family, Sex and Marriage*, 409–11. On kinship, see Miranda Chaytor, "Household and Kinship," and David Cressy, "Kinship and Kin Interaction." On communities, see Phil Withington and Alexandra Shepard (eds), *Communities in Early Modern England*. In *Incest and Agency*, Maureen Quilligan has recently argued that endogamy was a way in which families maintained and entrenched power, and that women—particularly women writers—used that power for their own ends.

[17] On literary communities in general, see Claude J. Summers and Ted-Larry Pebworth (eds), *Literary Circles and Cultural Communities in Renaissance England*: "Most often the literary circle is defined as a coterie whose members are linked by shared social, political, philosophical, or aesthetic interests or values, or who vie for the interests and attention of a particular patron, or who are drawn together by bonds of friendship, family, religion or location" ("Introduction," 1–2). On specific literary communities, see Sandra A. Burner, *James Shirley: A Study of Literary Coteries and Patronage in Seventeenth Century England*; Mary Hobbs, *Stoughton Manuscript: A Manuscript Miscellany of Poems by Henry King and his Circle*; B. H. Newdigate, *Michael Drayton and his Circle*; Arthur F. Marotti, *John Donne, Coterie Poet*; and Katherine Duncan-Jones, *Philip Sidney: Courtier Poet*. The Sidney family and circle has benefited from a particularly impressive number of studies, including Michael Brennan, *Literary Patronage in the English Renaissance* (1988); Mary Ellen Lamb, *Gender and Authorship in the Sidney Circle* (1990); Margaret P. Hannay, *Philip's Phoenix* (1990); and Gary Waller, *The Sidney Family Romance* (1993).

[18] Miner, *The Cavalier Modes from Jonson to Cotton*, 275.

Hoby's reading of puritan books in largely recusant Yorkshire, for example, endeavored to keep those ideas an active part of the regional and national conversations. Community is often seen as a positive term (Raymond Williams calls it a "warmly persuasive word"), but communities are, and were, nonetheless always marked by debate and conflict.[19] The production of literary texts could thus also challenge members of a given community to better adhere to a set of values.[20] When Mary Wroth invoked Susan Herbert and Mary Sidney Herbert in her romance, she was certainly imagining a same-sex "concentrate" of loyalty and political prudence particular to women, and useful for the purposes of political critique.[21] But she was also evoking the alliance between their families more generally, and attempting to shore up their commitment to a political cause.[22] Like the communities that produced them, literary texts were often more than merely affirmative; they were dialogic, contentious, even confrontational.[23] The communities discussed in this book produced a great deal of exciting and innovative literature, but they were by no means simply mutually supportive or hermetically sealed cultural enclaves. Regardless of the shared sympathies of their constituencies, they were made up of people who were at once allies and disputants, their very

---

[19] Raymond Williams, *Keywords*, 76. Withington and Shepard similarly refer to the term's vagueness and "rhetorical warmth" (*Communities in Early Modern England*, 2). On conflict as a defining feature rather than occasional side-effect of community, see Bob Scribner, "Communities and the Nature of Power." As Scribner writes, "concepts of community embodied universal, virtually hegemonic values, that led everyone to seek to appropriate them in social and political power plays in order to tilt the moral balance in their favour, or at least to disarm or comfort opponents" (317).

[20] On the ways in which coterie literary production serves "to confirm threatened social values and relationships," see Margaret J. M. Ezell, *Social Authorship and the Advent of Print*, 39.

[21] Laurie Shannon argues that chastity, configured as same-sex bonds, "harbors a heroic femininity similar to the 'gender concentrate' of male friendship," and thus that it is similarly useful as a limit case to male tyranny (*Sovereign Amity*, 69).

[22] Both Sidney and Wroth specifically alluded to female communities of readers within their respective romances, but their appeals were as strategic as they were flattering. Each author's understanding of the importance of women to their own literary and social ambitions was matched by their recognition that women's relationships were as politically engaged as those between men. Susan Frye and Karen Robertson use "alliance"—a term which "denotes a formally recognized relationship activated or chosen to the political advantage of its members"—in order to highlight the explicitly political aspects of the cultural networks forged by and between women. See the "Introduction" to Susan Frye and Karen Robertson (eds), *Maids and Mistresses, Cousins and Queens*, 4–5. As an example of such support, in the period following Walter Ralegh's imprisonment for treason, his wife, Elizabeth Throckmorton, relied on the help of other women. One of her petitioning letters to Robert Cecil included a list of eighteen women's names that clearly served to buttress her claims and illustrate her network of support (Robertson, "Tracing Women's Connections from a Letter by Elizabeth Ralegh").

[23] Literary coteries thus did not just "cohere social bonds among like-minded readers" (Ezell, *Social Authorship*, 42). As William H. Sherman puts it, every textual event represents "the voices of [an] argument" (*John Dee*, 58). Harold Love similarly claims that "the impetus

nature marked as much by conflict as by consensus. Rather than private and elite literary "coteries" exempt from wider political meanings, the communities I discuss in this book are best understood in terms of their religious and political commitments, of which the production and circulation of literary texts was an integral part.

Most of the interrelated communities I discuss here have been grouped under various aegeses before. Linda Levy Peck describes them as an "affinity network"; Mervyn James as an "oppositionist group"; Margaret P. Hannay as an "alliance"; and S. L. Adams as a "puritan faction."[24] The compound hyphenation of what is often refered to as the "Sidney alliance"'s reputed leaders—Leicester-Sidney-Essex-Herbert—goes some way towards explaining both its genealogy and its constituents, even as it marginalizes the women who were, as I argue here, often its anchoring forces and symbolic representatives. The alliance is often seen as having its origins under Robert Dudley, Earl of Leicester in the 1570s, centering for periods on Philip Sidney (d. 1586), Robert Devereux, Earl of Essex (d. 1601), and Prince Henry (d. 1612), and ending under the leadership of William Herbert, Earl of Pembroke, whose turn to Parliament signaled both an irreversible shift in English politics, and the end of the alliance's particular kind of activism.[25] While it was no means monolithic, nor, for that matter, consistent in either membership or approach, the alliance was committed to several things: a militant and internationalist Protestantism; a limited or mixed monarchy, particularly the political

to initiate an exchange of texts within a community (or to create a new community out of the exchange of texts) would frequently have a motive that was either reformist or reactionary" (*Scribal Publication*, 177, 179).

[24] Peck, "Benefits, Beneficiaries, and Brokers"; James, *Society, Politics and Culture*, 392; in *Philip's Phoenix*, Hannay refers to the "Dudley/Sidney alliance" (14), the "Protestant alliance" (21), and "the Protestant interventionist party" (81); and S. L. Adams, "Favourites and Factions," 272. Richard Helgerson refers to "the militant interventionist policy of the Leicester-Essex faction" (*Forms of Nationhood*, 53). Factions, in Peck's words, were "networks of patrons and clients who, at the least, were viewed by others as connecting and co-coordinating their political behavior. The faction might be animated not only by mutual self interest but by similar views on foreign policy and religion" (*Court Culture*, 53). "Faction" was a term of derogation and never used by group members to define themselves. In *Sonnets and the English Woman Writer*, Rosalind Smith refers to the alliance as "a group of aristocratic Protestant patrons perceived to be independent of courtly corruption and intrigue, often identified in terms of a physical withdrawal from the court to the country" (99). She is one of the few scholars to note, and take seriously, the women in the group, arguing that it "included a distinct sub-group of women courtiers: Susan Herbert Countess of Montgomery; Lucy Harington, Countess of Bedford; and Lady Mary Wroth" (99).

[25] For various accounts of this genealogy, see David Norbrook, *Poetry and Politics*; Vernon F. Snow, "Essex and the Aristocratic Opposition to the Early Stuarts" ("'Essex connection' constituted the nucleus of the aristocratic opposition to the early Stuarts," 224); Warren Boutcher, "Florio's Montaigne" ("The tradition of aristocratic political Puritanism that descended from...John Dudley, Earl of Northumberland, through the various branches

rights of the aristocracy, including the right to counsel; and the value of what has been called "practically active" or "political" humanism.[26] The alliance was at once oppositional and consiliary, and its members made use of literary texts both to oppose the current direction of royal policy, and to offer advice on how to do things better.[27] It expressed, in Patrick Collinson's words, "what is vulgarly called resistance theory, but is better described as the polemical critique of monarchy."[28] Its members sought a share in monarchical governance, that is, rather than its overthrow, and they sought to do so, in part, through the use of books.

Some of the books used by the members of the alliance have received a great deal of attention in this regard. Critics have pointed out, for example, that the Sidnean Psalms were modeled on Genevan and Huguenot translations which had expressed the political opinions of their translators

of the Dudley, Russell, Knollys, Sidney, Devereux and Herbert families, survived to find a figurehead in the Earl of Pembroke in the Jacobean era. The heirs to this tradition coalesced partly around the Virginia Company whose directors included the Earl [of Pembroke], Philip Herbert, Robert Sidney, Lord Harington and his sister": Boutcher, "Florio's Montaigne," 71); S. L. Adams, "The Protestant Cause," 4, 7 ("By the 1580s Leicester's clientage, originally inherited from his father, was beginning to adopt something of a party ethos; loyalty to the Earl himself was increasingly overshadowed by his identification with the cause" of the "advanced Protestants"); and Hannay, *Philip's Phoenix* ("Sir Philip Sidney, the hope of the alliance, died fighting its battles. Then the men of the powerful alliance of Leicester's own generation, died within ten years: Bedford in 1585, Henry Sidney in 1586, Leicester in 1588, Warwick and Walsingham in 1590; Huntingdon in 1595": 68). S. L. Adams argues that the "failure of Essex to achieve a similar position [as Leicester] and to extend a similar protection [to the cause] was to doom this form of organization...Only after the failure of Buckingham in 1625 and Pembroke in 1626 to provide adequate leadership did political puritanism turn...to the House of Commons and the 'country' and repudiate the court" ("The Protestant Cause," 35). As we will see in Ch. 4, Pembroke was working with the House of Commons in the early 1620s as well.

[26] On "practically active" humanism, see G. R. Elton, *Studies in Tudor and Stuart Politics and Government*, 220; on "political humanism," see F. J. Levy, "Francis Bacon and the Style of Politics," 147–9. See also S. L. Adams's account of "political Puritanism," which did its work under the leadership of the court aristocracy, and was concerned with aristocratic constitutionalism and in giving assistance to the Church abroad rather than rapprochement with Catholic powers. He also makes much of the alliance's investments in an ambitious foreign policy, specifically geared around resistance to the Habsburgs ("The Protestant Cause"). On religion, he argues that "As long as the magistrate was godly, Calvinism could function equally well within the autocracy of the Palatine, the semi-autocracy of Maurice of Nassau, the aristocratic constitutionalism of the English gentry or the French theorists of the 1570s, and the bourgeois republicanism of Geneva" (10).

[27] For the relationship between oppositionism and counsel, see S. L. Adams, "The Protestant Cause," 234. Adams (193) cites the argument of the *Vindiciae contra Tyrannos* that nobles are "obligated not only to perform their own duties, but also to hold the prince to his."

[28] Collinson, "The Monarchical Republic of Queen Elizabeth I," 44. See also Blair Worden: "In pre-civil war England it was the abuse of monarchy, not the principle, that attracted complaint" ("Republicanism, Regicide and Republic," 311). Collinson's focus is the 1584 anti-absolutist Bond of Association, an informal convocation of regional heads, earls, privy councilors, residents of Lincolns Inn, and bishops, who, given the absence of a plan for succession, established a republican plan of rule (48–50). Politics, argues Collinson,

and served as cautions for their monarchs. In Mary Sidney Herbert's rendering of Psalm 101, for example, King David promotes the value of his subaltern magistrates, vowing that "Such men with me my Counsailors shall sitt / such euermore my Officers shall be, / Men speaking right, and doing what is fitt."[29] Her contemporaries did not miss her point. In his manuscript copy of the poems, John Davies used gold capitals to emphasize the significance of "*Counsailors*" and "*Officers*." The works of Roman history and philosophy and British antiquarianism the members of the alliance read, translated, and published, are also frequently mentioned in political histories of the period.[30]

Yet many of the other texts produced by the alliance, including many of those I discuss in this book, have received almost no attention in these terms. (The *Urania*, most notably, is rarely mentioned in connection with "practically active" humanism.) Moreover, while some of the books associated with the alliance have also been associated with women—most critics, for example, note that Sidney wrote the *Arcadia* for his sister—this association is rarely seen in political terms, and the role of women thus remains, for the most part, both secondary and apolitical. *Mediatrix* argues that the texts discussed in its chapters were intimately related to the political concerns of the alliance that produced them, but it also argues that women played a crucial role both in the production of these texts, and in effecting the political goals they served. Rather than mere support staff, many of the women discussed in this book, including Mary Sidney Herbert and Lucy Harington Russell, served, at various points, as the leaders and spokespeople for the alliance.[31] This leadership, moreover, was both literal and symbolic. While they often had the "voice" or leadership of the alliance

"is now seen to have been one of differences and contentions within a regime, not of 'government' versus 'opposition'" (40).

[29] See Hannay's discussion of the psalms in ch. 4 of *Philip's Phoenix*, "This Moses and this Miriam." The quotation is from p. 105. Hannay provides the information about the Davies manuscript at p. 245 n. 78.

[30] See e.g. Malcolm Smuts, "Court Centered Politics and the Uses of Roman Historians"; and James, *Society Politics and Culture*. Vernon Snow also discusses the alliance's "use of the past" and their hiring of poets, historians, playwrights, and antiquarians: "They subsidized books and historical plays, many of which elevated honour and eulogized their lineal or titular ancestors. The antiquarians formed a society and presented research papers on such subjects as the origin of gentility, the etymology of honor, the antiquity of parliament and the dignity of titles. They attempted to prove that that the English constitution was a mixed monarchy; that conquest and counsel were the principal functions of the titled nobility; and that the House of Lords had once possessed untold privileges and greater jurisdiction when it was the *magnum concilium*" ("Essex and the Aristocratic Opposition to the Early Stuarts," 226). For oppositionist drama, see Margot Heinemann, *Puritanism and Theatre*; and Albert H. Tricomi, *Anti-Court Drama*.

[31] In a move characteristic of much history of the period, S. L. Adams simultaneously acknowledges the central role that women played in the alliance, and presumes that it could not possibly have been substantive. "It was from the second generation of the great puritan

in practical and political terms, women also frequently served as its representatives in a more figurative sense. As we will see in the pages that follow, the forms this representativeness took were varied and sometimes intimately related to one another. When Gervase Markham set out to publish his continuation of Philip Sidney's romance in 1607, for example, he entered it in the Stationers' Register as "The Countesse of BEDFORDES Arcadia Begynnynge where the Countesse of PEMBROOKES endes."[32] Like many others, Markham clearly saw Bedford as Pembroke's successor. The women discussed in this book performed in court masques as allegorized virtues; their miniatures were mounted on playing cards and used as symbolic bargaining tools in high stakes diplomatic negotiations; they were configured as "Pastorellas of *Arcadia*," and "starres" in an "Asterisme" that reflected the workings of their network; their celebrated constancy exemplified the neostoic fortitude and political disposition of their cause.[33] The women of the Sidney alliance were, in short, a crucial part of what has been called the "metaphorics" of a "discontented nobility," and like many metaphors, they found a logical home in books.[34] Their work as literary producers is thus registered not only in title-pages and dedications, but

families, such as Russells, that the strongest representation came," he writes. Political puritanism lost its leaders Warwick, Walsingham, Leicester, and Huntingdon by the mid-1590s, and "only the widows" like Anne, Countess of Warwick, remained ("Protestant Cause," 108). The Earl of Bedford's heir, he continues, had been killed in 1585 and his grandson was a minor. Even as he acknowledges the role of "a significant group of great ladies," including Margaret Russell, Mary Sidney, and Lucy Harington, Adams is nonetheless unable to see them as key factors in the alliance's activities, skipping over them to get to the next generation of men (182). At "the bare minimum," he continues, "the Virginia Company provided a medium for the association of the survivors of the Leicesterian and Essex parties with the younger men who would become the spokesmen for political Puritanism in the 1620s" (Adams, "Protestant Cause," 182). Yet even in the 1620s, as we will see in Ch. 3, loyalists located the center of oppositionism in the "ill councils of Bedford House"—one of the households over which Lucy Harington Russell, Countess of Bedford, reigned supreme.

[32] Cited in Gavin Alexander, *Writing After Sidney*, 141: "when Gervase Markham stopped reminisicing about the glory days of Essex's ascendancy and Penelope Rich's patronage, it was Lucy Harington to whom he considered dedicating his next-generation continuation of Sidney, *The English Arcadia*.

[33] For women as allegorized virtues, see Chs 1 and 3; for the use of miniatures, see Ch. 1; for neostoic constancy, see Chs 1 and 4. In his *Ourania* (1606), Nathaniel Baxter refers to Wroth and her sister Philippa as "Ladyes of worthe, and babes of *Sydneia*," "Pastorellas of *Arcadia*" and "blessed Nymphs/Neeces to Astrophell" (*Ourania*, B3ʳ, B4ʳ). In his dedicatory poem to Wroth in his *The Whole Works of Homer... in his Iliads and Odysses* (1616), George Chapman refers to her as part of the "Sydneian Asterisme": "TO THE HAPPY STARRE, DISCOUERED in our Sydneian Asterisme; comfort of learning, Sphere of all the vertues, the Lady Wrothe." (Pyrocles refers to Philoclea as his "Load-starre of comfort" in the *Arcadia* (*NA* 178, ed. 329)). Miniature portraits of both Dorothy Percy and Mary Sidney Herbert were mounted on playing cards (*Correspondence of Dorothy Percy Sidney*, 11 n. 26).

[34] This quotation is from Gordon Braden, *Renaissance Tragedy and the Senecan Tradition*, 77. I discuss this concept more fully in Ch. 1.

also within the texts themselves, where they and their work can be seen in figures ranging from the learned disputants in puritan treatises to the Roman heroines in neostoic tragedy and the ciphered heroines of chivalric romances.

Mary Sidney Herbert, Margaret Dakins Hoby, Lucy Harington Russell, and Mary Sidney Wroth are the central figures in this book, but other women make significant appearances as well: Penelope Devereux Rich and her sister Dorothy Devereux Perrot Percy; Margaret Russell Clifford, Countess of Cumberland, her sister, Anne Russell Dudley, Countess of Warwick, and her daughter, Anne Clifford, Countess of Dorset; Katherine Dudley Hastings, Countess of Huntingdon, sister of Robert Dudley and Mary Dudley Sidney; Margaret Hoby's mother-in-law, Elizabeth Cooke Hoby Russell; Mary Sidney Herbert's daughter-in-law (and Mary Wroth's ally), Susan de Vere Herbert, Countess of Montgomery; and, in the conclusion, Dorothy Devereux Percy's daughter Dorothy, who married Mary Wroth's brother, Robert Sidney, in 1615.[35] While the familial interrelationships are certainly part of the story I tell in this book, I am interested in these women less as mothers, daughters, and wives than as members of an alliance and heads of powerful households. In particular, I am interested in them as "almoners of ways"—mediatrixes who served as go-betweens for the various interests and offices that made up political life in early modern England.[36]

As Margaret Maurer puts it, the position that these women occupied was "theoretically non-existent" in the annals of political history, but "could be and often was, everything" in the political culture in which they actually

[35] In addition to these other women, this book also considers a much wider range of texts than the *Arcadia*, key militant Protestant treatises (including those of William Perkins, Richard Greenham, and Philip de Mornay), Donne's poems, and the *Urania*. Other works which are discussed in some detail include the poetry of Samuel Daniel, Michael Drayton, and Ben Jonson, and letters by Penelope Rich, Robert Devereux, Earl of Essex, and Fulke Greville.

[36] Scholars frequently assume that the family was a refuge from political life. See e.g. Hannay's claim that Wroth was "safe in her elite family circle" (*Mary Sidney*, p. xiv); Nandini Das's assumption that a focus on the familial connections between Sidney and Wroth risks keeping their work "cloistered within the aristocratic familial coterie of the Sidneys" (*Renaissance Romance*, 6–7); and Gavin Alexander's assumption about the "parochial nature of Pembroke's literary coterie" (*Writing After Sidney*, 82). Alexander is particularly (and peculiarly) insistent that Sidney Herbert's work should be considered solely in relationship to her brother: "[Philip Sidney] is subject and object enough"; "Sidney's endings are the focus of her grief, and both the beginning and the end of her art" (Alexander, *Writing After Sidney*, 111, 127). Scholars make similar claims about Wroth. See e.g. Elizabeth Mazzola's claim that "Wroth's subject is the confines of the family" (*Favorite Sons*, 79). The term "almoner of ways" was a contemporary term. (See e.g. Jane Nevill to the Earl of Salisbury, 27 January 1605–6 in *The Cecil Papers: Calendar of the Cecil Papers in Hatfield House*, xviii. *1606* (1940), 20–40: <http://www.british-history.ac.uk/report.aspx?compid=112278&strquery="almoner"> accessed September 2012).

lived.[37] Recent work on the female-centered courts of Queen Elizabeth I and Queen Anne has revealed the constitutive role that women played in the political life of early modern England.[38] (While scholars have long pointed out that influential courtiers like Robert Carr slept in the King's bedchamber, that is, they are now starting to look at the influence of women like Lucy Harington Russell who slept in the Queen's.) Yet while some of the women in this book served as attending gentlewomen—a position that was, and should be considered, a political office—others played less clearly defined roles, many of them away from the court altogether. The work these women did ranged from arranging marriages and the promotion of men to particular offices and benefices, to patronizing literary, religious, and political works, writing letters and presenting petitions, and mediating agreements and disputes.[39] (When Ben Jonson was arrested for

[37] Margaret Maurer, "The Real Presence of Lucy Russell, Countess of Bedford," 215. Hannay points out that when Robert Sidney and Rowland Whyte discuss "friends" at court, they were often refering to Katherine Dudley Hastings, Countess of Huntingdon; Elizabeth Cooke, Lady Russell; and Anne Russell Dudley, Countess of Warwick (*Philip's Phoenix*, 66). Rowland Whyte regularly advised Robert Sidney to take advantage of the power of his female relatives, telling him at one point that "the way to work it, is by your letter to my Lady your sister [Mary Sidney Herbert]" (*Philip's Phoenix*, 155).

[38] On Elizabeth's court, see Philippa Berry, *Of Chastity and Power*; Pam Wright, "A Change in Direction"; and Elizabeth Brown, "'Companion me with my Mistress': Cleopatra, Elizabeth I, and their Waiting Women." On Queen Anne, see Leeds Barroll, *Anna of Denmark*. Recent critics have worked hard to overturn Pam Wright's argument that the Privy Chamber "ceased to be a forum for independent initiatives in counseling the monarch over key political issues" when it came to be the forum of women. Nancy Mears has described Elizabeth's court as characterized by an "ad hoc" secretarial process facilitated in no small part by the intimate and consiliary services of women (*Queenship*, 46). Charlotte Merton and Joan Greenbaum Goldsmith have seen women as "points of contact" in the courtly circulation of news and information, and Mears has factored women's activity "into the wider workings of court politics—policy, debate, diplomacy" (Mears, "Politics," 68). See Charlotte Merton, "The Women Who Served Queen Mary and Queen Elizabeth: Ladies, Gentlewomen and Maids of the Privy Chamber, 1553–1603" (Ph.D. diss., Cambridge University, 1992); and J. B. Greenbaum Goldsmith, "All the Queen's Women: The Changing Place and Perception of Aristocratic Women in Elizabethan England, 1558–1620" (Ph.D. dissertation, Northwestern University, 1987). From at least 1566, Leicester's main contacts with Elizabeth were Dorothy Broadbent and Blanche Parry (Mears, "Politics," 73 n. 38). Privy Chamber servants like Broadbent and Parry facilitated access to Elizabeth for secretaries and courtiers; they managed petitions and delivered royal commands; they were also sources of information on the Queen and court, utilized not only by foreign ambassadors but by fellow members of the political elite.

[39] As Alison Wall points out in her *ODNB* entry on Penelope Rich, in 1599 "Rich asked Sir Julius Caesar, a judge of the admiralty court and master of requests, to continue his favour to a Captain Isard, for which she was beholden to Caesar." As we will see in Ch. 4, Mary Wroth supported the careers of—and attempted to mitigate the punishments for— officers in the English garrisons in Flushing (see also Hannay, *Mary Sidney*, 149). When he was in trouble for his part in the Essex conspiracy, Sir Charles Danvers appealed to the Countess of Warwick and Lady Hoby for help.

offending the King with *Eastward Ho* in 1605, for example, the Countess of Bedford was one of the people to whom he turned for help.[40])

The importance of such work was far from invisible to contemporaries. When Robert Sidney was seeking office in 1599, for example, the family secretary, Rowland Whyte, wrote to him at his wife's behest to tell him that she had had "much Speech" with "Lady Buckhurst" about (her husband) the "Lord Treasorer[s]" "love" for Sidney. Whyte concludes the letter by telling him that "Her Ladyship desires [him] to wryte unto these her Goships, for indeed they are worthy to have Thanks."[41] In another letter from the same year, Whyte informs Sidney of the work Penelope Devereux Rich has been doing to secure him the office of the Warden of the Cinque Ports, including keeping a letter of petition "in her bosom" and promising to deliver it to the Queen in the morning.[42] Such attention to the mediatrix's body served less as an inevitable form of sexualization than as an index of her status as a keeper and bearer of secrets—of the power she embodied in her very person and in her access to that of the Queen. The historian Thomas Fuller provides a perfect emblem of such power in his description of the rise of George Villers's as James I's favorite in 1615: "the *Lady* Lucy Countess of *Bedford* led him by the one hand, and William Earl of *Pembroke* by the other."[43] (Herbert would be made Lord Chamberlain the next year; on 11 September 1619, John Chamberlain wrote about a dispute between the Earl of Pembroke and Villiers which was "accorded mediation" by "the Lady of Bedford.")[44] The work that these women did, moreover, both at court and elsewhere, was carried out alongside their domestic, familial, and communal duties.[45] The great households with which they were associated are thus best understood not as "domestic sites"—particularly if we understand them as sites of separate-sphere

---

[40] On *Eastward Ho*, see Lewalski, *Writing Women*, 107; and Smith, *Women of Ben Jonson's Poetry*, 59.

[41] Collins, *Letters and Memorials*, ii. 153. In her *Life of Robert Sidney*, Millicent Hay points out that he sealed the letters he wrote to two of the Queen's maids with the Sidney arrowhead, suggesting that they solicited political, rather than romantic, assignations (154).

[42] Rowland Whyte often mentions Penelope Rich in his reports to Sir Robert Sidney. The letter is cited in Rawson, *Penelope Rich and her Circle*, 178. See also a 1599 letter to Robert Sidney in which Rowland Whyte discusses Barbara Gamage Sidney "present[ing] a petition with honest offers" to the Queen on behalf of her husband's rights to a park (cited in Hannay, *Mary Sidney*, 69).

[43] "Sir *Tho. Lake* may be said to have ushered him to the English Court, whilest the *Lady* Lucy Countess of *Bedford* led him by the one hand, and William Earl of *Pembroke* by the other, supplying him with a support far above his patrimonial income" (Fuller, *History of the worthies*, 130). See also Taylor, "The Masque and the Lance," 33. In April 1615, Villiers was knighted, installed in the privy chamber, and given a pension.

[44] Chamberlain, *Letters*, 61.

[45] In his discussion of John Dee's reading, Sherman points out that "Dee's base of operations was his own household, and his textual activities were carried out alongside

labor and containment—nor as "safe houses," somehow exempt from the machinations of political life.[46] Rather, the great houses with which these women were associated are best understood as bases of operations.

II. PLACE (AND PROPERTY)

> We cannot be so stupid as to imagine, that God gives ladies great estates, merely that they may eat, drink, sleep and rise up to play.
>
> (Bathsua Makin, *Essay to Revive the Antient Education of Gentlewomen*, 1673)

While the "private castles" of the ancient baronial nobility had become, under increasingly centralizing monarchs, the "private houses" of a somewhat diminished nobility, many of the great households of early modern England nonetheless retained their status as regional bases of power.[47] Through local governmental offices, such as Lord Lieutenant of the County, the household remained the basic unit of local government. It was, in Sir Henry Wotton's words, "a kind of private *Princedom*," and its lord "ruled his country almost as the king ruled the kingdom."[48] Indeed England itself was sometimes imagined as a "federation of noble fiefdoms," its rule effected as much by regional magnates and local office-holders as by an all-powerful monarch.[49] Understanding political governance as localized requires, once again, recognizing the centrality of women, who were often the owners, proprietors, administrators, and office-holders of

his domestic and communal duties" (*John Dee*, 69). This was certainly true for the women discussed in this book as well, and our difficulty in seeing this is often the result of an anachronistic sense of what "domestic life" comprised.

[46] Marion Wynne-Davies makes such an argument about "safe houses" in two related essays on Mary Wroth: "Penshurst, like all familial houses, functioned as a place where noble women could find pleasure in one another's company without the darker and more dangerous intrigues of the early seventeenth-century court" ("'For Worth, Not Weakness, Makes in Use But One,'" 170 n. 11). She also identifies Penshurst as a "safe house" in "'So much Worth as lives in you,'" 49.

[47] Between 1580 and 1629, Stone argues, "private castles gave way to private houses" and aristocratic rebellion petered out (Stone, *Crisis of the Aristocracy*, 15). For a brilliant discussion of the estate as a power base—what she calls a "princedom"—see Susan Wiseman, *Conspiracy and Virtue*, 80–94, esp. 88. On the shift from "magnate politics" to court-centered patronage, see Peck, *Court Corruption*.

[48] The first quotation is from Sir Henry Wotton, *The Elements of Architecture* (London, 1622), cited in Wiseman, *Conspiracy and Virtue*, 88; and the second from S. L. Adams, *Leicester and the Court*: "What distinguished the nobility was its superior power, as manifested in its affinities. The lord ruled his country almost as the king ruled the kingdom" (376).

[49] "In effect the country was divided into spheres of influence that could be displayed on maps; in some senses England was a federation of noble fiefdoms" (Bernard, *Power and Politics*, 31). See also Collinson, who argues that early modern England is best understood

these country estates. If, as some scholars have argued, England was a nation of office-holders, some of those office-holders were women.

The alliance discussed in this book held disproportionate sway in England's "federation of fiefdoms." In fact, by the 1570s, the Sidneys and their allies controlled over two-thirds of the property in England.[50] Their status as great magnates is well noted in literary history. Ben Jonson's "To Penshurst," to take the best known example, celebrates the Sidney estate in terms that both highlight and satirize the *noblesse oblige* of its owners. Wilton House, the Herbert seat in Wiltshire, was often praised as an "academy" for poets, and the Bedford estate of Twickenham Park and the Wroth estate of Loughton Hall were the subjects of well-known poems by John Donne and Ben Jonson respectively.

In some ways, women held unstable positions in these households. When Mary Sidney Herbert's husband died in 1601 and her son inherited his title, she (officially) lost her status as the mistress of Wilton.[51] Margaret Hoby fought with her husband about the future of the Yorkshire estate they lived and worked on, and after her death, and against her express

---

as "a series of overlapping, superimposed communities which are also semi-autonomous, self-governing political cultures or 'republics'" ("Monarchical Republic," 58). For local office-holding, see Mark Goldie, "The Unacknowledged Republic"; and Conal Condren, *Argument and Authority in Early Modern England*. Goldie points out that local officers were "agents of their communities as much as of the crown" (166). People saw themselves as "subjects of an anointed monarch who was armed with awesome prerogative powers yet also saw themselves as citizens of self-governing communities" (175–6).

[50] Hannay, *Philip's Phoenix*, 22. Mary Sidney's father, Henry Sidney, was Lord President of the Council of the Marches of Wales, and Lord Governor of Ireland. He alone "administered about one-quarter of the land under Elizabeth's rule" (20). By the 1560s, Robert Dudley, Earl of Leicester, and his brother Ambrose, Earl of Warwick, controlled most of Worcestershire. The power of the alliance was increased by consistent support in the Council from Mary's godfather, Henry Herbert, Earl of Pembroke, whose vast lands lay primarily in Wiltshire and in Glamorganshire. The other great Protestant earl was Francis Russell, Earl of Bedford; his daughter Anne married Ambrose Dudley, and his heir, Edward Russell, married Lucy Harington. When Mary Sidney married Henry Herbert, Earl of Pembroke (who succeeded Sir Henry Sidney as Lord President of the Council of the Marches of Wales), she married "the one great Protestant earl who was not [yet] a member of the Dudley family" (35). Herbert had inherited property in Wiltshire including Wilton (and eighteen other manors), as well as the town, castle, and borough of Cardiff with supporting estates, and more than half the land in Glamorganshire (36). In his history of Pembrokeshire, George Owen wrote that "you must understand that the earls of Pembroke of late time...were not earls only in name, as the rest of the earls of England were, but they were earls in deed." He goes on to describe "their royal jurisdiction, power and authority, *which they more like princes than subjects had over their people of this country in times past*" (cited in Helgerson, *Forms of Nationhood*, 136, emphasis added).

[51] While much has been made of her husband's dispossessing will—as John Chamberlain wrote to Dudley Carleton, "The erle of Pembroke died a fortnight since leaving his Lady as bare as he could and bestowing all on the young Lord even to her jewells" (cited in Hannay, *Philip's Phoenix*, 172)—her jointure was substantive. The list of properties in which she

wishes, he left it to his relatives rather than her own.[52] As a result of her husband's involvement in the Essex conspiracy (and general profligacy), Lucy Harington Russell spent her life encumbered by debt.[53] Mary Wroth was also afflicted by debt; when her husband died in 1614, she was famously left with a "£1200 fortune, a son a month old and £23 000" in debt.[54] His property, moreover, was entailed upon male heirs.

Yet none of these details dictates a straightforward story of female victimhood and dispossession. Indebtedness was often the default state of the propertied and ambitious in a credit economy like that of early modern England, and pleading for its amelioration was a standard means of socioeconomic and political negotiation and self-promotion. (Wroth, for example, successfully pleaded with Queen Anne to better the estate she would eventually hold in her own name; and Bedford's debts were but one of the many subjects of her myriad negotiations with various political parties.) Despite the law of *coverture*, moreover, many early modern women maintained substantial property interests of their own and were personally involved in the financial management of combined marital property.[55] Barbara Gamage, the Welsh heiress who married Robert Sidney in 1584 and became the mistress of Penshurst, brought financial stability to the Sidney family; indeed Jonson's allusion to her "linnen [and] plate" at the end of "To Penshurst" seems to hint at the female origins of the estate's functional wealth.[56] Her husband also consistently deferred to and relied on her in matters of estate management; "all things" concerning Penshurst, he wrote to her in 1609, "shall still be commanded by you."[57]

Women's governance of great estates, moreover, was not only a matter of money and ground-level husbandry. There is a remarkable moment in *De Republica Anglorum* (1584), when the political theorist Sir Thomas Smith states that while women should not, as a general rule, "medle with matters

---

was to retain life interest is given in a document entitled "Lands of the right honorable Henry Earle of Pembroke appointed for the ioynture of Marye nowe comtesse of Pembroke wife of the salde Earle and Daughter of the right honorable Sir Henrye Sidney, Knyght of the Garter and Lorde Presydent of Walles," and consists of ninety sheets (Hannay, *Philip's Phoenix*, 41). She was left holdings in Dorset, Wiltshire, Devon, Glamorgan, Monmouth, Sussex, Kent, and Surrey.

[52] See Sir Erskine Perry (ed.), *The Van den Bempde Papers*, 21; *Diary of Lady Margaret Hoby*, ed. Dorothy M. Meads, 43–4; and Ch. 2.

[53] See Margaret M. Byard, "The Trade of Courtship"; and Ch. 3.

[54] Cited in Josephine A. Roberts, "Introduction," *The Poems of Lady Mary Wroth*, 59–60. See also Hannay, *Mary Sidney*, 172.

[55] See Erickson, *Women and Property in Early Modern England*, 12 and throughout.

[56] Jonson, "To Penshurst," l. 86, p. 96. Hannay notes that Barbara was her father's "sole heir" and the properties she inherited provided half of the Sidneys' income (*Mary Sidney*, 11).

[57] *Report on the Manuscripts of Lord De L'Isle and Dudley Preserved at Penshurst Place, Kent*, vol. iv. See also *Domestic Politics and Family Absence*, 148.

abroade, nor to beare office in a citie or common wealth," there are excep-
tions "in such cases as the authoritie is annexed to the blood and progenie, as
the crowne, a dutchie, or an erledome, for there the blood is respected, not
the age nor ye sexe."[58] Women "which haue the name [of Queen, Duchess
or Countess] not by being maried to a king, duke, or erle, but by being the
true, right & next successors in the dignitie, and vpon whom by right of the
blood that title is descended," are "absolute"—the possessors of "the same
authoritie... in that kingdome, dutchie or earledome, as they shoulde haue
had if they had bin men of full age."[59] Noble women, in other words, could
govern as magistrates themselves. Even in cases in which they were not literally the "next successor[s] in the dignitie," noble women—particularly
those like Mary Sidney Wroth who were, as she herself reminded her readers,
"daughter[s] of an Earl"—nonetheless wielded considerable power within a
given "dutchie or erledome," even functioning in many cases as the heads of
great estates and families.

This was true of all the estates discussed in this book. It was under Mary
Sidney Herbert (not her husband) that Wilton House became known
as an academy for poets,[60] but she also made extensive improvements
to the estate, was involved in electing local Members of Parliament, and
appointed and protected radical members of the local ministry.[61] In addition, she the mistress of two lesser manor estates, Ivychurch and Ramsbury,
and of two castles: Baynard's, the Herberts' London seat, and Ludlow in
Wales, the seat of the Lord of the Council of the Marches (an office held

---

[58] *De Republica Anglorum*, ch. 16, "The diuision of the parts and persons of the common
wealth," 19.
[59] "For the right and honour of the blood, and the quietnes and suertie of the realme,
is more to be considered, than either the tender age as yet impotent to rule, or the sexe not
accustomed (otherwise) to intermeddle with publicke affaires, being by common intend-
ment vnderstood, that such personages neuer do lacke the counsell of such graue and discreete men as be able to supplie all other defectes" (19).
[60] Nicholas Breton claimed that Mary had more "servants" writing poetry to her at Wilton
than did Elizabetta Gonzaga, Duchess of Urbino, the patron celebrated in Castiglione's
Courtier (*The pilgrimage to paradise, ioyned with the Countesse of Penbrookes loue* (1592), sig.
A2) and Samuel Daniel claimed that he received "the first notion for the formall ordering of
[his poetic] compositions at Wilton, which I must ever acknowledge to have beene my best
Schoole" (*A panegyrike congratulatorie deliuered to the Kings most excellent Maiestie* (1603),
sig. G3). See Hannay, *Philip's Phoenix*, 202.
[61] See ch. 7 in Hannay, "A Most Heroical Spirit." The members of her household
included Thomas Moffet, the family physician; Gervase Babington, the chaplain; Sir John
Davies and Hugh Sanford (secretaries); Samuel Daniel (tutor); and William Browne, who
was one of William Herbert's retainers (Hannay, "A Most Heroical Spirit," 112). Each of
these men was also politically active: probably with Sidney Herbert's help, Moffett became
an MP; Babington was an active supporter of militant Protestantism; and, as we will see in
Ch. 4, William Browne was a lieutenant in Flushing who not only wrote Sidney Herbert's
epitaph, but listened to Mary Wroth's political advice about whom to appoint to military
positions. On Sidney Herbert's support of ministers, see Hannay, *Philip's Phoenix*, 132.

by her husband).[62] Poets' praise of her as a "Governor" or "Sov'raigne lady" who presides over her lands in a manner at once Diana-like and magisterial is thus more than merely metaphorical; it indicates her status as a kind of "Prince."[63] Abraham Fraunce, for example, celebrated Sidney Herbert as the "braue lady Regent of the... woods" of "Pembrokiana."[64] For Michael Drayton, she wore "the Laurell crown" of "The ancient glory of her noble Peeres," and served as "the glorious light, and load starre of our west."[65] Configuring her both as the new literary spokesperson for the Sidney alliance, and as the leader of the internationalist Protestant cause (the "load starre of our west"), Drayton represents Sidney Herbert sounding out the "sweet musick of the morrow" with the "Cleere bell of Rhetoricke"—a formulation that suggests the seriousness of her, and by extension his, work.[66] Sidney Herbert's patronage was, in fact, often explicitly political; Samuel Daniel credits her with encouraging him "To Sing of State and tragick notes to frame."[67] She herself translated a political tragedy originally written by a French magistrate and political activist to criticize the state.[68] When Sidney Herbert published her translation of Garnier's *Marc-Antoine* in the years following her brother's death, she explicitly associated it with her status as a great householder, locating its composition "At Ramsburie. 26. of November. 1590," and signaling her status as the new head of the alliance.[69]

Sidney Herbert was also a key mediator for her husband's political position, and most petitioning went through her; in 1599, for example, Rowland Whyte told Robert Sidney to "induce Lord Herbert and my Lady his mother to hearken to [Sidney's petition to obtain the presidency of Wales]. If anything advance you, it must be this, *for I see no other way*."[70] Even when the Earl of Pembroke died in 1601 and her son William (the "Lord Herbert" in this quotation) inherited the title, Mary Sidney Herbert

---

[62] Hannay suggests her position was "analogous to that of the medieval lady of the castle" (*Philip's Phoenix*, 106).

[63] Breton identifies her as a "governor" (Grosart, ii. 18–19).

[64] Fraunce, *The Countesse of Pembrokes Yuychurch*, sig. K4. Gavin Alexander points out that Mary Sidney's husband wrote a letter to the Lord Treasurer in 1590 recommending Fraunce to act as the Queen's solicitor in the Welsh Court where he practiced (*Writing After Sidney*, 135).

[65] Drayton, *Idea. the Shepheards Garland*, 40

[66] Drayton, *Idea. the Shepheards Garland*, 41.

[67] Daniel, "To the Right Honourable, the Lady Marie, Countesse of Pembrooke," *Collected Works*, 14. Hannay suggests that what he had in mind was his *Civile Wares betweene the Howses of Lancaster and Yorke* (*Philip's Phoenix*, 119).

[68] On Garnier, see Ch. 1.

[69] See Mary Sidney Herbert, *Collected Works*, 207; and the discussion in Ch. 1.

[70] Cited in Hannay, *Philip's Phoenix*, 167. In another letter, Rowland Whyte told Sidney that "the way to worke it, is by your letter to my Lady your sister" (*Philip's Phoenix*, 154).

held it in her son's minority, and continued to serve as an active local governor in a wide range of capacities. These capacities included managing an attempt by the citizens of Cardiff in Wales to break the seigneurial hold the Earls of Pembroke held over their lands. (Under her husband's will, Sidney Herbert inherited the castle and borough of Cardiff in satisfaction of her dower, held in trust for her son.) Sidney Herbert was not merely anadministrative force, that is, but an office-holder, and the records of the crisis bear the traces of this fact. The man who tried to set up a rival court to Sidney Herbert's was nonetheless identified as the "sworne Baylif unto her Ladyship"; and the town recorder who refused to acknowledge her authority as having "his place at her Ladyships pleasure."[71] The Ludlow castle walls that local advocates of Welsh self-government pulled down were identified as "*her Ladyships walles*," and the servants they sent away with the "blood running about their ears" were hers.[72] (In many ways, this final act of resistance seems to be a poetically vindicatory rebuttal of Ben Jonson's fantasy in "To Penshurst" that "There's none, that dwell about" the estate's walls that "wish them downe." Clearly there were many who wished to see Ludlow's razed to the ground.[73]) While the Herberts' seigneurial hold in Wales was challenged, these accounts nonetheless make it clear that Mary Sidney Herbert was seen as its reigning seigneur.

During the same period, Margaret Hoby and her husband lived and worked on a Yorkshire estate that was popularly known as her property rather than his.[74] Hoby's diary is full of the details of her hands-on management of her estate: working "in the granerie receiving Corne"; getting everyone "out to the hay"; receiving "Rentes"; paying "the sarvantes their wages."[75] The diary also reflects Hoby's sense of seigneurial proprietorship over her estate and the nearby properties in which she held rights: she refers to "my" servants in contradistinction to her husband's; she goes about her "fields" with her husband; "reeds abroad" with her cousin; and takes her coach "in to the feeldes" of her mother's nearby jointure property, which she, in turn, was due to inherit. (She eats "supper with my Mother and other friends" in those fields as a public sign of her proprietary rights.[76]) Although on a much smaller scale than Mary Sidney Herbert, Hoby also

---

[71] *Philip's Phoenix*, 179.   [72] *Philip's Phoenix*, 178–84.

[73] Jonson, "To Penshurst," l. 47, p. 94.   [74] See Ch. 2.

[75] Hoby, *Diary*, ed. Meads, for hay, see 131; for rents, 77.

[76] On her husband, see Hoby, *Diary*, 136; on her cousin, 176–7; on her mother, 130, 1505. Hoby makes numerous and pointed references in her diary to the fact that the tenants and workers are hers. She records many entries along the following lines: "walked to my workmen" (105); "went to my workmen" (108); "went with [a stranger] to my workmen" (108); "sitt a whill with my wemen talkinge of som principles unto them (130); "went abroad with my Maides that were busie pullinge hempe" (181). In each case cited, the possessive "my" is the labourers' defining characteristic, highlighting that Margaret Hoby,

understood herself as—and was understood to be—an office-holder: she gets "thinges readie against my Lord president [of the Council of the North's] Coming," and, as we will see in Chapter 2, keeps the manor court with her husband.[77]

Twickenham Park was also popularly known as Lucy Harington Russell's estate; her husband's name was never mentioned in relation to the property.[78] While Bedford leased, rather than owned, Twickenham, it nonetheless served as an important symbolic site of her power. Some of Bedford's contemporaries compared Twickenham to the royal residence that had been established for Princess Elizabeth at Kew, and John Donne, as we see in Chapter 3, identified it as a "Commonweale" over which Bedford ruled largely alone.[79] In Mary Wroth's case, the Loughton Hall estate she lived in was initially her husband's. In 1612, however, she successfully petitioned Queen Anne for the funds to rebuild it. Her letter makes much of her subordination to the crown—she professes her desire for "a house fitt for both your Majesties to rest in," and promises to let the King's "deere feede in his best grounds"—but it ends with an invocation of her own property rights.[80] Improving the estate, she tells the Queen "will be much for my good, mr. wrothe having promised to ad itt to my jointure, all the rest of his lande beeing entailed."[81] Loughton

rather than her husband, is their lord. These "my"s are not merely incidental; some workers on some properties were clearly identified as both hers and her husbands. See e.g. the entry for July 1605 about a property that her mother had recently transferred to her husband: "Mr Hoby and I walked to our Hay makers": 224) ... On 9 July, Hoby recounts taking her "cotch"—that most elaborate and public of liveried properties—with her mother to nearby Linton. Linton was her mother's jointure property, which Hoby was due to inherit, and whose sale to a Dakins cousin she ultimately helps orchestrate (see Hoby, *Diary*, 150–5). On one occasion she records writing "a perticuler," a detailed form of account, "of some thinges touching linton." Among other things, Hoby's diary served as a record of intended property transfer, and a paper trail of property rights.

[77] Hoby, *Diary*, 184.

[78] See Lawson, *Out of the Shadows*, 76. It was also near to Prince Henry's country court at Richmond Palace.

[79] This term, as Lawson points out, played directly on ideas of kingship and rule. She cites Thomas Wilson's *The Rule of Reason* (1551): "A common weale is deuided into the state of people whiche beare rule, & also into that power where the beste, and wisest, gave gouernance, and thirdly into ones hand whiche alone beareth the strike and is chief magistrate" (*Out of the Shadows*, 95).

[80] Cited in Wroth, *The Poems*, 233.

[81] Cited in Wroth, *The Poems*, 234. The Wroth's main family seat was Durance (Durants Place or Arbor), an ancient moated manor-house in Enfield in Middlesex (12 miles from London). Loughton Hall was both close to London and convenient for the hunting in the Forest of Essex (114). While her brother-in-law John Wroth still owned Loughton and officially served as lord of the manor, Wroth retained an interest in Loughton as part of her jointure, and was still its on-the-ground manager: people came to her for information about how to manage the forests and walks, and she sent a Loughton gamekeeper to Penhurst in 1621 (176).

was thus a focus of a great deal of Wroth's attentions, but she also staked her claim to the Sidney family properties in a variety of ways, including sending a poem called "Penshurst Mount" to the King's secretary Sir Edward Conway in 1616, and, as we will see in Chapter 4, shadowing Wilton and Penshurst (and Loughton) in her 1621 romance.[82]

Each of these estates, moreover, was associated not only with female proprietorship and governance, but with political opposition. In particular, the frequent poetic configuring of the estates as idealized retreats was often part of a "country versus court" discourse of political critique.[83] Sidney, to take a famous example, purportedly retreated to Wilton in the 1580s after displeasing the Queen with his unwanted counsel. Such retreats were often anti-courtly statements that intended, in Louis Montrose's words, to signal "the courtier's distance from the satisfaction of his ambitions." But Sidney's retreat also signaled Wilton's status as a site of "country" opposition, and the *Arcadia* as a "country" text with lessons to teach the court. As Montrose writes, "the 'covert intendments' of pastoral allegory are not only commentaries upon the specifics of court intrigue, but also the means by which a coterie is fostered."[84] The *Arcadia* served, in other words, to affirm both the alliance and its political commitments. By the time the *Arcadia* was printed, moreover, Wilton was recognized as the base of operations for the alliance for which Mary Sidney Herbert had become the acknowledged head.[85] If *Antonius* was published from Sidney Herbert's

[82] On "Penshurst Mount," see Hannay, *Mary Sidney*, 83. On the Wroth properties, see *Mary Sidney*, 110–30.

[83] See Derek Hirst, "Court, Country, and Politics before 1629," for a discussion of the dynamics of "court v. country" discourse.

[84] "Of Gentlemen and Shepherds," 426, 448. "Renaissance pastoral takes the court as its cynosure. Although many of these works direct criticism or hostility against courtly decadence or the inequities of courtly reward, such anti-courtliness tends to measure either the court's distance from its own high ideals or the courtier's distance from the satisfaction of his ambitions" (426). It is, Montrose insists, an "authorized mode of discontent, rather than a critique made in terms of a consciously articulated oppositional culture" ("Of Gentlemen and Shepherds," 427). On the association between the countryside and Stoic concepts of self-sufficiency and Epicurean ideas of self-cultivation, see Malcolm Smuts, *Culture*, 82. According to Smuts the "country" represented a "form of escapism and a means of dissimulating engagement in high politics, rather than a viable alternative system of values" (83). The alternative to court was not the country "but a wider field of action, especially international diplomacy and war" (84).

[85] On Mary Sidney Herbert's return to political society in 1588, see the report of the Spanish ambassador: "On Thursday the wife of the earl of Pembroke made a superb entrance into this city. She has been for more than a year on her estates in the country. Before her went 40 gentlemen on horseback, two by two, all very finely dressed with gold chains. Then came a coach in which was the Countess and a lady, then another coach with more ladies, and after that a little coach containing the children, and four ladies on horseback. After them came 40 or 50 servants in her livery with blue cassocks" (*CSP Spanish*, iv. 488, cited Hannay, *Philip's Phoenix*, 59–60). Citing Eleanor Rosenberg's insight about the importance of Mary

"Ramsburie" estate in 1590, the *Arcadia* was published under the "livery" of her name.

Hoby's Hackness estate also had an interesting political history. The Earls of Huntingdon and Essex had purchased it for her and her husband in 1589 when she married Walter Devereux, and they maintained an active interest in it throughout the period covered in this book. While Margaret Hoby was not a mediatrix of the same stature as Mary Sidney Herbert, and her estate a much smaller base of operations, her work in recusant Yorkshire was nonetheless intimately connected with that of the Essex alliance, and similarly critical of particular aspects of late Elizabethan and early Stuart rule. As we will see in Chapter 2, her powerful puritan mother-in-law Elizabeth Cooke Russell considered Hoby to be her political heir, and Hoby acted as a mediatrix for a related set of political and religious interests.

Twickenham Park was similarly politically charged. During the years in which Lucy Harington Russell "reigned" over Twickenham, it came to be known not only for its literary activities, but also for the political tenor of those activities. In her role as mediatrix, Bedford moved between country and court, protecting local puritan ministers in one venue, and, as we have seen, engineering the rise of Villiers in the other.[86] While she was a singularly influential figure at court, however, Bedford also "retired" to Twickenham in 1610 as part of the discourse and posture of political Protestantism, her retreat coding a similar kind of critique and counsel as Sidney's had in the 1580s, and positioning Twickenham as something of a counter-court.

While Loughton Hall did not function as a base of operations on the same level as Wilton, Hackness, or Twickenham, Mary Wroth was nonetheless a keeper of the powerful "Liverie" of her "noble name," and frequently associated with the anti-courtly posture of the alliance.[87] In an anonymous manuscript poem, "Ode to Lady Ma[ry] wrath," the speaker hopes to spend "the relique of myne age / Farre from the Court" and the

---

Sidney to the alliance, Hannay reiterates that the memorials to Philip Sidney were "part of a larger movement to revive the memory of the Dudleys and Sidneys and to celebrate the Countess of Pembroke as the chief surviving member of the line" (60).

[86] On Bedford's protection of radicals like Burges and Byfield, see Lawson, *Out of the Shadows*, 134. On the rise of Villiers, see *Out of the Shadows*, 137. For Bedford's attendance at the party celebrating the fall of the Somersets in 1615, see the Chamberlain letter cited in Lawson, which recounts a meeting attended by "the Lord Chamberlain [Pembroke], the earle of Mongomerie [Philip Herbert], the countesse of Bedford and I know not how many…more" (*Out of the Shadows*, 137).

[87] In *The Muses Gardin of Delights* (1610), Robert Jones asks for Wroth to "countenance" his work "with the faire Liverie of [her] noble name" (14).

"Frownes of our great Men," associating Wroth with the neostoic with-drawal characteristic of courtly critique.[88] Wroth's actual activities as a mediatrix, however—the De L'Isle and State papers are full of accounts of her presence at key meetings and details of her counsel in regard to political decisions—entailed her almost continual movement between the estates of Wilton, Penshurst, and Loughton, as well as Baynard's Castle in London. Wroth's consistent efforts to associate herself and her romance with these properties helped to establish her status as the rightful heir to the tradition of "political pastoral" that characterized her uncle's work, as well as to the kinds of political power associated with the landed nobility.

As neither the easy beneficiaries of the privileges of property nor wholly marginal to them, the women discussed in this book understood property as a matter of both local governance and broader political negotiation. The labors they practiced, enabled, and oversaw—each of the estates discussed in this book relied on the unseen and often highly exploited labor of others—were rarely separable into ready categories.[89] The regional location and concerns of these homes and estates influenced everything from an author's choice of genre and co-readers to the formats in which they published their texts.[90] The mediatrix's function was often carried out textually: through letters, news, petitions and pleas, contracts and orders, opinion papers and responses, and statements of intent. Many of the texts we now think of as "literary" reflect the same kinds of power-brokering we associate with these more direct forms of political engagement.

Sidney wrote the *Arcadia* in dialogue not only with his own letter of advice to the Queen, but with the Huguenot and neostoic texts he and his sister were reading and translating. Bedford read Donne's verses in the company of the other papers on her desk, including, as Donne himself pointed out, her own "compositions," and both Hoby and Wroth wrote letters in the same closets in which they read, and in Wroth's case, wrote, their books. Each chapter in this book thus pays close attention not only to the places in which texts were produced and read, but to the textual company they kept and the textual forms in which they circulated.

---

[88] Wroth, *The Poems*, 21.

[89] For popular protests at Wilton and Enfield (Wroth territory), see Norbrook, *Poetry and Politics*, 188–92). Local resistance to Sir Thomas Posthumous Hoby is discussed in Ch. 2.

[90] On the role the author's or intended audience's geographic location played in the author's choice of 'publication' practices, see Ezell, *Social Authorship*, 4, 18.

III. PUBLICATION: MANUSCRIPT AND PRINT, WRITTEN AND READ

No text exists outside of the support that enables it to be read.

(Roger Chartier, "Texts, Printing, Reading," 1989)

Some of the work discussed in this book appeared in print. After years of manuscript circulation the *Arcadia* was printed, in two different editions, in the early 1590s; Margaret Hoby read both printed and manuscript texts; and the first part of Mary Wroth's *Urania* appeared in print in 1621. Yet the majority of the work discussed, including the original text of Sidney's romance, Hoby's diary (and some of her reading), Donne and Bedford's poems, and the second part of Wroth's *Urania*, circulated in manuscript. Peter Beal refers to manuscript circulation as a form of "selective social bonding" particularly suited to exclusive communities, and Sidney, in particular, seems to have conceived of the *Arcadia*'s circulation in such a way.[91] Claiming that the safety of his romance "shall be the not walking abroad," Sidney asked his sister to keep the *Arcadia* close, reserving it for her "selfe, or to such friends, who will weigh errors in the balance of goodwill."[92] However, he also asked for her permission to dress it in her "liuerye," seeking both the cultural capital, as well as the protection, of her name.[93] The original, or *Old, Arcadia* was initially closely guarded among the intimates of Sidney Herbert's household; as Edmund Molyneux wrote in 1588, "A special dear friend he would be that could have a sight [of it] but much more dear that could once obtain a copy of it."[94] Yet Fulke Greville's claim that it had become "common" by 1586 suggests that it nonetheless circulated beyond the family bounds early in its textual life.[95] As these accounts suggest, manuscript publication was not always limited to a small sphere. In fact it often presumed—even courted—what Harold Love has called "user publication," the transfer of hand-written texts from one reader to another. Such practices frequently disseminated community-specific manuscripts far beyond their initial and designated audiences, their popular appeal explained largely by the presumed intimacy and exclusivity of their original context.[96]

[91] Peter Beal, *In Praise of Scribes*, p. viii.

[92] Philip Sidney, *The Countess of Pembroke's Arcadia (The Old Arcadia)*, ed. Katherine Duncan-Jones, 3.

[93] For a discussion of the power of Mary Herbert's name, see Hannay, "'Bearing the livery of your name.'"

[94] See H. R. Woudhuysen, *Sir Philip Sidney and the Circulation of Manuscripts*, 300.

[95] Woudhuysen, *Sir Philip Sidney*, 300.

[96] Love, *Scribal Publication*, 36–9. As Peter Beal's research has shown, there were more transcripts made of Donne's poems than of those of any other British poet of the 16th and

Manuscript was also frequently the chosen form of publication for politically sensitive texts, including those proffering political critique and guidance.[97] Sidney's notorious "Letter to Elizabeth" was among the most "scribally published" texts in early modern England.[98] While authors also used manuscript literary texts to flatter or influence monarchs, as Mary Sidney Herbert did when she offered a manuscript copy of the Psalms to Queen Elizabeth ("A King should onely to a Queene be sent"), they also used them to influence each other.[99] Donne's careful supervision and circulation of his poems in manuscript served to confirm or establish relationships with members of various political alliances, and Hoby's reading of the manuscript of a fellow northern puritan woman embodied her commitment to a regional form of godly activism.[100]

While printing played less of a role in the institutional exercise of power than manuscript, it could nonetheless get an author's name and message into the public realm. (As Margaret Cavendish put it in one of her prefaces, a printed book could "set every tongue to work."[101]) When Mary Wroth published the first part of her *Urania* in 1621, she chose not only folio, the biggest and most expensive print format, but notorious publishers as well. Rather than a sign of her relinquishment "of control over the further social use of" her work, Wroth's choice to print her romance was an extension of that control: an active decision to associate her romance with a tradition of dissent.[102] Printed texts, moreover, were neither separate from nor finalized

17th centuries. The large number of extant transcriptions reminds us not only that his verse belonged essentially to a manuscript culture, but that manuscript transcription was often a successful form of publication (see the *Index of English Literary Manuscripts*, 1.1.245, cited in Marotti, *Manuscript*, 147). As Ben Jonson observed of his own poems, "Being sent to one, they will be read of all" ("An epigram to my muse, the Lady Digby, on her husband Sir Kenelme Digby," *Works of Ben Jonson*, vol. 8, 263). While Love suggests that publication occurs when a text passes from the "private realm of creativity to the public realm of consumption," the work discussed in this book suggest that creativity was less a "private realm" than a collaborative one..

[97] Love, *Scribal Publication*, 160, 175. As David Carlson notes "handwritten works were particularly suitable for self-advancement" at the early Stuart court (*English Humanist Books*, cited in Woudhuysen, *Sir Philip Sidney*, 8). In contrast, printing, "however great its capacity to sway public opinion, was of minimal importance to the institutional exercise of power" (Love, *Scribal Publication*, 160).

[98] On the transmission of this letter, see Beal, *In Praise of Scribes*, 109–46.

[99] The line is from Sidney Herbert's dedicatory poem, "Even now that Care," cited in Hannay, " 'Bearing the livery of your name,' " 9.

[100] Love, *Scribal Publication*, 51–2. The term "politically active class" is Wallace MacCaffrey's. See "Place and Patronage in Elizabethan Politics," 99, cited in May, *The Elizabethan Courtier Poets*, 19. See also Marotti, *John Donne*; and, for other poets, May.

[101] *Poems and Fancies* (1653), A3ʳ. Cavendish also supported her texts' print publication with other, more performative, forms of self-presentation and promotion. See Crawford, "Preachers, Pleaders, and Players."

[102] Love, *Scribal Publication*, 39.

completions of manuscript texts.[103] As Wroth might well have expected, the 1621 publication of the *Urania* was greeted by a flurry of manuscript reactions: vitriolic poems exchanged between a shadowed character and Wroth; Wroth's own letters of self-exculpation and scandal-management; epistolary gossip between Sirs John Chamberlain and Dudley Carleton.[104] In addition, Wroth not only made corrections to printed copies of the *Urania*, but she continued the romance in manuscript. Similarly, while the majority of the texts Margaret Hoby read were printed, Hoby made them pertinent and alive for occasions and contexts other than the ones for which they were originally written, whether by reading them with others, or, in one exemplary case, marginally annotating them for future use. Hoby's reading practices illustrate the ways in which reading was an active form of literary production—as much a form of publication as either of its related, and arguably more permanent, technologies.[105]

The texts discussed in this book encoded, in ways both subtle and explicit, their affiliation with a given community and cause, and these codes depended on readers for their dilation and propagation. The literary strategies their authors used served both to advertise the authors' and communities' opinions and skills, and to solicit the attention and interpretive labor of readers—both inside and outside of those communities. As Stephen Dobranski has argued, many early modern texts counted on the active participation of readers (*Plutarch's Morals*, 1603, for example, points out how readers can uncover the "many profitable and holsome lessons" that are "covertly couched" in a literary work).[106] The impressive English history of encrypted texts—from the famous case of *Richard II* to Jonson's *Sejanus*—suggests that readers had "considerable experience interpreting [the] secretive language" of early modern literary texts.[107] The production of early modern literary texts was, as Annabel Patterson has argued, always intimately engaged with the specter of censorship.[108] Authors, she argues, encoded their own opinions in ways that simultaneously appealed

---

[103] For a discussion of print and manuscript as complementary, see David McKitterick, *Print, Manuscript and the Search for Order*.

[104] For transcripts of Wroth's letters, see "Appendix: The Correspondence of Lady Mary Wroth," in Wroth, *Poems*, 233–45.

[105] Readers, as a wide range of scholars have argued, participated directly in the making and meaning of early modern texts. In effect, readers were co-writers, or, at the very least, co-producers of the texts they read.

[106] *Plutarch's Morals* (1603), D1ʳ; cited in Stephen Dobranski, *Readers and Authorship in Early Modern England*, 44.

[107] Dobranski, *Readers and Authorship*, 44, referencing Lois Potter. See also Annabel Patterson, *Censorship and Interpretation*, 57.

[108] She argues that the "prevailing codes of communication, the implicit social contract between authors and authorities" were "intelligible to all parties at the time as being a fully deliberate and conscious arrangement" (Patterson, *Censorship and Interpretation*, 17).

to specific audiences—those who knew how to decode or interpret such opinions—and protected the authors both from possible unauthorized interpretation and from accusation by the authorities.[109] A larger community than the original or targeted audience shared some of the interpretive strategies associated with a specific text. In 1621, for example, Members of Parliament knew to read pastoral romance—especially one associated with the Sidneys—as political commentary.

Each of the communities discussed in this book used various forms of coded genre, terminology, or imagery in their textual exchanges. The codes both signaled factional and/or topical content and intentions, and provided the grounds for deniability in the face of unwanted interpretation. Sidney, for example, used a genre known, in his own words, for using "hidden forms [to] utter such matters as otherwise were not fit for their delivery."[110] In addition, the romance's pastoral names were often ciphers for real people and the existence of keys from the very beginning of its circulation suggests that it was associated with a specific sociopolitical milieu. Margaret Hoby's codes, if they can be called that, are more difficult to decipher; she promulgated her views through co-reading that was inextricable from other forms of sociability, and while I argue in Chapter 2 that her diary was the record of a public career, it still looks, to most people, like the diary of "a private Elizabethan gentlewoman." In the poems John Donne wrote to Lucy Harington Russell, his solicitation of her "grace" was at once a plea for patronage, and an engagement with the intra-Christian debate over the nature of grace in which they were both involved. The language of flattery in his poems was thus also an invitation to debate. Like Sidney, Mary Wroth chose to write a densely topical romance, at once epic and pastoral. Her protagonists, both male and female, exemplify the martial or chivalric heroisms that compensated for the loss of real power that the members of her alliance so lamented. In addition to "glauncing at greater matters," her use of pastoral also served to draw attention to the "country" interests of the *Urania*: particularly its promotion of the rights of the landed (or country) nobility. In each case, "the well-advertised secrecy" of such codes was designed to provoke interpretive effort from a range of readers.[111] Predicated on the mutually dependent labors of patrons, writers, dedicatees, and readers, the works discussed in this book sought to connect interpretive effort with sociopolitical effort in the public sphere.

---

[109] There "were conventions that both sides accepted as to how far a writer could go in explicit address to the contentious issues of his day, how he could encode his opinions so that nobody would be *required* to make an example of him" (Patterson, *Censorship and Interpretation*, 11).

[110] *Old Arcadia*, 50

[111] The term is Patterson's, *Censorship and Interpretation*, 40.

As Thomas Scott put it in *Vox Regis,* "sometimes Kings are content in Playes and Maskes to be admonished of divers things."[112] For each of the communities discussed in this book, the reform desired was both political and Protestant, and it was not only the King who required admonishing.

Yet at the same time as the individual chapters focus on the varied cultural and political activities of particular political alliances, they are equally conscious of the fact that literary texts are more than merely the carriers of relationships or ambitions.[113] The genres in which authors wrote carried histories and meanings beyond those of the present moment or cause, and the specific literary details that characterize individual texts are illustrative of their creators' learning and ingenuity as well as their political interests. As Pierre Bourdieu puts it, texts are the results both of their creators' positions in "a field of cultural production," and of their dispositions.[114] *Mediatrix* is thus equal parts literary history and literary criticism. It seeks to illuminate the central, political roles women played in the production of early modern literature, and to take seriously the material aspects of literary production, from the estates in which texts were produced to the material forms in which they circulated. Yet it is also a literary project, alive to authors' imaginative negotiations of inherited tropes and forms, the pleasure of what Mary Sidney Herbert called "this coupled worke," "theise dearest offrings of my hart / dissolv'd to Inke" and sent out into the world to do their work.[115]

---

[112] Cited in Patterson, *Censorship and Interpretation,* 53.

[113] Jonathan Crewe makes this point elegantly in *Hidden Designs:* "*Contra* historicism…the *object* of literary criticism is not the historical period or is particular ensemble of signification, and cultural political-strategies, but rather the phenomenon of *poesis* both in and *as* those significations and strategies" (17). No literary text i.e. is narrowly directed to one goal, nor merely the carrier of other, presumably more important, political intentions (74–5).

[114] Bourdieu, *The Field of Cultural Production,* passim.

[115] "To the Angell spirit of the most excellent Sir Phillip Sidney," *Collected Works of Mary Sidney Herbert,* 112, l. 2, ll. 78–9.

1

Female Constancy and *The Countess of Pembroke's Arcadia*

Sir Philip Sidney's *Arcadia* has long been read in terms of its coded political commentary. In particular, it has been associated with an aristocratic critique of monarchical absolutism and an insistence on the conciliary and magistral roles of that aristocracy.[1] Yet to date, no one has associated the *Arcadia*'s political concerns with aristocratic *women*, or rather not in any substantive way. A great deal of attention has been paid to the *Arcadia*'s

---

[1] Among the first to offer a political reading of the *Arcadia* was Fulke Greville, who maintained that Sidney's aim in writing the romance was "lively to represent the growth, state, and declination of Princes, change of Government, and lawes: vicissitudes of sedition, faction, succession, confederacies, plantations, with all other errors, or alterations in publique affaires" (Greville, *Dedication to Philip Sidney*, 18). Greville, Peter C. Herman argues, begins writing the *Dedication* in 1610, "just as the tension between James and the House of Commons concerning the delicate balance between royal prerogative and the subject's liberties began to spiral upward." "'Bastard Children of Tyranny': The Ancient Constitution and Fulke Greville's *A Dedication to Sir Philip Sidney*," 985. For contemporary readings of political ideas in the *Arcadia* (in roughly chronological order), see E. A. Greenlaw, "Sidney's *Arcadia* as an Example of Elizabethan Allegory" and "The Captivity Episode in Sidney's *Arcadia*"; W. D. Briggs, "Political Ideas in Sidney's *Arcadia*"; W. G. Zeeveld, "The Uprising of the Commons in Sidney's *Arcadia*"; I. Ribner, "Sir Philip Sidney on Civil Insurrection"; M. Bergbusch, "Rebellion in the *New Arcadia*"; Annabel Patterson, "'Under...Pretty Tales': Intention in Sidney's *Arcadia*"; W. R. Drennan, "'Or Know Your Strengths': Sidney's Attitude toward Rebellion in 'Ister Banke'"; Richard McCoy, *Sir Philip Sidney*; M. N. Raitiere, *Faire Bitts*; Mervyn James, *Society, Politics and Culture*; Blair Worden, *The Sound of Virtue*; David Norbrook, "Sidney and Political Pastoral," in *Poetry and Politics in the English Renaissance*; Deborah Shuger, "Castigating Livy"; Tracey Sedinger, "Sidney's *New Arcadia* and the Decay of Protestant Republicanism"; Victor Skretkowicz, *European Erotic Romance*; and Joel B. Davis, *The Countesse of Pembrokes Arcadia and the Invention of English Literature*. On Sidney's concerns about the decline of the nobility and the rise of the monarchy at its expense, see Worden, *Sound of Virtue*, 272–8; on the *Arcadia*'s valorization of the aristocracy, see Shuger: "One can, I think, see Sidney's drastic rewriting of Livy in terms of Lawrence Stone's familiar 'crisis of the aristocracy.' The Sidneys, from Sir Philip to Algernon, consistently supported the 'ancient powerful warlike nobility' of England as the natural guardians of 'the people's liberties' against over-mighty rulers" ("Castigating Livy," 23). Mervyn James sums up the argument as follows: "The *Arcadia* emerged from an oppositionist group intensely concerned about, but excluded from, political power" (*Society, Politics and Culture*, 392). While both the oppositionism and the exclusion of the Sidney circle may be exaggerated, the dynamic nonetheless still holds.

heroes, Pyrocles and Musidorus, particularly to their shifts from a (purportedly) pastoral mode of heroism in the *Old Arcadia* to a more chivalric heroic mode in the revised or *New Arcadia*.[2] This heroism has been seen as an exemplification of the symbolic representations of power that (in some part) compensated for the loss of real forms of power for aristocratic men under an increasingly centralized monarchy—a representational mode that was associated with men like Sidney and the Earl of Essex.[3] A far different kind of attention has been paid to the romance's heroines, Pamela and Philoclea. Their constancy and virtue are seen as in keeping with the limited roles of women under patriarchy, or they are seen as exemplars of "feminized virtue," a quality that caveats and/or corrects the masculine and martial *virtus* of the heroes.[4] In related formulations, they are seen as exemplars or allegories of Christian patience, stoicism, and constancy.[5] Yet

[2] See e.g. John Buxton, who characterizes the *Old Arcadia* as a "careless romance" written "to please the ladies," and the *New Arcadia* as a more "masculine" kind of book. *Elizabethan Taste*, 256–7.

[3] On the largely symbolic nature of authors' investment in a heroic aristocratic agency, see Andrew Shifflett, *Stoicism, Politics and Literature in the Age of Milton.* The real social conditions of substantive aristocratic power, he claims, were largely gone by the late 16th cent.

[4] For arguments that see the heroines, particularly in the *New Arcadia*, as correctives for the heroes, see William Craft, "Remaking the Heroic Self in the *New Arcadia*"; Myron Turner, who notes "a well-planned shift away from the exclusively male hero" in the *New Arcadia*, "The Heroic Ideal in Sidney's Revised *Arcadia*," 71; and A. C. Hamilton who argues that the heroines illuminate the "limitations of masculine virtue," *Sir Philip Sidney*, 163. Craft offers an excellent survey of criticism on the romance's heroines, pointing out that Jon S. Lawry (*Sidney's Two "Arcadias"*) sees Pamela as the chief exemplar of a new heroism "of patience" and argues that it replaces an older, chivalric ideal. Walter R. Davis, "A Map of *Arcadia*," argues on the basis of the composite text first published in 1593 that Sidney's princes ascend a platonic ladder from heroism (active public service), to love of the princesses, to love of God. Mark Rose argues that, through the example of the princesses, Pyrocles and Musidorus are led back from confusion and folly to a noble, classical rationality (*Heroic Love*, 59–73, summarized in Craft, "Remaking the Heroic Self," 48). Several writers praise Pamela's "feminine" or passively resistant virtue that exceeds the unsuccessful military virtue of the princes. See E. M. W. Tillyard, *The English Epic and its Background*, 308–9; Turner, "The Heroic Ideal," 71; Lawry, *Sidney's Two "Arcadias*," 268–9; and Hamilton, *Sir Philip Sidney*, 163. Thelma N. Greenfield suggests that Philoclea is the "sun and center" of the *New Arcadia*, calling her "a living picture of love and virtue made manifest through beauty" (*The Eye of Judgment*, 109, 108, cited in Craft, "Remaking the Heroic Self," 63). See also Mervyn James, who argues that "The two princely heroes of the *Arcadia* attain to wisdom, then to patience, by way of the *education sentimentale* which was the result of their respective love affairs" (*Society, Politics and Culture*, 389). A. C. Hamilton takes up a similar theme, arguing that book 3 of the *New Arcadia* showcases "masculine virtue" set against the foil of "feminine virtue" and "fulfils Sidney's intent to revise the *Old Arcadia* into an absolute heroical poem" embodied specifically in the 1590 *Arcadia* (*Sir Philip Sidney*, 160–72).

[5] Mary Ellen Lamb argues that in the *New Arcadia* the heroines move from object to subject status, and that their heroism draws from a range of sources, including romantic heroines who die for love, martyrs who die for their religious beliefs, and Stoic heroes who demonstrate their equanimity by dying well (*Gender and Authorship in the Sidney Circle*, 101). See Mary Beth Rose's take on "the heroicism of endurance" exemplified by Pamela and Philoclea. *Gender and Heroism in Early Modern English Literature*, p. xii. See also Melissa

while Pamela and Philoclea are read allegorically, this symbolism is seen as categorically different from that of Musidorus and Pyrocles, whose actions are associated, however indirectly, with political power and political critique. The author of one of the foundational books on the *Arcadia*'s politics, for example, sees Pamela and Philoclea's constancy as politically toothless, a form of "dangerous quietism."[6]

In this chapter, I argue instead that Pamela and Philoclea should be associated—as they were by early modern readers—with political power and political critique. Like most forms of Elizabethan power, this power was configured allegorically. In *The Arte of English Poesie* (1589), George Puttenham defines "the courtly figure" of Allegoria—when "our wordes and our meanings meete not"—in political terms.[7] "The use of this figure is so large, and his vertue of so great efficacie," he writes, that "it is supposed no man can pleasantly utter and perswade without it, but in effect is sure never or very seldome to thrive and prosper in the world, that cannot skillfull put in use, in so much as not onely every common Courtier, but also the gravest Counsellour, yea and the most noble and wisest Prince of them all are many times enforced to use it."[8] Sidney's *Arcadia* is certainly allegorical in this sense, and its configuration of women was central to its particular mode of political persuasion and counsel. In the *Arcadia*, I argue, female constancy, particularly in the face of male tyranny, serves as an allegory for aristocratic power, resilience, and critique. This configuration, moreover, was not unique to the romance, but in keeping with the politically symbolic role female constancy played in late Elizabethan culture more broadly. Finally, the consistent associations between the *Arcadia* and women, particularly those women associated with the Sidney circle and its established modes of political critique, indicate the extent to which the symbolic formulation and political purchase of what Mary Ellen Lamb has called "the heroics of constancy" was intimately related to the sociopolitical and cultural work of actual women.[9] The allegory of female constancy was

Sanchez, who focuses on the *Arcadia*'s "hagiographic" accounts of the female character's erotic ordeals to argue that characters "who accept physical torment gain a moral authority that retroactively legitimates rebellion against both patriarchal and political hierarchy" (*Erotic Politics*, 35).

[6] McCoy, *Sir Philip Sidney*, 206, 212. See also Worden, who writes that in the *Arcadia* "Philoclea's passivity... offers an image of peace" and that "[t]here is no room for femininity in politics" (*Sound of Virtue*, 331).

[7] George Puttenham, *The Arte of English Poesie*, 186.

[8] Puttenham, *The Arte of English Poesie*, 186. Louis Adrian Montrose discusses this passage in "Celebration and Insinuation: Sir Philip Sidney and the Motives of Elizabethan Courtship." See also Sidney's defense of poetry as something "not affirmatively but allegorically and figuratively written." *A Defence of Poetry*, ed. Jan Van Dorsten, 53. "There are many mysteries contained in poetry," he writes later in the *Defence*, "which of purpose were written darkly, lest by profane wits it should be abused" (75).

[9] Lamb uses the term in the title of her chapter on Mary Wroth, but she also uses it in her discussion of the *Arcadia*, 101.

a mode of political persuasion associated with some of the most powerful women and political alliances in late Elizabethan England, and it is the story this chapter takes as its subject.

I. A LADY'S TEXT

The *Arcadia* has long been understood as a "ladies' text."[10] Much like Sidney's widely circulated "Letter to Elizabeth," which advised her against marriage with the duc d'Alençon, the *Arcadia* is frequently read as a form of advice for the Queen herself. "[G]launcing" as it does "at greater matters under the vaile of homely persons," pastoral romance was the privileged genre for such political commentary.[11] The *Arcadia's* concerns with right rule, and the grounds of resistance and rebellion, reflected those of the members of the Sidney alliance concerned with militant international Protestantism, and with the aforementioned rights of the nobility not only to provide counsel to the Prince—in this case, Elizabeth I—but to share in the governance of the kingdom under a mixed, or limited, monarchy.[12]

The *Arcadia* is also explicitly dedicated to a lady, or, more accurately, placed under her aegis. This is done both titularly—the romance's full

---

[10] The term is Juliet Fleming's, see "The Ladies' Man and the Age of Elizabeth," 158.

[11] Puttenham, *The Arte of English Poesie*, 53. Shepherds "sometimes, again, under hidden forms utter such matters as otherwise were not fit for their delivery" (*OA* 50). See also Annabel Patterson, "'Under...Pretty Tales,'" who cites Sidney's *Defence*: "Is the poor pipe disdained, which sometime out of Meliboeus' mouth can show the misery of people under hard lords or ravening soldiers, and again, by Tityrus, what blessedness is derived to them that lie lowest from the goodness of them that sit highest; sometimes, under the pretty tales of wolves and sheep, can include the whole considerations of wrong-doing and patience" (Sidney, *Defence of Poetry*, 43).

[12] See Mervyn James's account of the "political stance with which Sidney so enthusiastically identified himself—that of the Leicester-Walsingham policy of Protestant activism which was inherited by the second earl of Essex, also the legatee of Sidnean chivalric romanticism. This involved a European Protestant league, a larger investment of resources in the war with Spain, wider military commitments abroad, westward oceanic expansion, and an extended naval assault on the Spanish empire. At home, the keynote of the policy was bitter opposition to the dominant Cecil faction, and alliance with Puritanism" (*Society, Politics and Culture*, 391). For a more recent formulation, see Simon Adams, *Leicester and the Court*, passim. For the influence on Sidney of the Huguenot aristocracy, particularly their efforts to secure independence from a centralized Catholic monarchy and share in the governance of the commonwealth, see Briggs, "Political Ideas," who quotes the following line from the *New Arcadia*: "those, who being subaltern magistrates and officers of the crowne, were to be employed as from the Prince, so for the people" (*NA* 372). Sidney's knowledge of this doctrine is attributed to his knowledge of François Hotman's *Franco-Gallia* and the *Vindiciae Contra Tyrannos*, presumably written by his friends Philippe de Mornay and Hubert Languet. Both works oppose the nobility's constitutional claims to the potentially tyrannical impulses of the crown, cautiously explaining their own right to resistance. See Briggs, "Political Ideas," cited in McCoy, *Sir Philip Sidney*, 185.

title is *The Countess of Pembroke's Arcadia*—and via its production and circulation.[13] In his famous dedicatory epistle to his sister, Mary Sidney Herbert, Countess of Pembroke, Sidney said that he wrote the *Arcadia* for her, "in loose sheetes of paper, most of it in your presence, the rest, by sheetes, sent vnto you, as fast as they were done."[14] When he goes on to ask her permission to allow his romance to circulate "bearing the liuerye" of her name (*OA* 3), Sidney acknowledges both her constitutive role in the *Arcadia's* production, and her substantial influence in Elizabethan culture and politics.[15] In many ways, the *Arcadia* is the Countess of Pembroke's book as much as it is her brother's, and her livery, or familial insignia, is its calling card.

In its original form, the *Arcadia* is also directly addressed to "fair ladies." These addresses are made by the narrator himself, who invites the "fair ladies" to identify with matters of desire—"you ladies know best whether sometimes you feel impression of that passion" (*OA* 35)—and guides them through a number of narrative turns and surprises.[16] These "ladies," moreover, are often identified with the women who were part of Mary Sidney Herbert's circle at Wilton house, where Sidney composed the *Arcadia*, and who, it has been argued, comprised its original audience.[17] Readers have frequently commented that these extra-narrative appeals to women readers cease in the last two books of the *Old Arcadia*, and are wholly absent from the *New*.[18] But few have noted that many of the important episodes

[13] The title spawned others, including Abraham Fraunce's *The Countesse of Pembrokes Emmanuel* (1591) and *The Countesse of Pembrokes Ivychurch* (1591). The editors of *The Collected Works of Mary Sidney Herbert*, 12, point out that Franklin Williams demonstrates that the only aristocratic woman to receive more dedications than Pembroke was her second cousin, Lucy Harington Russell, Countess of Bedford, who received thirty-eight. (Their sources are "The Literary Patronesses of Renaissance England," and the *Index of Dedications and Commendatory Verses in English Books Before 1641*, and supplement, *The Library*, London, 1975.) The Countess of Bedford is the subject of Chapter 3 in this book.

[14] Sir Philip Sidney, *The Countess of Pembroke's Arcadia (The Old Arcadia)*, ed. Katherine Duncan-Jones (Oxford: Oxford University Press, 1985), 3. All subsequent references to this text, *OA*, will be cited in parentheses.

[15] Samuel Daniel's dedication of *Delia. Contayning certayne sonnets* (1592) to "Ladie Mary Countess of Pembroke" expresses a similar sentiment: "I desire only to be graced by the countenance of your protection: whome the fortune of our time hath made the happie and iudiciall Patronesse of the Muses." *The Complete Works in Verse and Prose of Samuel Daniel*, ed. A. B. Grosart. 5 vols (London, 1885–96; repr. 1963), 33.

[16] For the addresses to "fair ladies," see *OA* 25, 26, 34, 35, 36, 41, 44, 46, 49, 151, and 152. For a discussion of these addresses, see Lamb, *Gender and Authorship*, 72–115; and Crawford, "Sidney's Sapphics."

[17] These ladies are alluded to in Thomas Moffet's *The Silkewormes and their Flies*, 36–40. See also Lamb, *Gender and Authorship*, 175. Moffet lived near Wilton, and had recently, with the help of the Herberts, been elected its MP.

[18] Bertram Dobell, who discovered the first manuscripts of the *Old Arcadia*, was the first to note this. See "New Light Upon Sir Philip Sidney's *Arcadia*," 82. See also Lamb, *Gender and Authorship*, 74–5, on the lack of references to "fair ladies" in the last two books. Worden

in both the original and the revised editions are recounted within the narrative itself to women characters, chiefly Philoclea and Pamela, who serve both as evaluators and, frequently, as politic decipherers, of the stories they are told. Women, in other words, hold key symbolic and interpretive roles in both versions of the romance.

The *Arcadia*'s use of ciphers, pastoral names that served in part as codes for actual living persons, was also associated with women—including the "fair ladies" addressed by and in the text. While some of the ciphers in the *Arcadia* are more obvious than others—"Philisides," is almost universally seen as a cipher for Philip Sidney himself—others are more ambiguous.[19] The "Mira," to whom Philisides sings a song of devotion in the fourth eclogues of the *Old Arcadia*, has been identified with Queen Elizabeth, but it is more likely that she is an anagrammatic figure for "Mari" Sidney Herbert—a reading that fits with Sidney's consistent presentation of his sister as his poetic and familial organizing principle. (At the end of his song, a poetic variation on the Judgment of Paris, Philisides chooses Mira over Venus and Diana, and "her shape sanke in [his] brest" (*OA* 293).[20] Thereafter, she serves as a kind of internalized muse.) Contemporary readers associated the most famous addition to the *New Arcadia*, the story of the constant lovers Argalus and Parthenia, with both Philip and Mary Sidney's parents, Sir Henry and Lady Mary Sidney, and Mary Sidney Herbert and

sees the addresses to "fair ladies" in the *Old Arcadia* as a "decoy" designed to distract attention from the inflammatory material concerning government and topical concerns. The address to his sister, he argued, "intended less to convey his purpose than to protect it" (Worden, *Sound of Virtue*, 20, cited in Hackett, *Women and Romance Fiction*, 104). While I also argue that her name served as protection, the protection I am arguing for is in keeping with the political intentions of the *Arcadia*, rather than a way of disguising them.

[19] On Philisides as "Sidney's fictionalised self-portrait," see Dobell, "New Light Upon Sir Philip Sidney's *Arcadia*," 91–2; and *The Poems of Sir Philip Sidney*, ed. Ringler, 418.

[20] For an argument identifying Mira with Elizabeth, see Dennis Moore, "Philisides and Mira." The "Mira" episode takes place in "Samothea" (a name for ancient Britain), further highlighting the political topicality of the poem. See Katherine Duncan-Jones, "Sidney in Samothea," 174–7. Holinshed describes Samothea as a proto-Christian land of learning and justice—a British civilization believed to be older than Greece and the source of Greek letters—which declined under the conqueror Albion. As Duncan-Jones puts it, "The fact that the melancholy Philisides comes from Samothea is thus perhaps a sign of Sidney's discontent with contemporary England" ("Sidney in Samothea," 176). Dobell suggests that Mira (and Philoclea) portray aspects of Penelope Devereux ("New Light Upon Sir Philip Sidney's *Arcadia*," 93–4). For Mira as Mary, see *The Silkewormes and their Flies* (1599), in which Mary is addressed as Mira, a shepherdess with a train of "Virgins white" whom Geoffrey Hiller identifies as Mary Sidney Herbert's daughter Anne and her attendant gentlewomen. "'Where thou doost live, there let all graces be,'" 43. On Tudor treatments of the judgment of Paris, see John D. Reeves, "The Judgment of Paris as a Device of Tudor Flattery," *Notes and Queries*, ns 1 (1954): 7–11; Louis Adrian Montrose, "Gifts and Reasons: The Contexts of Peele's *Araygnement of Paris*," *English Literary History*, 47 (1980): 433–61; and Curt Breight, "Realpolitik and Elizabethan Ceremony: The Earl of Hertford's Entertainment of Elizabeth at Elvetham, 1591," *Renaissance Quarterly*, 45 (1992): 20–48.

her husband Henry Herbert, second Earl of Pembroke.[21] Each couple, crucially, served at different times as the anchoring unit for the religious and political interests of what has been called the Dudley-Leicester-Sidney alliance.

While identifications of the heroes Pyrocles and Musidorus vary—contemporary (and subsequent) readers identified them with figures ranging from Sidney himself to the husbands of the Devereux sisters—those of the heroines Philoclea and Pamela are surprisingly consistent.[22] They are identified with Penelope Devereux Rich and Dorothy Devereux Perrot Percy, sisters of the famous Elizabethan courtier and Sidney ally, Robert Devereux, Earl of Essex, and notable figures in late Elizabethan social,

---

[21] On Argalus and Parthenia as Mary Sidney Herbert and her husband, see William Dean, "Henry Oxinden's Key (1628) to *The Countess of Pembroke's Arcadia*," 14–21: "it would be natural for early readers to perceive that in these characters Sidney was paying a high compliment to his beloved sister and her husband" (18). Oxinden himself identifies Argalus with Henry Herbert, second Earl of Pembroke. See also Marcus S. Goldman, "Sir Philip Sidney and the 'Arcadia,'" 173; and Katherine Duncan-Jones, *Sir Philip Sidney: Courtier Poet*, 3–5.

[22] The key that appears in a copy of the 1598 folio owned by letter writer and neo-Latin poet Henry Oxinden (1609–70) makes the following identifications:

> Philisides Sr. Philip Sydney himselfe
> Basilius the old Earle of Essex
> Gynecia the countess [of Essex]
> Miso the Lady corke
> Mopsa the Ladie Lucie
> Philoclea the Ladie Rich
> Pamela the Lady Northumberland
> Argalus one what Sr. Philips mother loued who was my lord of Pembroke
> Parthenia the countesse of Pembroke who was Sr. Philips sister
> Helen queen Elizabeth
> Quaere who Pyrocles (Dean, "Henry Oxinden's Key," 16)

The manuscript commonplace book of Sir Francis Castillion, the son of Elizabeth's Italian tutor, identifies Pyrocles as Sidney, Musidorus as his friend Sir Edward Dyer, Philoclea as Penelope Rich, and Pamela as her sister Dorothy (summarized in Schurink, " 'Like a Hand in the Margine of a Booke,' " 14). D. Tyndale, who is quoted in Aubrey's *Lives*, also read the *Arcadia* as a *roman à clef*, identifying Kalandar as Henry Sidney, Pamela as "my Lady Northumberland," Philoclea as "My lady Rich," and Musidorus and Pyrocles as their husbands ("some others I have herd guessed at"). On Tyndale's key, particularly as it concerns Rich, see Goldman: "the only one of the identifications which has had a steady appeal to the imagination of readers of the *Arcadia* is that of Philoclea as Penelope Devereux... it was general and persistent enough to receive a kind of permanent sanction in the list of characters printed at the beginning of the third volume of the 1724–25 edition of Sidney's works" ("Sir Philip Sidney and the 'Arcadia,'" 176). For a discussion of the possible references to Penelope Rich as Philoclea in the *Arcadia*, see Ephim G. Fogel, "The Personal References in the Fiction and Poetry of Sir Philip Sidney," 90. W. H. Bond reports that the William Andrews Clark Library has William Herbert's copy of the 1593 *Arcadia*, with a key ("The Reputation and Influence of Sir Philip Sidney" (unpublished doctoral dissertation, Harvard University, 1941), 93–5—cited in Alexander, *Writing After Sidney*, 301 n. 40).

cultural, and political life.[23] The existence of keys to the *Arcadia* from the very beginning of its circulation indicate that perceived connections between characters and real historical figures were structural, rather than merely ornamental, to the *Arcadia*'s meaning; the consistency of certain identifications suggests, moreover, that the romance was associated with a specific sociocultural milieu or community. While the keys do not securely fix given ciphers to actual historical subjects, they nonetheless testify that this mode of interpretation was an integral part of the experience of reading the *Arcadia*.

My argument in this chapter is that this recursive mode of reading—what we might call the *Arcadia*'s deciphering imperative—was intimately related to an extant and more broadly allegorical mode in late Elizabethan English culture in which women functioned as the exemplars of a principled constancy: the Christian neostoic constancy associated with aristocratic critique. This mode, in which the neostoically constant and providentially minded woman served as the exemplary figure for aristocratic power, was associated with the Sidney circle, and anchored, in many ways, by women, particularly Mary Sidney Herbert and Penelope Devereux Rich. While the personal biographies of these two women in relation to Philip Sidney are so frequently repeated as to have been rendered almost completely anodyne—Sidney "retreated" from court to his sister's house to write his romance; Penelope Rich is the "Stella" of Sidney's frustrated love—their importance as cultural and, more pertinently for my purposes, political figures has received far less attention.[24]

While the Dudley-Leicester-Sidney-Essex alliance was, as its (heuristically) hyphenated name suggests, associated with men who held (or sought) office, women, including Mary Sidney Herbert and Penelope Devereux Rich, were frequently identified as the scions of these same families, and often served as their most powerful agents or brokers. In his response to the scurrilous *Leicester's Commonwealth* (1584), for example, Philip Sidney defended his own right to aristocratic prominence through

---

[23] Dorothy Devereux married Sir Thomas Perrot in 1583. He fought with Sidney at Zutphen and was one of the knights who walked in state by his coffin. He and Dorothy had a daughter they called Penelope. After Perrot's death in 1594, Dorothy married Henry Percy, ninth Earl of Northumberland and became the Countess of Northumberland. They had a daughter, Dorothy (1598–1659), who later married Robert Sidney, earl of Leicester. See Sally Varlow, *The Lady Penelope*, passim.

[24] The connections between Sidney's Stella and Penelope Devereux Rich are longstanding. See e.g. Walter G. Friedrich, "The Stella of Astrophel" (1936). As Ringler puts it in his edn of Sidney's poems, "the legitimate procedure is not to ignore the biography but to find out what kind of biography it is" (170). Friedrich asks a similar question: "Spenser says that Astrophel did love Stella—but how?" ("The Stella of Astrophel," 116).

his mother's line ("my chiefest honour is to be a Dudley");[25] Mary Sidney Herbert's "liuerye," as we have seen, was the one under which Sidney sought protection for the *Arcadia*; and Penelope Devereux Rich played a crucial role in the political machinations of her brother's, and indeed the whole alliance's, activities, throughout the late sixteenth and early seventeenth centuries. Indeed in one of her letters to the Huguenot Jean Hotman, written when she was involved in clandestine communication with James VI of Scotland about his pursuit of the English throne, Rich explicitly evokes the politically symbolic idea of female constancy. She encourages Hotman's constancy to his own wife, and attests, in what is clearly a kind of political code, to her own. At the end of her letter she identifies herself as "la plus constante de ceux qui sont nommez en ce papier"—a list comprised largely of international diplomats.[26]

One of the reasons these women played such potently symbolic roles in the political culture of late Elizabethan England was because of the early modern political analogy between women and political subjects. A woman's constancy configured not just her own relationship to her lord (father or husband), but also that of the subject to his or her lord: the prince. Similarly, attitudes towards women—attacks on and defenses of women—were frequently analogized to monarchical attitudes toward their subjects. Misogyny was associated with tyranny, whereas those who took the side of women—as both Pyrocles, and, eventually, Musidorus do at the beginning of the *Arcadia*—were associated with the rights of the subject, and, crucially, with limitations on the monarch's power. When the *New Arcadia*'s tyrant Cecropia refers to the "imperious maisterfulnesse, which nature giues to men aboue women" (*NA* 534), she evokes precisely

---

[25] "The Discourse in Defense of the Earl of Leicester," in *The Miscellaneous Works of Sir Philip Sidney*, 314. Leicester was Sidney's mother's brother, and Sidney was heir to both his Dudley uncles, the Earls of Leicester and Warwick.

[26] Rich's letters are in the Teyler Museum in Haarlem, see MSS. Hotomaniora, nos. 41, 42, 43, 44 and 45, included in P. J. Blok, *Correspondence inédite de Robert Dudley*. The cited letter reads in full: "Je baisse en toute humilité les mains de ma cherre Clarté, et à Monsieur de Busanval je luy souhaitte les bonnes graces de sa Maistresse, et à monsieur Palevesin bon vant, et à monsieur de Sidnye, qui ne croye pas tout ce que l'on luy dict, et à monsieur Constable qu'il ne soit plus amoureux, et à vous mesme d'aymer bien vostre femme, et à tous d'estre constants jusques à vanderdy. La plus constante de ceux qui sont nommez en ce papier hors mins une, Penelope de Riche" (178). (It translates thus: "I kiss in all humility the hands of my dear Light, and to Monsieur de Busanval I wish the good graces of his Mistress, and to monsieur Palevesin good wind, and to monsieur de Sidnye that he wouldn't believe everything people tell him, and to monsieur Constable that he wouldn't be in love anymore, and to yourself to love your wife, and to everybody to be constant till Friday. The most constant of those who are in this paper with one exception, Penelope Riche.") I am grateful to Nicolae-Alexandru Virastau, Ph.D. candidate in the Department of French and Romance Philology at Columbia University, for his help with these letters. Unless indicated, all translations are his.

the analogy that solicited the kinds of politically meaningful defenses of women we see in a wide range of late Elizabethan and early Jacobean texts, including the *Arcadia*.[27]

Women's constancy was thus concerned not only with gender roles and family loyalty, but also with the relationship between subjects and their monarch more broadly. While the *Arcadia* is critical of many aspects of monarchical rule—the Arcadian ruler Basilius's impolitic retreat from active political life; his and other kings' susceptibility to the "poysonous sugar of flatterie" (*NA* 228); the evil monarch Cecropia's Machiavellianism—it is also, as numerous critics have pointed out, consistently and carefully pro-monarchy. The romance spends a great deal of time articulating the differences between popular rebellion (the "many-headed multitude, whom inconstancy only doth guide": *OA* 115), and that headed by aristocratic magistrates.[28] The latter form was concerned not with getting rid of monarchy *per se*, but rather with opposing tyranny and (re)establishing ideal forms of monarchy: people- and law-based; substantively and structurally conciliary; limited rather than absolutist. What critics have not noted is that the *Arcadia*'s mode of holding up the monarchy in its ideal— that is, mixed—form, is predicated, both structurally and symbolically, on the constancy of women. The relationship between the symbolic forms of

[27] For a brilliant reading of *querelle des femmes* texts as coded critique of absolute monarchy, see Christina Luckyj, "*A Mouzell for Melastomus* in Context." She argues that the analogy between marriage and politics served as the foundation for resistance theory—i.e. that a woman's rights within marriage signified the rights of the subject under a monarch.

[28] On resistance being rightfully entrusted to the nobility rather than "initiatives by private persons," see Worden, *Sound of Virtue*, 282–4. In reproaching the rebels in book 2 of the *New Arcadia*, Pyrocles, Worden argues, adopts Languet's stance in *Vindiciae contra tyrannos*: "there could be no...obedience where every one upon his own private passion may interpret the doings of the rulers": *NA* cited in *Sound of Virtue*, 284. On the other hand, as Worden wryly notes, "Elizabethan propaganda about the divinity of kingship and about the place of kings in a divinely appointed hierarchy, left no mark on Sidney's writings" (*Sound of Virtue*, 285). David Norbrook makes a similar observation about the limits of resistance and the rights of the aristocracy: "The Leicester circle had supported the Dutch rebels against Philip II, but William of Orange had been careful to emphasize that this was a rebellion with strong feudal precedents and with aristocratic leaders." In the Netherlands, he recommended that only the nobility of the land or other learned persons, well versed in matters of state, should be appointed to the country's councils" ("Sidney and Political Pastoral," in *Poetry and Politics in the English Renaissance*, 91). See also McCoy, *Sir Philip Sidney*, 186–94. At one crucial point Musidorus resists his own election as monarch, arguing instead for monarchical succession. When "some of the wisest (seeing that a popular licence is indeede the many-headed tyranny) preuailed with the rest to make Musidorus their chiefe," Musidorus, "vnderstanding that there was left of the bloud Roiall, & next to the succession, an aged Gentleman of approued goodness" conferred the power to him, "but with such conditions, & cautions of the conditions, as might assure the people (with as much assurance as worldly matters beare) that not onely that gouernour, of whom indeed they looked for al good, but the nature of the gouernment, should be no way apt to decline to Tyranny" (*NA* 138, ed. 271).

female constancy and the actual women who played out this symbolism in the public sphere of late Elizabethan England is precisely what the deciphering imperative of the *Arcadia* illustrates. The political nature of female constancy is thus what has been missing from our analyses of the romance.

II. "CONSTANT IN THE MIDST OF INCONSTANCEY"

In recent years, critics have turned their attention to the political roles that women played in the period, particularly those of the ladies of Elizabeth's Privy and Bedchambers.[29] Many of these women were extremely powerful. Like Elizabeth I, whose motto was *semper eadem*, some of them blazoned their political strength, claiming the qualities of inward strength and resolution in the face of outside accidents that Sidney famously encouraged in his letter to the Queen.[30] Such constancy was often understood as an attestation of loyalty to Elizabeth, but it also sometimes served as sign of independence, even as a caution on the Queen's power. In a Latin elegy presented to Philip Sidney in "the center of Dutch Protestantism" (Ghent) in 1579, for example, "Divine Eliza" is presented with a train of allegorical counselors: Religion, Justice, Prudence, and "brave Constancy who fortifies the mind and holds forth the laurel wreath towards victorious heads."[31] The "bevy of illustrious Heroines" which follows, including Sidney's mother and sister, the Countess of Huntingdon (identified as Sidney's "second mother"), and "Lady Russell" (Elizabeth Cooke Hoby Russell) ("the goddess's equal in wit, features and manners"), buttresses Sidney in his promotion of English Protestantism ("Religion, dressed in modest rites, will firmly and with a pure voice establish God in his churches!") and in his own as-yet-tender "Constancy."[32] Each of these women did actually

---

[29] See e.g. James Daybell (ed.), *Women and Politics in Early Modern England* and *Women Letter Writers in Tudor England*, Charlotte Merton, "The Women Who Served Queen Mary and Queen Elizabeth," and Natalie Mears, *Queenship and Political Discourse*. Earlier, groundbreaking work includes Pam Wright, "A Change in Direction"; and Barbara J. Harris, "Women and Politics in Early Tudor England."

[30] The 1580 letter is included in *The Miscellaneous Works of Sir Philip Sidney*. "For neither outward accidents do much prevail against a true inward strength," he writes at one point (293). "And as to your person, in the scale of your happiness, what good there may come by it [by this marriage], to balance with the loss of so honourable a constancy; truly yet I perceive not" (295).

[31] J. A. Van Dorsten's *Poets, Patrons and Professors* includes a translation of Daniel Rogers's Latin elegy "To Philip Sidney, a young man of renowned wit and virtue" written on his last day in Ghent with Hubert Languet in January 1579 (*Poets*, 62–5).

[32] Van Dorsten, *Poets*, 62, 64.

Figure 1.1 Portrait miniature of Margaret Clifford, Countess of Cumberland, with the motto "Constant in the Midst of Inconstancey," by Laurence Hilliard. Reproduced by permission of the Victoria and Albert Museum.

play such a role in Elizabethan England; all were committed Protestant activists and key figures in the Leicester-Sidney alliance, and their presence in this scene illustrates the fusion of symbolic and literal constancy that characterized the alliance's activism.

Another of these women, Margaret Russell Clifford, Countess of Cumberland, was frequently heralded by her contemporaries for her constancy, particularly in the face of the personal obstacles she faced. Her own miniature (see Figure 1.1) bore the motto "Constant in the Midst of Inconstancey."[33] To date, these qualities have been read solely in light

[33] On this inscription on a Laurence Hilliard portrait of Clifford, see Yvonne Bruce, "'That which Marreth All,'" 46.

of Clifford's response to her husband's infidelities—that is, as personal characteristics—yet a number of late Elizabethan texts suggest that her constancy was something more than marital fidelity. In one of these texts, a heroic epistle by Samuel Daniel, she is characterized as an exemplary Christian neostoic, unmoved by "all the thunder-cracks / Of Tyrants threats," and looking "upon the mightiest monarchs warres / But only as on stately robberies."[34] "[S]ecur'd within the brazen walles / Of a cleere conscience," and trusting in "all-guiding Providence," Daniel's Clifford looks on as "man doth ransacke man" "[a]s from the shore of peace with unwet eie" (205).

Fulke Greville's little-known "Letter to an Honourable Lady," which advises a (pointedly) unnamed woman how to survive her unfaithful and tyrannical husband, has also long been associated with Margaret Clifford.[35] The letter is dedicated to her, and many saw her relationship with her husband—whose profligacy was the subject of popular knowledge—as appropriately analogous to that between the "Honourable Lady" and her profligate husband. Yet Greville's letter is also a coded piece of Christian neostoic advice for elite subjects living under a too-absolutist monarch; Greville himself explicitly highlights the analogy between the relations between husbands and wives and sovereigns and subjects. Towards the beginning of the letter, he promises to "lay before [the Lady] the opinions of worthie men, borne under Tyrants, and bound to obay, though they could not please: the comparison holdinge in some affinitie betweene a wives subjection to a husband, and a subjects obedience to his soveraigne" (154). Presuming that women always configure private histories rather than political rights more broadly, critics have failed to see a connection between the Letter's dedication to a woman and its political commentary. Yet Greville's letter articulates the political analogy between the position of women and the rights of noble subjects that was central both to the

---

[34] The epistles, which were not published until 1603, are included in *The Complete Works*, vol. 1. The cited lines appear on p. 204. All subsequent references to the poem will be cited parenthetically within the text. Daniel was also working on another poem at the same time, "A Letter from Octavia to Marcus Antonius" (1599), which tells a similar story of female constancy. Written in *ottava rima*, the poem is a letter of complaint to Mark Antony while he is living in Egypt with Cleopatra, asking him to "Do, as the best men do, bound thine owne will" (ll. 41, 134). Here Octavia is the exemplar of constancy. This letter has also been seen as in "some sense a representation of the marital difficulties of his patron, Margaret Clifford." See Martha Hale Shackford, "Samuel Daniel's Poetical 'Epistles,'" 182–3; and John Pitcher, "Negotiating a Marriage for Lady Anne Clifford: Samuel Daniel's Advice," 784–7.

[35] The "Letter to an Honourable Lady" is included in *The Prose Works of Fulke Greville*. It was not published until 1633, but was probably written before 1589. All subsequent references to the letter will be cited parenthetically within the text. On the letter, see Ronald A. Rebholz, *The Life of Fulke Greville*, and Bruce, "'That which Marreth All,'" 273.

period and, as we will see, to Sidney's particular mode of political allegory in the *Arcadia*.

In the story Greville recounts in the "Letter to an Honourable Lady," the lady's marriage begins as it should, in "equalitie guided without absolutenesse" (138). Yet finding himself in a context in which "the ends of societie are no more nowe to love, or equallie partycipate, but absolutely to rule," the Lady's husband "beganne to thincke of somethinge more then mutuall enjoyinge," and moves towards the "affected absolutenesse of a husbands power" (140). The better part of the letter advises the Lady how she might endure this situation, and promotes constancy as the answer: "But who are they that can walke this milkie way? Not those unconstant spiritts, which are wandered into the wildernesse of desire" (140). Greville advises the lady that "instead of mastering" her husband, she should master herself: "My councell is therefore *Madame!* that you enrich your selfe upon your owne stocke, not lookinge outwardlie, but inwardlie for the fruite of true peace" (154). Patience, he asserts, is an "armor against oppression."[36]

Yet lest we perceive this advice as politically quietist, the "Letter" characterizes the patient and obedient stoicism it promotes as a form of counsel. "Pleasing," Greville points out, "is good, not least because the meanes that are used in it, as vowes, prayers, sacrifice, obedience &c, are all milde councells; and such, as rather enrich, then enpoverishe those that use them" (146). Greville's stoic vision is, moreover, more than implicitly conciliary. He also offers the Lady a piece of advice familiar to any reader of Sidney's *Arcadia*:

> Therefore *Madame!* untill the smartes of sense have so united will, and understandinge, as all men, in like fortunes, may have like ends; *till the beasts beginne to knowe their strengthes*; the unwritten lawes blott out the written; and the temporal cease under the eternall; there is neither in yours, nor in any other subjection, any true peace to be gotten by trust of Superiors; nor honor by strife against them. (158, emphasis added)

The Lady must neither "complaine, or mutinie," he advises, "but rather as vegetable thinges in the wisdome of nature doe [...] which is, drawe all your sappe in this winter of thoughts downe to the roote; and be content to want leaves, till the sweet springe of time, or occasion come, to invite them up againe" (159).

---

[36] *A Defence of Poetry* identifies the teaching of "patience" as one of the ends of political pastoral: "under the pretty tales of wolves and sheep," pastoral poetry "can include the whole considerations of wrong-doing and patience" (43). Justus Lipsius writes that "the true mother of Constancie is PATIENCE, and lowlinesse of mind, which is A voluntarie sufferance without grudging of all things whatsoeuer can happen to, or in a man" (cited in Bruce, "'That which Marreth All,'" 45).

In this advice, Greville promotes the ancient constitution (the "unwritten laws" of the nation), and divine providence (the "eternall" that trumps the "temporal"), but he also explicitly cites the "Ister Bank" poem that Philisides, Sidney's cipher, recites in the *Arcadia*. This poem, a beast fable that Sidney credits, in the only explicitly topical allusion in the romance, to the Huguenot tyrannomach Hubert Languet, functions as a barely coded comment on the rights of the nobility to resist, within limits, the powers of the king.[37] (The newly appointed king, Man, begins his reign by destroying the power of the nobility.[38]) The final stanza of the poem, in which Philisides advises Man to "[d]eeme it no gloire to swell in tyrannie," ends with a famously ambiguous piece of advice to the noble "beastes" who live under his (tyrannical) sway: "And you poore beastes, in patience bide your hell, / Or know your strengths, and then you shall do well" (*OA* 93).[39] Greville's explicit allusion to and pointed emendation of Sidney's words— "*till* the beasts beginne to knowe their strengthes"; there is no "or"—and his placement of it in an (idealized) future in which men of "like fortunes" have "like ends," suggest the political stakes of his advice to the "Lady."

---

[37] Involved with international Protestant politics, Languet helped to draft the Apology with which William of Orange justified his rebellion against Philip II. His and Philippe Duplessis-Mornay's *Vindiciae Contra Tyrannos* was published in 1579. As Blair Worden suggests, to name Languet was to bring the *Vindiciae* to the fore: "No Elizabethan courtier could have referred to the *Vindiciae* openly. But the 'hidden forms' of pastoral and of Aesopian beast-fables at once gave their authors license and alerted their readers to the exercise of it" (*Sound of Virtue*, 288–9). In his discussion of the poet as a "popular philosopher" in his *Defence*, Sidney refers to Aesop's tales as a proof, "whose pretty allegories, stealing under the formal tales of beasts, make many, more beastly than beasts, begin to hear the sound of virtue from these dumb speakers" (*Defence*, 34). The response to the Ister Bank poem within the *Arcadia* itself highlights its charged status: "According to the nature of diuerse eares, diuerse iudgements streight followed: some praising his voice, others his words fit to frame a pastorall stile, others the strangenes of the tale, and scanning what he shuld meane by it" (*OA* 225).

[38] Norbrook notes: "At first the people are delighted to have lost their noble oppressors, but they learn by bitter experience that the aristocracy at least acted as a buffer between themselves and the tyrant, who now proceeds to enslave them" ("Sidney and Political Pastoral," in *Poetry and Politics in the English Renaissance*, 87–8). The Huguenot Henri Estienne ascribed to Anjou's mother, Catherine de Medici, a wish to "root out the chief of the nobility" (Worden, *Sound of Virtue*, 272).

[39] William Ringler claimed "know your strength" means "be aware that the aristocrats are the protectors of the commons against tyranny" (414, cited in Worden, *Sound of Virtue*, 291). While everyone was enjoined to patience under tyranny (one could legitimately resist only before tyranny was established). Once a people has consented they must bear the new ruler "with a patient heart" (*Sound of Virtue*, 292). Worden argues that the final couplet goes beyond a mean: Sidney "threatens to take up not only his pen but his sword" (*Sound of Virtue*, 293). Skretkowicz suggests that the placement of the "Ister Bank" poem in the First Eclogues of the 1590 *Arcadia* was the work of Fulke Greville, who "shared Sidney's disposition for parable as [a] method of teaching" (*European Erotic Romance*, 178–9). In the 1593 *Arcadia*, the Philisides-Languet poem is relocated by the editors in the Third Eclogues (*European Erotic Romance*, 179). (The poem also appears in the Third Eclogues in the *OA*.)

Like Sidney, Greville uses a discourse associated with aristocratic political critique and resistance.[40] He uses it, moreover, both to recommend a kind of political "winter" during which the nobility must drawe their sap "downe to the roote; and be content to want leaves, till the sweet springe of time, or occasion come, to invite them up againe," and to promote a particular political agenda of noble "strength." Greville's encouragement of the Lady's patient obedience is thus less about her subjection to patriarchy *per se* than about her disposition in relation to political power. The "Honourable Lady" at once configures the nature of the "subjects obedience to his sovereign" and the political disposition of the Sidney alliance.

As Greville's account suggests, constancy is best understood not as passive or patient suffering, but rather as an active achievement of the will, and thus as a statement of power.[41] Its chief spokesperson in the period, Philip Sidney's friend the Flemish humanist Justus Lipsius, argued for stoic resolve as a way to survive civil war and other extreme forms of political difficulty (what Samuel Daniel calls the "thunder-cracks / Of Tyrants threats").[42] Blending Senecan stoicism with Tacitean political pragmatism, Lipsius attempted to answer "the crucial question of how individuals might remain politically engaged and morally virtuous in an age in which politics had become unstable and violent and morally debased."[43] (As Greville puts it to the Honourable Lady, "there is neither in yours, nor in any other subjection, any true peace to be gotten by trust of Superiors; nor honor by strife against them"). In *De Constantia* (1584, translated into English in 1591), Lipsius defines constancy as "a right and immoveable strength of the minde, neither lifted up, nor pressed down with external or casuall accidentes" which gives those who possess it "that great title, the nearest that man can have to God, *To be immooueable.*"[44] Even in a

---

[40] Joel B. Davis looks at the relationship between the *Arcadia* and Greville's "Letter" as well, comparing the Lady's husband to Sidney's Cecropia, the evil queen who tries to usurp the crown of Arcadia for her son, the prince Amphialus. Greville advises his Lady, "remember the image of Cecropia: in whose narrow, and unloving nature, there is yet expressed an unmeasurable, and bewitched love of her own" (161. 31–3), "Multiple Arcadias," 413. Davis also argues that, for Greville, "the reactions of Pamela and Philoclea to their captivity and torture in book 3 of the *New Arcadia* provide direct examples of the passive female stoicism he advocates in his *Letter*" (414). With the *NA* Sidney in effect "becomes a courtier-soldier who had rejected the effeminate lures of pastoralism to embrace a stern Stoic moral and political philosophy" (415).

[41] On stoicism as a philosophy of the will, see Gordon Braden, *Renaissance Tragedy and the Senecan Tradition*, 20.

[42] Daniel, "To the Countess of Cumberland," 204. Lipsius was also friends with Robert Sidney, Philip's younger brother (see HMC, 2.662, cited in Alexander, *Writing After Sidney*, 151: In 1602 Sidney's deputy in Flushing, Sir William Browne, referred to "your Lordships old friend Lypsius").

[43] Adriana McCrea. *Constant Minds*, 10.   [44] Lipsius, *Two Bookes of Constancie*, 83.

situation in which they are "pressed down" by fortune, that is, constancy renders subjects both ethically and dispositionally powerful.

Gordon Braden has suggested that "stoicism's central strength was its calculus of adaptation to unchanging realities," a fact that made it particularly useful for those living under a monarchy.[45] But stoicism was also, crucially, a doctrine of those who perceived themselves to be disenfranchised or dispossessed; Braden calls it the "creed of discomfited aristocrats," and Andrew Shifflett "the rhetoric of malcontents."[46] The concept of self-sovereignty—the idea that one has power over one's passions and will even if one has power over nothing else—thus served as both political ethos and covert form of political resistance. Rather than being "the language of docile subjects," Stoicism was, in Shifflet's words, "a subtle casuistry of political activism" (*Stoicism*, 32, 1). This activism was complicated; Stoic retirement often meant retreat from the state rather than from political action, "a decisive act of political rhetoric and a tacit but hard to ignore plea for a return to virtue-centered politics" (*Stoicism*, 3). When the Christianization of Stoicism replaced fate with providence, moreover, it also posited a power greater than the monarch: God. In Lipsius's words, constancy gives man the great "title" of being "immoveable," "the nearest that man can have to God." The value of being ethically autonomous and spiritually obligated to no one but God was of inestimable symbolic value to those who were both subject to a monarch and committed to a political worldview that that monarch did not, in their view, support with sufficient dedication. Neostoic constancy is thus best understood as a vow rather than a capitulation, a symbolic form of resistance to the consolidation of monarchical power and an assertion of the immanent power—what Sidney calls the "strength"—of the nobility. If the early modern aristocracy countered the erosion of its real political power with the symbolic power of neostoicism—as Braden puts it "stoicism enters Renaissance literature as part of the metaphorics of the nobility"—this symbolic power

---

[45] Braden, *Renaissance Tragedy*, 17.

[46] Braden, *Renaissance Tragedy*, 16. Shifflett argues that a stoical Protestant militarism had been espoused by Sir Philip Sidney in the 1580s; later Essex and his intellectuals "combined a warlike Protestantism with Senecan and Tacitean critiques of the late Elizabethan court" (*Stoicism*, 340). "Stoicism remained an important rhetorical means for noble English malcontents and their intellectual retainers to reclaim honor over and against institutional authorities" (Shifflett, *Stoicism*, 15). The struggle was fought in the name of "constancy," a term which asserted "the honor of the willful, aristocratic self amid factional and ideological struggles," and was pleasingly gender equitable (*Stoicism*, 32). "For all their talk about the masculinity of virtue," Shifflett argues, "ancient and early modern Stoics tended to emphasize the intellectual equivalency of the sexes" (*Stoicism*, 6). Subsequent references to Shifflet will be cited parenthetically within the text.

was based in large part on female constancy.[47] And as the examples given illustrate, women were both the symbolic and literal agents of its cultural and political purchase.

During the period in which Sidney was writing the *Arcadia*, the Earl of Essex's sisters, Penelope Devereux Rich and Dorothy Devereux Perrot, wielded considerable cultural and political power. Like Margaret Clifford, they were associated with both the symbolism of constancy and the Sidney alliance—their brother Essex would, quite literally, take over Sidney's mantle at his death.[48] During the 1580s, Penelope Rich frequently mediated with Lord Burghley and other powerful figures for people seeking political favours, including Robert Sidney.[49] Contemporaries considered the marriage Leicester proposed between Penelope Devereux and Philip Sidney in 1581 a "Treaty" with serious political repercussions.[50] Something of what one biographer has called "a cult of Penelope Rich" also developed in the period, and numerous songs and poems with a pointedly oppositional flavor were dedicated to her.[51] Paying homage to this cult was a way of courting the favor of, or attesting loyalty to, the Sidney, and, later, the Essex alliance, and the symbolics of female constancy played a notable role in its culture. The composer William Byrd included the song "Constant Penelope," in his 1588 *Psalmes*, for example, casting Sidney's muse as Ulysses's faithful wife.[52] She is also featured in Thomas Morley's collection of madrigals as "Diana," a figure who evokes not only the goddess of chastity, but the constant virgin heroine of the romance *Amadis de Gaul*, who,

---

[47] Braden, *Renaissance Tragedy*, 77. See also Davis: "the erosion of the military function and power of the nobility generated an increased interest in the symbolic representation of its status," particularly via vernacular translations of Stoic tracts ("Multiple Arcadias," 407).

[48] James VI himself best articulated the view espoused by so many others: "In him [Essex] we have recovered the person of Sir Philip Sidney" (cited in J. L. Smith, "Music and Late Elizabethan Politics," 523). On Essex as the "heir to Sir Philip Sidney," see Paul E. J. Hammer, *Polarisation of Elizabethan Politics*, 51–4.

[49] On Rich, see Alison Wall's entry in the *Oxford Dictionary of National Biography*; Maud Stepney Rawson, *Penelope Rich and her Circle*; S. Freedman, *Poor Penelope*; and Varlow, *Lady Penelope*. On her power at court, see Freedman, *Poor Penelope*, 65. On Sir Robert Sidney's case specifically, see Rawson, *Penelope Rich and her Circle*, 178. Penelope Rich also had a "small army of godchildren": Dorothy's daughter Penelope, two of Essex's children, Sir Robert Sidney's son and Hilliard's daughter (Varlow, *Lady Penelope*, 118).

[50] After the death of the first Earl of Essex in 1576, Edward Waterhouse wrote to Sir Henry Sidney: "The Lords do generally favour and furder [the young Earl of Essex, Penelope's bother]...And all thes Lords that wishe well to the Children, and I suppose, all the best Sort of the *Englishe* Lords besides, doe expect what will become of the Treaty between Mr. *Phillip* and my Lady *Penelope*. Truly, my Lord, I must saie to your Lordship, as I have said to my Lord of *Lecester*, and Mr. *Phillip*, the Breaking of from this Match, if the Default be on your Parts, will turne to more Dishonour, then can be repaired with eny other Mariage in *England*" (23, Collins, *Letters and Memorials of State*, 1: 147).

[51] On the relationship between music and the Essexians, see L. M. Ruff and D. Arnold Wilson, "The Madrigal, the Lute Song, and Elizabethan Politics."

[52] On Byrd, see Smith, "Music," 530.

like the *Arcadia*'s Philoclea, is first locked up and then defended by a man dressed as an Amazon. (Bartholomew Yong also dedicated his translation of Jorge de Montemayor's *Diana* to Rich in 1598.)[53]

Perhaps the most explicit illustration of the political significance of female constancy I have been arguing for occurred in 1589, when the poet Henry Constable carried a (now lost) Hilliard miniature of Penelope Rich to James VI in Scotland as a sign of the alliance's support for his candidacy as England's next monarch. In the same year, Rich herself began writing ciphered letters to the King in the hopes of securing his political approbation for her family and religious and political viewpoints.[54] It was during this time that she wrote the aforementioned letter to Jean Hotman, son of the Huguenot jurist and tyrannomach, François Hotman, and secretary to the Earl of Leicester from 1582 until Leicester's death in 1588, playing on her status as "the most constant of those who are named in this paper."[55] Those named included Sir Horatio Plaviciso, Elizabeth's ambassador to Germany on behalf of Henry of Navarre, and Sir Robert Sidney, the new Earl of Leicester, whom she encourages not only to be "constant," but "not to believe everything he hears."[56] Her work as a mediatrix and as a constant woman consistently shored up both the values and the men of the alliance.

As she puts it in another letter to Hotman, Rich sent her letters to a "prince caché," or a hidden prince, a sign of the dangerous nature of the game they were playing. The letters themselves were appropriately and elaborately ciphered: the queen was "Venus," King James, "Victor," the

---

[53] For the identification of Rich with Diana, see Smith, "Music." On Yong's dedication to "my very good Lady, the Lady Rich," see Smith, "Music," 532. (Smith claims the translation was ongoing in 1583.) The *Amadis de Gaul* is the romance Sidney says has the ability to move men's hearts "to the exercise of courtesy, liberality, and especially courage" (*Defence*, 40–1). Mary Sidney Herbert had a copy of the *Amadis de Gaul* in her library (Smith, "Music," 519).

[54] See Michele Margetts, "Lady Penelope Rich." Claiming that her "influence in the political sphere cannot be ignored," Freedman argues that Rich "played a part in smoothing King James's path to the English throne" (*Poor Penelope*, 204). On the exchange of the letters, see Freedman, *Poor Penelope*, 82–3. She refers in one letter to having sent Hotman an answer for the Hidden Prince ("le prince caché") (cited in Varlow, *Lady Penelope*, 113). On the Constable connection, see *The Poems of Henry Constable*, ed. Joan Grundy. On Hotman hoping to use Rich's influence to receive from King James I the promised reward for his French translation of the *Basilicon Doron*, see Van Dorsten, *Poets*, 85.

[55] Quoted in Freedman, *Poor Penelope*, 82. For the French, see Blok, *Correspondence*, 256.

[56] Rich's letters to Hotman's wife, her own former lady-in-waiting, the Huguenot Jeanne de Saint-Martin, also frequently refer to constancy. "[T]here is no vice in the world that I hate more than inconstancy," she writes in one letter, vowing "that the friendship I dedicated to you couldn't diminish but with life," and in another that Jeanne not think "I had ever thought of giving you the occasion of considering me inconstant toward you"(cited in Varlow, *Lady Penelope*, 86). For the French, see Folio 45, "ne pence point que j'avois jamais pencé, de vous donner occasion de m'estimer inconstante en vostre endroit car je vous aime, et vous aimera toute ma vie, et en ceste assurance, je vous souhaite au tant de bien que vous peut desirer, cele que vous aime infiniment").

Earl of Essex, "the weary knight" (abbreviated to "TWK"), and Penelope herself "Ryalta," a term that evokes Venice's rialto and the trade for which it was famous.[57] In many ways, the ciphering in these letters echoes that in the *Arcadia*; the "weary knight" seems to cite the various personas characters take on in the *Arcadia*, including the "Forsaken knight" (a disguised Musidorus) who defends Philoclea and Pamela against their would-be attackers in the third book (*NA* 314, ed. 534 on).[58] Penelope Rich—ciphered in the *Arcadia* as the constant Philoclea—thus seems to have deployed an allegorical mode of political persuasion similar to the one Sidney uses in the *Arcadia*, making use of one of the key aspects of the "metaphorics of the nobility" for high-level political ends. Essex's own letters to his sister also reveal that the language of stoicism and the trope of female constancy—in his case the negative example of proverbial female *in*constancy—were central to the Devereux conversations about political ambition.[59] While constancy was hard to maintain, it was nonetheless a key term for political integrity

Penelope's sister Dorothy, the most frequent referent for Pamela in contemporary keys to the *Arcadia*, also played a notable role in late Elizabethan political life. According to the Spanish ambassador and spy Mendoza, Leicester at one point proposed marrying Dorothy to King James of Scotland as a way of cementing the family's future political prospects.[60] (The sisters

---

[57] As Freedman points out, "she had a nickname for everyone involved, and there was a long scroll of these names in the possession of Richard Douglas, nephew of the Scottish Ambassador in London, Archibald Douglas (Hatfield Cecil Papers, XVIII, cited in Freedman, *Poor Penelope*, 83). The participants, as Freedman puts it, "seemed to have been concerned to secure their own positions in the event of James's succession" (*Poor Penelope*, 83).

[58] On the "forsaken Knight, attired in his owne liuerie, as blacke, as sorrowe it selfe could see it selfe in the blackest glasse," and who had "in his headpiece, a whippe, to witnesse a selfe-punishing repentaunce," see Sidney, *NA* 315, ed. 536. (Goldman points out that when Sidney made peace with Elizabeth on New Year's Day 1581, he gave her "a iuel of gold, being a whippe garnished with small diamonds" as a token of submission: "Sir Philip Sidney and the 'Arcadia,'" 177.) One of the "forsaken knight's" companions is a knight all in green whose shield bears a picture of a sheep "feeding in a pleasant field, with this word, *Without feare, or enuie*," the classic motto of Stoic constancy (*NA* 320ᵛ, ed. 543). He is soon identified as Philisides: the Knight of the Sheep.

[59] On these letters, see Michele Margetts, "'The wayes of mine owne hart,'" 101–10, and K. Duncan-Jones, "Notable Accessions: Western Manuscripts." Oxford, Bodleian Library MS Don. c. 188 [early 1598; before 1593]. As Daybell writes "The coded nature of these highly stylized fraternal missives, while rendering their meaning rather elusive, is also suggestive of Lady Rich's role as political confidante to her brother, and her interest and involvement in his court career" (Daybell, "Lady Rich's Letter," 118). See also *Essex to Stella. Two letters from the Earl of Essex to Penelope Rich*, ed. Freeman. "The Court," Essex writes in his second letter, is "of as many humors as the rayne bow hath collores. The tyme wherin we liue, more vnconstant then womens thoughts." The proverbiality of women's inconstancy was the negative norm against which the constancy of women like Penelope Rich herself was measured.

[60] See the *Calendar of State Papers Spanish*, III, 1550–86, 477, cited in Freedman, *Poor Penelope*, 70. Leicester left £2,000 to further the match (Longleat, Dudley MSS Box 3

thus shared a romantic history, no matter how imaginative, with the King.)
Dorothy's eventual marriage to the soldier and Sidney ally Sir Thomas
Perrot in 1583—a controversial marriage which Penelope Rich facilitated in
secrecy—may well be alluded to in the *Arcadia*.[61] (In one of the many scenes
attesting to the "gender concentrate" of female same-sex chastity that characterizes the bond between Philoclea and Pamela, Philoclea goes to visit her sister and finds her weeping.[62] "[I]mpouerish[ing themselves of their] cloathes
to inriche their bed," "and there cherishing one another with deare, though
chaste embracements," the sisters have a conversation in which Pamela con-
fesses to her love for Dorus—though "held continually in due limits" (*NA*
120; ed. 245–6). Philoclea vows to help Pamela in much the same way as
Penelope helped Dorothy to marry Perrot.) The bond between Penelope and
Dorothy Devereux was certainly one of which the world took note. Shortly
after their arrival at court in 1581, the two women were painted together in
a remarkable portrait that cites, among other things, the likeness topos at the
center of positive ideas about union (Figure 1.2). The portrait represents not
only a powerful female bond, but also one of the emblematic forces of female
power and loyalty that undergirded the Sidney alliance. It also serves, I want
to argue, as an emblem for the *Arcadia* itself: the constancy of two sisters
serves as the crux around which the whole romance turns.

III. "UNJUST CONQUEST" AND
FEMALE CONSTANCY

Constancy is one of the *Arcadia*'s key values.[63] As Pyrocles puts it in the
Old Arcadia,

> A mind well trained and long exercised in virtue…doth not easily change
> any course it once undertakes but upon well grounded and well weighed

---

no. 56, cited in Hammer, *Polarisation*, 52. On this proposed match, see also Michele
Margetts, "Stella Britannia," 353–61, and Varlow, *Lady Penelope*, 88.

   [61] In June 1583, Perrot wrote to Penelope seeking her help in support of his suit for her
sister's hand (Elizabeth I disapproved of the match) (see the *Calendar of State Papers Domestic*,
1581–90, CLXI, 22, cited in Freedman, *Poor Penelope*, 70–1). After the couple eloped, Perrot
was sent to Fleet prison and Rich wrote to Lord Burghley asking for help to get him out of
prison (Freedman, *Poor Penelope*, 71). See also Margetts, "Stella Britannia," 251–2.
   [62] Laurie Shannon argues that female same-sex chastity "harbors a heroic femininity
similar to the 'gender concentrate' of male friendship," and thus that it could serve as a
caution on political tyranny (*Sovereign Amity*, 69). On the relationship between Aristotle's
belief that "friendship appears to be the bond of the state," and the *Arcadia* more generally,
see Craft, "Remaking the Heroic Self," 54–5.
   [63] I am not the first to point out that constancy is the *Arcadia*'s key value, nor that
this constancy is characterized in explicitly neostoic, even Lipsian, terms. See e.g.

Figure 1.2 Portrait of Dorothy and Penelope Devereux. © Reproduced by permission of the Marquess of Bath, Longleat House, Warminster, Wiltshire, Great Britain.

causes; for being witness to itself of his own inward good, it finds nothing without it of so high a price for which it should be altered. Even the very countenance and behavior of such a man doth show forth images of the same constancy in maintaining a right harmony betwixt it and the inward good in yielding itself suitable to the virtuous resolutions of the mind. (*OA* 12)

Constancy plays an even more central role in the revised, or *New Arcadia*. Following their princely education, the two heroes head off into a heavily symbolic storm that represents the misfortune that tests and teaches neostoic constancy.[64] The storm leaves them "neither power to stay, nor way to escape," and, in what amounts to a parable of political fortune, the princes "carried by the tyrannie of the winde, and the treason of the sea," are at last "driuen vpon a rocke" (*NA* 121, 132, ed. 261, 262). While the majority of their fellow sailors weep, pray, or attempt suicide, the heroes, protected by their "power of reason," the "rule of vertue," and their refusal "to abandon ones selfe," survive (*NA* 133, ed. 263). (The entire episode seems to be undergirded by the Lipsian image: "let showres, thunders, lighteninges, and tempestes fall round about thee, thou shalt crie boldlie with a loude voyce, *I lie at rest amid the waves.*"[65]) Stoicism, in this episode and throughout the romance, is the basis for Pyrocles and Musidorus's heroism.

Lipsius offers neostoic advice to noble subjects in *On Constancy* and to princes in his *Politics*, and both forms are prevalent in the *Arcadia*. As Musidorus puts it, with "contentment of mind" "no state is miserable," and without it "no prince's seat restful" (*OA* 40).[66] Good kings in the *Arcadia* are characterized by their constancy. We are told, for example, that

McCoy: "Constancy is the principal virtue in the *Arcadia*, a condition of moral balance and sanity to which all the characters aspire" (*Sir Philip Sidney*, 42). "Thematically," he writes, "Sidney seeks to project an image of constancy and balance in a context of expanding contingency. This process corresponds to the narrative's formal development in which a unified organization is supposed to keep pace with expansive amplification" (*Sir Philip Sidney*, 171). Joel B. Davis points out that, in 1590, "Greville likely saw Sidney's revised *Arcadia* as a compendium of examples of constancy. He would write later that Sidney had intended his *Arcadia* to teach men 'how to set a good countenance on all the discountenances of adversity'" (Davis, "Multiple Arcadias," n. 28).

[64] The storm is characterized as a tragedy, the genre that teaches kings not to be tyrants. As they sail off, "a vaile of darke cloudes" appears before the sun, "which shortly (like inck powred into water) had blacked ouer all the face of heauen; preparing (as it were) a mournefull stage for a Tragedie to be plaied on," *The Countesse of Pembrokes Arcadia, Written by Sir Philippe Sidnei* (London: Printed by Iohn Windet for William Ponsonbie, 1590), 131. All subsequent references to this text, *NA*, will be cited parenthetically within the text, along with comparable references to Maurice Evans's edn of the 1593 edition.

[65] Lipsius, *Two bookes of constancie*, 84, italics in the original. In case the story was not sufficiently clear, the "storme deliuer[s] sweete Pyrocles to the stormie minde of that Tyrant" of Phrygia, who "hauing quite loste the way of noblenes...straue to clime to the height of terribleness." His vow to kill Pyrocles highlights the latter's glory: "Princely youth of inuincible valour, yet so vniustly subiected to such outragious wrong, carrying himselfe in all his demeanure so *constantly*, abiding extremitie, that one might see it was the cutting away of the greatest hope of the world, and destroying vertue in his sweetest grouth" (*NA* 135, ed. 266, emphasis added). It is passages like these that Greville accentuates both in the chapter headings of his edn of the *Arcadia*, and, later, in his *Life of Sidney*, in which he argues that Sidney's purpose in the *Arcadia* was to "limn out such exact pictures, of every posture in the minde, that any man being forced, in the straites of this life, to pass through any straights, or latitudes of good, or ill fortune, might...see how to set a good countenance upon all the discountenances of adversitie, and a stay upon the exorbitant smilings of chance," cited in James, *Society, Politics and Culture*, 388.

[66] Sidney's fiction, Greville tells us, offers guidance on two fronts: "first on the monarch's part," and "then again, in the subject's case" (cited in Worden, *Sound of Virtue*, 280).

the exemplary king of Macedon Euarchus's "line of action" is "straight and always like itself, no worldly thing being able to shake the constancy of it" (*OA* 357–8).[67] Bad kings, conversely, are characterized by their change-ability and susceptibility to passion. The *New Arcadia*'s Antiphilus, for example, can imagine "no so true propertie of souereigntie, as to do what he listed" (*NA* 228; ed. 398). Being "borne into an vnknowne Ocean of absolute power," he rules "as euerie winde of passions puffed him" (*NA* 228, ed. 398).[68] For Lipsius, the way to prevent a monarch from abusing his power was not to threaten him with revolt or tyrannicide, but rather to educate him thoroughly in Stoic ethics. Lipsius's ideal monarchy—and the *Arcadia*'s—is based on neostoic moral philosophy, whose precepts and doctrines ensure that the unruly passions—of both king and subjects—are governed by reason. In the *Arcadia*, it is constant women, even more than the heroes themselves, who provide this education.

Both Lipsius's *Politics* and Sidney's *Arcadia* focus on the key virtue of the prince, political prudence, which is located both within himself and in his aristocratic advisors. In the *Arcadia*, the ruler Basilius ("not the sharp-est pearcer into masked minds") is criticized for his impolitic choice of the "flattering courtier" Dametas as an advisor (*NA* 223, ed. 392; *NA* 13, ed. 79). His chief noble advisor, Philanax, however, gives him honest, error-correcting advice that is wholly in keeping with the neostoic advice Lipsius and Sidney offer to their princes.[69] Among other things, Philanax tells Basilius that the "heavens have left us in ourselves sufficient guides"; that "a constant virtue, well settled" is not victimized by a change in for-tune; that subjects will not "stick" to a leader who "abandons himself"; and that whether Basilius's time calls him "to live or die," he should "do both like a prince."[70] In addition to speaking truth to power, the noble Philanax

[67] See also Davis's account of the 1593 *Arcadia*'s additions to this portrait of Euarchus, where he is "foremost, a statesman" and "prudent and even Machiavellian in his foreign pol-icy," forestalling conflict between Greeks and their "would-be conquerors from the Italian peninsula" (Davis, *The Countesse of Pembrokes Arcadia*, 173).

[68] It continues: "Whereto nothing helped him better, then that poysonous sugar of flat-terie" (*NA* 228, ed. 398). Antiphilus "that had no greatnesse but outwarde," collapses in the face of calamity: "like a bladder, sweld redie to breake, while it was full of the winde of prosperitie, that being out, was so abiected, as apt to be trode on by euery bodie" (*NA* 231, ed. 402).

[69] According to Goldman, Philanax is a cipher for Sir Francis Walsingham, Elizabeth's Secretary of State: "The resemblances between Walsingham and Philanax...fairly shriek from the page" ("Sir Philip Sidney and the 'Arcadia,'" 183).

[70] The following dialogue between Basilius and Philanax beautifully captures Lipsian philosophy:

'And would you, then,' said [Basilius], 'that in change of fortune I shall not change my determination, as we do our apparel according to the air, and as the ship doth her course with the wind?'

also wields considerable power of his own. At a key point of crisis—a popular rebellion—he comes "accompanied with divers of the principal Arcadian lords," and with "five hundred horse" at the ready (*OA* 247–8). A note about his "incomparable loyalty" to Basilius reassures readers of his—and Sidney's—pro-monarchical stance, but the *Arcadia*'s consistent focus on the value and necessity of both his counsel and his lordly power (his "five hundred horse") indicate more specifically the kind of mixed monarchy Sidney promoted. Like Lipsius's, the power of Sidney's ruler is located both within himself and in his noble magistrates.

The *Old Arcadia* begins with an account of Basilius's decision to retreat from active political life in order to protect his daughters from the events prophesied by a Delphic oracle. (He plans, essentially, to lock them up.) Almost immediately, the reader is presented with a seemingly unprompted defense of said daughters in the manner of the *querelle des femmes*, or debate on women. Pamela and Philoclea, we are told, "seemed to be born for a sufficient proof that nature is no stepmother to that sex, how much soever the rugged disposition of some men, sharp-witted only in evil speaking, hath sought to disgrace them" (*OA* 4). Pamela and Philoclea's story, in other words, is framed by a defense of women. Immediately afterwards, we learn that the *Arcadia*'s concern with women is directly related to its central concern with right rule and just counsel. While Basilius initially seeks counsel for the "confirmation of fancies [rather] than correcting of errors," Philanax, as we have seen, nonetheless gives him honest, error-correcting advice in a neostoic vein (*OA* 5). This advice, moreover, is specifically concerned with the treatment of women. "[E]ven the same mind hold I as touching my ladies, your daughters," he tells Basilius in the course of his advice, "in whom nature promiseth nothing but goodness, and their education by your fatherly care hath been hitherto such as hath been most fit to restrain all evil, giving their minds virtuous delight, and not grieving them for want of well-ruled liberty" (*OA* 7). "Now to fall to a sudden straitening them," he tells Basilius, "what can it do but argue suspicion, the most venomous gall to virtue: Leave women's minds, the most untamed that way of any; see whether any cage can please a bird, or whether a dog grow not fiercer with tying" (*OA* 7). In this speech, particularly in the

---

'Truly sir,' answered [Philanax], 'neither do I as yet see any change; and though I did, yet would I think a constant virtue, well settled, little subject unto it [...]'

'To give place to blows,' said the duke, 'is thought no small wisdom.'

'That is true,' said Philanax, 'but to give place before they come takes away the occasion, when they come, to give place.'

'Yet the reeds stand with yielding,' said the duke.

'And so are they but reeds, most worthy prince,' said Philanax, 'but the rocks stand still and are rocks.' (*OA* 8)

final and rather wonderfully sententious clause, Philanax configures women's liberty in precisely the terms in which men like Sidney configured aristocratic liberty: noble birth and education warrant subjects a certain amount of liberty within a well-ruled regime; tying them up—limiting their liberty—only renders them a ("fiercer") threat. By configuring women's rights in terms of "well-ruled liberty"—and in the face of limitations on that liberty—the *Arcadia* thus identifies them as a matter of political concern. The analogy between women and subjects that undergirds these configurations is, as I have suggested, an essential aspect of the political critique the *Arcadia* offers "under the vaile of homely persons."

It is thus notable that the romance's heroes have their own debate on women. When Pyrocles first falls in love with Philoclea (and crossdresses as the amazon "Cleophila," an inversion of her name), Musidorus sees it as "a slackening" of Pyrocles's "main career": "better your mind to seek the familiarity of excellent men in learning and soldiery," he advises (*OA* 12–13). A man "formed by nature, and framed by education to the true exercise of virtue," he continues, should resist "sensual weakness": "it utterly subverts the course of nature in making reason give place to sense, and man to woman" (*OA* 17, 18). Cleophila's defense against this attack is explicitly feminist—"I am not yet come to that degree of wisdom to think lightly of the sex of whom I have my life"—but it is also political (*OA* 19). "It is strange to see the unmanlike cruelty of mankind," she continues, "who, not content with their tyrannous ambition to have brought the others' virtuous patience under them, like childish masters, think their masterhood nothing without doing injury to them who (if we will argue by reason) are framed of nature with the same parts of the mind for the exercise of virtue as we are" (*OA* 19).[71] The assertion of equality in this

---

[71] In the *New Arcadia*, Pamela and Philoclea are introduced in the context of valiant virgins (Kalandar shows Zelmane a painting of Philoclea with her parents that hangs alongside portraits of Diana, Atalanta, and "many more": *NA* 10, ed. 74), and via a proto-feminist defense. They are described as "so beyond measure excellent in all the gifts allotted to reasonable creatures, that wee may thinke they were borne to shewe, that Nature is no stepmother to that sex, how much so euer some men (sharpe witted onely in euill speaking) haue sought to disgrace them" (*NA* 12, ed. 76). In the catalogue of praises Pamela is described as "of high thoughts, who auoides not pride with not knowing her excellencies, but by making that one of her excellencies to be voide of pride; her mothers wisdome, greatnesse, nobilitie, but (if I can ghesse aright) knit with *a more constant temper*" (*NA* 12, ed. 76, emphasis added). It is notable that the love the heroes feel for the heroines is initially conceived of as an assault on a particular characterization of agentive heroism predicated on reason and against passion. As Musidorus tells Pyrocles, who is now not only in love with a woman, but dressed as one, "Remember (for I know you know it) that if we will be men, the reasonable parte of our soule, is to haue absolute commaundement; against which if any sensuall weaknes arise, we are to yeelde all our sounde forces to the ouerthrowing of so vnnaturall a rebellion, wherein how can we wante courage, since we are to deale against so weake an aduersary, that in it selfe is nothing but weakenesse?" (*NA*

formulation serves to counter a dynamic in which "tyrannous" power subjects "virtuous patience" to its mastery. Virtuous and reasonable women, by way of analogy, are virtuous and reasonable subjects, and as such, they deserve love, not tyranny. "Let this suffice," Cleophila concludes her defense, "that [women] are capable of virtue. And virtue, you yourself say, is to be loved" (*OA* 20).[72] There are certainly other symbolic registers at work in this scene, notably concerned with the necessary conjoining of reason and (com)passion in a virtuous man. (When Musidorus asserts that "the head gives you direction," Cleophila replies, "And the heart gives me life": *OA* 21). Indeed scholars have long pointed to the ways in which the love of virtuous women "unbends" the heroes from a too rigid, or militarized, sense of honor.[73] Yet Pyrocles's education via the love of a virtuous woman is also a crucial part of the education of princes, and an analogous configuration of a prince's relationships to his subjects.[74] In learning to love, rather than master or tyrannize over, women/subjects, the prince also learns the limits of his prerogative.

When Philoclea and Pamela become the heroes' beloveds, and thus the guides for their actions, their constancy configures aristocratic political

52; ed. 132–3). (Note, in contrast,Sidney's claim that his sister's requests are "to his heart an absolute commaundement," 3.) For Musidorus, women represent, more than anything else, inconstancy: male "resolve" must stand up against women's "peeuish affections" or it is a slippery slide to "vitiousnes" (*NA* 52; ed. 133). It is this argument to which Pyrocles offer his feminist response.

[72] "For, if we love virtue," she asks, "in whom shall we love it but in virtuous creatures" (*OA* 20; *NA* 53, ed. 136). It "likes me much better," she adds, "when I finde vertue in a faire lodging, then when I am bound to seeke it in an ill fauoured creature, like a pearle in a dounghill." In the *Defence*, Sidney praises poetry for setting "virtue so out in her best colours, making Fortune her well-waiting handmaid, that one must needs be enamoured of her" (37). In the *Arcadia*, the feminine allegory of virtue is annexed to the defense of women that itself serves as a political allegory.

[73] See Turner, "Heroic Ideal," 76. See also Pyrocles's defense of love: "the minde it selfe must (like other thinges) sometimes be vnbent, or else it will be either weakned, or broken. And these knowledges, as they are of good vse, so are they not all the minde may stretch it selfe vnto: who knowes whether I feede not my minde with higher thoughts" (*OA* 13). Eventually, Musidorus supports Pyrocles in his pursuit of his desires, and comes to recognize that " 'Strength' means something more than force . . . the strengths of reason and virtue within each one of us, which flourish when they prevail over passion and fortune" (Worden, *Sound of Virtue*, 288).

[74] In characterizing men in terms of "tyrannous ambition" and women in terms of "virtuous patience under them," Sidney, like Greville, is articulating a political parallel between men and women and rulers and subjects. He is also, however, articulating a particular gendered mode of characterizing virtue. The love for a virtuous woman also serves as a symbolic organizing principle for political energies. Musidorus tells Pyrocles, first to grieve no more, second to love Philoclea, and finally that Pyrocles should "command me to do you what service I can towards the attaining of your desires" (*OA* 23). Similarly, in the *New Arcadia*, Dorus (the peasant-dressed Musidorus) tells Pamela that her "commandement doth not onely giue me the wil, but the power to obey you, such influence hath your excellencie" (*NA* 126, ed. 253).

power as much as sexual loyalty or gender submission. Pamela's emblem
for her "estate," much like Margaret Clifford's, is a symbol of constancy: a
"perfect white lamb tied at a stake with a great number of chains" (*OA* 34).
(In the *New Arcadia*, it is "a very riche Diamond set but in a blacke horne,"
which reads "*yet stil my selfe*" (*NA* 60, ed. 146, emphasis added), a motto
much like Elizabeth's own *semper eadem*.) While politickly "scanning" the
crossdressed Musidorus's words about his own situation for a "second meaning" (*OA* 87) (he is dressed as the shepherd, Dorus), Pamela also offers him
classic Lipsian advice about achieving constancy himself: "'Master Dorus,'
said the fair Pamela, 'methinks you blame your fortune very wrongfully,
since the fault is not in your fortune but in you that cannot frame yourself
to your fortune'" (*OA* 88). From the very beginning of their relationship,
that is, and in very structural ways, Pamela shores up Dorus's constancy not
only with her own, but with explicit articulations of its utility.

When Dorus commences to tell Pamela the story of Musidorus, gear-
ing it specifically towards his auditor—he "stayed his speech till Pamela
showing by countenance that such was her pleasure, he thus continued
it" (*OA* 92)—he also offers her the opportunity to decipher political pastoral. He presents his account of "Musidorus's" pastoral crossdressing in
terms similar to those Puttenham uses to define pastoral: as an estate "not
always to be rejected, since under that veil there may be hidden things to
be esteemed" (*OA* 93). Pamela, of course, "well found he meant the tale
by himself, and that he did under that covert manner make her know the
great nobleness of his birth" (*OA* 93). Political pastoral, in other words,
tells a veiled story about nobility, and it is a woman who holds the key.

This mode of intratextual deciphering plays an even more prevalent
role in the *New Arcadia* than it does in the *Old*. As in the *Old Arcadia*, the
shepherd "Dorus" tells Musidorus's story to Pamela in the *New Arcadia*,
suggesting that "this estate [of shepherd] is not alwayes to be reiected, since
vnder that vaile there may be hidden things to be esteemed" (*NA* 109–10,
ed. 230). After Dorus delivers his "prettie tale" in such a manner that "the
Princesse might iudge that he ment himselfe," Pamela asks: "Doo you not
know further (saide she, with a setled countenance not accusing any kind
of inwarde motion) of that storie?" (*NA* 111, ed. 232). In drawing attention to Pamela's politic "countenance"—indeed, the parentheses mimic
what the clause describes—Sidney indicates both that Pamela is adept at
reading political pastoral, and that she is politically circumspect as well. In
a number of other scenes, Pamela actively—and with some irony—solicits
Dorus for accounts of Musidorus and Pyrocles. On one occasion she asks
him to tell her about Pyrocles ("Truely (said *Pamela*) *Dorus* I like well your
minde, that can raise it selfe out of so base a fortune, as yours is, to thinke of
the imitating so excellent a Prince, as *Pyrocles* was": *NA* 126, ed. 253). She

also serves as the politic decipher of both biographical and political codes. At one exemplary moment, Pamela asks Dorus about Pyrocles's father, and the account he offers of Euarchus's ideal governance, which highlights the fact that he "neuer restrain[s]" his nobility's liberty, is presented specifically to her: "I might as easily sette downe the whole Arte of gouernement," he says, "as to lay before your eyes the picture of his proceedings" (*NA* 128, ed. 256). In this account, Pamela's "countenance"—both her face and her approbation—is imagined as the witness and guarantor for the ideal "Arte of gouernement." "Dorus," moreover, finally reveals his real identity to Pamela when he is recounting a story in which Musidorus and Pyrocles fight tyranny, slipping in an "I" in place of a "he," and a "me" in place of a "him."[75] Musidorus's and Pamela's complicity in maintaining the "vaile" of pastoral—he blushes and she smiles—even while Sidney clearly plays with its uncovering, underscores that Musidorus's story has a political component. Indeed after this slip, Dorus "turned againe her thoughts from his cheekes to his tongue," focusing on the cries of "Libertie" that the "yong men of the brauest minds" offer against their tyrant. In the end, even though the people seek to crown Musidorus in return for freeing them from their tyrant, he gives the rule to "a Gentleman of approued goodness" who was "of the bloud Roiall, & next to the succession," assuring both the (people of) Phrygia and Sidney's readers that anti-tyranny is not the same thing as anti-monarchy, and that there is a limit to both aristocratic power and critique (*NA* 138, ed. 270). The central role Pamela plays in these stories—as both politic decipherer and keeper of political secrets—suggests the importance of female constancy and female interpretation.

While the *Old Arcadia*'s Pamela is glad to have "a reasonable ground to build her love upon" when she learns of Musidorus's nobility, she is also cautious about his intentions vis-à-vis her virtue. She moderates her own feelings "with great constancy," thinking it safest "to divert" Musidorus's desirous attentions "*lest in parley the castle might be given up*" (*OA* 94, emphasis added). Her characterization of her chastity as a castle—the synecdoche and symbol for the power of the baronial nobility—highlights the political nature of Pamela's constancy.[76] Unmoved in the face

---

[75] Pyrocles, Dorus recounts, appears at a crucial moment to encourage Musidorus's heroic resolve: "*Musidorus* (said he) die nobly." "In truth," Dorus continues, "neuer man betweene ioy before knowledge what to be glad of, and feare after considering his case, had such a confusion of thoughts, as I had, when I saw *Pyrocles*, so neare me." "But with that," we are told, "*Dorus* blushed, and *Pamela* smiled: and *Dorus* the more blushed at her smiling, and she the more smiled at his blushing; because he had (with the remembraunce of that plight was in) forgotten in speaking of him selfe to vse the therd person" (*NA* 137, ed. 268).

[76] On castles as "the fortified bastions of the medieval nobility" and thus as symbols of aristocratic power, see J. S. A. Adamson, "The Baronial Context of the English Civil War," 119.

of Musidorus's sexual aggression, her constancy evokes the relationship between the nobility and the prince in Lipsian theory, in which constancy serves as an implicit caution to and critique of unfettered monarchical will.

Shortly after this scene in which Pamela defends her "castle" from Musidorus's sexual aggression, she has the occasion to do so again with much higher stakes. Having arranged with Pamela to "steal... her away to the next seaport, under vehement oath to offer no force unto her till he had invested her in the duchy of Thessalia" (*OA* 152), Musidorus, nonetheless, resorts to force before fulfilling his promise. (There's a wonderfully anti-lawyerly moment when Sidney describes Pamela "bending herself towards [Musidorus] like the client that commits the cause of all his worth to a well-trusted advocate": *OA* 172.) Pamela makes it clear that she has agreed to come with him for one reason only: because he is a "Prince," "with no other my heart would ever have yielded to go" (*OA* 172). Her belief in both the legitimacy, and the value, of his princeliness provides the grounds for her agreement. Her honor, she makes clear, is in his hands: "Let me be your own (as I am) but by no unjust conquest," she concludes, "I have yielded to be your wife; stay then till the time that I may rightly be so" (*OA* 173). Warning him against the tyrannical use of force—the "unjust conquest" of rape—Pamela presses instead for the just contract of marriage. Yet while Pamela writes the following couplet upon the root of a tree: "Sweet root, say thou, the root of my desire / Was virtue clad in constant love's attire" (*OA* 174), Musidorus's temporary promise to restrain from sexual conquest begins to have "fainting force" in the face of his desire (*OA* 177). Passion, in other words, begins to trump reason, and rape, always a sign of political tyranny, encroaches upon the promise of an equitable marital contract.

Philoclea and Pyrocles engage in a similar debate about castles and conquests at a similar point in their romance. When Pyrocles finally abandons his Amazonian disguise and proclaims his love for her, Philoclea feels a "spark of honour arise in her well disposed mind, which bred a starting fear to be now in secret with him" (*OA* 106). She expresses concern that her "affection ill hid hath given [Pyrocles] this last assurance." "If *my castle had not seemed weak*," she continues, "[he] would never have brought these disguised forces" (*OA* 106, emphasis added). Like her sister, Philoclea presents her virtue as a "castle," similarly evoking the symbolic power base and (im)pregnability of the nobility.[77] Like the contract that Pamela elicits from Musidorus, the "promise of marriage" (*OA* 107) Philoclea solicits

---

[77] Philoclea questions herself and Pyrocles more rigorously after observing his affections toward her mother, worrying about his motivations and faithfulness: "Was all this to win the undefended castle of a friend," she wonders, "which, being won, thou wouldst after

from Pyrocles is more than a romantic alliance; it too (re)configures the contract between ruler and subject. As Victoria Kahn has argued, a contract promised a more egalitarian model of political rule than that of absolutism. In this scene, as in the one with Pamela and Musidorus, female constancy serves both to limit the tyranny of passion and as the grounds for an equitable contract.[78]

In a much-discussed episode, when Pyrocles tries to secure the sexual rights of marriage on the basis of the given promise of marriage, he is interrupted, quite literally, by a rebellion. As many critics have pointed out, the popular rebellion of the Phagonians serves as the antitype to the kind of political critique Sidney was offering in the *Arcadia*. The revolt of the "many-headed multitude, whom inconstancy only doth guide," occupies the negative place of rebellion in a way that allows for and shores up the legitimacy of the kinds of (aristocratic) critique and resistance the *Arcadia* does offer (*OA* 115). When Cleophila crushes the rebels, moreover, she is "valiantly seconded by Philisides," Sidney's cipher and the spokesperson for the most explicit political critique in the *Arcadia*: the aforementioned Ister Bank poem (*OA* 111). In crushing a rebellion in which "everyone rules and no one follows," the noble princes both enact and promote their right to govern as subaltern magistrates, even as they shore up monarchical power. Why, Cleophila asks, "instead of a duke delivered unto [them] by so many royal ancestors" would they "take the tyrranous yoke of [their] fellow subject, in whom the innate meanness will bring forth ravenous covetousness, and the newness of his estate suspectful cruelty?" (*OA* 114).[79]

Yet by having a populist rebellion interrupt such politically allegorical scenes of near-rape—Musidorus's imminent breaking of his promise

---

raze?" (*OA* 184–5). Immediately afterwards she expresses her anguish "Under [the] veil" of a song (*OA* 185).

[78] On the political implications of the marital contract, see Victoria Kahn, "Margaret Cavendish and the Romance of Contract"; and Belinda Peters, *Marriage in Seventeenth-Century Political Thought*, 6.

[79] The rebellion itself is carefully presented as having some legitimate grounds of critique, but motivated largely by drunkenness (the rebels were "chafed with wine and emboldened with the duke's absented manner of living": [111]), and self-interest ("Public affairs were mingled with private grudge"). The fact that "the prince's person fell to be their table-talk" (111) is presented with regret, and the people's political claims—"What were the shows of his estate if their arms maintained him not? Who would call him duke if he had not a people?" (*OA* 111)—ultimately lead to an unacceptable end: first, we are told, the rebels "pretended to succour [Basilius], then to reform him, now thought no safety to themselves without killing him" (*OA* 113). In contrast to the "disagreeing sound of so many voices," Cleophila's defense of monarchy rings out loud and clear. While it makes some sense that the "uncertainty" of the Duke's "estate" led them take arms, it is clear that the "weak trust of the many-headed multitude, whom inconstancy only doth guide at any time to well doing" (*OA* 115) is not a viable alternative.

to Pamela is similarly interrupted by "a dozen clownish villains, armed with diver sorts of weapons" (*OA* 177), whom we later find out to be the "scummy remnant of those Phagonian rebels" (*OA* 265)—Sidney seems to be making a related point about the education of princes. While the inconstancy of the "many-headed multitude" is certainly a threat, and can momentarily deter a prince from egregious abuses of power, the real threat to just rule comes from immoderate passions—what Lipsius calls "rebellious affections"—and the threat of "unjust conquest" and tyranny.[80]

Much scholarly attention has been devoted to the subject of rape in the *Arcadia*. Deborah Shuger has argued that, despite the fact that rape, and the lascivious energies of aristocrats more generally, had long symbolized monarchical abuse, Sidney's portrayal of rape in the *Old Arcadia* and the heroes' ultimate vindication in its final book serve instead to legitimate the rights of those very aristocrats.[81] Yet as I have argued here, the specter of rape functions more explicitly as a sign of princely abuse—an impulse to tyranny, "unjust conquest," and force—that stands in explicit contradistinction to contract. It is also an oddly undernoted fact that it is the intended victims of these rapes—the constant women—who determine the meanings of the actual encounters and who serve as the guarantors for the eventual contracts that are their results.

When all four protagonists are imprisoned for breaking Arcadian laws about pre-marital sex, Pamela and Philoclea handle it far better than Musidorus and Pyrocles do. Adhering to the basic tenets of Christian neostoicism, they advise the princes against suicide on the grounds of providence ("to prejudicate [God's] determination is but a doubt of goodness in him": *OA* 258) and argue that suicide is, in effect, merely a poorly disguised assertion of passion and will. (Since suicide "hath not his ground in an assured virtue," Philoclea argues, "it proceeds rather of some other disguised passion": *OA* 258.) They assert the value of a clear conscience (man is to think of honor, shame, and pain as "nothing in regard of an unspotted conscience"· *OA* 258) and of resolution and constancy in the face of misfortune. Pamela also speaks against her own purported victimization, begging Musidorus not to think her "so basely

---

[80] Lipsius, *Two Bookes of Constancie*, 81. See also his discussions of the "furious assaultes of lustes," and of the particular dangers of "DESIRE, JOY, FEAR and SORROW," which are uniformly destructive to men, "some of them by puffing vp the minde, other by pressing it downe too much" (77, 85).

[81] Shuger, "Castigating Livy," passim. Shuger argues that "Sidney subverts Livy's narrative, metamorphosing his republican myth celebrating the triumph of law over libido into an *apologia* for aristocratic liberty, an *apologia* that draws on the Elizabethan chivalric revival and the *avant-garde* political thought of the late sixteenth century. These shape the climax of *The Arcadia*: its valorization of equity over law, clemency over strict justice, noble natures over impersonal codes, aristocratic privilege over legalistic impartiality" (542).

disposed as to let [her] heart be overthrown, standing upon itself in so unspotted a pureness" (*OA* 270). Her love for him "can no more be diminished by these showers of ill hap than flowers are marred with the timely rains of April" (*OA* 270). "For how can I want comfort that have the true and living comfort of my unblemished virtue," she asks, "and how can I want honour as long as Musidorus (in whom indeed honour is) doth honour me? Nothing bred from myself can discomfort me, and fools' opinions I will not reckon as dishonour" (*OA* 270). Musidorus's resulting vow, "Whatsoever I be, let it be to her service," formalizes the achievement of contract and testifies to Pamela's determining power within that contract: he will work, as all good princes should, in "her service" not through "unjust conquest" and force (*OA* 270).

As it has throughout the romance, Pamela and Philoclea's constancy in the final scenes of the *Arcadia* enables that of Pyrocles and Musidorus. Following the example of their beloveds, Pyrocles vows the following to Musidorus: "Let us prove our minds are no slaves to fortune, but in adversity can triumph over adversity" (*OA* 275). Together they sing a song that concludes with a couplet of unimpeachable stoicism: "Then let us hold the bliss of peaceful mind, / Since this we feel, great loss we cannot find" (*OA* 323). Ultimately it is official letters from the princesses, rather than their own claims, that establish Pyrocles and Musidorus's status as princes and legitimate their right to rule. Philoclea asserts that Pyrocles is "a great prince," and Pamela, who is herself, crucially, the heir to the Dukedom of Arcadia, vows that Musidorus "is a prince and worthy to be my husband. And so is he my husband by me worthily chosen" (*OA* 343).[82] Their

---

[82] Pyrocles inherits from his father the whole kingdom of Thrace (*OA* 361). For a discussion of the range of options for rule discussed at the end of the *OA*, see Skretkowicz, *European Erotic Romance*, 212: "Owing to the centralization of a monarch's power, on the death of Basilius no one in Arcadia is left who is practiced in the science of governing: 'for now their prince and guide had left them, they had not experience to rule, and had not whom to obey. Public matters had ever been privately governed, so that they had no lively taste what was good for themselves'" (*OA* 277). The *res publica* is paralyzed by "an extreme medley of diversified thoughts" (*OA* 277): republicanism ("the Lacedemonian government of few chosen senators," "the Athenian, where the peoples voice held the chief authority"), hereditary monarchy (some want to promote Pamela or Philoclea), and elective monarchy or monarchical republicanism (others want to elect Philanax as "lieutenant of the state": *OA* 278). See also Davis, who points out that this "anatomy of political discord" in book 4 first appeared in print in the 1593 *Arcadia* (*The Countesse of Pembrokes Arcadia*, 170–1). He particularly focuses on Timautus, a Sejanus-like figure "cunning to creep into men's favours" (*OA* 279), who is a stirrer of rebellion far more dangerous than that of the Phagonians (Davis, 171–2). For the debate in Mary Sidney Herbert's 1593 edn, see *NA* ed. 765–73. Among other things, Timautus tries to get Philanax to bend to his will by suggesting the two of them marry Pamela and Philoclea and divide the kingdom between them, a travesty, as Davis argues, "of the friendship between Musidorus and Pyrocles" (172). Skretkowicz points out that building a "philhellene Protestant league" relies on "the intermarriage of political allies" (*European Erotic Romance*, 214) and, although he does not point it out, this is what we see between Musidorus and Pamela and Pyrocles and Philoclea.

example makes the princes worthy of their titles, and their words make their rule possible. Pamela, in fact, makes it clear that it is her choice ("so is he my husband by me worthily *chosen*") that makes Musidorus worthy of and legitimate in his role. Female constancy is the grounds upon which the entire political order is restored, and female consent is the means.

IV. AN "VNLIMITTED MONARCHIE"

It has long been argued that the *New Arcadia* corrects, even erases, the scenes of rape that so characterize and (putatively) trouble the *Old*.[83] Yet I would argue that the *New Arcadia* actually entrenches the lessons I have delineated. In the scene in which the *New Arcadia's* Pyrocles finally reveals himself to Philoclea, explicitly acknowledging her central role as his "Load-starre of comfort" and "Princesse of felicitie," he presses his sexual advantage in much the same way he does in the *Old Arcadia*, pleading with her not to be "the Rocke of shipwracke" by resisting his desires (*NA* 178, ed. 329). Much as she does in the earlier version, Philoclea responds by expressing her concern that it was the "weakenesse of [her] gouernment" (*NA* 178ᵛ–9, ed. 330) that made him assume his disguise and make his advances. "Doost thou loue me?" she asks, commanding him, by logical contingency, to "keepe me then still worthy to be beloued" (*NA* 179, ed. 330). In pursuing her consent, Pyrocles presents her with "iewels of right princely value, as some litle tokens of his loue, & qualitie," a strategy that highlights his power as giver and thus the inequality of the exchange. He also shows her status-assuring letters from his father (*NA* 179, ed. 330). Yet although "*Pyrocles* would [fain] haue sealed [their souls' meeting] with the chiefe armes of his desire," "*Philoclea* commaund[s] the contrary," and "they pass…the promise of mariage" (*NA* 179ᵛ, ed. 331). The result of these sexual negotiations, in which honor, virtue, and reason temper passion, is, as it is in the *Old Arcadia*, a contract: "the promise of mariage."

[83] See Dobell, "New Light Upon Sir Philip Sidney's *Arcadia*," 99–100. In his edn of the *New Arcadia*, Maurice Evans claims that Sidney Herbert "suppressed the more disreputable episodes: the scene where Pyrocles consummates his love with Philoclea was changed to one in which the two spend the night in virtuous chastity and Musidorus's rape of Pamela is quietly omitted" (12). Shuger argues that "the *New Arcadia* largely erases the Livian subtext of the earlier version: because the princes do not violate their ladies' chastity, the analogy with Livy's aristocratic libertines vanishes—or rather seems to be transferred to Amphialus, whose forcible abduction of an unwilling Philoclea seems closer to Tarquin's rape than to the youthful erotic freedoms that Brutus's sons claim as their birthright" ("Castigating Livy," 544).

When Musidorus officially reveals his true identity to Pamela in the revised *Arcadia*, he also attempts to take advantage of the situation. Subject to the tyranny of passion, Musidorus declares in an illustrative series of formulations that he "could not set bounds vpon his happines, nor be content to giue Desire a kingdome, but that it must be an *vnlimitted Monarchie*" (*NA* 244^v, ed. 435, emphasis added). He takes Pamela "in his arms, offering to kisse her, and, as it were, to establish a trophee of his victorie" (*NA* 244^v, ed. 435). Pamela's rejection of this would-be sexual conquest is swift and categorical. "Away (said she) vnworthy man to loue, or to be loued . . . Let me see thee no more" (*NA* 245, ed. 436). Musidorus's pursuit of an "vnlimited Monarchy" of male desire solicits correction via Pamela's constancy. And, much like Pyrocles, he learns to seek her consent to a contract rather than force her subjection.

In seeking this consent, moreover, Musidorus offers Pamela something other than jewels or letters. Looking for "some meanes by writing to shew his sorrow, & testifie his repentance," he writes an "elegy," hoping that verse "would draw her on to read the more," and that counterfeiting his hand would keep her from throwing it away (*NA* 245^v, ed. 437). Labouring over each word ("this word was not significant, that word was too plain: this would not be conceiued; the other would be il conceiued": *NA* 245^v, ed. 437), Musidorus writes his poem and then steals "vp into Pamelaes chamber." He leaves the poem "in her standish (which first he kissed; and craued of it a safe and friendly keeping) . . . to be seene at her next vsing her inke," and places the standish "vpon her beds head, to giue her the more occasion to marke it" (*NA* 246, ed. 437).

This rather remarkable scene references a convention of poetic circulation best evoked by Thomas Nashe, when he describes Philip Sidney's sonnets, newly liberated in Nashe's printed edition, as having been too long "imprisoned in Ladyes casks."[84] In this formulation, women are the

---

[84] When Thomas Nashe dedicated the first edn of *Astrophel and Stella* (1591) to the Countess of Pembroke, he described his publication of the sonnet sequence as liberatory: "although it be oftentimes imprisoned in Ladyes casks, & the president bookes of such as cannot see without another mans spectacles, yet at length it breakes foorth in spight of his keepers." *Elizabethan Critical Essays*, 2: 224. The "Ladyes casks" are the private repositories for the poems, but they can also be understood as the veils for the meanings; to have another man's spectacles is to have access to what he sees, to understand the allusions and the relationships the poems encode. Like *Astrophel and Stella*, the poems in the *Arcadia* were clearly seen as "ladies' texts" in a way that was specific to that female audience as well as a possible cover for other male homosocial or sociopolitical motivations. The poems had been locked in "Ladyes casks," not *a* lady's; they were addressed to women, but they were also written for women. It is thus important to consider that the secret relationships they encode are not simply between male poet and lady dedicatee, but among a whole network of "Ladyes," women friends, perhaps, "who will weigh errors in the balance of good will." On these issues, see Chapter 4.

privileged audience for poems: the guardians of their (limited) circulation, and the keepers of their meanings. The "standish" that Musidorus leaves the poem in, a stand containing ink, pens, and other writing materials and accessories, evokes Pamela's own textual production, and her ability not only to determine the meaning and purchase of others' writings, but to respond in kind. (It is notable that a standish is listed in a later household inventory of the woman for whom Pamela serves as a cipher: Dorothy Devereux Perrot Percy.[85])

When Pamela wonders whether she should "second his boldnesse" by reading Musidorus's "presumptuous letters," and determines that she "might out of his wordes picke some further quarrell against him," she illustrates the extent to which a literary text is a kind of negotiation, or transaction (*NA* 246, ed. 438). Musidorus's poem, an apology for yielding his "reason" to "passion," as well as a promise that from here on her "will" will be to him "more then a lawe," attests to his turn from "vnlimited Monarchy" to what Greville in the "Letter to an Honourable Lady" calls "equalitie guided without absolutenesse" (138). It offers a political allegory that unfolds along two familiar fronts: a neostoic focus on reason over passion, and the promotion of a constitutional and contractual basis of rule over an absolutist one. In this crucial scene, conducted through the exchange of a literary text, Musidorus learns not to be a tyrant. His temporary desire for an "vnlimited Monarchy," signaled by (attempted) rape, is corrected by a constant woman whose words, and literary perspicuity, configure precisely the mixed monarchy the Sidney circle so actively promoted with its own literary work. In both revised rape scenes, the woman/subject corrects the unbridled will of her "lord," creating a relationship characterized not by tyranny or absolutism, but by a (re)negotiated contract. Musidorus and Pyrocles are less "peerless princes" than appropriately counseled and contracted ones.

Immediately after this last scene, the *New Arcadia*'s much discussed "captivity episode," which takes up the entirety of the third and final book of the revised romance, commences. In this story, Pamela, Philoclea, and Zelmane (the crossdressed Pyrocles) are kidnapped by the tyrant queen Cecropia and imprisoned in an "impregnable" castle (*NA* 250, ed. 443). There, the two heroines are enjoined to marry Cecropia's son Amphialus (who is in love with Philoclea) and, upon their refusal, subjected to a series of increasingly violent torments. Scholars have long noted the similarities

---

[85] Under the listing "The Inventory of Plate Bought 1617–22" in the household accounts of Dorothy Percy's husband is a folio list of "Plate which was my Ladye's," including amidst its "Sawcers" and "Candlesticks," a "Standish, I, 016 oz. ¼." *The Household Papers of Henry Percy*, 112.

between Cecropia and Amphialus and Catherine de Medici and the duc d'Anjou—enemies of the Huguenots, perpetrators of the Bartholomew Day massacre, and foils for Elizabeth I.[86] Invested in the (Catholic) pomp and raw violence of power, Cecropia's intrigues against the Arcadian monarch—she believes she has the right to Basilius's throne—evoke the widespread belief that the papacy plotted against Protestant sovereigns such as Queen Elizabeth.[87]

But Cecropia's mode of rule is also the antithesis of the kind that Lipsius and Sidney advise, and hyperbolizes the themes we see in the princes' would-be rape scenes. Most notably, Cecropia wishes that her son would hate rather than love Philoclea ("[f]or Hate often begetteth victory; Loue commonly is the instrument of subiection") and she promotes abduction and rape as the grounds upon which her son can "build [his] soueraigntie" (*NA* 252^v, ed. 447). Amphialus, for his part, is the political antithesis of the Lipsian prince: he wears a "brode & gorgeous coller" fastened with jewels "which he thought pictured the two passions of Feare and Desire, wherein he was enchained."[88] (In one of the most famous passages from Lipsius's *De Constantia*, he asks beleaguered aristocrats a question that clearly informs Sidney's portrait of Amphialus. "Have you not seen in the proclamations and on the shields of some of today's rulers that sublime and enviable *Nec spe nec metu* [with neither hope nor fear]?" "It will suit you who, truly a king, truly free, submit only to God, immune from the yoke of the emotions and fortune."[89] When dressed as the shepherd knight—and in direct contrast to Amphialus—Sidney's cipher Philisides wears this same motto, "*Without feare, or enuie*" (*NA* 320, ed. 543), as a sign of his political disposition. (Amphialus, in other words, is the anti-Philisides.)

When the inconstant Amphialus visits the imprisoned Philoclea, on the other hand, she is an emblem of resolution, her eyes "fixed . . . vpon the wall . . . with so steddie a maner, as if in that place they might well chaunge,

---

[86] See Greenlaw, "The Captivity Episode in Sidney's Arcadia," 54–63, 57–8; Raitiere, *Faire Bitts*, 27; and Barbara Brumbaugh, "Cecropia and the Church of Antichrist in Sir Philip Sidney's *New Arcadia*." Briggs, on the other hand, sees Cecropia as Mary Stuart and Amphialus as the young James VI.

[87] As Brumbaugh puts it, "Perhaps the success of Cecropia's agents in abducting the Arcadians should be read as a warning of the menace posed to the Protestant 'Cause' by the refusal of Queen Elizabeth and other rulers to support it at a level considered satisfactory by devotees such as Sidney, Philippe du Plessis-Mornay, and Hubert Languet" ("Cecropia and the Church of Antichrist," 31).

[88] "[T]he one was of Diamonds and pearle, set with a white enamell, so as by the cunning of the workman it seemed like a shining ice, and the other piece being of Rubies, and Opalles, had a fierie glistring, which he thought pictured the two passions of Feare and Desire, wherein he was enchained" (*NA* 253^{r-v}, ed. 448).

[89] The passage is cited in Braden, *Renaissance Tragedy*, 76; and Davis, "Multiple Arcadias," 407.

but not mende their obiect" (*NA* 253ᵛ, ed. 449). An extreme version of Pyrocles and Musidorus's pre-contracted selves, Amphialus identifies himself as subject to the "Tyrant Loue, (which now possesseth the holde of all my life and reason)" (*NA* 255, ed. 450–1). Philoclea, in turn, resists his protestations of love and debunks his rhetoric: "you say, you loue me, and yet do the effectes of enmitie," she tells him, and "while you say I am mistresse of your life, I am not mistresse of mine owne."[90] In keeping with her Lucrecian exemplar, Philoclea vows that she would commit suicide rather than consent to Amphialus's attentions. During her own back-up visit, Cecropia is also rejected. Her characterization of Philoclea as an "vnexpert virgin, who had alreadie with subtiltie and impudencie begun to vndermine a monarchy," captures with perfect economy the political allegory of female constancy.[91]

Cecropia's visit to Pamela is no more successful. Like Philoclea, Pamela is presented as an exemplum of constancy, pacing in her chamber, "full of deep (though patient) thoughts. For her look and countenance was setled, her pace soft, and almost still of one measure, without any passionate gesture, or violent motion" (*NA* 264, ed. 463.) At length "awaking, & strengthning her selfe," and "sure, that how soeuer [her oppressors] wrong me, they cannot ouer-master God," Pamela goes on to speak a set piece of providential neostoicism.[92] Praying that "calamitie be the exercise, but not the ouerthrowe of my vertue," she attests to both her love for Musidorus

---

[90] In response to his claims that he is soliciting her love, Philoclea drily responds that "If then violence, iniurie, terror, and depriuing of that which is more dear then life it selfe, libertie, be fit orators for affection, you may expect that I will be easily perswaded" (*NA* 254, ed. 449–50).

[91] Cecropia promises that her son will give Philoclea the "castell" if she marries him—a rhetoric of gifts that belies the contractual model espoused elsewhere in the romance. In the debate that then ensues over marriage, Philoclea scarcely listens, "listing not to dispute in a matter whereof her selfe was resolute, and desired not to enforme the other, she onely told her, that whilest she was so captiued, she could not conceiue of any such persuasions (though neuer so reasonable) any otherwise, then as constraints: and as constraints must needs euer in nature abhor them, which at her libertie, in their owne force of reason, might more preuaile with her" (*NA* 262ᵛ–3, ed. 462).

[92] In a famous debate with Cecropia Pamela offers the following defense of providence: "You say yesterday was as to day. O foolish woman...What dooth that argue, but that there is a constancie in the euerlasting gouernour?...This worlde therefore cannot otherwise consist but by a minde of Wisedome, whiche gouernes it, which whether you wil allow to be the Creator thereof, as vndoubtedly he is, or the soule and gouernour thereof, most certaine it is that whether he gouerne all, or make all, his power is aboue either his creatures, or his gouernement.... assure thy selfe, most wicked woman (that hast so plaguily a corrupted minde, as thou canst not keepe thy sickenesse to thy selfe, but must most wickedly infect others) assure thy selfe, I say, (for what I say dependes of euerlasting and vnremooueable causes) that the time will come, when thou shalt knowe that power by feeling it, when thou shalt see his wisedome in the manifesting thy ougly shamelesnesse, and shalt onely perceiue him to haue bene a Creator in thy destruction" (*NA* 284).

and her own constancy: "gracious Lord (said she) what euer become of me, preserue the vertuous *Musidorus*" (*NA* 264ᵛ, ed. 464). Her debate with Cecropia ends, famously, with Pamela's display of "so faire a maiestie of vnconquered vertue, that captiuitie might seeme to haue authoritie ouer tyrannie" (*NA* 284, ed. 492).[93] If "Philoclea with sweete and humble dealing did auoid their assaults," the narrator avers, Pamela "with the Maiestie of Vertue did beate them of[f]" (*NA* 265ᵛ, ed. 465). In these characterizations, we see two sides of female constancy, neither of which could be characterized as quietist.[94] Rather, both are associated with political efficacy, using the "Maiestie of Vertue" to "undermine" a tyrannical "monarchy."

At the same time as the sisters' constancy has political purchase, though, it does not lead to violent political action—that is, to tyrannicide. Even when presented with a strategy by which they might kill Amphialus, Philoclea "(in whose cleere minde treason could finde no hiding place": *NA* 303, ed. 519) refuses to support the plan. She "would rather yeeld to perpetuall imprisonment, then consent to the destroying her cosin, who (she knewe) loued her, though wronged her" (*NA* 303, ed. 519). Sidney and the political theorists he most admired were what Victor Skretkowicz calls "selective monarchomachs," and Philoclea is as well. Tyrannicide, in other words, serves as the limit to the episode's political allegory of resistance.[95] While Sidney levies a critique of tyranny, and idealizes the stoic and providentially minded characters who resist its worst abuses, killing the tyrant is never presented as a viable solution to the problem.

Eventually, as we might expect, Cecropia advises that her son stop "seeking to haue that by praier, which he should haue taken by authoritie," and take Philoclea by force (*NA* 313, ed. 532). ("No, is no negatiue in a womans mouth," she rather memorably informs him (*NA* 313ᵛ, ed. 533)). Cecropia's promotion of what Pamela earlier identified as "unjust conquest" features a fascinating list of rape stories that resulted in famed unions ("doo you thinke *Theseus* should euer haue gotten

---

[93] Indeed Pamela's prayer is explicitly characterized as a *representation* of vertue: "But this prayer, sent to heauen, from so heauenly a creature, with such a feruent grace, as if Deuotion had borowed her bodie, to make of it self a most beautifull representation; with her eyes so lifted to the skieward, that one would haue thought they had begunne to flie thetherward, to take their place among their fellow stars" (*NA* 264–5, ed. 464).

[94] Following Turner, McCoy highlights the heroines' superiority in the *New Arcadia*: "Neither Sidney nor his heroes can emulate the women's rigor" (*Sir Philip Sidney*, 205). "Yet," he goes on, "their exemplary virtue remains essentially passive, tending near the very end toward dangerous quietism" (McCoy, *Sir Philip Sidney*, 206–7). McCoy uses the same term a few pages letter, arguing that while the women's "saintly zeal tends towards a dangerous quietism," the men's "virile identity emerges from its oppressive disguise" into action. "Just before the narrative abruptly ends," he writes, "the hero's aggressive potency is dramatically expressed and morally vindicated" (*Sir Philip Sidney*, 212).

[95] Skretkowicz, *European Erotic Romance*, 177.

Antiope with sighing, & crossing his armes?" (*NA* 313ᵛ, ed. 533)),⁹⁶ and concludes with the account of a much sought after lady who was won not by "over-suspicious" soliciting, but by "that imperious maisterful-nesse, which nature giues to men aboue women" (*NA* 314, ed. 534).⁹⁷ Amphialus's response to this misogynist claim shows that while Pamela and Philoclea's example may be lost on his mother, it has had an effect on him: "Did euer mans eye looke thorough loue vpon the maiesty of vertue," he asks, "but that he became (as it wel became him) a captiue?" "[I]s it the stile of a captiue, "he asks," to write, *Our will and pleasure?*" (*NA* 313, ed. 532). In becoming a subject, or "seruant" to his beloved, rather than seeking to master her with his "will and pleasure," the prince Amphialus learns a crucial lesson not only in neostoic constancy but in political governance as well.

Despite Amphialus's reformation, however, Cecropia is still sovereign, and she remains a tyrant. Giving up on "eloquent praying, and flattering perswasion," she turns to other, increasingly violent, means to "winn the castle of [the sisters'] Resolution" (*NA* 325, ed. 550). We are reminded, in sententious stoic formulations, that "*Pamelaes* determination was built vpon so brave a Rock, that no shot of [Cecropia's] could reach vnto it," and that "*Philoclea* (though humbly seated) was so inuironed with sweete riuers of cleere vertue, as could neither be battred, nor vndermined" (*NA* 326, ed. 550). When Cecropia, in response, is carried by "abhominable rage...to absolute tyrannies" and subjects the two women to violent beatings, and, eventually, threats of death, this increasingly tyrannical treatment merely shores up their constant resolve (*NA* 326, ed. 551).⁹⁸ Every day Philoclea is "further of-minded from becomming his wife, who vseth [her] like a slaue" (*NA* 327, ed. 552), and Pamela's heroic *aristeia* is

---

⁹⁶ She also gives the examples of Iole and Hercules; and Helen ("who could neuer brooke her manerly-wooing Menelaus") and Paris (*NA* 313, ed. 533).

⁹⁷ Cecropia argues for male superiority at length: "in our very creation [women] are seru-ants," she tells her son, "and who prayseth his seruaunts shall neuer be well obeyed: but as a ready horse streight yeeldes, when he findes one that will haue him yeelde; the same fals to boundes when he feeles a fearefull horseman...Thinke, she would not striue, but that she meanes to trie thy force: and my Amphialus, know thy selfe a man, and shew thy selfe a man: and (beleeue me vpon my word) a woman is a woman" (*NA* 314).

⁹⁸ Finding "her threatnings repelled with disdaine in the one, & patience in the other," Cecropia increasingly ups her "tyrannicall authoritie," "doubling and redoubling her threat-nings," then "dishonorably vsing them both in dyet, and lodging," hoping, "by a contempt to pull downe their thoughts to yielding," then resorting to random acts of terrorism ("sometimes with voices of horror, sometimes with suddaine frightings in the night"), beat-ings and threats of death (*NA* 326, ed. 551). See also the following description of Pamela, only in the 1593 *Arcadia*: "(like a rock amidst the sea, beaten both with the winds and with the waves, yet itself immoveable) did receive this rigorous charge with a constant, though sad, countenance, and with fixed eyes witnessing the moving of her mind" (*NA*, ed. 606).

presented in even more hyperbolic terms. If "euer Vertue tooke a bodie to shewe his (els vnconceaueable) beautie," we are told, "it was in *Pamela*":

> For when Reason taught her there was no resistance, (for to iust resistance first her harte was enclined) then with so heauenly a quietnes, and so gracefull a calmenes, did she suffer the diuers kindes of torments they vsed to her, that while they vexed her faire bodie, it seemed, that she rather directed, then obeyed the vexation. And when *Cecropia* ended, and asked whether her harte woulde yeelde: she a little smiled, but such a smiling as shewed no loue, and yet coulde not but be louelie. And then, Beastly woman (saide she) followe on, doo what thou wilt, and canst vpon me: *for I know thy power is not vnlimited.* Thou maist well wracke this sillie bodie, but me thou canst neuer ouerthrowe. For my part, I will not doo thee the pleasure to desire death of thee: but assure thy self, both my life and death, shall triumph with honour, laying shame vpon thy detestable tyranny. (*NA* 328, ed. 553–4, emphasis added)

This speech, one of the most famous in the *Arcadia*, is the romance's most powerful articulation of the political allegory of female constancy. Its key words—"*thy power is not vnlimited*"—articulate precisely the political philosophy of limited monarchy that the *Arcadia* so actively promotes via the example of female constancy.

During what Cecropia calls "the last parte of the play," Cecropia tells Philoclea she will cut her sister's head off before her eyes (*NA* 389ᵛ, ed. 556). Philoclea's "Lieutenant Resolution" helps her withstand this assault, reminding her that "since in her selfe she preferred death before such a base seruitude, loue did teach her to wish the same to her sister." "Do what you wil…with vs," she tells Cecropia, "for my part, heauen shall melt before I be remoued" (*NA* 390, ed. 556). When Pyrocles tries to "perswade [Philoclea] to saue [her] life with the ransome of [her] honour," she refuses (*NA* 334, ed. 561). "Trouble me not," she tells him, "by tormenting my resolution: since I cannot liue with thee, I wil dye for thee" (*NA* 334, ed. 562). In the captivity narrative, familiar stories of female constancy are told as Senecan (near) tragedy—the genre that Sidney claims "makes kings fear to be tyrants."[99] Yet rather than featuring rape as the catalyst

---

[99] "Tragedy," he writes, "openeth the greatest wounds, and showeth forth the ulcers that are covered with tissue; that maketh kings fear to be tyrants, and tyrants manifest their tyrannical humours; that, with stirring the affects of admiration and commiseration, teacheth the uncertainty of this world, and upon how weak foundations gilden roofs are builded; that make us know

> Qui sceptra saevus duro imperio regit
> Timet timentes; metus in auctorem redit." (*Defence*, 45)

Van Dorsten translates the quotation, which is from Seneca's *Oedipus*, thus: "Who harshly wields the scepter with tyrannic sway, fears those who fear: terror recoils upon its author's head."

for republican reform, female constancy serves as the supreme representation of aristocratic virtue. Immediately after this scene, Pyrocles makes a hyperbolically ridiculous attempt at suicide: "he ranne as hard as euer he could, with his head against the wall, with intention to braine himself," but in "the haste to doo it," tripped, and only "depriue[d] him of his sense" (*NA* 335, ed. 564). This lapse into passion and despair contrasts with the resolution of the two women, who simply refuse to give in. In the end, Cecropia's subjects stop their "obedience to her tyranny" and she kills herself (*NA* 342, ed. 573). Amphialus, crazed with remorse, stabs himself, and Queen Helen of Corinth, in what may well represent an Elizabethan compromise, comes to his aid. (A number of critics argue that Helen is a figure for Elizabeth.) Thus while their kingdom is left in a perilous state, it is clear that, if he lives, Amphialus will no longer endeavor to love, or rule, by force, knowing as he does that his "power is not vnlimited."

Yet the *New Arcadia*'s obsession with tyranny does not end with the death of Cecropia and the attempted suicide of her son. As Pamela points out to her sister, their "Tragedy" has "many acts" (*NA* 349, ed. 580). Pyrocles's long-time foe, Anaxius, threatens the women with death as revenge for the attack on Amphialus (*NA* 349, ed. 579). Anaxius's tyranny, as is so often the case in the romance, is signaled by his misogyny: he scorns women as a "peeuish paltrie sexe, not woorthie to communicate with [his] vertues" (*NA* 305, ed. 522), and his plan of revenge soon incorporates threats of rape. This, in turn, provides Philoclea and Pamela with another opportunity to display the heroics of constancy ("a shippe," Pamela points out, "is not counted strong for byding one storme" [*NA* 349, ed. 580]). Both sisters again refuse to give in to their tyrant captor, but Anaxius, who "made Fortune his creator, and Force his God" refuses to give up (*NA* 355, ed. 587). The revised portion of the *Arcadia* ends with Zelmane fighting Pamela and Philoclea's would-be rapists (Anaxius's brothers join him in his assault) under an explicitly feminist aegis, the misogynist tyrant "punished by the weak sex which [he] most contemnest" (*NA* 360, ed. 594). The specter of rape, the harbinger of tyranny, thus haunts the very last pages of the revised *Arcadia*, suggesting that Sidney believed both in the recursiveness of political absolutism, and in the power of the forces levied against it.[100] Female constancy, which, as I have been arguing, configured such resistance both allegorically and through the representative power of

---

[100] Greville claimed that "The original's subsequent developments, such as the resumption of responsibility by Basilius and the 'marriage of the two sisters with the two excellent princes,'" were "ideas" that could have been realized, "if this excellent Image-maker had liv'd to finish, and bring to perfection, this extraordinary frame of his own Commonwealth" (Greville, *Life*, 14–15, cited in McCoy, *Sir Philip Sidney*, 133).

actual women, was Sidney's central structural principle in the *Arcadia*. This centrality, moreover, offers us another possible explanation for Mary Sidney Herbert's desire to keep the romance under the "liverye" of her name when it was published in the years following Sidney's death.

V. THE COUNTESS OF PEMBROKE'S ARCADIA

After the deaths of her brother and her parents in 1586, Mary Sidney Herbert withdrew from public life. When she rejoined society in November 1588, she returned with a vengeance, riding into London with an extensive entourage wearing her blue and gold livery and proclaiming both the return of her alliance and her status as its head.[101] Joel B. Davis has pointed out that her return coincided with the date Fulke Greville entered what would become the 1590 *Arcadia*—the first printed version of the romance—in the Stationers' Register. The work Sidney Herbert published in the years before releasing her own edition of the *Arcadia* in 1593 was, he argues, geared toward authorizing her superior edition of the romance and keeping it in a particular conversation.[102] Sidney Herbert explicitly locates the two translations she published during this time under her aegis: the translation of Philippe de Mornay's treatise on death was completed, she tells us on its final page, "The 13. of May 1590. At Wilton," and the translation of Robert Garnier's neo-Senecan play *Marc Antoine* "At Rambsurie 26 of November 1590." By locating this work in her estates, both of which served as gathering places for the alliance, Sidney Herbert indicates that, like the *Arcadia*, it was created under her control and was meant to circulate under her "liuerye." By explicitly dating both translations before the Greville *Arcadia*, she simultaneously authorized the contexts for her own edition and associated it with the politically attuned neostoicism her translations express.

As the editors of Sidney Herbert's collected works put it, the work she published in these years offers "a Senecan philosophical approach to

---

[101] This entrance is described in Michael G. Brennan, *The Sidneys of Penshurst and the Monarchy*, 100. I have argued elsewhere that her liveried return to London signaled Sidney Herbert's new status ("Literary Circles," 47–8). Margaret P. Hannay notes that Eleanor Rosenberg was the first to recognize Mary Sidney Herbert's importance to the family, arguing that that the memorials to her brother were "part of a larger movement to revive the memory of the Dudleys and Sidneys and to celebrate the Countess of Pembroke as the chief surviving member of the line." Sidney Herbert was, in Hannay's words, the "Primary female patron of Protestant Letters." See "'This Moses and This Miriam,'" 60.

[102] "[W]ithin a month of *The Countess of Pembroke's Arcadia*'s entry into the Stationers' Register in 1588, the Countess emerged from mourning, returned to the court in London, and began her most productive period of writing" (Davis, *The Countess of Pembrokes Arcadia*, 147).

the problems of life and death, warning of the dangers of avarice, ambition, and illicit passion, and advocating a life ruled by Reason."[103] As such, her work has been characterized as an avowal of her investment in continental intellectual and theological movements, including international Protestantism and stoic philosophy (the latter particularly for the "passive heroism" it enabled women).[104] Yet the translations are also forms of political commentary; stoicism, as we have seen, was part of the metaphorics of a discontented nobility, and both French Huguenots like de Mornay and neo-Senecan dramatists like Garnier used their work for these purposes. Sidney Herbert's translations, moreover, are centrally concerned with precisely the kind of neostoic constancy that is so central to the *Arcadia*, and the Garnier translation is specifically concerned with the *female* constancy that I have been arguing is the anchoring value for both the *Arcadia* and for the Sidney alliance's literary mode of political critique.

De Mornay's *Discourse de la vie et de la mort* is about the battle between "tyrannical passion" and reason in human life, but it is also an indictment of court life and ambition, particularly for those who live "at the pleasure of a Prince."[105] Life, de Mornay argues in a familiarly neostoic formulation, is a tempest, and death the "entraunce of the porte where wee shall ride in safetie from all windes"—provided, that is, that we come in with "quietnesse of mind, constancie, and full resolution" (247). It is, as we have seen, with exactly such a disposition that Pamela faces her own imminent death in the captivity episode of the *New Arcadia*—a disposition she

---

[103] *Collected Works*, 267.

[104] For the former, see *Collected Works*, 267; for the latter, Lamb, *Gender and Authorship*, 119. Traditionally, scholars have associated this work with Sidney himself—"Sidney and his continental allies"—and less with Mary herself. On the other hand, while feminists have looked at the extent to which this work was concerned with women, they have made no connection between this fact and the larger political concerns of the texts, seeing it instead as concerned primarily with Mary Sidney's own concerns about gender. Lamb e.g. suggests that the *Discourse* is about female grief and proposes that Cleopatra exemplifies a "heroics of constancy" acceptable for a woman because tied to the memory of a beloved man (*Gender and Authorship*, 119, 140–1).

[105] *Discourse*, 233–5. All future references will be cited in the text. A courtier, de Mornay argues in a wonderful formulation, is like a "Lions keeper, who by long patience, a thousand feedings and a thousand clawings hath made a fierce Lion familiar, yet geves him never meate, but with pulling backe his hand" (237). During the end times, God will laugh at the presumptions of princes, "breaking in shivers their scepters in their hands, and oftentimes intrapping them in their owne crownes" (240). Hannay argues that Sidney Herbert's translation of the *Discourse* was one of a series of translations of the Huguenot leader's works undertaken by Philip Sidney and his continental allies in order to disseminate de Mornay's works and support the Huguenot cause (Hannay, "This Moses and This Miriam," 220–1). Philip Sidney began a translation of de Mornay's *De la vérité de la religion chrestienne* that was eventually published as *A Worke concerning the Trewnesse of the Christian Religion* by Arthur Golding in 1587.

too compares to a ship sailing in rough waters. The *Discourse*'s defense against suicide—while we must seek "to cast the world out of us," we may under no circumstances "cast our selves out of the world"—similarly echoes Philoclea's argument in the *New Arcadia* (253). De Mornay's insistence that it is "cowardly to runne away" (253) is reflected in Pyrocles's ridiculous suicide attempt in which he quite literally "runs" into a wall.

The tragedy *Antonius* is based on similar neostoic values: "*In this our world nothing is stedfast found,*" we are told in an italicized sententia, "*In vaine he hopes, who here his hopes doth ground*" (887–8, p. 177). The play, moreover, is a tragedy about a woman, focusing on Cleopatra as a figure of constancy in the midst of political turmoil. As Davis points out, both Antony and Caesar are foils for Cleopatra's constancy. Anthony "can not rule himselfe" (l. 939, p. 178), "betraying the fundamental neostoic maxim *imperare sibi maximum imperium est* (rule over oneself is the greatest empire)."[106] Caesar, for his part, is a tyrant who vows, in an explicitly anti-Elizabethan formulation added by Sidney Herbert, to rule by fear rather than the love of his people.[107] He is also, crucially, a man who would sooner "*permit another should / Love her [he] love[s], then weare the Crowne he weares,*" a value set that evokes the parallels between the treatment of women and political ambition (1027–8, p. 181, emphasis in original). The play begins with Antony believing Cleopatra has betrayed him ("Nor constant is, even as I constant am": 143, p. 157) and offering the kind of misogynistic views similarly associated with tyranny in the *Arcadia*: "*But ah! by nature women wav'ring are, / Each moment changing and rechanging mindes*" (146–7, p. 157, sententious emphasis in the original). Cleopatra's first speech in the play is, like Pamela's very similar

---

[106] *The Countess of Pembrokes Arcadia*, 154.

[107] In Caesar's rule "[E]qual Justice wandreth banished, / And in her seat sits greedy Tyranny" (1201–2, p. 155). Sidney Herbert adds the Elizabethan reference to a debate between Caesar and Agrippa about kings ruling by fear:

AG. A feared Prince hath oft his death desir'd.
CAE. A Prince not fear'd hath oft his wrong conspir'de.
AG. No guard so sure, no forte so strong doth prove,
No such defence, *as is the people's love.*
CAE. Nought more unsure more weak, more like the winde,
Then *Peoples* favor still to chaunge enclinde.
AG. Good Gods! what love to gracious Prince men beare!
CAE. What honor to the Prince that is severe! (1527–34, p. 194, emphasis added)

See the editors' note on l. 1530 on p. 335: "Traditional debate over clemency or severity as the best policy for a ruler is given topical resonance by Pembroke's adaptation of Queen Elizabeth's assertion that she ruled by the love of her people."

speech in the *Arcadia*, a defense of her constancy, even in the face of—in her case inviting—torture:

> That I would breake my vowed faith to thee?
> Leave thee? deceive thee? yeelde thee to the rage
> Of mightie foe? I ever had that hart?
> Rather sharpe lightning lighten on my head:
> Rather may I to deepest mischiefe fall:
> Rather the opend earth devower me:
> Rather fierce *Tigers* feed them on my flesh. (397–403, p. 164)

When her adviser Charmian tells her to free herself from Antony and submit to Caesar, Cleopatra refuses.

> In that faire fortune [of his power] had I him exchaung'd
> For *Caesar*, then, men would have counted me
> Faithles, unconstant, light: but now the storme,
> And blustering tempest driving on his face,
> Readie to drowne, *Alas!* What would they saie?
> (580–84, p. 169)

Having established herself as Antony's "wife" and "friend," Cleopatra concludes the play surrounded by her women, the "gender concentrate" that signifies both loyalty and resistance to tyranny.[108] She ends the play, moreover, by thinking about her people's future. When her own death seems inevitable, she wonders if in "stede of" the "Scepters promis'd [to them by] imperiouse *Rome*," her children "shall crooked shepehookes beare" (ll. 1882–3, p. 204).[109] While the statement explicitly expresses Cleopatra's concerns for her children's future, its allusion to the bearing of "shepehookes" in the future also nods towards political pastoral, including, perhaps, the *Arcadia*. Cleopatra advises her children to "learne t'endure" and to "forget" their "birth and high estate" in order not to fall into Caesar's "Tyrantes handes" (ll. 1885–6, 1860). She prays, instead, that they will flee Egypt and live "In free estate devoid of servile dread" under the aegis of divine providence (ll. 1871–2, p. 203).[110] This kind of critique of imperial rule is often written from the perspective of a disenfranchised but still ambitious upper class, and in many ways it echoes Ister Bank's recommendation that the nobility "bide" its hell "in patience" or know its strengths and "do well." Under the veil of pastoral, Sidney Herbert alludes to the allegory of neostoic "patience" and noble strength

---

[108] When her women want to die with her, Cleopatra says "Live sisters, live" (676, p. 171).

[109] The editors of the play note that "Cleopatra evidences the "traditional ambiguity inherent in pastoral, which is a fall in rank for the nobility and yet a safe retreat" (336).

[110] Euphron tells the children that "The Gods shall guide us" (1896, p. 204).

that is also the subject of the *Arcadia*. It is in such subtle ways that the constant woman in Sidney Herbert's play resonates intertextually across the Sidneian corpus.[111]

Mary Sidney Herbert published her corrected version of the *Arcadia* in 1593, appending the last two unrevised books of the original version of the *Arcadia* to the first three revised ones. (Greville only published the first three books). She also included a cover that highlighted her "liuerye."[112] (The title-page features both the Dudley bear and the Sidney porcupine. The armed Pyrocles is balanced by a sheephook-holding Musidorus. See Figure 1.3.) While Sidney Herbert undoubtedly had many motivations for publishing this corrected version, I want to argue for three crucial ones. First, the final two books of the original *Arcadia* are the ones in which

---

[111] Samuel Daniel's own neo-Senecan play, *The Tragedy of Cleopatra*, was registered on 19 October 1593 and published the following year. Identifying it as a work "which she did impose" upon him, Daniel dedicated it to Mary Sidney Herbert, crediting her with encouraging him to "sing of state" (*Delia & Cleopatra*, sig H6, cited in *Collected Works*, 14). Most intriguing is the lost "Anthony and Cleopatra" of Fulke Greville, which he said was "sacrificed in the fire" because its presentation of the "irregular passions in forsaking empire to follow sensuality" could be "construed or strained to a personating of vice in the present governours and government"—apparently a reference to the fall of Essex, mentioned in the next paragraph (*Dedication to Philip Sidney*, in *Prose Works*, 93, cited in *Collected Works*, 43).
Another Sidney Herbert work—an undated and unprinted translation of Petrarch's *Trionfo della Morte*—resonates in similar ways with the works discussed so far. By the time of her translation, the treatise had been long been appropriated as a Protestant allegory by reformers like John Bale and John Foxe, and Sidney Herbert added her own tenor to this history. The Laura in her translation is, like her Cleopatra, a figure of neostoic constancy. By resisting Petrarch's "passion" with her "reason," Laura attempts to bring about Petrarch's "salvation" even after her death (280). "[F]eare and desire," she tells him in the familiar neostoic formulation, are "ill providers" (280). Like Pamela, when threatened by Death Laura is unbowed ("I knowe, whose safetie on my life depends" (l. 52, p. 274)), and like Pamela, she is an emblem of constancy. She speaks "with devoutlie-fixed eyes / Upon the Heavens" and claims that while "Torments, invented by the Tyrants old" "extreemelie martireth," death itself is a form of "heavenlie rest" (279). The editors' claim that Sidney Herbert's *Triumph* was "haphazardly preserved in a transcript of papers sent by John Harington to Lucy, Countess of Bedford" is one with which I would vehemently disagree (264). Rather than a haphazard accident, it seems like that Harington was sending the work of one godly Protestant activist-writer to another, passing the torch.
[112] As Blair Worden has pointed out, the title-page for the 1593 *Arcadia* associates Musidorus with Leicester's Dudley arms, and Pyrocles with Sidney's family crest (*Sound of Virtue*, 313). "The two brave knights," observes Sidney's friend Gabriel Harvey, are "combined in one excellent knight, Sir Philip Sidney" (cited in Worden, *Sound of Virtue*, 313). See also Davis: "The Pyrocles figure, in the upper right corner of the page, wears armor, bears a sword, and stands beneath a charging lion; this part of the page signifies the more heroic martial and political aspects of the *Arcadia*, while simultaneously alluding to the beast Pyrocles slays to save Philoclea in book 1. Musidorus holds a sheephook and stands under a bear in the upper left corner of the title page, signifying the pastoral aspects of the *Arcadia* and representing the beast that Musidorus slays in book 1. Perhaps more important, the bear is part of the Dudley family crest, and next to it stands the Sidney family crest, the porcupine," together they signify the Dudley-Sidney alliance ("Multiple Arcadias," 429).

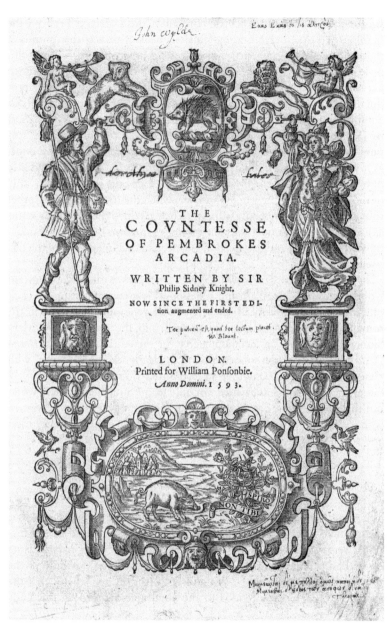

Figure 1.3 Title-page of *The Countess of Pembroke's Arcadia* (1593). © Reproduced by permission of the Folger Shakespeare Library.

we see the vindication of female constancy: the marriages between the heroines and their buttressed-by-female-constancy princes that promise a mode of rule based on contract and consent rather than force. Secondly, by keeping the *Arcadia* under her aegis, Mary Sidney Herbert proclaimed her status as the new head of the Sidney alliance, and of the literary production that was their calling card. As the Pembroke secretary Hugh Sanford put it in his letter to the new edition, the work was done "most by [Sidney Herbert's] doing, all by her directing," concluding that "it is now by more than one interest *The Countess of Pembroke's Arcadia*: done, as it was for her: as it is, by her."[113] Finally by insisting on the importance of what we might call the liveried text, one which bore the values not only of the author but of the whole cause for which the text was, among other things, a political statement, Sidney Herbert retained the romance's status as an allegory told "under the vaile of homely persons": a literary transaction dependent on and defended by the deciphering imperative of the text itself.

In seeming accordance with Sidney Herbert's wishes, the constant women who both populate and function as referent points for the deciphering imperative of the *Arcadia* remained determinative agents in the romance's circulation and meanings well into the next century. Mary Sidney Herbert was in fact responsible for the edition of *Astrophel and Stella* that included the sonnets that most clearly identified "Stella" with Penelope Devereux Rich (they were omitted from the first edition).[114] Sidney Herbert thus endeavored not only to continue her brother's work, but that of the whole community, including that of the constant women who served—and would continue to serve—as its politically allegorical and actual spokespeople.

VI. READING THE *ARCADIA*

The *Arcadia* retained its status as a ladies' text—particularly a Sidney ladies's text—well into the Jacobean period. A remarkable pair of fictional verse letters Josephine A. Roberts called the "Imaginary Epistles of Sir Philip Sidney and Lady Penelope Rich," alludes not only to the relationship between the *Arcadia* and Rich (the author tells us that the romance was "chiefly intended to the honorable memory of this Lady

---

[113] H.S. "To the Reader," Sidney, *Arcadia*, sig A4, cited in *Collected Works*, 7.

[114] In her 1598 edn, Mary Sidney Herbert included Sonnet 37 with its identification of Stella as Penelope Devereux Rich, a woman who "Hath no misfortune but that Rich she is." Hannay, *Philip's Phoenix*, 69. Notably, this is also the edn in the Penhurst library.

Penelope"),[115] but also to the romance's political allegory.[116] At one point in his letter "Sidney" writes that "I might haue had a queene vnto myne Aunt" (l. 62), referring to the notorious bond between Elizabeth and his uncle, the Earl of Leicester. He also alludes to his other relatives, including those of the "honnord house of Huntington" (l. 65), in whose household Penelope and Dorothy Devereux were educated, and his maternal uncle, Ambrose Dudley, Earl of Warwick (l. 60), whose title Penelope Rich's son would one day bear (Roberts, "Imaginary Epistles," 69). He tells Rich that if she had married him, "old Carmarden [the Earl of Huntingdon] needed not repent / the League with Penshurst notable in Kent" (ll. 69–70, p. 69).[117] (Sidney's 1581 betrothal to Penelope Devereux was arguably thwarted by his (temporary) loss of his status as Leicester's heir.) The explicit subject of the letters is the aftermath of Penelope's subsequent marriage to Lord Rich, and the letters take the form of a debate between lovers centered on the concept of constancy. Like the other heroic epistles that take female constancy as their subject, including Samuel Daniel's and Fulke Greville's, the Sidney/Rich letters offer a similar commentary on monarchical absolutism. In much the same way as *Astrophel and Stella* and the (*New*) *Arcadia* feature "star-crossed lovers, caught under the spell of a tyrannical Queen," the letters cast the relationship between Sidney and Rich as one thwarted—but by no means doomed—by the "wrathfull fury of an Angry queene" (Roberts, "Imaginary Epistles," 65).

Sidney's first letter to Rich in the exchange attests to his "constant love" for her, and to her "vnconstant change" in marrying another. In a by-now-familiar statement, Sidney swears that

> Death, torment, horror; prude*n*ce, endurance
> shall neuer drawe mee from my loues assurance

---

[115] In his own letter "Sidney" tells Rich that he has printed her "name in everlasting writs"

so longe as doth Arcadias name suruiue
so longe thy graces in *that* name shall lue
By which all readers shall deride as strange
My constant loue, *and* thy vnconstant change.
If Idle poeme make vs live foreuer
then Stella shall in Astrophel dy neuer. (ll. 74–9, Roberts, "Imaginary Epistles," 69)

All subsequent references to the letters will be cited parenthetically within the text.

[116] The epistles date after Rich's death in 1607, but allude to events in 1581, including Sidney's participation in the Fortress of Perfect Beauty. The letters survived in a (single) miscellany that includes works by other members of the Sidney alliance, including William Herbert (Mary Sidney Herbert's son) and the Herbert agent Benjamin Rudyerd, and lines from William Browne of Tavistock's "Elegy to the Countess of Pembroke" (Roberts, "Imaginary Epistles," 66). They also allude to both Sidney's connections and the political power of the alliance.

[117] The letter also alludes to the "pearled Medway," the river in Kent that runs by Penshurst (ll. 167, Roberts, "Imaginary Epistles," 71).

No threate of frendes; no Princes angry browe.
No change of state should force mee breake my vow.
(ll. 11–14, p. 67)

He imagines that she, on the other hand, will say that "the Queene did
force [her] *and* [she] must obay" (l. 155, Roberts, "Imaginary Epistles,"
71). But, he asserts, there is no such thing as "must":

Princes may force the body not the mind
The mind's a temple, free *and* hallowed Cell
W*hi*ch Tirantes cannot raze, nor strength compell.
(ll. 157–9, p. 71).

In her letter of response "Rich" seems to concur with Sidney's judgment: "the fault was mine," she claims, "I should haue beene tormented /
even vnto death *and* yet not haue consented" (ll. 9–10, Roberts, "Imaginary
Epistles," 73–4). However, she insists that although she was unable to resist
the "wrathfull fury of an Angry queene," she was and is constant to Sidney
in her "hart" (ll. 42, 46; Roberts, "Imaginary Epistles," 74). "But say *tha*t
I am maried as I am," she writes, "Can that forbid mee to bee still the
same"? (ll. 69–70; Roberts, "Imaginary Epistles," 75). Her articulation
of the familiar Elizabethan motto "still the same" (*semper eadem*) asserts
her constancy as a limit case for monarchical absolutism. By the time the
"imaginary epistles" were circulating in manuscript, Rich had quite literally become a figure of aristocratic resistance. In arguably the most notorious example of the Elizabethan nobility "show[ing their] strength" through
outright resistance, her brother, the Earl of Essex, attempted a rebellion
against the Queen in 1601. In the trial that followed, Penelope Rich was
named one of the chief conspirators, her name printed as "La. Rich" on the
writ of indictment, the only woman in a long list of rebels.[118]

When James came to the throne in 1603, Rich's work aligning herself
and her people with the King when he was still a "prince caché" paid
off handsomely. Penelope Rich was among the first women to welcome
Queen Anne when she arrived in England in 1603. Shortly thereafter,
Rich was given the precedence of the Earldom of Essex, signifying the alliance's political rehabilitation and revivified power, as well as her status as

---

[118] The Privy Council convened to read the indictments of the conspirators on
17 February "There is a long roll of a names of those involved in the rebellion. At the head
of the list appear the following names:

Earl of Essex	Earl of Bedford
Earl of Rutland	Earl of Sussex
Earl of Southampton	La. Rich

(HMC Salisbury XI.44 cited in Freedman, *Poor Penelope*, 141.) See also the account in the
Calendar of State Papers Domestic (1598–1601), 542–602.

its head. (Freedman points out that Rich had "precedence over all the bar-
onesses in the Kingdom and of the daughters of all earls except four."[119])
She was, as Lady Anne Clifford put it, so "great a woman with the Queen
as everybody much respected her."[120] Her role as one of the gentlewoman
of Queen Anne's Bedchamber was one whose own "gender concentrate"
often served, somewhat ironically, as a limit on James I's own absolutist tendencies. The fact that the "imaginary epistles" appeared long after
Rich's death suggest not only the semi-legendary status of her story, but
its ongoing association with the Sidney alliance and the literary texts that
so often heralded its work. As the imaginary Sidney claims in his letter to
the imaginary Penelope Rich, he has put her "name in euerlasting writtes
/ so longe as doth Arcadias name suruiue" (ll. 73–4; Roberts, "Imaginary
Epistles," 69). The other names that survived along with it—the "honnord
house of Huntington," "Leicester," and "Penshurst notable in Kent"—are
all traceable through the romance's deciphering imperative as well, and
remain integral to its meanings.

   In August 1617, Margaret Clifford's daughter, Lady Anne Clifford,
Countess of Dorset, made an entry in her diary about being kept from a
big gathering at Penshurst. (She herself was also living in Kent, at the property of her husband's family, Dorset House, and the couple was fighting
bitterly about her pursuit of her Clifford inheritance.) Clifford's husband
traveled to Penshurst on 4 August, Clifford recounted, "but would not
suffer me to go with him, although my Lord and my Lady Lisle [Robert
and Barbara Gamage Sidney] sent a man on purpose to desire me to come"
(143).[121] The reasons that her husband prevented this visit are obscure, but
the diary reports that a few days earlier Clifford had visited with "Lady
Wroth [Robert and Barbara Sidney's daughter; Margaret Sidney Herbert's
niece], whither my Lady Rich [Penelope Rich's daughter-in-law, Frances
Rich, in many ways the inheritor of Penelope's social and political posi-
tion] came from London to see me" (143). Although Clifford docs not
report what the women discussed, their meeting may well be the reason
her husband wanted to keep her away from the later Penshurst gathering;
these women were both her kin and her allies.[122]

[119] After she became a Lady of the Drawing Chamber, James I conferred on her the "place
and rank of the ancientest earl of Essex called Bourchier" (*Calendar of State Papers Domestic
1603–10*, p. 32 (17 August 1603) cited in Freedman, *Poor Penelope*, 155). Sir Humphrey
Ferrers considered her powerful enough to ask the king or queen to procure him a barony
(BL, Stowe MS 150, fol. 192). See Alison Wall's entry on Rich in the *ODNB*.

[120] Anne Clifford, *The Memoir of 1603 and The Diary of 1616–1619*, 49. All subsequent
references to this work will be cited parenthetically within the text.

[121] For a discussion of this prohibited visit, see Crawford, "Literary Circles," 52.

[122] A few weeks before, after Clifford had spent "the most part of the day" weeping,
"seeing [that her] enemies had the upper hand of [her]," the same Lady Rich "sent a man

During the time that her husband is at Penshurst without her, Clifford reports keeping largely to her chamber, and spending "most of the time in playing glecko and hearing [one of the members of her household] Moll Neville read the Arcadia" (145)—perhaps the manuscript copy of the *Old Arcadia* that we know the Cliffords owned.[123] What seem here like harmless leisure activities are nonetheless intimately related to the combative backdrop of the forestalled visit. (They are also of a piece with the stoic withdrawal of their practitioner; Clifford always "ke[pt] to her chamber" when making a point to her husband.[124]) Clifford's reading of the *Arcadia* during this specific moment suggests that she considered the romance a kind of compensatory placeholder for not being with the Sidneys themselves, and that she associated it with a particular kind of ethical and political disposition. In her marginal comment for the same entry, Clifford notes that she was thinking "much of religion" at the time, and that she persuaded herself "that this religion in which my mother brought me up in is the true and undoubted religion" (144). Her mother's religion was, as we have seen, both militantly Protestant and neostoically flavored, and it is likely that Clifford was vowing her loyalty to a disposition as much as a faith. Much like Fulke Greville before her, Anne Clifford portrays her mother as an exemplar of constancy, heroically resolute in the face of male tyranny—including that of the King.[125] In Anne Clifford's "Great Picture," her mother, featured in the center of the triptych (pregnant with Anne), is represented holding a Psalter—the key text of international Protestantism associated most famously with Mary Sidney Herbert (see Figure 1.4). To her right are three other books that advertise her chief interests and commitments: a book of alchemy, a Holy Bible, and a copy of "Senakes Workes."[126] (See Figure 1.5.)

Clifford records her own similar reading habits in her own portraits in the two outer panels of the tryptich as well as in her diary. At one point during a particularly difficult negotiation with her husband over her rights

---

hither with a letter of kindness" (141). Later, when she records the death of the first Lord of Warwick, Clifford notes that he left "a great estate to my Lord Rich and my good friend his Lady" (163).

[123] Anne Clifford's parents owned one of the manuscripts of the *Old Arcadia* (Hackett, *Women and Romance Fiction*, 108). "The scribe of the Clifford manuscript of the *Old Arcadia* (now in the Folger Shakespeare Library) can be identified as Richard Robinson, who recorded that Sidney and his father were 'many tymes benevolent unto my pore study'" (BL, Royal MS 18 A.lxvi, fol. 5ᵛ, cited in Davis, "Multiple Arcadias").

[124] On Clifford's keeping to her bedchamber, see Crawford, "The Case of Lady Anne Clifford."

[125] See Crawford, "Lady Anne Clifford and the Uses of Christian Warfare."

[126] Crawford, "Lady Anne Clifford," 115–17.

Figure 1.4 Center panel from the "Great Picture" attributed to Jan can Belcamp. Reproduced by courtesy of Abbot Hall Art Gallery, Kendal, Cumbria. © Lakeland Arts Trust.

to the Clifford properties, she recounts reading a book she identifies as "my Lady's book in the praise of a Solitary Life."[127] This volume, whose title alone provides evidence of the political allegory I have been illuminating here, was given to Margaret Clifford by the same Samuel Daniel who praised her neostoicism in the epistle cited in the beginning of this chapter. Clifford's strategic use of "my Lady's book in the praise of a Solitary Life" suggests the

---

[127] For an excellent account of Clifford's legal battles, see Acheson's introduction in her edn of the diary. Clifford, *The Memoir*, 9–36. For "my Lady's book in the praise of a Solitary Life" see British Museum Addit. MS. 30161, reproduced in *The Letters and Epigrams of Sir John Harington*. The work is based on Petrarch's *De Vita Solitaria*, but includes quotations

A Written hand Booke of Alkijume Extractions, of Diftillations,. And Excellent Medicines.

All Senakes Workes translated out of Latine into English

The Holy Bible the old and new Testament

Figure 1.5 Detail from the "Great Picture," "All Senakes Workes translated out of Latine into English." Reproduced by courtesy of Abbot Hall Art Gallery, Kendal, Cumbria. © Lakeland Arts Trust.

extent to which female constancy had become a recognizable sign of political integrity and resistance. Her reading of the *Arcadia*, I want to suggest, served a similar purpose, evoking both a family—the Sidneys—and a particular religious and political disposition.

A short while after the forestalled visit, Clifford records making another visit to Penshurst, visiting with Lady Lisle, Lady Dorothy Sidney, Lady Manners, Lady Norris, her "cousin Barbara Sidney," and, in particular, Mary Wroth, "who told me a great deal of news from beyond sea" (145). This scene is reminiscent of the "fair ladies" evoked by the *Arcadia*, as well

from Roman authors as well, particularly Seneca. For a discussion of the transmission of *The Prayse of Private Life*, see Sir John Harington, 45. See also Crawford, "Lady Anne Clifford," 116–20. In the "Great Picture," Clifford represents herself with the English translation of Pierre Charron's *De la sagesse* (*On Wisdom*, 1601), a neostoic text based on Lipsius and similarly associated with both aristocratic critique and the Sidney alliance (Crawford, "Lady Anne Clifford," 121).

as by its deciphering imperative.[128] These women were the new mediatrixes of the Sidney alliance, and Wroth's "news from beyond the sea" was
undoubtedly concerned with the Thirty Years War and the cause of international Protestantism. A few years later, Mary Wroth would publish her
own romance. Like the *Arcadia*, it too would be concerned with the rights
of the nobility and make creative use of the political allegory of female
constancy. And, like the *Arcadia*, it would circulate wearing the "liuerye"
of a woman's name.

---

[128] Heidi Brayman Hackel points out that half of the surviving copies of the *Arcadia* have
women's signatures in them (*Reading Material*, 154).

2

How Margaret Hoby Read
her De Mornay

[T]his after none, [I] tooke a Lecture of Rhetorick
(Diary of Lady Margaret Hoby, 14 May 1601)

The "honnord house of Huntingdon" in Yorkshire provided godly training
for the children of those who "fear[ed] God, love[d] the gospel, and hate[d]
popery," many of whom were members of the Sidney-Essex alliance.[1] Its
mistress, Katherine Dudley Hastings, Countess of Huntingdon, claimed
in a letter to Sir Julius Caesar in 1618 that she knew "how to breed and
gouern young gentlewomen."[2] Among these young gentlewomen were
Penelope and Dorothy Devereux and a young Yorkshire heiress named
Margaret Dakins. Dakins's wealth, education, and connections made her
a desirable match for many notable families, including the Devereux, and
she was married to Walter, the younger brother of Penelope, Dorothy,
and Robert, sometime before she was 18. After Walter Devereux died
fighting under his brother for the Protestant cause in Rouen in 1591,
there was something of a competition for Margaret's hand. Two of the
most powerful families in late Elizabethan politics—what one scholar has
rather evocatively referred to as "hives"—wanted her for themselves: the
Huntingdons wanted her to marry a Sidney, the Cecils, a young man
named Sir Thomas Posthumous Hoby.[3] While Thomas Sidney became
Margaret's second husband in 1591, after his equally premature death in
1595, she was married, for the third and last time, to the losing candidate
in the previous round: the (posthumous) son of the Hoby who translated Castliglione and, more importantly for the purposes of this book, of

<hr />

[1] Cited in Claire Cross, *The Puritan Earl,* 59; and *Diary of Lady Margaret Hoby, 1599–
1605,* ed. Dorothy M. Meads, 7.
[2] See Hoby, *Diary,* ed. Meads, 7. See also Cross, *Puritan Earl,* ch. 2: "The Godly
Household," 22–60. Lawrence Stone describes the Huntingdon household as "a Protestant
Seminary in miniature" (*Crisis of the Aristocracy,* 737).
[3] On "hives," see Hoby, *Diary,* ed. Meads, 11.

Elizabeth Cooke Hoby Russell, a Protestant activist and influential media-trix.[4] Sir Thomas Hoby himself was of dubious moral character—his mother described him as having "infirmytyes and insufficiency by want of stature, learning, and otherwise"—but he had both a godly pedigree and powerful political connections.[5] Ultimately, the Earl of Huntingdon encouraged Margaret to accept Sir Thomas for "God's cawse," and they were married in 1596.[6]

Huntingdon's insistence that Margaret marry Hoby for "God's cawse" has solicited some comment. Claire Cross has suggested, for example, that Huntingdon, who was then the President of the Council of the North, wanted to plant Sir Thomas Hoby as his agent in the north of England in order to militate against the recusancy of the region.[7] Yet while Thomas brought important connections with him, it seems more likely that both the Huntingdons and Elizabeth Russell viewed Margaret Hoby, rather than her husband, as the key factor in this plan.[8] According to Sir Edward Stanhope, an Essex ally and member of the Council of the North, by 1596, Margaret had already "carved" herself a reputation for "good wisdome and honorable government" in Yorkshire.[9] While

---

[4] On Elizabeth Russell as a mediatrix, see Felicity Heal, "Reputation and Honour in Court and Country." Her sister, Mildred, was the wife of Queen Elizabeth's chief councilor, William Cecil. In 1574, Elizabeth married John Lord Russell, the son of Francis, Earl of Bedford, with whom she had two daughters. (His sister was Margaret Russell, eventually Countess of Cumberland: Hoby, *Diary*, ed. Meads, 13.) On Russell's 1592 entertainment for the Queen, in which she encourages a militant international Protestantism and imagines Elizabeth stretching one hand to France "to weaken rebels," and "the other to *Flaunders* to strengthen Religion"), see Crawford, "Literary Circles," 42–3. On Russell's involvement in the puritan activism of 1570, see Crawford, "Literary Circles," 41.

[5] Russell has more to say about her son's "vnnaturall bad nature and insolency" and his envy of her love "to his poore wronged sistars" (Hoby, *Diary*, ed. Meads, p. 24 n. 71). In the face of Margaret's (understandable) resistance to marrying him, Hoby thus received support from a number of corners, including Dorothy Devereux Perrot, who advocated on his behalf. See Elizabeth Russell's letter to her son describing "I.a. Perrott" as "the wisest, surest, and fittest to [Hoby's] good" (*The Private Life of an Elizabethan Lady: The Diary of Lady Margaret Hoby 1599–1605*, ed. Joanna Moody, 231–2). Thomas Hoby wrote to the Countess of Huntingdon in June 1596, thanking her for her "favorable coorse helde in [his] present sute" of Margaret, and expresses his hope that he "wyll be fownde as dutyfully servyceable, as if I wer a naturall branch of the stocke yt self, whereto I shall then be but grafted" (26 June 1596, full letter in Hoby, *Private Life*, ed. Moody, 236–7).

[6] Huntingdon's 9 December 1595 letter to Margaret is printed in full in Hoby, *Private Life*, ed. Moody, 235.

[7] Cross, *Puritan Earl*, 172.

[8] On Elizabeth's pursuit of Margaret and disappointment in her son, see Elizabeth Farber, "The Letters of Lady Elizabeth Russell," 111–14.

[9] Stanhope's letter is cited in full in Hoby, *Private Life*, ed. Moody, 236. Stanhope, who had been admitted to the Council of the North in 1587 through the Earl of Leicester's influence, was still "attached to his step-son's [Essex's] party" (Reid, *The King's Council of the North*, 227). Stanhope was a frequent visitor to Hackness; see Hoby, *Diary*, ed. Meads, 74, 146, 157, 188, and 204 for other mentions of Stanhope.

Elizabeth Russell promised a "good portione and lyvelod" to Margaret when she married her son, moreover, the estate the couple would live on was Margaret's, purchased for her and Walter Devereux by her father, the Earl of Huntingdon, and the Earl of Essex in 1589.[10] Hackness was thus more than a godly household in the recusant north—it was an outpost of one of the most powerful political alliances in England, and Margaret Hoby was its acknowledged keeper.

Margaret Hoby is known to us by a diary she kept between 9 August 1599 and 21 July 1605, a period covering, among other things, the Essex rebellion, the death of Elizabeth I, and the accession of James I. The diary is comprised of 59 folios (118 pages) and written in her own hand—a hand, as the diary's editor points out, "well accustomed to the use of the pen."[11] For the most part, Hoby's diary has been seen as the life record of a "private Elizabethan lady," a document "kept largely as a means of assisting in the religious exercise of self-examination," or as part of the "self-imposed career" of a "Puritan saint."[12] It has been of interest to literary scholars largely for its account of Hoby's reading habits, which were both capacious and communal. Recently, it has been suggested that Hoby's reading shows that she was "intellectually engaged in some of the most controversial theological issues of the day," and that it is best understood as a "familial" or "sociable" practice characteristic of godly life.[13] In this chapter I want to

[10] On Hoby's "good portione of lyvelod," see Hoby, *Diary,* ed. Meads, 25. On the purchase of Hackness, see Hoby, *Diary*, ed. Meads, 4.

[11] The diary, MS Egerton 2614, is currently at the British Library. In addition to the two scholarly edns by Dorothy M. Meads and Joanna Moody already cited, a facsimile of the manuscript is available through the Perdita Project, <http://www.perditamanuscripts.amdigital.co.uk>. All references to the diary itself will be to the Meads edn. On Hoby's hand, see Hoby, *Diary*, ed. Meads, p. x.

[12] The title of Joanna Moody's edn of the diary is *The Private Life of an Elizabethan Lady*, and she describes it as "a collection of private meditations and secret recollections" (p. xv). The second quotation is from Hoby, *Diary*, ed. Meads, "Introduction," 47. On Hoby's "self-imposed career," see Sara Heller Mendelson, "Stuart Women's Diaries and Occasional Memoirs," 189, and for her status as a "puritan saint," Diane Willen, "Godly Women in Early Modern England." See also Peter Lake, "Feminine Piety and Personal Potency," at 155 (on Jane Ratcliffe of Chester and the "cult of personal godliness"), and Michael Winship, "Bridget Cooke and the Art of Godly Female Self-Advancement." For other accounts of the diary as primarily an exercise in the puritan discipline of self-examination, see the new *ODNB* entry on Margaret Hoby by Paul Slack, and Mary Ellen Lamb, "Margaret Hoby's Diary," 64. For a thoughtful set of reflections on what a diary was—less a transparent reflection of actual events and feelings than a genre with its own conventions and mediations—see Kunin, "From the Desk of Anne Clifford."

[13] On Hoby's "intellectual engagement," see Hoby, *Private Life*, ed. Moody, p. xvi, and on sociable reading, see Andrew Cambers, "Reading, the Godly and Self-Writing in England, Circa 1580–1720." Cambers locates diaries and autobiographies "as much in the public context of the religious community as in the realm of the private self" and focuses on such writings as "familial" and "sociable" practices (p. 796).

argue that Hoby's diary was something far more complicated than any of these descriptions allow.

Hoby undoubtedly had devotional and sociable purposes in mind when she chose what books to read, and with whom, but she also sought to influence those readers in certain directions, particularly in regard to what she calls "principles of relegion" (62). She also sought to make herself convincing. On two occasions in May 1601, for example, Hoby records taking "a lecture in Rhetorick," the art of public persuasion and influence (172, 173).[14] Hoby read with a wide range of people, from the members of her extended household to her tenants, neighbours, local and visiting clergymen, and "strangres as Came to [her]" (71).[15] She also read a wide range of books with them, including the Bible and the "book of Marters" with the men and women in her household (74, 75, 82, 111, 175); the "diatt of the soule" by the Yorkshire-based anti-Romanist and former chaplain to the Earl of Huntingdon, Thomas Morton (68);[16] Hugh Latimer's sermons; a sermon of the puritan controversialist John Udall (with her husband, 163); the work of the former Sidney/Herbert chaplain, Gervase Babington (77); a book by the anti-Whitgiftian "Mr [Hugh] Browghton" (114, 263 n. 326); the John Whitgift and Thomas Cartwright disputation itself (with both her minister, Richard Rhodes, and her husband, 67, 97); the writings of the puritan William Perkins (87, 97, 101, 104, 170, 178); the work of another anti-Whitgiftian, George Gifford (both by herself and with Rhodes, 68, 72); "a good man's book" who "proveth" truths against the arguments of the anti-puritan Thomas Bilson, Bishop of Winchester (with Rhodes, 97, 259 n. 282); the works of the puritan Richard Greenham (with at least six other people, 86, 93); "some notes of [the renowned London puritan activist] Mr Egertons Lecturs" (193); "a

---

[14] Meads suggests that Hoby was perhaps reading Thomas Wilson's *The Arte of Rhetorique* (1552) (Hoby, *Diary*, 279 n. 466), but in the entries she uses the verb "took" (as in "I tooke a Lecture of Rhe;"), suggesting, at the very least, an active lesson. Regardless of the exact form it took, Hoby's study of rhetoric was, as I will argue further, intimately related to her communal reading practices.

[15] "[A]fter the sarmone ended" on Sunday, 7 October 1599 e.g. she reports reading "a whill of the Bible" to Mrs Ormston, one of the members of her household (76). On 10 August 1599, she "went about the house, and instructed Tomson wiffe in som principles of relegion" (62). Hoby regularly reads with her husband, and reports "instruct[ing] som of [her] famelie" on 30 August 1599 (67) and reading books and discussing sermons with her own "wemen," "workwemen," "olde wemen" (130, 81, 117)—women who worked as servants, tenants, or workers in her fields—as well as local "good wiffes" and "gentlewomen" (136, 131, 169, 189, 190), and "neighbours" (133, 190).

[16] The full title is: Thomas Morton, *Two Treatises Concerning Regeneration, 1. Of repentance, 2. Of the diet of the soule shewing the one, how it ought to be sought after and may be attained vnto, the other, how it being gotten, is to be preserued and continued* (London, 1597).

Little of Mr Rogers book to Anne france" (210); at least one Catholic book
(120); the Earl of Essex's "defense of his own causes" and Francis Bacon's
account of Essex's "treason" (132, 172); and a number of unnamed books,
both print and manuscript, given to her by her cousin, Arthur Dakins, her
minister's wife, and a fellow northern puritan woman.[17] Her reading was
familial and sociable, that is, but it was also public, interpellative, inter-
confessional, and, as I will argue here, political.

At once theologically controversial and "sociable," Margaret Hoby's
reading habits were geared toward influencing both local sentiment and
belief and religious and political action. While they were not exactly
"scholarly transactions" in the sense that Lisa Jardine and William
H. Sherman have outlined—as far as we know, Hoby did not hire a secretary to read to her—her reading habits were nonetheless "goal-directed"
in that they sought real-world effects.[18] Many of the books Hoby read
were by local authors, and while her reading corresponded with specific
regional concerns with which she was actively involved, it was also concerned with English religion and politics more broadly. Hoby did her
reading in Yorkshire, a region notorious for recusancy and embroiled in
power struggles that played out both internally (largely on the Council of
the North), and between the country and London, during a particularly
fraught period of religious and political transition. Hoby may not have
had the same political influence as Mary Sidney Herbert or the Devereux
sisters, but she did nonetheless serve as a mediatrix for shared political
interests—at one point she referred to herself as a "mediator" on behalf of
Robert Sidney—and her reading was concerned with similar religious and
political ends. Like Gabriel Harvey and Philip Sidney's, Margaret Hoby's
reading was a form of "jostl[ing] for power," concerned, like theirs, with
nothing less than "the exercise of government."[19] Rather than a record of
the "self-imposed career" of a "puritan saint," Hoby's diary is thus best
understood as a record of a public career, and her reading as a form of
political activism.

---

[17] Hoby mentions a book Rhodes's brother Edward brought to her "from his wife" (23
April 1601; 169). Hoby records getting a book from her cousin on 20 June 1602 (198).
I will discuss the northern puritan woman, Isabel, Lady Bowes, further. For a list of the texts
Hoby mentions reading, see the appendix to Mary Ellen Lamb's essay, "Margaret Hoby's
Diary," 87–91.

[18] On the term "goal-directed," see Lisa Jardine and Anthony Grafton, "'Studied
for Action': How Gabriel Harvey Read his Livy," 31. See also Lisa Jardine and William
H. Sherman, "Pragmatic Readers."

[19] Jardine and Sherman, "Pragmatic Readers," 102, 106.

I. "[T]HE MOST DANGEROUS PART OF YORKSHIRE FOR HOLLOW HEARTS, FOR POPERY"

On 27 August 1599, during the same month that Margaret Hoby began keeping her diary, the Archbishop of Canterbury, John Whitgift, wrote to the Archbishop of York, Mathew Hutton, about the "informations given that recusants are of late increased in that province, and that you are to[o] milde with them."[20] (Hutton, whom Peter Lake has described as a "puritan Bishop," was in Yorkshire largely due to the influence of the Earl of Essex. Like his patron, he supported toleration in religion.[21]) Whitgift was right about Yorkshire. By the end of 1595, thirty priests had been executed in the north (mostly in York) and eight laypeople had been convicted of harboring priests.[22] Whitby, the hundred in which Hackness was situated, had thirty-two recusants and four non-communicants listed in the Presentment book for 1595–6.[23] When Thomas Hoby arrived in the North Riding of Yorkshire in 1596 and assumed a series of local political offices, he thus took up recusant hunting as a means of "winn[ing] . . . commendation" for himself from the court.[24] (Margaret Hoby makes frequent records of her husband's anti-recusancy efforts in her diary.[25]) Thomas

---

[20] "Some of your ministers doe also affirme the same to be trewe," Whitgift continues, "My advice therefore ys, that your Lordship make a true declaration in writing how that province standeth in that pynte and this tyme." *The Correspondence of Dr. Matthew Hutton*, 147. Subsequent references to Hutton's correspondence will be cited in the text.

[21] Lake, "Matthew Hutton—A Puritan Bishop?" On Hutton's opposition to compulsion in religion, see Reid, *King's Council*, 227.

[22] Cross, *Puritan Earl*, 243.

[23] J. S. Purvis, *Tudor Parish Documents of the Diocese of York*, 48. The standard account of Catholicism in the region is Hugh Aveling's *Northern Catholics*.

[24] In his letter to Hutton about recusancy, Whitgift went on to suggest that recusant-hunting could be a tool of political ambition: "for it may be some men's pollicie to make things worse then they are, to effect there desyers and to winne the commendation to themselfes" (Hutton, *Correspondence*, 147). Within a short period of time, Hoby became known as an "industrious" justice of the peace; recording warrants for arrests in a "booke" he kept with him at all times. See "Journal of Sir William Brereton," *North Country Diaries* (2nd series), ed. J. C. Hodgson (Durham: Surtees Society 124; 1915), quoted in Hoby, *Diary*, ed. Meads, "Introduction," 34–5. Within a few years he had become a commissioner of the peace for the North and East Ridings of Yorkshire, had been recommended for election to the Council of the North, and was listed as a high commissioner for the Province of York. On Hoby's frequent and litigious bids and campaigns for office, as well as the offices he held, see Hoby, *Diary*, ed. Meads, "Introduction," 35–7.

[25] She reports that Sir Thomas received "Leters, touching Recusants, from the Counsill [of the North]" on 17 April 1605, and notes a number of occasions on which he traveled to nearby towns "to take order for recusants" or "to sitt upon a Comition for recusantes" (218, 219, 220). In 1615, Hoby launched a suit in Star Chamber against the East Riding Quarter Sessions, "alleging various malpractices in the conduct of business, unruly behavior and partiality toward recusants," and complaining against several prominent local recusants,

Hoby quickly became known for his efforts. When an attack was to be made on a house suspected of harboring papists in April 1599, for example, the man in charge of the raid told Sir Robert Cecil that, with Sir Thomas Hoby away in London, he knew "of no faithfull assistance in the country."[26] Indeed, Thomas Hoby's interactions with his recusant neighbors were conducted primarily in two ways: through the exacting local administration of justice and persecution.

In her diary Margaret Hoby frequently records the duties she and her husband performed together as godly householders. One day in August 1599, for example, Hoby reports that she "walked with Mr Hoby about the toune to spye out the best places where Cotiges might be builded," and, later in the evening, "helped Mr Hoby to Looke over some papers" (65). She notes in an early entry in her diary (25 August 1599) that she spoke "privately, with Mr. Hoby, of matters concerninge Conscience and our estates," and, on another occasion, that she helped "to read of the book for the placing of the people in the church to Mr Hoby" (66, 69). She makes a record on 4 September 1601 of talking with Sir Thomas "of some Complaintes made to him," and then "Cop[ying] out a letter which [he] had wretten to the Busshopp of Limbricke [Limerick]," John Thornborough (185). On 23 August 1601, she writes that she was "gett[ing] some thinges readie against my Lord presedent Cominge" (184), referring to a visit from Thomas Cecil, Lord Burghley, who had taken over the presidency of the Council of the North after Huntingdon's death and a brief stint in which Matthew Hutton, at once too tolerant and too much Essex's man, had been in charge.[27]

Hoby also recounted her role in keeping the sessions of the Hackness Manor Court, a court of special sessions held for the inhabitants of the manor of Hackness by the owner of the manor, and attended by justices of the peace from the immediate district.[28] As she writes on 4 August 1601, "this day I was busie in the house, havinge manie strangers, because of the Courte that was kept after Mr Hoby and my self, by godes goodness, had gotten thestate [the estate] of Hackness" (181). The gratitude Hoby expresses for "godes goodness" refers to his providential assurance of their victory in a battle with their recusant neighbors over the right to hold such a court. (These neighbours, the Cholmleys, had claimed the historical right

including Sir William Constable and Sir William Hildyard (G. C. F. Forster, "Faction and County Government in Early Stuart Yorkshire," 82, 83).

[26] *Calendar of State Papers Domestic: Elizabeth, 1598–1601*, vol. 270, no. 99; cited in Hoby, *Diary*, ed. Meads, "Introduction," 35 (see also 35 n. 112).

[27] Hutton had taken over in February 1596, after Huntingdon's death, but had been dismissed because of his "overmuch toleration used to recusants." See Reid, *King's Council*, 230.

[28] Hoby, *Diary*, ed. Meads, 280.

to hold the manor courts as well, and there had been a protracted court battle between the two families.[29]) The fact that Hoby points out that the court
was kept "after Mr Hoby and *my self*...had gotten thestate of Hackness"
indicates that she considered herself an office holder as well. In the period
in which Hoby was writing, manor houses served as regional headquarters,
places from which those who held the rights of the manor courts governed
the estate and its surrounding demesnes.[30] Manor courts, moreover, were
one of the venues in which women were able to hold office, and Hoby's
diary indicates that she took her co-governance of Hackness seriously. In
one entry she records a visit from a man who came "to see Mr. Hoby *only*, as
he saied," a request that highlights, by its notable rarity, the habitual nature
of the Hobys' shared governance (187, emphasis added).

Yet despite their habitual co-governance, Margaret Hoby considered
Hackness to be her own property. (It had been purchased, as I mentioned,
for her and Devereux.) Throughout her diary, Hoby frequently refers to
the estate's workers and tenants as "hers," often in explicit contrast to those
who worked for her husband.[31] Her contemporaries seemed to see it in this
way as well. Hugh Cholmley, a member of the family who had fought the
Hobys over the rights to the manor court, referred to Hackness as belonging to "Sir Thomas's lady."[32] The diary also indicates Hoby's differences
from her husband, particularly in matters spiritual. Perhaps more than
anything else, Hoby differed from her husband in the way she dealt with
her neighbours' Catholicism. She seems to have handled it largely through
co-reading and conversation. On 16 May 1600, for example, Hoby makes
a record in her diary of hearing her personal chaplain "Mr. Rhodes read of
the principles of poperie out of one of their owne bookes" (120), a practice

[29] See *Diary*, ed. Meads, 3 and 280–1 n. 487.

[30] Hackness was a sizable estate, comprised of "the Manor of Hacknes," "200 messuages
and 4 mills with lands there and in Silpho, Suffielde, Everle, Hacknes Dale, Harewoode
Dale, Brexay, Burneston, Huton Bushell, and Ayton," and "the rectory and advowson of the
vicarage of Hacknes als. Hacknesse church" (Hoby, *Diary*, ed. Meads, 9 n. 31). On manor
courts, see Goldie, "The Unacknowledged Republic."

[31] For examples of Hoby's differentiation between their workers, which Meads also
notes, see 81, 123, 265 n. 348, and Introduction, 20–21, n. 76.

[32] Cholmley had little respect for Sir Thomas himself, alluding in his memoir to the fact
that Hoby sold his wife's property to his relatives despite her express wishes that it go to her
own. Sir Erskine Perry, *The Van den Bempde Papers*, 21: "The Sydenhams, now possessed
of Hackness, may in some sort thank me for it; for Sir Thomas Hobby, to make the Lord
Coventry his friend, against me, proposed his cousin Sydenham in marriage to my Lord's
grandchild, and so settled Hackness on him, which in right belonged to Mr. Dakins, next to
Sir Thomas's lady, whose land that was." Sir Thomas left the bulk of estate to his own cousin
and heir John Sydenham in 1640, along with "the flaggon bracelet of gold with the picture
of my late most dear and only wife in which is fastened there unto and which I do purpose, if
God shall permit, to wear about mine arm untill and at the time of my death" (Hoby, *Private
Life*, ed. Moody, epilogue, 224–6). See also Hoby, *Diary*, ed. Meads, "Introduction," 43–5.

in which they, like many politically active Protestants, engaged intently for a few days.[33] The day after reading a (perhaps the same) "popeshe booke," Hoby records talking "with a good Christian touchinge sundrie infirmetes that our humaine nature is subject to" (121), a topic, as her use of the term "good Christian" suggests, familiar across confessional lines. On 24 February 1599, Hoby records spending her evening in the following way: "saluted some strangers: after praied and then dined: after, I kept Companie tell they departed and, after, reed and talked with a yonge papest maide" (105).

"[P]apest maide[s]" were in many ways responsible for keeping Catholicism alive in Protestant England, and Yorkshire in particular boasted far more recusant women than men.[34] Many of these women were famed for their intellectual and theological acumen. Sir Edward Stanhope left a particularly telling record of spying on and eventually capturing and executing a group of recusants, in which he notes that the women in the group were particularly "perilous," "not only for their recusancy, but for speaking boldly against the state, persuading others, and dealing abroad with women."[35] Hoby notes nothing of the content—or purpose—of her conversation with the "yonge papest maide," what text(s) they read, or what points of controversy or commonality they touched upon. Yet her reading and talking with a young Catholic woman stands in sharp relief to the bare note she made the following month: "Mr Hoby that night went to search a house for papists" (24 March 1600; 110), an enterprise that was doubtlessly more violently persecutory than dialogic.

---

[33] See also the entry for 19 May, three days later: "Hard Mr Rhodes read of a popeshe booke": 120). Many English Protestants believed Catholic books to be dangerous, at least for certain readers; see e.g. Hutton, *Correspondence*, 167. Sir Edward Stanhope also read Catholic texts that it would be treasonable for anyone else to have, and may have shared them with Hoby. See John Barnard and Maureen Bell, *The Early Seventeenth Century York Book Trade*, 30. For other Protestant women who read Catholic books, see David McKitterick, "Women and their Books in Seventeenth-Century England"; and Arnold Hunt, "The Books, Manuscripts, and Literary Patronage of Mrs. Anne Sadleir."

[34] The 1604 recusant rolls for Yorkshire list almost 400 more women than men who were presented for recusancy. See Sarah L. Bastow, "Worth Nothing, But Very Wilful," 597. For English recusant women generally, see Marie B. Rowlands, "Recusant Women, 1560–1640."

[35] Katharine M. Longley, "Blessed George Errington," 43, 44. In 1609, Sir Edward Hoby, Margaret Hoby's brother-in-law (and a puritan lobbyist himself) dedicated a polemical letter to a newly converted Jesuit, "To All Romish Collapsed Ladies of Great Britanie," joking that the fastest way to get his castigatory missive to its addressee at St. Omer is "by your Ladiships meanes, as having weekely newes from the English house"; *A Letter to Mr. T.H. Late Minister: now fugitiue*, A2. Hoby's concern with the intellectual attentions and activities of women in this work acknowledges the central role that women played in keeping Catholicism alive in post-Reformation England. See also his later pamphlet, *A Curry-combe for a Coxe-combe* (London, 1615), in which he contrasts Protestant and Catholic women's religious understanding.

On 26/27 August 1600, a hunting visit to Hackness manor by the members of two of the most powerful Catholic families in the area, the Eures and the aforementioned Cholmleys, went terribly awry.[36] There is some evidence that it was motivated by hostility against Thomas Hoby. As he wrote to Sir Robert Cecil following the incident, problems had been brewing between the families before the visit: "there has been some dryness in the Lord Ewre (whose tenants are my next neighbours) almost ever since I was employed as a commissioner in these parts."[37] A hostile witness claimed that, well before the incident, Sir Christopher Hillyard had said "there was a sorte of younge fellowes in Yorkshire wolled plaie him [Hoby] a tricke were it were longe and when it were done he shoud not mende himselfe." He also reported that another visitor had proposed to pull down the local church because he knew "the Lord of the Mannor [Hoby] was tyed to buyld yt agayne."[38] Sir Thomas Hoby, whom one local man described as "the busiest saucy little Jack in all the country [who] would have an oar in anybody's boat," thus seems to have been the target of some local animosity.[39]

During their visit, the visiting party reportedly interrupted prayers with rude noises, including a "black sanctus," or burlesque hymn.[40] While aggressive festivity characterized the visit in general—the party also played cards and got drunk—the singing of the "black sanctus" was a direct attack on the Hobys' godliness. (Hoby frequently records singing psalms with the members of her household in her diary). Yet despite the fact that she was a psalm singer herself, the visitors' depositions were, as Felicity Heal puts it, "at pains to stress that no insult was intended to Lady Margaret, indeed some comments suggest that she was respected by her neighbours" (173). While Heal claims that the Hobys "made no secret of their alienation from the values of local society," the account itself suggests that Margaret Hoby behaved very differently from her husband.[41] In a telling phrase in his deposition, William Eure reports that Thomas Hoby's behavior was "not answerable to our northern entertainments." Margaret Hoby, on the other

---

[36] On the visit and its litigated aftermath, see Royal Commission on Historical Manuscripts, *Calendar of the Manuscripts of the Most Honourable, the Marquess of Salisbury Preserved at Hatfield House, Hertfordshire, Part X* (London, 1904), 302–4; Aveling, *Northern Catholics*, 118–20; Heal, "Reputation"; Forster, "Faction"; and Meads, "Introduction," 40–3; and Hoby, *Diary*, ed. Meads, 269–72 n. 368. Joanna Moody also provides some extracts from the correspondence and evidence relating to the case in appendix 2 of her edn of the diary. Thomas Hoby charged the hunting party with "riotous assault" before the Council of the North, and, eventually, the Star Chamber (Hoby, *Diary*, ed. Meads, 270 n. 368). His account mentions "cards," "lascivious talk where every sentence was begun or ended with a great oath," and "inordinate drinking unto healths, abuses" he never practiced himself (Hoby, *Private Life*, ed. Moody, 240).

[37] Quoted in Hoby, *Diary*, ed. Meads, 270 n. 368.

[38] Heal, "Reputation," 170–1.   [39] Quoted in Forster, "Faction," 74.

[40] Heal, "Reputation," 171.   [41] Heal, "Reputation," 173, 171, 163.

hand, was less hostile and even "shew[ed] some dislike of her husband's strange behavior."[42] Eure's evaluation was perhaps influenced by Margaret Hoby's greater sociability. While Thomas Hoby singled out both the Eure and Cholmley families for persecution, Margaret Hoby had numerous social interactions with both families.[43] On several occasions she mentions writing "to my Lady Ewre" and, on others, visiting her in person (69). (On 18 September 1599, for example, Hoby "took my Cocth, and wente to malton to salute my Lady Ewre, with whom I staied about:2: houres" (73). She visited her again on 30 May 1600, less than two months before the hunting visit (123).)

While one might be tempted to characterize these visits as forms of female socializing irrelevant to the public and political affairs of men, on 29 April 1600, a month before the above visit with Lady Eure, Lady Hoby records that she "kept Companie with Mr Cholmley, [the head of the most powerful local Catholic family], tell allmost night" (117).[44] Hoby records at least two earlier visits with the same man: on 27 August 1599, she records talking "a little with Mr Cholmley" during an evening when her husband is away in York, and on 26 December 1599, talking with Mr Cholmley "of diverse thinges" (67, 92). While she gives no account of what they talked of during these visits, Margaret Hoby's "talking" was almost always tied to religious and intellectual exchange. Cholmley, moreover, was a dangerous man to be talking with in late 1599.

In the late sixteenth century, northern politics, particularly in the Council of the North, were deeply affected by the battle between Essex and Cecil. In order to counter Cecil's influence, Essex had his own agents on the Council of the North. (Matthew Hutton, as I suggested earlier, was an Essex loyalist.[45]) But Essex was also corresponding with northern Catholics, including Richard Cholmley, about a northern rising geared towards securing the succession of James and, it was hoped, toleration in religion.[46] Cholmley, in fact, was eventually indicted for his role in the

---

[42] *Manuscripts of the...Marquess of Salisbury*, 302–4.

[43] Meads, "Introduction," 34, see also 237–8 n. 109. Sir Thomas, on the other hand, presented Henry Cholmley to the recusancy commission, and alienated the leading magnate of the area, Ralph, third Lord Eure with his zealous Protestantism" (Heal, "Reputation," 169).

[44] James Daybell similarly challenges the tendency to see early modern women's and men's sociability outside the home as qualitatively different, pointing out that "Whereas women are traditionally seen as 'gossips,' peddlers of ephemeral and trifling tittletattle, men are described as 'intelligencers,' suppliers of information of serious import"; " 'Suche newes as on the Quenes hye wayes we have mett,'" 116.

[45] On 20 May 1601, Mathew Hutton wrote to Whitgift asking him to plead with the Queen to "stretch forthe the goulden scepter" to Essex, who was "abiding the frownes of fortune, and to cause a sure and hartie reconciliation" (Hutton, *Correspondence*, 155).

[46] Reid, *King's Council*, 230. As we saw in Ch. 1, Essex and his sister were also corresponding with James VI about his succession to the English throne.

Essex conspiracy.[47] (Sir William Eure was also "caught in its fringes".) Essex, as we saw in the last chapter, had taken over from Sidney as the leader of the advanced reformers, but he also advocated toleration in religion, a position that appealed to those who felt alienated from the Elizabethan settlement—including Catholics like the Cholmleys and Eures and puritans like Hoby. In 1599, Essex was in trouble with the law, and his sister, Penelope Devereux Rich, was busy defending his reputation and position. (Early in 1600, she would be arrested for writing a critical letter to Queen Elizabeth.[48]) Both Hoby and Cholmley would thus have been paying close attention to Essex's activities in 1599, and he might well have been one of the "diverse thinges" they talked about during their visits.

We know from her diary that Hoby followed Essex's doings attentively. In July 1600, she records spending "the after none in my Chamber" and hearing "Mr Rhodes read a book that was mad, it was saied, by my lord of Essex in defense of his own causes" (132). This book, known as Essex's "Apology," was written against those who "falsely and maliciously tax[d] him to be the only hinderer of the peace and quiet of this kingdom," and it was printed, and then suppressed, when Essex was in trouble with the Queen in June 1600 for arguing against peace with Spain. As we saw in the last chapter, opposition to Spain was a central tenet of the Sidney-Essex alliance, and Essex's "Apology," much like his sister's letter to Elizabeth, actually circulated more as an oppositional treatise than as a genuine apology. Among other things, it featured a number of cautions on overweening royal authority, including Essex's oft-cited question: "Cannot subjects receive wrong? Is an earthly power or authority infinite?"[49] On 12 May 1601, less than a month after her last visit with Cholmley, Hoby records hearing Mr Rhodes read another book about Essex, this time "the booke

---

[47] Heal points out that Cholmley was eventually released with a £200 fine, although Thomas Hoby characteristically tried to prove that he had the "hollow hearts" of the country behind him ("Reputation," 175). There was, in the end, no breaking of the peace in the north, and, because Cecil wanted to keep his own correspondence with the King of Scotland secret, and make sure that the Catholics did not revolt out of despair, the northern gentlemen associated with Essex, including Richard Cholmley, were let off with fines (Reid, *King's Council*, 234).

[48] In February 1600 Whyte wrote: "I hear that my Lady Rich was called before my Lord Treasurer or Mr Secretary for a letter she had written to Her Majesty" (Freedman, *Poor Penelope*, 134). Later in the month he wrote that "My Lady Rich is commanded to keep her house; the cause is thought to be that by her means certain copies of a letter she writ to the queen is published abroad" (135). Bacon called her letter "an insolent, saucy, malapert action" (136).

[49] Essex, *Lives and Letters of the Devereux*, 501. The book that Hoby was reading may well have included not only Penelope Rich's own letter to the Queen, but also Essex's letters of resistance, criticizing the absoluteness of Elizabeth's power. Like Sidney's, these letters circulated widely in manuscript.

of my lord of Esixe treason," Francis Bacon's account of the Earl's January 1601 rebellion.[50] She reads the book intently for several days. It is after reading this book, it is worth noting, that Hoby records taking her first "Lecture of Rhetoricke" (172).

While Hoby read many books with many different people, her most frequent reading, writing, and discussion partner was her personal chaplain, Richard Rhodes. In meetings recounted in her diary, many of which take place in her "Closet" or "Chamber" (122, 123), Hoby examines "that I had wreten with Mr Rhodes" (63); has "Mr Rhodes read" the Bible or "read a chapter" to her (120, 121, 124, 130, 64); "hard Mr Rhodes read 2 chapters of the Testament" (138); "wrought and hard Mr Rhodes read of the testement and other good bookes" (121); talks "of good matters with Mr Rhodes and Mr Maude, a younge devine, a exceedinge good Christian" (89); and hears him read numerous books, including "a sarmon booke" (129, 133), "Latimers sarmons" (129), "Cartwright," "Mr Cartwright and the Bushoppe of Canterberies booke," a "popeshe booke" (120), and "a booke against some newe sprange up heresies" (67, 99, 98). Hoby, as I indicated earlier, read a wide range of religious texts, and most were concerned with theological and doctrinal controversy. "Mr Cartwright and the Bushoppe of Canterberies booke," for example, recorded the central Presbyterian debate of the 1570s. Thomas Cartwright, who was on the radical side of the debate, received the protection of both Elizabeth Hoby Russell and the Earl of Essex for precisely those controversial opinions.[51] Texts like the Cartwright/Whitgift dispute were records of discussion and debate, and models for the same. They undoubtedly influenced the way that Hoby herself read. The verbs she uses to describe her work with Rhodes—"read," "meditate," "examine," "talk," "hear," "write"—suggest the range and variety of their interactions, and Hoby consistently presents herself as an active interlocutor. In particular, she frequently notes the occasions on which she "has" Rhodes read her a given text, a verb that suggests the choices were her own, and that she was as much a director of Rhodes's reading as he was of hers.[52]

---

[50] Francis Bacon, *A declaration of the practises & treasons attempted and committed by Robert late Earle of Essex and his complices, against her Maiestie and her kingdoms and of the proceedings as well at the arraignments & conuictions of the said late Earle, and his adherents.* See also William Barlow, *A sermon preached at Paules Crosse, on the first Sunday in Lent: Martij 1. 1600 With a short discourse of the late Earle of Essex his confession, and penitence, before and at the time of his death…Whereunto is annexed a true copie, in substance, of the behauiour, speache, and prayer of the said Earle at the time of his execution.* Both were published in 1601.

[51] For details of the 1572 Presbyterian *Admonition* of the Church of England and Whitgift's response, see A. F. Scott Pearson, *Thomas Cartwright and Elizabethan Puritanism,* 58–75.

[52] e.g. on 16 August 1599, she "*hadd* Mr Rhodes read a chapter" to her before going to bed (64). Lamb "describes Hoby as listening to a reader about 34 times of the 54 times" she reads ("Margaret Hoby's Diary," 75). In an essay on Hoby's marginalia, Andrew Cambers

Hoby's co-reading with Rhodes was by no means solely or even primarily concerned with her personal salvation or education. One night in August 1599, for example, Hoby records that she and Rhodes "had som speech with the poore and Ignorant of the som princeples of religion," and on other occasions she works, both with Rhodes and on her own, to convince her neighbors of matters of godly concern (65–6). On 11 March 1599/1600, for example, she writes of a visit with "some of my neighbours, with whom I took occasion to speak of divers nedfull dutes to be knowne: as of parence Chousinge for their children, of the charge of godfathers, and of the first instructing of them" (107). On another occasion, she declines an invitation "to be a witness at [Mr Daunie's] childes baptisinge...in regard that my Conscience was not perswaded of the charge I was to undertake, nor Throughly taught touchinge the parvartinge the ende of witnesses from a christiane instetution" (118). Her belief that the established church had "perverted" the original intentions of baptism leads her to "inquire more of this matter, god willinge, with the next faithfull devine, beinge loth to denie, if I may, any freind such a Curtesie" (118). A few days later, she records that she "walked with Mr Hoby and Mr Rhodes and talked touchinge baptismie" (118). Her navigation of a controversial matter thus involves not only deference to a godly authority—she waits to inquire of the matter with a "faithfull" divine—but also a circumspect blend of informed conversation and sociopolitical delicacy: the "freind" to whom she did not want to deny a "Curtesie" was a member of the Eure family.[53] The practices she resists were among those practices of the established church most frequently attacked by puritans.

Hoby's reading and discussion is thus best understood as a form of local puritan activism, mediated by factors ranging from neighborliness to "Conscience"-keeping. Effective Protestant proselytizing relied, as one polemicist put it, on "able ministers over the land, applying themselves in every case of conscience, as godly casuists unto all the distressed in mind."[54] While the Protestant ecclesiastical establishment certainly sought to make local ministers more learned and abler instructors of their congregations, reform could not be effected by the ministry alone.[55] If, as Claire Cross has

sees Rhodes as Hoby's spiritual director and considers the diary as "part of the regime of self examination which Richard Rhodes brought to her as chaplain." "Readers' Marks and Religious Practice," 211.

[53] See Hoby, *Diary*, ed. Meads, 264 n. 337.

[54] W. Loe, *Vox clamatis* (1621), 30, quoted in Keith Thomas, "Cases of Conscience," 37.

[55] The means by which the Reformation was sought—lectureships, sermons, books, conversations—were both actively dialogic and deeply partisan. On the education of the ministry, see Peter Marshall, *The Face of the Pastoral Ministry*, 14. Cross notes that the central government was much more tolerant of Nonconformity in the north because of the struggle against recusants there and permitted the continuing education of clergy in Yorkshire when it was prohibited elsewhere. See *Puritan Earl*, 259.

suggested, the success of Protestantism in England lay in the alliance of laypeople with the clergy, then Margaret Hoby's relationship with Richard Rhodes is an exemplary instance of such an alliance—a partnership deeply affected, as we have seen, both by its recusant northern context and the godliness of its practitioners.[56] Hoby may well have sought to counsel the "distressed in mind," but she also sought to affect what people believed and what they read. Her diary is a record of her relentless efforts not only to battle Catholicism, but also to change how Protestantism was lived and practiced in England. While Hoby concerns herself with Catholics and "the good of the paritioners" of her own church, she also seeks to change people's ideas about the "princeples" of religion and, above all, to introduce godly books into her community (102).

Many of the godly books Hoby read were explicitly associated with the militant Protestantism espoused by her patrons and allies. Many of them were also explicitly associated with the Sidney alliance. The "diatt of the soul" was the work of a former Huntingdon chaplain, Thomas Morton, and both John Udall and Richard Greenham were Huntingdon protégés. Others, including Hugh Broughton, George Gifford, Thomas Cartwright, and Stephen Egerton, were supported directly by the Earl of Essex. Many of the works Hoby reads were associated with puritan Presbyterian activism of the 1570s (such as the debate between Cartwright and Whitgift) and the 1590s, movements supported in no small part by members of the Sidney-Essex alliance, including Elizabeth Russell.

Hoby's reading of these books was often aggressively communal. This was particularly true of her reading of Richard Greenham, a defender of Cartwright whose 1599 *Works* were dedicated to the Countess of Huntingdon. Hoby records a number of occasions on which she "reed[s] of Greenhame" alone (69, 71), but also records having others read him to her: Rhodes (86, 125), his relative "Megg Rhodes" (85), "Averill," a member of her household who was also the daughter of the Yorkshire High Sheriff (80);[57] the visiting preacher "Mr Ardington" (142–3), to whom I will return shortly, and an influential local landowner, Mr Stillington (168). Indeed Hoby's presentation of this last readerly transaction—"I

[56] Claire Cross, *Church and People*. For contrasting views of relationships between clergy and laywomen in the period, see Diane Willen, "Godly Women in Early Modern England," and Patrick Collinson, "'Not Sexual in the Ordinary Sense.'"

[57] Everill Aske was the daughter of Robert Aske of Aughton, the Yorkshire High Sheriff from 1588 (see Hoby, *Diary*, ed. Meads, 256 n. 246). Lamb sees Aske and Hoby as forming a network of gentlewomen, but while she sees it as a "female subculture," I see the women's reading as part of a wider vision of religio-political influence ("Margaret Hoby's Diary," 78). Like the Countess of Huntingdon, Hoby took many young women into "service" in her household.

Came home and *Caused* Mr Stillington to Read of Grenhame" (168, emphasis mine)—indicates the ways in which she created a community of readers around a text through a kind of willful interpellation.[58] Greenham's *Works* were themselves specifically concerned with the proper reading and teaching of godly texts and doctrine.[59] The "Preface to the Reader" opens with Proverbs 10: 21, "The lippes of the righteous feede many," but warns that those lips should not want the "art and good experience" of holy books and learning. In order to minister to others, Greenham argues, one must "know how to proceede by any certaine rule of art, and well grounded practice."[60] Through "causing" others to read Greenham's work with her, Hoby enacts the kind of practice Greenham encourages, enabling both herself and her community to come prepared for a dialogue on religion, "the want of which," as Greenham puts it, "maketh much janglings and wranglings in companie" (394). Margaret Hoby used Greenham in the same way that she used many other books, sermons, and discussions: to shift local religious conversation in the direction of Presbyterian-minded puritanism, keeping books and beliefs alive that had, according to most historians, gone "underground" for much of the period during which Hoby kept her diary.[61] The diversity of her co-readers and discussants, who ranged from local women and landowners to representatives of the local ministry and magistracy—those who "jostl[ed] for power"—suggest that she sought to normalize this critical tradition and promote its reformist ends through the use of books.

II. HOW MARGARET HOBY READ HER DE MORNAY

Hoby left other traces of her reading in addition to those she recorded in her diary. A number of books owned and signed by Margaret Hoby and

---

[58] Hoby read this way with her husband as well. See e.g. the following entry: "I *gott* Mr Hoby to Read some of perkines to me" (107, emphasis added). On Robert Stillington, see Robert Glover, *The Visitation of Yorkshire*, 633. Hoby is carefully sociable with the Stillingtons, talking with his wife, and on 30 October 1601 "sett[ing] some trees which Mr Stillington sent me" (*Diary*, 190).

[59] On Greenham, see Eric Carlson's entry in *ODNB*, and Paul S. Seaver, *The Puritan Lectureships*, 218–19. Mary Ellen Lamb points out that Greenham, like William Perkins, was "at the forefront in the Protestant movement to apply abstract doctrine to the practices of everyday life," and sees Hoby's reading of him as part of this discipline ("Margaret Hoby's Diary," 68). I suggest that Hoby had a more outward-reaching kind of reading practice.

[60] *The Workes of the Reuerend and Faithfull Seruant of Iesus Christ M. Richard Greenham*, A4, A4ᵛ. All subsequent references will be cited parenthetically in the text.

[61] The standard account of the movement remains Patrick Collinson, *The Elizabethan Puritan Movement*.

her husband and kept in the Hackness parish library remained together as a collection.[62] Those signed by Sir Thomas Hoby include one of John Whitgift's responses to Thomas Cartwright's *Second Admonition to the Parliament* (1574), an edition of Foxe's *Acts and Monuments* (1610), a 1611 translation of Calvin's *Institution,* and Thomas Morton's *A Catholike Appeale for Protestants* (1610).[63] The three books signed by Margaret Hoby herself are John Donne's notorious *Pseudo-Martyr,* a 1606 edition of the translation by puritan activist John Field of Philippe de Mornay's *A Treatise of the Church* (a book originally dedicated to the Earl of Leicester), and a heavily annotated copy of the 1600 translation of de Mornay's *Fowre Bookes, of the Institution, Use and Doctrine of the Holy Sacrament of the Eucharist in the Old Church.*[64]

It is this final book, wholly concerned with the Christian controversy about "the Use and Doctrine... of the Eucharist," in which we see Hoby actively reading de Mornay.[65] The extensive marginalia in the book may be in Hoby's own hand (it matches her signature in the front of the book, as

[62] The Hackness church library (now lodged in York Minster Library), comprising 116 volumes as listed in a catalogue of 1701 (Hoby, *Private Life,* ed. Moody, p. xxii).

[63] John Whitgift, *The Defense of the Aunswere to the Admonition, against the replie of T. C[artwright]* (London, 1574), York Minster Library (YML), shelfmark: Hackness 45; John Foxe, *Actes and Monuments of Matters Most Speciall and Memorable, Happening in the Church,* 7th edn (London, 1610), YML, Hackness 2 (1). John Calvin, *The Institution of Christian Religion... translated into English... by Thomas Norton* (London, 1611), YML, Hackness 19; and Thomas Morton, *A Catholike Appeale for Protestants, out of the Confessions of the Romane Doctors* (London, 1610), YML, Hackness 51. The other books signed by Sir Thomas are John White, *The Evokes* (London, 1624), YML, Hackness 42; Thomas Morton, *Of the Institution of the Sacrament of the Blessed Bodie and Blood of Christ* (London, 1631), YML, Hackness 44; Edward Coke, *Quinta pars relationum Edwardi Coke Equitis aurati* (London, 1605), YML, Old Library XI I 10; Gerhard Mercator, *Atlas sive Cosmographicae meditationes* (Duisberg, Germany, 1595), YML, Old Library III A 8; and Abraham Ortelius, *Theatrvm orbis terrarvm* (Antwerp, 1592), YML, Old Library III A 4/2.

[64] Donne, *Pseudo-Martyr* (London, 1610), YML, Hackness 57. Phillippe du Plessis de Mornay, *A Treatise of the Church,* 2nd edn (London, 1606), YML, Hackness 66; de Mornay, *Fowre Bookes, of the Institution, Use and Doctrine of the Holy Sacrament of the Eucharist in the Old Church,* 2nd edn (London, 1600 [STC 18142]), YML, Hackness 47. References to Hoby's marginalia in the pages of *Fowre Bookes* will be given in the text. On the controversy the latter attracted when it was published, see Peter Milward, *Religious Controversies of the Elizabethan Age,* 139–41. Moody notes that Hoby's interest in these books "may well have been inspired by her sister-in-law, the Countess of Pembroke" (Hoby, *Private Life,* p. xxxii), and it certainly seems probable to me that this was one of the reasons that Hoby read her de Mornay so carefully. Margaret Russell Clifford, moreover, left a copy of this same book ("Duplesses Booke of the Masse") to "Lady Herbert," Elizabeth Russell's daughter, in her will, a bequest that highlights the alliance's ongoing commitment to Huguenot and godly reading (Williamson, *Lady Anne Clifford,* 458).

[65] See Crawford, "Reconsidering Early Modern Women's Reading, or How Margaret Hoby Read her De Mornay." The argument there and here engages with the Anthony Grafton and Lisa Jardine essay, "'Studied for Action.'"

well as her handwriting in her diary),[66] yet whether or not Hoby wrote the marginalia herself, it is just as important that it was made, and remains, under her aegis—the signature "Margaret Hoby, 1600" that appears on the title-page of the book (Figures 2.1 and 2.2).[67] In many ways marginalia are less the trace of an individual's reading *per se* than the trace of reading under, or in service to, a name—that of a person, family, household, "liuerye," alliance, or cause. Hoby's diary reveals not only that she read and discussed dozens of books that did not survive in (or even make it into) her library, but that she read others' books as well. Book ownership was a "privy" activity rather than a "private" one, and signs of book ownership were not signs of exclusivity.[68] In particular, her diary tells us that she read books signed by her husband; the book she reads with Rhodes on 28 December 1599, "Mr Cartwright and the Bushoppe of Canterberies booke," is likely one of those bearing her husband's signature in their library. As Hoby's large number of reading partners suggests, a wide range of people could have made marginal marks in Hoby's books, and they may well have done so. Hoby's co-readers were working in the service of, or at least in active conversation with her, and it follows, at least to some extent, that they were also reading in conversation with the ideas those books addressed, and the causes for which they were produced and reproduced.

In "The Preface of the Author upon this Second Edition" of *A Treatise of the Church* (1606), a book signed but not annotated by Margaret Hoby, Philippe de Mornay acknowledges both the controversy that greeted the original publication of this work, and the selective ways in which people read. Readers would have done better, he insists, "to follow this Treatise (as they were required) from reason to reason, and from page to page" (B^v). By encouraging people to read from argument to argument, de Mornay promotes critical engagement not only with his own text, but with those from which he cites. He encourages a comparative reading of learned opinion on church history, including his own. In his epistle "To the Reader" de

---

[66] Deirdre Mortimer, curator of rare books, and Peter Young, paleographer and curator of manuscripts, both at the York Minster Library, also believe the marginalia to be Hoby's. See also Cambers, "Readers' Marks and Religious Practice."

[67] For the observation that early modern women were generally "silent" readers, who refrained from annotating the books they signed, see Brayman Hackel, "'Boasting of Silence," 101, 107.

[68] Brayman Hackel notes that "ownership marks, which seem to be competing for possession of the book, suggest a fluidity of ownership and access within a household" (*Reading Material*, 161). Since readers may contribute to marginalia even when they do not write them themselves, marginalia in books in family libraries, even when not linked paleographically to a given woman, thus may testify to women's reading. See also Brayman Hackel's discussion of Anne Clifford, who both wrote and dictated her marginalia (*Reading Material*, 49). On "privy" ("less asocial and apolitical than selectively social and political") versus "private," see Sherman, *John Dee*, 50.

FOWRE BOOKES,

OF

THE INSTITVTION, VSE

AND DOCTRINE OF THE

HOLY SACRAMENT OF THE
EVCHARIST IN THE OLD
CHVRCH.

AS LIKEWISE, HOW, WHEN,
And by what Degrees the Maſſe is brought
in, in place thereof.

By my Lord P H I L I P of Mornai, Lord of Pleſsis-
Marli, Councellour to the King in his Councell of Eſtate, Captaine
of fiftie men at armes at the Kings paie, Gouernour of his towne
and Caſtle of Samur, Ouerſeer of his houſe
and Crowne of Nauarre.

The ſecond edition, reuiewed by the
Author.

Saint Cyprian, in the treatiſe of the Sacrament of the Cup of the Lord.

We ought not herein to regard what any man hath iudged meete to bee done, but rather, what he which was be-
fore all men, euen Ieſus Chriſt our Sauiour hath done himſelfe, and commaunded vnto vs doe : For we follow
not the cuſtome of man, but the truth of God.

A L S O;

If ſome one of our predeceſſors haue not ſo obſerued and kept it : God may haue pardoned him in his mercie: but
for vs, from henceforth there will remaine no place for pardon , we hauing beene inſtructed and admoniſhed
by him.

LONDON
Printed by I O H N W I N D E T, for I. B.   T. M. and W. P.   1 6 0 0.

nai, Lord of Plefsis-
incell of Eftate, Captaine
ouernour of his towne
: of his houfe
:re.

d by the

of the Cup of the Lord.

ee done; but rather, what he which may be-
d commaunded others to doe : For we follow

Figure 2.2 Close up of Margaret Hoby's signature on the title-page of Philippe de Mornay seigneur du Plessis-Marly, *Fowre bookes*. Reproduced by kind permission of the Dean and Chapter of York.

Mornay asks the reader to read not as one "hauing already found the truth, but as one that seeketh after it," and asks those who are critical "to answere it point by point," "in the spirit of sinceritie and mildnesse, seeking…the salvation of the people" (B2). While he asks people to read and annotate with a greater cause in mind—"the salvation of the people"—de Mornay also encourages them to read for dialogue (to "answere" "point by point"). Margaret Hoby seems to follow these directions in her reading and annotation of his book on the Eucharist.

While the de Mornay includes the only substantive Hoby marginalia yet discovered, Hoby records reading and taking notes in intimate relationship to each other throughout her diary, and she refers to a number of manuscript books that have not survived, including a "table book" (97), a "Houshould book" (104), a "Common place book" (67, 81, 95, 144), a "book framed by Mr Rhodes" (95), and a "sermon book" (66, 67, 96, 108, 128, 133, 138, 143). She also makes numerous records of writing notes in books in response to hearing sermons and reading other works. Most often she records writing "notes" in her "testament" (64, 68, 71, 75, 76, 77, 79, and passim), Bible (66, 67, 69, 70, 96, and passim), and sermon book (128, 129, 131, 142), but she also frequently characterizes her note-taking as a record of multiple kinds of theological, doctrinal, and scholarly exchange. For example, she makes the following entry on

7 September 1599: "After privat praiers I wrett notes in my testement, which I geathered out of the Lector the night before" (70), and a similar entry in January 1599/1600: "I reed of the testement, and wrett notes in itt and upon Perknes [William Perkins]" (101). Both records suggest a comparative and intertextual process; rather than marking the end of her intellectual or theological engagement, the note-taking provides the basis for further consideration.[69]

The marginal notes and comments in Margaret Hoby's copy of de Mornay's *Fowre Bookes* seem to be a kind of preparation for debate, a practice fully in keeping with the kinds of reading, note-taking, and conversation she describes in her diary. Scribal marginalia were themselves a record of active reading, and readers used them to correct, elaborate on, or otherwise engage with a text; to identify difficult, ambiguous, or controversial claims; to serve as a record of a dialogue, service, or training in *adversaria*; to function as a reference guide for future reading; or to mark particular rhetorical maneuvers or modes of expression which the reader sought to commit to memory, excerpt for commonplacing, and/or make use of in conversation or debate.[70] (Mary, Countess of Warwick, for example, kept a book of apothegms in order that she might use them to "suitably lard her conversation," and Frances Wolfreston prefaced her copy of a *querelle des femmes* treatise with the phrase "in prais of women, a good one," suggesting she might have planned to use it in just such an argument.[71]) Marginal comments in religious texts were particularly likely to be geared towards polemical or disputative ends.

Hoby's marginalia call attention to subjects of puritan controversy, seeking to record or establish the history of the primitive church and single out its Romish corruptions. Her more specific strategy seems to have been to adduce strong proofs and points of argument in these matters of controversy. Her most frequent annotations highlight moments at which the corruptions most decried by reform-minded Protestants were first introduced into the primitive church: "four hundred years after Christe, or ever

[69] When Hoby writes on 4 February 1599 of going "to privat praier and examenation, then to supper, after to the lector : after that, to my Closit, where I praied and Writt som thinge for mine owne privat Conscience" (101), she points out the (much rarer) "privat" nature of what is usually for her a practice oriented toward further exchange with others.

[70] On the polemical uses to which readers put marginalia, see Joad Raymond, "Irrational, Impractical and Unprofitable." On the influence of religious controversy on the practice, see Steven N. Zwicker, "Reading the Margins"; Brayman Hackel, *Reading Material*, 31; and Hunt, "Mrs. Anne Sadleir," 210. In *Used Books*, William H. Sherman notes that literary texts were annotated less than texts associated with religious controversy (p. xiii).

[71] On Warwick, see McKitterick, "Women and their Books," 365. On Wolfreston, see Morgan, "Frances Wolfreston and 'Hor Bouks,'" 204.

ye worde Masse was used" (33); "ye first occasion of using ye crosse" (49); "how ye table came to carry ye name of an altar" (109); and "how images firste got footing in ye church" (121). She also notes (contested) points of Protestant belief—"sygnes have no other power than that which ye lorde giveth them" (161)—and occasionally emends de Mornay's own printed marginalia to further highlight the puritan view. To de Mornay's own marginal note indicating his topic, "The Priestlie garments," to take a notable example, she adds the words "which in ye oulde church were none but ordinary attire" (163). Hoby is not averse to pointing out the inferiority of the Catholic Church ("ye church of Rome did not bringe forthe one doctor of note in ye tyme of all ye council in former ages": 44), and indulges in the occasional mockery of its practices and beliefs. At one point, for example, she underlines a number of benefits Catholics superstitiously believe the Mass could achieve, including that it's "good for warres" and "saveth cattell" She also adds her own sarcastic note in the margin highlighting a belief that was a frequent target of Protestant criticism: "St Gregoryes masse delivers soules out of purgatorye" (72). Hoby's marginal summaries of de Mornay's arguments are often judgmental: the "muttering used by ye romish priests in ye consecration," she tells us in one note, is "directly contrary to christs institution" (158). Yet at other times, she edits her own marginalia to avoid sweeping condemnation of Catholicism as a whole. It is in these moments that we see her preparing for what Greenham calls a "dialogue in religion."

In summarizing one section, for example, Hoby originally wrote: "A rehearsall of ye principall errours in *popery*," but later crossed out the final word (one neither de Mornay nor his translator uses), and amended her notation to "A rehearsal of ye principall errours in *ye masse*" (235, my emphasis; see Figure 2.3). In this revision we see Hoby's desire to specify exactly what she is arguing against and about, and her (ultimate) resistance to her own urge to subsume points of doctrinal controversy, and thus of potentially fruitful engagement, under a sweeping term of opprobrium ("popery"). This is not to say her marginalia avoid making judgments in excess of de Mornay's (she notes next to one description of a ritual, "ye grosse prayer yt is made att ye consecrating of ye crosse," and "grosse" is not used in the text itself (136)), but her marginal comments are often careful summaries of the "reason" at hand, and they are often geared for argument. Next to de Mornay's own printed marginal reference to 2 King 22: 20, for example, Hoby originally wrote "a good place to *know* tht ye saints know nothing done upon earth," yet once again, she edited her own marginalia to read "a good place to *prove* tht ye saints know nothing done upon earth" (305, my emphasis; see Figure 2.4). In replacing "know" with "prove," Hoby indicates that her reading was intended not (or not only)

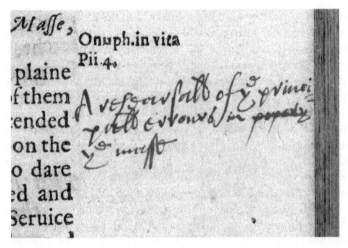

Figure 2.3 Detail of de Mornay, *Fowre Bookes*, 235, showing Margaret Hoby's marginal note and correction. York Minster Library, Hackness 47. Reproduced by kind permission of the Dean and Chapter of York.

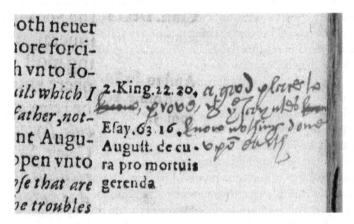

Figure 2.4 Detail of de Mornay, *Fowre Bookes*, 305, showing Margaret Hoby's marginal note and correction. York Minster Library, Hackness 47. Reproduced by kind permission of the Dean and Chapter of York.

for personal assurance or edification, but rather for argumentative communication, to prove a point to others via considered reading and engagement. Her use of the term "prove" suggests that she views de Mornay's explanation as an arsenal of argument, in keeping with a spiritual practice centered on preaching, disputation, and "sociable" reading.

Hoby uses other, equally argument-ready, terms throughout the book, and summarizes key arguments via a range of polemical terms noted in the margins. These terms include "allegations" ("Allegations for Images," "Allegations agaynste images, & ye adoring of them" (129)), "answers" ("an answere to Gen. 14 and yt filthy stuffe which from ye falsification of that claim they bringe" (201); "a good answere to ye popish shift of ye sayntes seeing our thoughts in god" (304)); and "proofs" ("a proofe, yt Christe did administer ye cupp unto his disciples not as preistes consecratinge, but as faythfull men receivinge" (93)). (See Figure 2.5.) As it turns out, this last "proofe" was a matter of particular concern for Hoby. In chapter 10 of *Fowre Bookes*, which argues "That the communion under both kindes [bread and wine] was practiced all in the old Church" (75), Hoby pays particular attention to the cup, adding to de Mornay's own printed marginal note, "The foolish reasons of the Councell," the words "why ye givinge ye cup to ye laity should be cutt of[f]" (89). While de Mornay mocks the reasons given by Catholics—the fear "*That a licour may be shed*" by clumsy laypeople—Hoby is more forceful in her judgment, condemning in the margin the "blasphemous councell of papists" who made the decision to keep the cup from the people (89). Hoby acted on the anger she expresses in her marginalia in quite material ways. In October 1605, five years after the publication of de Mornay's book on the Mass, the Hobys gave to Hackness parish church "One Comunion Cupp with a cover weyinge 12 oz.," a material sign of their commitment to the communion under "both kinds."[72] If the bulk of Margaret Hoby's reading of de Mornay seems to be a page-by-page and "reason by reason" "study for argument," the gift of the cup seems to be an argument of a very particular kind, giving to the people of Hackness, much as de Mornay and Hoby wanted, a communal and participatory means of taking communion.[73]

Unsurprisingly, Hoby's marginalia frequently suggest criticism of the Elizabethan Prayer Book service and ecclesiastical hierarchy. Some of the most heavily annotated sections concern the ministry, and she takes particular care with the sections in which de Mornay outlines a pattern for the "generall agreement and consent of the people and ecclesiasticall order" about who was to "bee chosen Bishoppe or Elder" (161, Hoby's emphasis). In the margin next to a discussion of elders and deacons, she wrote, "How bishops were chosen in ye oulde church," and on the next page, "bishopps in the firste ordination not above other ministers" (162). Hoby is

---

[72] See *The Register of the Parish of Hackness*, 75.

[73] For Hoby, the most important aspect of the Mass—and one she underlined in de Mornay's text—is that it was: "an assemblie of Christians, calling uppon the name of God by Jesus Christ." It included "singing his prayeses, hearing his worde, [and] attending unto the expounding of the same, as it was delivered them by the Pastors" (52).

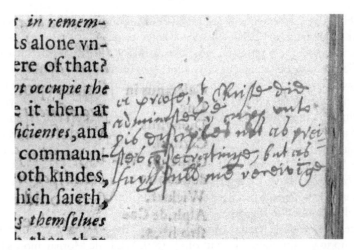

Figure 2.5 Detail of de Mornay, *Fowre Bookes*, 93, showing Margaret Hoby's marginal note. York Minster Library, Hackness 47. Reproduced by kind permission of the Dean and Chapter of York.

equally critical of the ecclesiastical hierarchy in her diary: on 1 April 1601, she records Rhodes reading to her "that no Callinge is lawfull with out a grown[d]e for itt in godes word," and that "the title of Lord Archbusshopes are Vlawfull" (166). She also records hearing "Mr Rhodes read of the true diCeplen of christes church" (181), or the Book of Discipline, the surreptitiously circulated Presbyterian guidebook that outlined, among other things, the unlawfulness of bishops and the desirability of electing elders in a reformed church.[74] Her reading of de Mornay was an integrated part of her habitual practices of reading, discussion, and argument, with "papests" and Protestants, and with those who sought further reformation.

III. THE PRESBYTERIAN UNDERGROUND

Like the other members of her alliance, Hoby carefully navigated between maintaining good relations with members of the established church and

[74] The Book of Discipline circulated, usually in manuscript, throughout the English countryside in the 1580s and 1590s. It was at St John's College, Cambridge, where many of the men Hoby supports were educated, that the Book of Discipline was allegedly revised for the last time in 1589. On the Book of Discipline, see the *ODNB* for Thomas Cartwright and the chapter on the Book of Discipline in Patrick Collinson, *The Elizabethan Puritan Movement*, particularly 291–302. Hoby read or heard sermons by several ministers who subscribed to a survey indicting bishops presented to the 1586 Parliament, including George Gifford, John Udall, Cartwright, Field, and Egerton.

supporting its critics. Her diary records frequent visits with the Dean of York and Bishop of Limerick, John Thornborough, and his wife, and in her visits to London she appears with Mrs Thornborough at public places such as the Exchange and Lincoln's Inn.[75] She also makes frequent visits to the Archbishop of York, Matthew Hutton, at Bishopthorpe (including a visit in which she "talked with Mrs Hutten of religion": 73). After visiting the home of the new lord president of the Council of the North, Lord Burghley, on 21 September, 1599, on the following evening she receives his chaplain, Mr Fuller, whom she evaluates as "a godly and relegous young man" (73). These visits do not simply testify to an easy alliance of gentry and ecclesiastical establishment; both Hoby and the chaplain seem to understand that he is subject to her approbation. Fuller's subsequent "Christian Conference" with Hoby, an exposition of a psalm, seems to be something of a job interview.[76] And sometimes approbation was not forthcoming. Her judgment of William Palmer, the conformist chancellor of York Minster from 1571 to 1605, is scathing: "I went to the church, wher I hardd Mr Palmer speak, but to small profitte to any" (73). His words, in fact, make her "lament the misirie of godes visible Church" (73).[77] While Fuller passes inspection, Palmer is found wanting, a sign of the "small profitte" a poor preacher—and, frequently, the established church—can offer the people.

Margaret Hoby records hearing and taking notes on the sermons and "disputations" of a wide variety of Yorkshire preachers, including those who were outside of the ecclesiastical establishment.[78] Often her readings

---

[75] On Yorkshire visits with the Thornboroughs, see e.g. *Diary*, 146, 147. During one of the London visits, on 16 December 1600, Hoby goes with Mrs Thornborough and her mother "in a Cotch in to the feeldes and there walked" (158); Moody guesses the area was Lincoln's Inn (Hoby, *Private Life*, ed. Moody, 129 n. 229). On the 20th she "went wth Mrs Thornborow to the exchang" (p. 159).

[76] On the afternoon of 16 January 1600, Hoby records that Fuller "expounded, [a psalm] unto me, and tould me his praier was to god that, in the actions of god which he was to perform, none of his owne affections might be mingled" (p. 162).

[77] Hoby also criticizes the ungodly magistracy: "Mr pollard the Head Constable, dined wt us: stronge is the force of vanitie but the Lord is greater then all" (208).

[78] Her diary also records her frequent conversations with and judgments of these men. For example, on 10 April 1600, Hoby went to the minster "wher I hard Mr Smith defend the truth against the papest, the question beinge whether the regenerate doe sinne: after I Came home I went to diner: I went to the church where I hard Mr Stuard handle this question between the papists and us—whether we were Iustefied by faith or workes" (113). On 13 April 600: "[Hoby] went to Mr Harwoodes sermon, in which he deliuered this faulse possi[t]on, that, for necessetie, a minister might buye church liuinges, for necessetie had no lawe" (75). On 26 October 1599, she "hard a great disputation between 2: preachers" (80). Hoby frequently judged ministers based not on their positions in the church, but on their preaching and opinions. To take only two examples, "Mr Wilsone" is termed "a godly preacher," and Mr. Maude, an "exceedinge good Christian" (78, 88).

of or with these men occur in sequence and within specific communities. On 7 December 1599, for example, Hoby records talking "of good maters with Mr Maud," a puritan educated at St John's College Cambridge and affiliated with the Wakefield Grammar School in the West Riding of Yorkshire—a venue known for its puritan library and teaching (88).[79] The day after, she records hearing "one read of ardentons book" (88). This book was the work of Henry Arthington, a Yorkshire man, also from Wakefield, famous for his association with the executed Presbyterian William Hacket and, according to his own published account, for being "a detector of Seminaries, olde massing Priestes, and *Jesuits.*"[80] (Not coincidentally, the Arthington/Hacket case was used against Thomas Cartwright in 1591 when the Star Chamber was trying to determine if he was the author of the Book of Discipline—a book, as we have seen, that Hoby also read.[81]) Hoby reads Arthington again on 7 September 1600 ("I reed of Mr Ardingtons booke": 143), and "Ardington" reads to her several times in March and again in August of the same year (see 165–6, and 181–3). "Ardington," moreover, is also one of the men Hoby "has" read Greenham to her.[82]

When Hoby is reading most actively with Arthington in the summer of 1601, she also records a series of engagements with a woman she identifies as "Lady Bowes" (183). Like Margaret Hoby, Isabel, Lady Bowes was a northern puritan woman of an activist bent. Like Hoby's, Bowes's husband was a member of the Council of the North and a devoted recusant-chaser. Bowes herself patronized puritan and Nonconformist divines; provided venues for puritan disputations and discussions in both Derbyshire and Yorkshire; and was an outspoken critic of the established church. (She was, again like Hoby, particularly active during the crucial years of the transition from Elizabeth to James.[83]) Margaret Hoby corresponds with

---

[79] This is probably Edward Mawde or Maude, on whom, see Ronald A. Marchant, *The Puritans and the Church Courts*, 263; and J. Venn and J. A. Venn, *Alumni Cantabrigienses*, 3: 447. Like Rhodes, Mawde attended St John's. Following her first mention of "Maud," Hoby records talking "of good matters with Mr Rhodes and Mr Maude, a younge devine, a exceedinge good Christian," and, the following day, notes that she "hard Mr Maud read of a sarmon book" (89).

[80] Henry Arthington, *The Seduction of Arthington by Hacket*, 42. Arthington was also the author of *The Exhortation of Salomon* (1594); *Principall Points of Holy Profession* (1607); and *Prouision for the Poore* (1597). On Arthington, see A. G. Dickens, "The Writers of Tudor Yorkshire," 63.

[81] On the use of the Arthington/Hacket case against Thomas Cartwright in 1591, see *ODNB* entry for Cartwright.

[82] Beginning in November 1601, Arthington "wintered" in the Hoby household (Hoby, *Diary*, ed. Meads, 191).

[83] On Lady Bowes's role in local religious politics, see Christine M. Newman, "An Honourable and Elect Lady," 409, 413, 414. Sir William Bowes himself also enjoyed the favor and patronage of the puritan Earl of Huntingdon and supported the millenary Petition (Newman, pp. 412–13). In a heated exchange with the Earl of Shrewsbury, Sir

Lady Bowes (on both 14 and 17 August 1601 she records writing "a letter to my lady Bowes": 183, 184), and on 10 November she records "reed[ing] some meditations of the Lady Bowes hir Makinge" (191). Her reading of Bowes's "meditations" at the same time as she was reading, Arthington suggests the regional nature of Hoby's interests and reading practices.

As her relationships with Maude, Arthington, Bowes, and in particular Rhodes indicate, Hoby spent a great deal of time with radical, unbeneficed, and often divested, preachers: Yorkshire men educated at the puritan Cambridge college that fostered the Book of Discipline, and committed to a more radical reformation of the church. Hoby rarely recorded the subjects of the myriad sermons and conversations she heard or participated in in her diary, but those she did record were all matters of godly controversy that Whitgift feared were gaining purchase in Yorkshire in the period.[84] In addition to the debate about bishops already discussed, Hoby records talking with a "godly preacher" about another controversial matter singled out by Whitgift: justification. (The "godly preacher" tells her that "Iustefecation" was conferred "by and in christes Righteousness" and that those who "grounded their Iuestefaction on workes, did denie so farr the truth in the foundation of christian religion": 114.) Like her reading, Hoby's discussions with preachers empowered her in her judgments of and interventions into matters of religious controversy. She frequently defends precisely those things which Cartwright disputed with Whitgift.

The Hobys offered Hackness as a refuge for a number of deprived ministers, including the only Yorkshire minister Matthew Hutton ever deprived for Nonconformity.[85] Margaret Hoby also intervened for Richard Rhodes, who was on a number of occasions brought up for preaching

William noted how he had expressly sought his wife's opinion in defending the Petition since "She is verie wyse and especially in things of this kynde." In particular, he notes her defense of the rights of subjects to "compleyn" by petitions. Isabel added her own postscript at the end of her husband's letter, "stressing that the Earl should read the 'good King Hesekiah,' a reference to Ezekias, the Old Testament King of Judah who had returned his heathen country to the worship of the true God" (Lambeth Palace Library, Talbot Papers, MS 3203, fol. 166, cited in Newman, p. 413). Shrewsbury replied that the couple should "feare God and your King and meddle not with them that are seditious" (Lambeth Palace Library, Talbot Papers, MS 3201, fol. 173). All Lady Bowes's preachers "were silenced men by reasons of non-conformity" (Newman, p. 415).

[84] See *Diary*, 90 (on grace); 114 (on justification). Hoby also records a sermon on the controversial practice of buying livings (113). On the Archbishop's letter to Hutton expressing his concerns, see Hutton, *Correspondence*, 155.

[85] On this minister, Richard Stainforth, also a graduate of St John's, see Marchant, *The Puritans*, 26, 282. The Hobys also had frequent interactions with William Ward of Scarborough, who was eventually punished in the 1604 visitation for refusing to wear the surplice (see *Diary*, 174, 219, 290; and Marchant, *The Puritans*, 290). Along with Sir Thomas, Ward eventually became a member of a commission for prosecuting recusants (*Diary*, 220).

in unsanctioned venues and without the Book of Common Prayer. (He would eventually be arrested for holding illegal conventicles in his own house.[86]) While Hoby records many examples of Rhodes co-reading with herself and the citizens of the North Riding of Yorkshire, she also records some of the work she had to do to keep him within the bounds of the acceptable. On 12 April 1600, for example, she records having "speaches with Mrs fearne of Mr Rhodes, and how much she had mistaken him" (113). "Mrs fearne's" husband, John Ferne, was a member of the Council of the North whom Robert Cecil had appointed to keep an eye on Essex's people.[87] It thus makes sense that Rhodes would have aroused the Fernes' suspicions. Rhodes also seems to have been a target in the Eure and Cholmley "visit" to the Hoby household. William Eure was reported to have said that, had Rhodes been present in his lady's chamber when he entered it, "he woold have gelded him."[88] As Eure's desire to castrate Rhodes indicates, Hoby's reading partners were among the most controversial, and occasionally unpopular, men in Yorkshire.

Hoby's reading practices were in many ways specific to the north, but the worlds of Yorkshire and London intersected in crucial ways. In the course of her long visit to London from October 1600 to March 1601, during which time Essex was tried and executed, Hoby frequently attended the sermons of Stephen Egerton, a man who had been supported by the Earl of Essex throughout his controversial career. Like Cartwright, Egerton refused to subscribe to Whitgift's articles in 1584, and would soon be silenced again for petitioning the lower house for a reformed prayer book. During her time in London, Hoby frequently attended his sermons at St Anne's in Blackfriars, a location known for puritan sermonizing. Her public patronage of Egerton's sermons was in many ways itself a statement of puritan oppositionism. (It's telling that her visit to Westminster is comparatively disappointing: "I went to the minster and hard one Mr Smith preach," she writes, "wher I hard, to my knowledge, nothinge worth the notinge": 151.)

---

[86] Ordained in 1597, Rhodes served as chaplain to the Hobys from 1599 to 1605, and from 1605 to 1614 he served as perpetual curate (a minister in charge of a parish that lacks either a rectory or vicarage) of Hackness. On Rhodes's career and his chastisement by the courts for his unconventional ministry, see Marchant, *The Puritans*, 26, 37–8, 48.

[87] Cecil secured the appointment of John Ferne as secretary to the Council in August 1595. As Ferne had had a bitter contest with Stanhope, Essex's man, for the Recordership of Doncaster in 1590 and 1592, "he could be trusted to keep a watchful eye on Essex's friends, and on Stanhope in particular" (Reid, *King's Council*, 228). Cecil, for his part, was reported to have laughed when William Eure mimicked Rhodes "by using such gestures as his preacher did use in his evening exercises" (271).

[88] Heal, "Reputation," 172.

Hoby's visits to Elizabeth Russell's house in Blackfriars often involved an Egerton sermon. On 19 October, for example, Hoby "went to Mr Egertons sermon, and after Came to my lady Russils to Diner: After, I went againe to his exercise and thence home to my lodginge, wher I wrett some of his notes in my testement" (150). On the 26th she "went by water to the blake friers and hard Mr Egerton: after, I saw my lady Russill" (151). (See also 16 and 17 October, and 30 November, where she again "sett downe in my testement the cheffe notes deliuered by Mr Egertone (156), and 7 and 14 December and 4 and 18 January.[89]) During the same period, she visits with numerous members of the Sidney alliance: Robert Sidney's secretary "Mr Roland whitt" pays her a visit; she visits her "sistere [Barbara Garage] Sidne" (157); and goes to "walsinghams house," wher she sees "my lady [Penelope] Rich, my lady Ruttland, [Philip Sidney's daughter], and my Lady walsingame [Lady Walsingham, the mother of Philip Sidney's widow, Frances]" (161). Like Anne Clifford's meetings with many of the same women discussed in the previous chapter, Hoby's were something of a regathering of the forces or rallying of the alliance; all of these visits take place in the weeks leading up to Essex's rebellion and, in turn, to his trial.

When Hoby records Essex's trial for treason in January 1601, she reports being "so ill that I could not goe out of my chamber" (164). Unlike the rest of the diary, moreover, this entry runs right across the page for nine lines, leaving no margin whatsoever (Figure 2.6). The diary's editor Dorothy M. Meads suggests that this unusual layout "may betray, as no words do, Lady Hoby's feelings," reminding readers that Essex was her brother-in-law (278 n. 436). But I would suggest further than the "feelings" evinced in this entry are also for a central figure of an alliance in which Hoby herself was invested. Two days after she records Essex's death in the Tower on 25 February 1601, Hoby reports going to "the Court to se my Lady warwick" (Anne Russell Dudley), Margaret Clifford's sister, and one of Essex's chief supporters (165).

Hoby's later visits to London after the accession of James I (in April–June 1603 and November 1604–February 1605) also seem to have been motivated by current events.[90] Her commitment to Egerton both increased and became more public. She went to hear him preach in London less than a month after James became king, and in the midst of the millenary petition scandal (12 April 1603; 202). She heard him again on 21 November

<hr />

[89] She revisited his sermons on 29 November 1601, after returning to Yorkshire: "This day I went to the church and hard both the Lecturs: and at Night went to privatt praier, after Mr Hoby had reed unto me some notes of Mr Egertons Lecturs" (193). On Egerton, see Hoby, *Private Life*, ed. Moody, 209 n. 366, and the *ODNB*.

[90] For a contrasting reading to my own, see Pauline Croft's argument about the Hobys' visits to London ("Capital Life," 69–73).

Figure 2.6 Margaret Hoby's diary entry on Essex's trial for treason, from Egerton MS 2614, 69ᵛ. Reproduced by permission of the British Library.

1604 ("I waited on my Lady Russill to Mr Egerton's Lecture": 214), and again on the following Sunday. After attending this last sermon, Hoby records that "Mistress Cartwright came to se my Lady [Russell]" (214). "Mistress Cartwright" was Thomas Cartwright's widow, the equally radical Alice Cartwright, and this meeting of two powerful puritan women is interesting in its own right. Yet immediately following her account of the meeting Hoby notes that she "delivered Sir Arthure Dakins message" to Mrs Cartwright (214). Hoby considered the contents of this message to be worthy of note, leaving a large blank space in her diary for its inclusion (Figure 2.7).[91] Perhaps, in the end, the message was too controversial or

<hr />

[91] Alice Stubbs Cartwright was sister to John Stubbs, author of *The Gaping Gulfe* (see *ODNB* for Cartwright). In November 1603, Cartwright was involved in the renewed

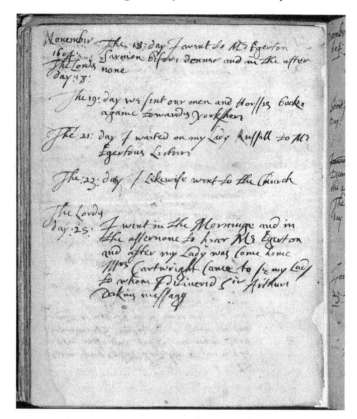

Figure 2.7 Space in Margaret Hoby's diary for "Sir Arthure Dakins message" to Mrs Cartwright, from Egerton MS 2614, 109ᵛ. Reproduced by permission of the British Library.

incriminating to include, but its empty space remains as a marker of its significance.

Sir Arthur Dakins was Margaret Hoby's first cousin and an influential local politician; the fact that she served as his emissary—indeed, as a secretary of sorts—suggests a familial and regional commitment to the renascence of the puritan cause.[92] Hoby recounts frequent meetings with

campaign for further reformation upon the accession of James. He was meant to be at Hampton Court in January 1604, but died in December 1603.

[92] On Dakins's activities, see *The North Riding Record Society for the publication of Original Documents Relating to the North Riding of the County of York*, vol. 4, Quarter Session Records, ed. J. C. Atkinson. (London: Printed for the Society, 1886), passim.

Arthur Dakins in her diary, some of which are characterized by a kind of perambulatory readerly practice which Hoby herself calls "reed[ing] abroad." On 22 June 1601 Hoby records that she "reed abroad wth my Cosine Dakine: after I Came home and that I had dined, I talked of good matters wth him, and he reed to me" (22 June 1601; 176–7). Hoby's sequential pun—"reed" evokes both "ride" and "read"—highlights the mobile nature of the proprietary and readerly habits by which Hoby and Dakins both publicly advertised their family' commitments and endeavored to bring the community into alignment with their views.[93] When Hoby records giving Cartwright Arthur Dakins's message in London, she leaves a trace of the traffic between godly activists in the recusant north and the "underground" forces that were again working, this time in the first hopeful years of James's reign, for further reformation.[94]

Margaret Hoby's diary provides evidence of her involvement in this resurgence. In April 1603, right after the accession of James and six months before she passed Arthur Dakins's message to Alice Cartwright, Hoby reports that "Lady Russill," "required the names of such as I would trust to passe some Livinge, after hirr death, unto me" (203).[95] Famous herself for arranging for the ministerial appointments, or "Livinge[s]," of puritan preachers, Elizabeth Russell evidently felt that Margaret Hoby— rather than her own son—should be responsible for continuing this practice.[96] (There is some evidence that Hoby did take on this mantle; in 1603 the Hobys nominated a godly minister whom they heard preach at Thorpbassitt and then hosted at Winteringham, Margaret Hoby's mother's parish, in 1603, for a much more influential living (205).[97]) It was after this exchange with Elizabeth Russell about "Livinge[s]," moreover, that Richard Rhodes obtained his official benefice as rector of Hackness, the Hoby vicarage. Margaret Hoby thus played a role both in fomenting

---

[93] Her interactions with Arthur Dakins were particularly bookish. In addition to having him read to her, at one point she records "readinge of a book [Arthur Dakins] sent me" (198).

[94] On Hoby's reading of Cartwright, see *Diary*, 67, 97, 99. She was also visited by Job Throckmorton, another influential puritan controversialist, in December 1600 (see Hoby, *Private Life*, ed. Moody, 127 n. 224; and Hoby, *Diary*, ed. Meads, 274–5 n. 409). When she returns to Yorkshire from London in March 1604, she stays with Arthur Dakins in Linton (Hoby, *Diary*, ed. Meads, 216).

[95] This note is syntactically cryptic; both of Hoby's editors see it as a sign of Russell reflecting on her own mortality. The term "Livinge," however, suggests that the women are talking about church livings, and thus of the appointments of the right kind of preachers to these livings or benefices.

[96] For a discussion of the Cooke sisters, Hoby, and women's intellectual circles, see Crawford, "Literary Circles."

[97] On John Philips, rector of Thorpe Basset, Margaret's mother's seat, from 1582 to 1605, see Marchant, *The Puritans*, 27, 269.

the new energy of Presbyterian reformists in London, and in changing the ministerial face of her corner of Yorkshire.

Like many puritans, the Hobys looked forward to the accession of James I with both trepidation and hope.[98] Her diary entry on 26 March 1603 sounds a rather cautious note of celebration: "our now kinge Iames of Scotland proclaimed kinge...god send him a long and Hapie Raign, amen" (202). In April, Hoby records receiving a letter from the King "that euerie Counsiller and other offecer should Continew in their places vntill his further pleasur were knowne" (202). In May, she records kissing the new Queen's hand. Yet Hoby's hopes for further reform were soon dashed. On 17 November 1603, she records that "Mr Netelton brought us the Kinges proclimation for the restraininge some Combustious persones that sought reformation"—a proclamation followed by the deprivation of multiple ministers (208). On 8 January 1604, Hoby makes the following terse record: "This day was Mr Egerton, wt diuers others, silenced by the Bisshoppe of London": 215). The Hampton Court Conference, held in the same month, further silenced the renewed activism of Presbyterian-minded puritans, and even Yorkshire felt the turn. While the Archbishop of York, Mathew Hutton, refused to see puritans as the real threat to regional security, the King disagreed. In February 1604, James wrote to Hutton ordering him to bring Yorkshire puritans into conformity with the church.[99] The puritans' focus on papists, he argued, has diverted "our lookes from them selves, while they were plotting and contriveing all thinges that could be imagined likelie to deprive that state of the Church as it is established in our kingdome, and *to bring in a forme of presbyterie*, to the utter dissolucion of all monarchies" (174, emphasis added). James insisted that Hutton must suppress and bring to conformity all those "malitious contentions againste the Bishops and ecclesiasticall pollicy here by lawe established," and deprive any ministers "not conforming to the Booke of Common Prayer and ceremonies of the Church" (174, 175). Less than two months after this letter, on Sunday, 14 April 1605, Hoby made the following entry in her diary: "This day was the first day that the Commune praier Booke was read in our Church" (217). Meads suggests this was a positive comment: 1605 was the first year in which Richard Rhodes, taking over from his "unsatisfactory" predecessor, signed

[98] On the Hoby household's anxiety about the accession of James, see 27 March 1603: "went Mr Hoby and myselfe towardes Yorke, thinkinge to Continewe there vntill all thinges were established" (202).

[99] For Hutton's defense of all but the most radical puritans, see Lake, "Matthew Hutton—A Puritan Bishop?" and Hutton, *Correspondence*, 25. This letter, dated 19 February 1604, is in Hutton, *Correspondence*, 171–5. Subsequent references to this letter will be cited parenthetically within the text.

the register as parish priest (289 n. 612). Yet I see it as a sign of the exact opposite, a record of her own church's necessary capitulation to the newly strict enforcement of anti-puritan ecclesiastical policy. The "Commune praier Booke"—a text specifically designed to foster Church of England conformity in the diverse parishes of England—was the antithesis of the varied practices of reading and disputation Margaret Hoby practiced so assiduously. That these practices were aimed, in persistent if subtly executed ways, at encouraging Presbyterian thinking, suggests that James was right: whether or not they were committed to the "dissollucion of all monarchies," people like Hoby did want "to bring in some forme of presbyterie" in England. Reading, moreover, was one of the means by which they sought to do so.

As Elizabeth Clarke has argued, early modern women's spiritual journals were not always private documents. Many, in fact, were used for public and polemical purposes; some were even meant to be read aloud in congregations as hagiography for their authors and buttressing for their Nonconformist faith.[100] Whether or not Hoby intended for her diary to be read in this way, her simultaneous avowal of puritan opinions and politic circumspection about such matters as the Book of Common Prayer, the Essex rebellion, the nature of her household's often conventicle-like religious practices, and the contents of Dakins's letter to Alice Cartwright, suggest that she understood her diary, like her reading, as something of a public act—the record less of a private individual, than of a collective, social, religious, and political struggle. Hoby may well have seen her diary as subject to potential scrutiny as well as approbation; she may even have imagined that some day it would be subject to the kind of reading I have made in this chapter. In much the same way that Hoby's reading of de Mornay provides evidence that women read for action, her diary suggests that recording one's reading was a way of registering and affirming religious and political alliances, and a means of working towards those alliances' goals. It is only later readers who could mistake Margaret Hoby's diary as the record of a "private Elizabethan gentlewoman."

---

[100] Elizabeth Clarke, "Beyond Microhistory," 217. See also Elizabeth Clarke, "Elizabeth Jekyll's Spiritual Diary."

3

"His Factor for our loves": The Countess of Bedford and John Donne

The first of John Donne's many verse letters to Lucy Harington Russell, Countess of Bedford, begins with the following lines:

> MADAME,
> Reason is our Soules left hand, Faith her right,
> By these wee reach divinity, that's you;
> Their loves, who have the blessings of your light,
> Grew from their reason, mine from faire faith grew.[1]

While Bedford would become one of Donne's greatest patrons and one of the most frequent recipients of his verse letters in the years between 1608 and 1614, this poem suggests that they had not yet met. In seeking Bedford's patronage, Donne frames his desire in theological terms: while others approach divinity—the Countess—through first-hand knowledge, or reason, Donne's love for her comes from faith alone—he believes, that is, without seeing.[2] He continues the conceit in the next stanza in which he claims that, although "a squint lefthandednesse / Be'ungracious, yet we cannot want that hand," suggesting both that human reason is limited, even ungenerous, in its purview, and that while it is not the same thing as grace, or salvation, it is still a necessary means of understanding or

---

[1] Grierson, *The Poems of John Donne*, 1: ll. 1–4, 189–90. 5. All subsequent references to Donne's poems will be to this edn and will be cited parenthetically in the body of the text. In his edn of the *Satires, epigrams and verse letters*, Wesley Milgate suggests that the poem "To the Countess of Bedford, on New Year's Day" may be the first verse letter Donne wrote to her. In a letter of 6 August 1608 Donne refers to being in London "when I shall use that favour which my Lady Bedford hath afforded me, of giving her name to my daughter; which I mention to you, as well to shew that I covet any occasion of a gratefull speaking of her favours." Donne, *Letters to Severall Persons of Honour*, 119. All subsequent references to the letters will be cited parenthetically in the body of the text. Donne wrote six verse letters and two occasional poems to the Countess of Bedford, titled a poem after her estate, and wrote funeral elegies for her friends Lady Markham and Lady Cecilia Bulstrode, as well as for her brother, Sir John Harington.

[2] Milgate points out that the line includes a reference to John 20: 29: "blessed are they that have not seen, and yet have believed (*Satires*, 253). See also Helen Gardner, "Notes on Donne's Verse Letters."

working toward faith (ll. 5–6)—a combination Donne promotes in much of his writing.

In the stanzas that follow, Donne claims to pursue first-hand knowledge of Bedford in order to buttress his "faith." He promises to "study [her] first in her Saints, / Those friends, whom [her] election glorifies"; in her "deeds, accesses, and restraints" (the ideas and people whom she welcomes and rebuffs); and, finally, in what she herself "reade[s]" and "devize[s]" (ll. 9–10, 11, 12). When the reasons why she is loved grow infinite, Donne continues, and "passe reasons reach," he will fall back on "implicite faith," "And rest on what the Catholique voice doth teach" (ll. 14–16). "That you are good," he affirms, "not one Heretique / Denies" (ll. 17–18). Even if someone did divert from "Catholique" or universal opinion, moreover, such a controversial judgment—which Donne imagines, in a stoic metaphor familiar to us from Chapter 1, as the futile washing of waves—would simply be ignored: Bedford's goodness is as a rock "which high top'd and deep rooted" will never be undermined by the faithless or misled (l. 19). She is "the first good Angell, since the world's frame stood, / That ever did in womans shape appeare" (ll. 31–2).

The final stanza brings the theological language of the poem to its ideal hoped-for conclusion. "Since you are then Gods masterpeece," he tells her, "and so

> His Factor for our loves; do as you doe
> Make your returne home gracious; and bestow
> This life on that; so make one life of two.
> For so God help mee, 'I would not misse you there
> For all the good which you can do me here.'" (ll. 33–8)[3]

In addition to painting Bedford as "God's Factor," or agent, sent to solicit the love and devotion of others like himself, Donne puns on her graciousness, alluding both to her ability to proffer grace, or favor, to Donne himself, and to her own guaranteed salvation, or state of grace. While Donne hopes for earthly favor or patronage—"all the good" that she can do him "here"—he also suggests that he will, with both God's help and Bedford's, be "there" with her among the elect in the afterlife. The idea that grace, the divine imputation and promise of salvation, is in his future as well as hers imagines a proximity between poet and patron, putting them on equal footing in the realm that matters most.

---

[3] See also: "Her return home to her native heaven will be blessed, for she will be accompanied by the souls she had helped to save" (*Satires*, ed. Milgate, 255). In his "Obsequies" on Bedford's brother's death, Donne similarly complains that Sir John Harington did not "stay, t'enlarge God's kingdome" "By making others what [he] didst, to do" (213).

Donne's verse letter to Bedford thus equates the process by which a patron selects which poets to support to the process by which God elects Christians for salvation—her "Saints" are those friends whom she has rendered "elect" by her support. In the poem's final stanza, Donne intentionally confuses the agentive meaning of grace—the favor or privilege a person can confer on or offer to others—with its unagentive meaning—the infusion of divine grace into the regenerate Christian. Evoking the intra-Christian debate over the status of "works" in salvation, Donne repeats both "do" and "make" twice in the final stanza of the poem. Bedford, Donne suggests, can "make" her own return home gracious, and he hopes that she will help him do the same.[4] The poem, as even this brief reading attests, is both theologically complex and witty.

But it is according to this latter judgment that the poem, like all of Donne's verse letters to women, has been read: as an ingenious display of Donne's wit, flattering to its recipient, and self-promoting of its author. In a formulation later echoed with differing degrees of feminist or historicist rigor by critics as disparate as Barbara Lewalski and David Aers, Wesley Milgate suggests that the " 'valters sombersalts' of intellect which the lady [dedicatee of the verse poem] is supposed to be able to appreciate are no less flattering to her powers of mind than the genuine moral ardour of Donne's references to virtue and beauty are to her character."[5] Patricia Thomson similarly sees the verse letters as complimentary acts in that they presume that Bedford "could follow the intricacies of [Donne's] ingenious arguments."[6] On a slightly less laudatory note, Arthur F. Marotti has backed up John Buxton's suggestion that Bedford may have "been as much bewildered as flattered" by Donne's verse letters.[7] We are well aware, however, that many early modern women actively sought out "ingenious arguments." The poet Katherine Philips, for example, wrote in her own verse letter to the poet Henry Vaughan that she is reminded in "the charming rigor [his] muse brings, / That there's no pleasure but in serious things."[8] Donne himself expressed admiration for women engaged in "serious things," reportedly praising Anne Clifford as someone who "knew well how

---

[4] See also Patricia Thomson: "Donne does not let himself forget permanently, however far his religious speculations carry him, the practical aspect of the situation, 'all the good which you can do me here.' The Countess is a 'factor for our loves,' giving access to God, and she is also, it may be cautiously suggested, fulfilling a similar role on earth, giving access to the benefits of James I's court" ("Donne and the Poetry of Patronage," 318).

[5] *Satires*, ed. Milgate, pp. xxxviii–xxxix.

[6] Thomson, "Donne and the Poetry of Patronage," 316.

[7] Buxton, *Sir Philip Sidney and the English Renaissance*, p. 230, cited in Marotti, *John Donne: Coterie Poet*, 335 n. 144.

[8] Making a similar point, Janel Mueller cites these lines in "Women among the Metaphysicals," 38.

to discourse of all things, from Predestination, to Slea-silk." ("Meaning," as her eulogist put it, "that although she was skilful in Houswifry, and in such things in which Women are conversant . . . her penetrating Wit soar'd up to pry into the highest Mysteries."[9]) Donne professed great respect for Bedford's intelligence in particular, claiming in a letter to his friend, and Bedford's intimate and courtier, Sir Henry Goodere, that he reserved all his "thoughts of women's worthiness" for Bedford "alone" (*Letters*, 107).[10]

This verse letter, in which Donne applies ideas about the strange power-lessness of the Christian seeking salvation to the strange powerlessness of the poet seeking patronage, does not merely flatter Bedford's ability to follow Donne's ingenious logic. Nor, as I will argue, does it just deploy theological language as an analogy for the pursuit of patronage. Writing about another verse letter to Bedford, Margaret Maurer has argued that Donne's verse letters "borrow" terms from religious and ethical systems, particularly the idea of grace, in order to explain the workings of a political-religious order in which human effort is necessary but does not necessarily promise reward. "Donne's style," she writes, "intensifies both the impression of the poet's effort (wit) and the absolute supremacy of the reader's decision (grace) to accommodate it."[11] This style, as Maurer understands it, mimics the dynamic of royal prerogative, where it is not the poet's skill that matters so much as the patron's power to reward it. Linda Levy Peck has similarly pointed out how common Donne's mode of petitioning was in the period, arguing that in a divine right monarchy court patrons or brokers were often seen as saints who could intercede "with an all-knowing God to bring salvation and favor to the supplicant and himself."[12] In Jacobean

---

[9] Edward Rainbow, Lord Bishop of Carlisle, *A Sermon Preached at the Funeral of the Right Honorable Anne Countess of Pembroke, Dorset and Montgomery*, 38.

[10] As he puts it in another letter, Donne wrote not for all women, but for "those of sincerer palates" (*Letters*, 108).

[11] Maurer, "The Real Presence of Lucy Russell, Countess of Bedford," 224. "Donne's best interests are served by a system that accommodates the absolute whim of a patron's prerogative without discounting the importance of a suitor's effort" (224). "From his position with respect to her and from hers on his behalf with respect to others Donne and his patroness must agree: indiscretion will not prosper unless a risk succeeds; and if it does, the accomplishment will be named, not for the skill that earned it, but for the power that granted it" (224).

[12] Peck does not write about Donne himself, but her arguments certainly bear on his poem. *Court Patronage and Court Corruption*, 17. (Intercession was a form of (Catholic) prayer in which one could seek mercy or divine benefits from God for another. Saints, who had "accumulated benefits beyond those necessary for salvation," were thus able to intercede on behalf of others: *Court Patronage*, 114). For a poetic example, see Robert Herrick, "His Prayer to Ben Jonson":

> When I a verse shall make,
> Know I have prayed thee,
> For old religion's sake,
> Saint Ben to aid me. (*The Poetical Works of Robert Herrick*, 1: ll. 1–4).

England, seekers of various kinds were thus advised to direct themselves to the right "saint," or "angel," at court. (Unlike saints, angels—God's servants in the court of heaven—were transdenominational, and thus made the petitionary trope palatable for everyone. "Even Calvinists did not have to rely upon grace alone in this world," Peck writes, "good works and the intercession of intermediaries provided access to advancement."[13]) When Donne refers to Bedford as an "Angel" (with its contingent joke about women's general inapplicability for the role), he relies on this transdenominational reference point; the Countess of Bedford was certainly a powerful "saint" at court, but it was clear to everyone who knew her that James I was in no way analogous to her God.[14] As Donne's modification of the trope acknowledges, if Bedford considered herself a "saint" of any kind, it was the puritan kind.

More than simply a deployment of the trope outlined by Maurer and Peck, the insistently theological language in Donne's verse letter was in fact precisely the means by which he sought to engage his would-be patron. As George Puttenham puts it, "it behooveth the maker or Poet to follow the nature of his subiect," and the language in Donne'spoem was acutely attuned to its godly subject.[15] But the poem, whose tone is both self- and subject-mocking, was also a challenge, and an invitation to dialogue. While many of the poem's religious terms are familiarly hyperbolic, such as the claim that Bedford is divine, most are also explicitly controversial. When Donne refers to Bedford's current "friends"—only most obviously the poets she already supports—as "Saints" chosen by "election," he uses godly terms; his reference to "the Catholique voice" evokes both the term's universal or consensual meaning and its Romish one; and his numerous puns on "grace" highlight the doctrinal controversy over whether or not it can be solicited by human merit or "works," and whether or not it can save every Christian or only a few. In using these terms, Donne intentionally invoked a particular set of controversial theological issues of pressing religious and political concern in early seventeenth-century England and with which both he and Bedford—and their supporters and detractors—were actively involved.

In this chapter, I argue that the verse letter known as "Reason is our Soules left hand" was one of many elements of a politically and religiously charged sustained literary transaction conducted between Donne and

[13] Peck, "Benefits, Brokers and Beneficiaries," 114.

[14] Interestingly, at Christmas 1599, Donne wrote to a friend describing the various activities taking place about the court, adding, "My lorde of Essex and his trayne are no more mist here then the Aungells which were cast downe from heaven," cited in Carey, *John Donne*, 71.

[15] Cited in Maurer, "John Donne's Verse Letters," 236.

Bedford, and their shifting and interrelated communities and alliances, during the period between their introduction in 1608 and Bedford's death in 1627. (Their relationship did not end, as is often suggested, with Donne's last verse letter in 1614, but rather continued into the early years of Charles's reign.) Donne's verse letters were meant to, and did, circulate as part of a wider system of textual exchange with Bedford which included non-verse letters, religious and political news, politically topical literary games, religious treatises and rebuttals, translations, and poetry.[16] The exchange was facilitated largely through Donne's friend and conduit Henry Goodere, gentleman of James's Privy Chamber, Bedford's courtier and a frequent presence in Bedfords' country house of Twickenham Park—a site that also plays an important role in this story.[17]

The years in which Donne was closest to Bedford, part of the literary and political culture of Twickenham Park, and constantly soliciting her favor and intervention, were also the years in which he was actively reading divinity and canon law and defending James's notorious Oath of Allegiance. This work would culminate in the 1610 publication of *Pseudo-Martyr* and, in some ways, in his 1615 ordination. It was also the period in which he was writing about the similarities and differences between Christian denominations: the Roman Catholicism of his family, the orthodox Protestantism of the English church, and the more puritan-leaning or militantly Calvinist Protestantism professed by Bedford and her allies. Frequently, Donne encourages unity in the face of such divisions, officially and publicly avowing an ecumenicist, Erastian, one-Christendom vision that may itself be a polemical position.[18] Like "Reason is our Soules left hand," many of Donne's verse letters allude both directly and indirectly to controversies in which Donne and Bedford frequently stood on opposing sides. Reading Donne's verse letters and related poems in this light allows us, as William H. Sherman puts it, to "hear the voices of the argument represented by every textual event."[19] As we saw in the last chapter, the reading and exchange of texts was in many ways the grounds of Protestant reform, and active debate and mutual correction were the means by which conversion or "consensus" could be reached.[20] Donne's

---

[16] There are numerous other signs of Donne's textual exchanges with Bedford and her circle that I do not take up in this chapter. For example, we know that Donne gave Bedford a copy of a book by the Calvinist Denis Godefroy who moved to Heidelberg at the invitation of the Elector Palatine in 1600.

[17] On Goodere and the family estate of Polesworth, see Lesley Lawson, *Out of the Shadows*, 70; and the *ODNB*.

[18] In *Inventing Polemic*, Jesse Lander points out that this position was itself a form of polemic, and not necessarily one that Donne held himself.

[19] Sherman, *John Dee*, 58.   [20] See Dobranski, *Readers and Authorship*, 29–30.

epistolary and literary relationship with the Countess of Bedford is thus best understood as a form of (highly mediated) co-reading, an often provocative transaction or negotiation in which the matters of difference between them were subject to their joint interpretation.

Near the beginning of his courtship of Bedford as a patron, Donne wrote a letter to Henry Goodere in which he asserted that, despite the claims of "inobedient Puritans" and "over-obedient Papists," "in all Christian professions there is way to salvation" (*Letters*, 101).[21] Confessional suspicion, he claims, hits people "not in their conscience, nor ends, but in their reputation," a matter which had serious implications not only for Goodere, who was, as Donne put it, susceptible to "Sophisters in Religion," but for the Catholic-born Donne and the puritan-leaning Bedford as well (*Letters*, 101). As Donne well knew, Bedford's reputation had already been compromised. She and her husband had been implicated in and punished for Essex's rebellion (it was, notably, Penelope Rich who brought the Earl of Bedford to Essex House on the day of the uprising); she promoted the often oppositional interests of the alliance for which Essex had served as the figurehead; and she was known for her support of radical ministers.[22] Donne alludes to wounded reputation twice in "Reason is our Soules left hand": first when he refers to the potential knocks Bedford might take

---

[21] Donne despaired over the tone of much of the writing on religion. In another letter to Goodere he criticizes those who "write for Religion, without it," claiming instead that "both sides may be in justice, and innocence" (*Letters*, 160). "You know I never fettered nor imprisoned the word Religion," he writes in yet another letter, "not straightning it Frierly, *ad Religiones factitias* (as the *Romans* call well their orders of Religion) nor immuring it in a *Rome* or a *Wittenberg*, or a *Geneva*." All religions, he continues, are "virtuall beams of one Sun" (*Letters*, 29).

[22] In 1605 Robert Cecil, as Lewalski puts it, "paid grudging tribute to the Countess's tenacity of purpose and family loyalty (if not diplomatic delicacy) in a letter to Lord Harington calling a halt to her efforts to arrange a marriage between his daughter and her brother":

> I must be thus far bowld with my Lady the Countesse, as to say that if she hathe not more resembled her sex in loving her owne will than she dothe in those other noble and discrett parts of her mynd (wherein she hath so great a portion beyond most of those that I have knowne) she might have moved you to suspend the sending upp of any particularities at this tyme...I have not hidd it from herselfe, that I have found her so absolutely fixed upon a resolution to allow of no reason which she finds not justly concurrent with your satisfaction.

Hatfield, Cecil Papers 114, fol. 130, cited in Barbara Lewalski, *Writing Women in Jacobean England*, 98–9. On her politics more generally, see also Lewalski, p. 117. On her support of ministers, see Francis Bacon's June 1613 letter "concerning the restoring to preach of a famous preacher, one Doctor Burgess" which "hath been laboured by my Lady of Bedford and put in good way to the Bishop of Bath and Well." (J. Spedding, *Letters and Life of Bacon*, 5: 372–3, cited in Thomson, "John Donne and the Countess of Bedford," 334). She also recommended an English preacher going to The Hague on the "good aprobacion from Doctor Burges & Mr Preston" (PRO S.P. 84/103/127, April 1622, cited Thomson, "John Donne and the Countess of Bedford," 334).

from "heretics" and their inability to affect her stoic rock-like self, and secondly when he characterizes her "learning and religion" as a "methridate,"
or antidote, which can "[k]eepe [off], or cure what can be done or said"
(26–7).[23] Discretion was thus a recurrent concern in Donne's verse letters
to Bedford not only because they were invested in each other's behavior as
part of the complex political dance of court life, but also because both had
been associated with unpopular or resistant positions.

In the letter to Goodere, Donne warns, in particular, against taking
"indifferent things," the *adiaphora* of intra-Christian debate, too seriously.
"[L]abour to keep your alacrity and dignity in an even temper," he argues
"for in a dark sadnesse, indifferent things seem abominable, or necessary,
being neither" (103). He encourages Goodere instead to remember that
the "channels of Gods mercies run through both fields: and they are sister
teats of his graces" (101). For Donne, focusing on "indifferent" matters
of doctrine confuses both the central issue of salvation and the central
commonality—his favored term is "unity"—between Christians. At
the conclusion of this discussion, Donne refers directly to the Countess
of Bedford, and in terms much like those of "Reason is our Soules left
hand." Although he first based his belief in Bedford's worthiness on
Goodere's praise of her, he writes, "I have had since an explicit faith, and
now a knowledge: and for her delight (since she descends to them) I had
reserved not only all the verses, which I should make, but all the thoughts
of womens worthiness" (104). In his use of the terms "faith" and "knowledge," the two concepts with which he begins his verse letter, Donne both
alludes to his poem—in all likelihood the poem that accompanied this
letter as its "companion and supplement" (104)—and to the matters of
potentially divisive religious faith and practice he discusses in the letter as
a whole. In the vision expressed in this letter, the way to salvation is broad
and only the most "inobedient Puritans" and "over-obedient Papists"
would fight over the means. Like many of his letters to Goodere, Donne
intended this letter to be shared with Bedford, and we can understand his
plea for ignoring "indifferent things" to have been directed towards her
as well as Goodere.

---

[23] Two other verse letters Donne sent to Bedford in this period are similarly concerned
with reputation, controversy, and concomitant (and coded) advice about discretion. In "On
New-yeares day," he suggests that while God has given Bedford "innocence" for her conscience, he has also given her "a discreet wariness" for her fame: "And though to 'scape,
than to revenge offence / Be better He shows both" (ll. 56, 57, 58–9). A third verse letter, "Honour is so sublime perfection," explicitly associates discretion with religion: "discretion," he writes, "Must not grudge zeal a place," nor "banish" itself (ll. 37–9, p. 219).
Religion, he reminds her, hath "Wrought your ends, / and your wayes discretion," and thus
she should "goe the same way [she] went" (ll. 51, 52, p. 220).

When understood in the context of the letters which accompanied and framed them, Donne's "flattering" references to Bedford in his verse letters thus take on a different cast. The theological frame of "Reason is our Soules left hand" is not a "borrowing" of theological terms so much as an engagement with them, and the letter is best understood as an invitation to a conversation about religion. Again and again, Donne showed himself willing to enter into a "serious consideration" of religion, even with those whose positions differed from his own. Many of his letters reflect an empathetic concern for those like Goodere and the Catholic Tobie Matthew whose beliefs and affiliations might have brought them into conflict with authority.[24] Bedford was one of the most important of Donne's heterodox interlocutors, with whom he engaged in substantive textual exchange. In the letters, poems, and other texts that traveled between them, we can see poet and patron forging a relationship that was based less on flattery than on an intellectual dialogue that could encompass agreement and disagreement, consensus and debate. It sought, in other words, to "stand inquiring right" while gently mocking the righteousness that so often characterized the enterprise.[25]

I. MEDIATRIX

When Donne identified the Countess of Bedford as God's "Factor for our loves" in "Reason is our Soules left hand," he chose his term well. By the early 1600s, the Countess of Bedford was a "Factor," or agent, of signal importance in Stuart England. Among other things, a "factor" was a maker, performer, and "author of a literary work," and Bedford was all of these (*OED* 1). She commissioned and performed in court masques and was widely known as an "author"—in the broad sense this book has been arguing for—of a wide range of texts, from Florio's Montaigne to poems, religious treatises, and a translation of Lucan's *Pharsalia*. She was also a "factor" in the sense that she had the "charge and management of the affairs of an estate" (*OED* 5a). Following her husband's involvement in, and punishment for the Essex rebellion, the Countess became

---

[24] For Donne's letter to the courtier turned Catholic priest Tobie Matthew, see *A Collection of Letters Made by Sir Tobie Mathews*, 67–9: "I never mis-interpreted your way; nor suffered it to be so, wheresoever I found it in discourse. For I was sure, you took not up your Religion upon trust, but payed ready money for it, and at a high Rate. And this taste of mine towards you, makes me hope for, and claime the same disposition in you towards me" (68–9).

[25] In Satire 3, Donne writes that "in a strange way / To stand inquiring right, is not to stray; / To sleep, or run wrong is" (ll. 77–9).

what the *OED* calls a "land-steward," managing almost all of the family and estate affairs, including holding her husband's proxy in Parliament (*OED* 5a). Bedford was also a powerful political "Factor" or go-between in the Stuart court; as we saw in the Introduction, Donne referred to her as a "Mediatrix" (*Letters*, 193). Along with her husband's aunts, the aforementioned Countesses of Cumberland and Warwick, and Penelope Rich, Bedford was among the first women to greet Queen Anne when she arrived in England in 1603. She immediately became the Queen's chief courtier, and was thereafter able to, quite literally, determine the "accesses and restraints" of myriad petitioners.[26] In her 1603 *Memoir*, Lady Anne Clifford noted that no one is "so great a woman with the Queen, as Bedford," and in 1604 Chief Justice Edward Coke described her to Fulke Greville in politically loaded (if somewhat ironic) terms that captured the extent of her political power: "Lady Bedford," he wrote, "keepeth her prerogative of greatness at Court."[27]

Through her parents, the guardians of the future Elizabeth of Bohemia (her mother was Elizabeth's governess), and her brother, Prince Henry's main companion until the latter's death in 1612, she was also a key "Factor" in creating a web of connections across the Privy Council and the various and often contentious Stuart households.[28] Using her position in court, Bedford also worked to maintain the interests of the affinity network discussed in the last two chapters—occasionally in some tension with a more strictly court-centered sense of obligation.[29] Like many aristocratic magnates and courtiers, Bedford was aware of the differences between a powerful nobility and court-dependent favorites, and, like many members of her alliance, she played a crucial role in both "court" and "country," as both insider and critic.

[26] As Leeds Barroll has pointed out, Queen Anne's household was dominated by former followers of the Earl of Essex, including Penelope Devereux Rich, Lucy, Countess of Bedford, and Sir Robert Sidney, her household chamberlain. See Barroll, *Anna of Denmark*; and Peck, *Court Patronage*, 68 n. 116.

[27] In her 1603 *Memoir*, Clifford describes Lady Bedford as being "so great a woman with the Queen as every body much respected her, she having attended the Queen from out of Scotland" (p. 49). In the margin she notes that the Queen "showed no favour to the elderly Ladies, but to my Lady Rich and such-like company" (p. 50). Clifford also highlights Bedford's status as a "Mediatrix": "my mother wrote letters to the King, and her means was by my Lord Fenton and to the Queen by my Lady of Bedford" (p. 57). The night before Clifford is called before the King about her court case, her husband "went up to the King's side about his business" and she "went up to my Lady Bedford in her Lodgings" (113). Coke is cited in Florence Humphrey Morgan, "A Biography of Lucy Countess of Bedford," 74.

[28] See Peck, *Court Patronage*, passim.

[29] On the "web of political connections" that women like Bedford "wove across the Privy Council and royal Households," see Peck, *Court Patronage*, 47–8. See also her discussion of the transformation of "magnate politics into court-centered patronage" (p. 48). (A powerful nobility independent of the crown was far more threatening to the monarch than the favorites who were his "creatures," p. 49.)

As Donne's allusion to her ability to "cure" whatever "can be done or said" about her in his verse letter suggests, Bedford was also a "Factor" in the sense derived from the Latin *facere cum aliquo*: "someone who takes a side, a partisan, or adherent" (*OED* 2). Along with Mary Sidney Herbert's son William Herbert, Earl of Pembroke, Bedford had quickly become a leader of the anti-Spanish, pro-Protestant alliance that cohered around the former followers of Sidney and Essex in the early seventeenth century. She was the creator, as Peck puts it, of networks of politically coordinated action among the various members of the alliance.[30] In seeking Bedford's patronage, Donne certainly knew that men like William Herbert were among the "friends" she had elected, and thus to whom she was likely to give "access" and whom she was likely to "restrain." His reference to Bedford's "deep rooted" resistance to the washing of waves in "Reason is our Soules left hand," a standard stoic trope and, as we saw in Chapter 1, one associated specifically with the women of the Essex party, indicates how well Donne had in fact studied her "Saints." (Donne wrote verse letters to some of these other women as well. In 1612 he wrote a poem to Penelope Rich's daughters, Lettice Rich Carey and Essex Rich, in which he similarly identified them as "saints."[31]) The verse letter's theological cast, moreover, evokes not only Bedford's beliefs, but her activism as well. Among those likely to gain "access" and "elect[ion]" were the unbeneficed and Nonconformist ministers for whom Bedford, as a "partisan" of militant Protestantism, also frequently served as a "Factor": men who considered themselves, quite literally, to be the "elect," and who worked on behalf of the militant Protestantism supported by the alliance.[32]

Petitioners of all kinds usually inform themselves about those whom they hope to impress, and it is thus more than likely that Donne did in fact "study" Bedford in all the ways he promises in his poem. While his plan to study Bedford in her "Saints" evokes those whom she patronizes in a broad sense, including those of similar religious and political convictions, and his vow to study her "accesses and restraints" refers to his necessary awareness of the kinds of networks she endeavored to foster, his plan to

[31] In this poem, "A Letter to the Lady Carey, and Mrs. Essex Riche, from Amyens," he plays on his fate in a Catholic state where "by All All Saints invoked are" and thus the necessity of his turning to the Rich sisters as his only "saints." If he did not do so, he claims, it would make "my schisme [non-Catholicism], heresie [a crime]" (ll. 1, 6, p. 221). As in his poems to Bedford, Donne's poem to Rich's daughters plays both with the dominant language of courtiership and with terms of religious divisiveness ("schism," "heresie," and "faith alone") in a way that illustrates both his knowledge of their contexts, and his own Catholic past.

[32] See e.g. Samuel Clarke's *Eminent Divines*, for the entry on "The Life of Doctor [John] Preston": "The Earl of Pembroke and the Countesse of Bedford had a great interest in him," Clarke writes, "and he in them, and all men looked on him as a rising man" (119).

study what she "read[s]" and "devize[s]" is the most suggestive of all. In a broader sense, to "devise" meant to plan, determine, or resolve (*OED* 6a). It also meant to write, invent, design, or to arrange the plot of (*OED* 5). The things Bedford devised in this broad sense ranged from marriages and the promotion of men to particular offices and benefices to writing poems and letters and commissioning and patronizing masques and, as we will see in some detail, patronizing works of religious and political commentary. To "devise" also meant to divide or distinguish, even to arrange "in battle array"; and it is this aspect of Bedford's "deviz[ing]" to which Donne must have devoted the greatest attention (*OED* 1a, b, 2). Donne's vow to "study" Bedford in what she "devize[s]" acknowledges her role not only as a "Mediatrix," but as a "Factor" in what had been, and might again be, a faction. This faction, moreover, was one with which Donne himself had frequent interactions, and for which his writing was sometimes used as support. Donne had attended the Earl of Essex in his expeditions against Cadiz and the Azores Islands in 1596 and 1597, and he remained friends with Sir Henry Wotton, who continued to serve Essex in a scholarly capacity. Ernest W. Sullivan II argues that the Dalhousie manuscripts, a pair of poetic compilations heavily featuring the poetry of John Donne (as well as the neostoic discourse of the "discontented nobility") were the work of the Sidney-Essex faction, and were intended to both reflect and serve their interests.[33] Donne's concern about Bedford's "discretion" or "reputation" was thus conscious of the kinds of activism with which she was involved, as well as the kinds of texts she and her allies lined up in battle array.

As patron, dedicatee, and reader, Lucy Harington Russell "read" and "devize[d]" an impressive arsenal of texts. Indeed her status as a reader was almost iconic in the period. In the Samuel Daniel masque she commissioned (or "devize[d]") in 1604, *The Vision of the Twelve Goddesses*—based, notably, on Seneca's "tres Gratiae"—Bedford appears as Vesta, the

---

[33] Ernest W. Sullivan (ed.), *The First and Second Dalhousie Manuscripts*, passim. For recent work on Donne's politics, see David Norbrook's "The Monarchy of Wit and the Republic of Letters"; and Annabel Patterson's "John Donne, Kingsman?" Resisting the then standard account of Donne, Norbrook argues that, while "as a Catholic in origin, Donne lacked the Puritan conviction that was an essential component of radical ideology," his politics were nonetheless far more complicated than the standard account of him as "conservative coterie poet, [and] the monarch of an exclusive inner circle of wits who disdained the wider republic of letters" (pp. 4, 5). While not a "full-fledged oppositional figure," Donne sought to "maintain a critical distance, a standpoint outside the existing social order from which he can criticize it" (p. 6). His satires e.g. were often critical of an unlimited monarchy. Norbrook suggests that Donne "kept a certain distance from the Essex circle," but he also had an ongoing correspondence with Wotton, who had, among other things, written a lengthy defense of the Aragonese rebellion against Philip II as part of Essex's "campaign to unify anti-Hapsburg forces" (p. 12). He also points out that Donne evinced "muted sympathy" with Essex in *The Courtier's Library* (12).

Goddess of Religion, holding a "burning Lampe in one hand, and a Booke in the other."[34] Books, as the allegory suggests, were integral to the kind of international "amitie" the masque idealizes and promotes, but they were also recognized as the tools of Bedford's trade.[35]

Perhaps the best known book that Bedford received in the period was Ben Jonson's gift of Donne's satires. ("Rare poemes," Jonson wrote in his dedicatory poem, "aske rare friends."[36]) But in December 1600, Bedford's cousin Sir John Harington of Kelston sent her a similarly important gift: a presentation copy of three of the Countess of Pembroke's paraphrases of the Psalms: Psalms 51, 104, and 137.[37] In many ways, these poems were the calling card of the godly, used to encourage "Princes," in Mary Sidney Herbert's words, to "doo what [godly, Sidnean] men may sing."[38] The Psalms Harington chose to send to Bedford were particularly godly and politically charged: Psalm 51 focuses on human dependence upon divine grace (the theme Donne plays on in his verse letter); Psalm 104 presents God as the only king to whom "roiall pompes belonge," an implicit caution on monarchical power; and Psalm 137, "By the waters of Babylon we sat down and wept," was habitually deployed by reform-minded Protestants to provide consolation for political and religious exiles, including the (internally exiled) godly.[39] Harington's gift can thus be seen both as

---

[34] Daniel, *The vision of the 12. goddesses,* sig. A5^r. In a letter to John Chamberlain, Sir Dudley Carleton identified Bedford as the masque's "*rector chori*" (cited in Lewalski, "Lucy, Countess of Bedford," 307 n. 19). For another visual emblem of Bedford, see Nicholas Breton's *Religions love in wisedomes worth, the truest beauty, best sets forth* (London, 1615). On Bedford's support of Daniel, see Lewalski, *Writing Women,* 105.

[35] Daniel, *The vision of the 12. Goddesses,* passim. See also Ruth Stagen's discussion of the 1605 Masque in which the French ambassador credited Lady Bedford with the fortunate outcome of his mission ("Lucy, Countess of Bedford," 35). Lewalski points out (*Writing Women,* 96; see also p. 99) that Bedford "associated herself closely with Queen Anne's subversive masques" and (at p. 100) notes: "Lady Bedford's role as Vesta-Religion associated her closely with the Queen (who portrayed Pallas) and her gift was specified as the primary support of the realm:

> Whose maine support, holy Religion frame:
> And *1 Wisdome, 2 Courage, 3 Temperance,* and *4 Right,*
> Make seem the Pillars that sustaine the same.
> (Daniel, *Whole Workes,* 413)"

[36] The poem's title is "To Lucy, Countesse of Bedford, with Mr. Donnes Satyres," Jonson, *Works of Ben Jonson,* vol. 8, 60–61. On Bedford's relationship with Jonson, see Riggs, *Ben Jonson,* 118–62; and Robert C. Evans, *Ben Jonson and the Politics of Patronage,* 48–51.

[37] See Jason Scott-Warren, *Sir John Harington and the Book as Gift,* 146–53.

[38] Sidney Herbert, *Collected Works,* 104. The Psalms also presented a historical drama involving the persecution of the godly under a court tyranny, and as such they were appropriate reading for the godly in England as well.

[39] See Hannibal Hamlin, "Psalm Culture in the English Renaissance." Gavin Alexander points out that these were the three Psalms Harington quoted in the commentary to his translation of the *Aeneid,* a work he dedicated to Prince Henry (*Writing After Sidney,* 132).

a recognition of Bedford's religious and political beliefs, and as a figurative passing of the torch. Among other things, the gift acknowledged Bedford's role in promoting the concerns and values associated with the Sidney alliance, particularly, as was the case with the Sidneys themselves, through the production and exchange of literary texts.[40]

After her marriage to Edward Russell, third Earl of Bedford in 1594, Lucy Harington Russell had access to the renowned Bedford library.[41] According to a 1584 inventory, the collection included multiple editions of Calvin (including the versions published by the puritan John Field and dedicated to the (senior) Earl and Countess of Bedford, whom he identifies as God's "adopted children"); texts dedicated to their children, the aforementioned Countesses of Warwick and Cumberland, including a sermon celebrating the latter's "welcome coming into these rude and desert partes" of Craven, Yorkshire, which, the author claimed, "ministered great solace to the godly"; anti-Catholic tracts; and many controversial intra-Protestant texts.[42] This last group of texts includes "The B. of Caunterburies awnswere to Ste. Gardiner touchinge the doctrine of ye L. Supp." and "Ye 2^{d} replie of T. Cartwright against D. Whitgift of church disciplyne," as well as numerous anti-Catholic and pro-Calvinist "disputacions," "defenses," "answers," "dialogues," "replies," and "confucations."[43] As their titles indicate, these latter texts both model and provide the resources for the kinds of dialogic reading Margaret Hoby was

[40] Harington's letter to Bedford reads thus: "I have sent you heere the devine, and trulie devine translation of three of Davids psalms, donne by that Excellent Countesse, and in Poesie the mirroir of our Age; whom, as you are neere unto in blood, of like degree in Honor; not unlike in favore; so I suppose none coms more neere hir then your self in those, now rare, and admirable guifts of the mynde, that clothe Nobilitie with vertue" (Harington, *The Letters and Epigrams*, 87). See also Scott-Warren, *Sir John Harington*, 146. Scott-Warren argues that the volume for the Countess of Bedford outlines the terms on which Harington is prepared to accept puritanism in religion, and that it may have included Mary Sidney's translation of Petrarch's *Triumph of Death* (*Sir John Harington*, 148, 151–2).

[41] For an account of the library, see M. St. Clare Byrne and Gladys Scott Thomson, "My Lord's Books," 385–405.

[42] The puritan John Field dedicated his translation of the *Thirteene Sermons of Maister John Calvine* (1579) to the Earl and his wife: "As God hath called you to the knowledge of his glorious Gospel, which is a token of your election, so goe forwarde more and more in the grouth therof.... God hath called you to high honor, not so much by your places and calling amongst men...but in that he hath made you his adopted children" (Byrne and Thomson, "My Lord's Books," 393). The sermon was by Christopher Shutte, *A verie godlie and necessary sermon preached before the yong countesse of Cumberland in the North, the 14 of Nouember, 1577*, item 141 in the inventory. Clifford left a Bible to "Mr Shute, a preacher" in her will (Williamson, *Lady Anne Clifford*, 459).

[43] Canterbury is item 18 in the inventory, and Cartwright 81. See e.g. the following entries in the inventory: item 24, "Disputacion wth Campion in the Tower," 35; "Defense of the doctrine of the L. Supp.," 97; "Awnswer by Wal. Travers to an epistle for ye catholickes," 125; "A dialogue betweene a gent. & a popish priest," 142; "An other of Charkes awnsweres to a seditiocose [*sic*] pamphlet"; and 134, "A confutacion of ye reall presence by P. Whyte."

doing in Yorkshire. (As we saw in the last chapter, the Hobys owned Field's translations of Calvin and de Mornay as well, and Hoby read, with some intensity, the same version of the Cartwright/Whitgift disputation as the one in the Bedford library.) Many of the "answers," "dialogues," "replies," and "confutacions" in the Bedford library, moreover, were specifically concerned with the issues of "election & reprobation" that animate Donne's poetic exchanges with Bedford.[44]

In addition to the books which were given to her, and those which we can presume she read in family libraries, Bedford was also the dedicatee of over fifty works—more than any other non-royal patron in the period.[45] Many of these books were religious, and many were directly concerned with the anti-Catholic and puritan-sympathizing values held by the Haringtons, Russells, and Sidneys. (An early book dedicated to Lucy Harington was by the French Huguenot, Claudius Hollyband.[46]) As Michael G. Brennan argues, "the dissemination of propaganda was the most powerful single purpose behind the production of patronized religious writing in the period," and Donne undoubtedly knew that Bedford's patronage of these kinds of texts was unparalleled.[47] Many of those who dedicated their work to Bedford did not, like Donne, know her from "faire faith," but rather had written directly under her or her family's aegis. (As I have argued throughout this book, many authors and translators credited their patrons with a role in "deviz[ing]" the books they dedicated to them.) Nicholas Byfield, whose godly work was also supported by Sir Thomas and Margaret Hoby, dedicated three treatises to Bedford.[48] In one volume, he thanks her and her husband specifically for clearing his "reputation from

---

[44] See e.g. item 36, "Calvines Sermons of election & reprobation," 49; "An other of Calvins sermons of election & reprobation," 135; "A consolacion for a troubled conscience," 92; "Th'image of nature & grace by Richard Candish"; and 147, "iiij Sermons of M. G. Gifford" (*Foure Sermons upon the seaven chiefe vertues or principall effectes of fayth, and the doctrine of election*).

[45] See Franklin B. Williams's *Index of Dedications and Commendatory Verses in English Books Before 1641*. In 1616, Bedford's mother donated 200 Latin and Greek folios "consisting chiefly of Fathers, Councils, School-men, and Divines" to the local parish library for the use of the vicar of the church of Oakham parish and the neighboring clergy." See Anne. L. Herbert, "Oakham Parish Library," 6. While most of them were by the church fathers, the collection also included the work of the major reformers and Cardinal Bellarmine's *Disputations*, the book to which Donne was devoting so much time to refuting while seeking Bedford's patronage. Bedford and her mother also gave 218 books to Sidney Sussex College.

[46] See Williams, *Index of Dedications*, 160: STC 6735.

[47] Brennan, *Literary Patronage*, 88.

[48] See Byfield, *An Exposition upon the Epistle to the Colossians* (1615) (dedicated to the Earl and Countess); *The Marrow of the Oracles of God* (1630); and *A commentary upon the three first chapters of the first Epistle generall of St. Peter* (1637). See also *ODNB*.

the vnjust aspersionof [his] adversaries."[49] In another, Byfield alludes to his trouble with the established church (he refers to "having suffered an involuntary vacation") and expresses his desire to be helpful "to the Church of God abroad," a reference to the cause of international Protestantism supported by Bedford and her allies.[50] In "seeke[ing] shelter" from Bedford for his books, Byfield simultaneously signals the contentious nature of his work (it has suffered from "assaults and calumnies") and seeks the protection of Bedford's powerful name. (In *A commentary* he asks her to "grace these notes with the liberty to passe under the protection of [her] name, and favour": A[v].) Many dedications, moreover, referred to Bedford's theological engagement with their volume's concerns and assumed its continuation. William Perkins, for example, identified her as the logical recipient of "the summe and chiefe heads" of his "thinking," and Thomas Draxe presumed that Bedford would "make vse" of the treatise he dedicated to her.[51]

The vast majority of the books dedicated to Bedford were by ministers whom the *Oxford Dictionary of National Biography* identifies as "severe Calvinists" and "unrepentant" puritans.[52] And like those in the Bedford library, many of these books were specifically concerned with matters of election and reprobation. William Perkins's treatise on "the order of the causes of Saluation and Damnation," for example, discusses the four "opinions of the order of Gods predestination," a debate that informs the terms of Donne's poetic engagement with Bedford not only in "Reason is our Soules left hand" but, as we will see, across a range of exchanges.[53] The

---

[49] Byfield, epistle dedicatory to *An Exposition vpon Colossians*, n.p. Referring to "the assaults and calumnies" which were "powred out vpon" his work, Byfield suggests that there is "great cause...that it comming out now to a more publike view, should seeke shelter." With their history of clearing his "reputation from the vniust aspersions of my aduersaries, and that by the mouth and pen of the Lords Annointed, my most dread Soueraigne," Byfield sees Bedford and her husband as the best providers of that shelter. On the Hobys, see J. T. Cliffe: "Byfield was held in high esteem among the laity, including some of the puritan gentry. At Isleworth Sir Thomas Hoby and his wife were among Byfield's most appreciative listeners" (*Puritan Gentry*, 38).

[50] Epistle dedicatory (dated 1617) to *A commentary*, A[v].

[51] Perkins, *A Golden Chaine*, epistle dedicatory to *A Salve for a Sick Man*, p. 421. Draxe, epistle dedicatory to *The Worldes Resurrection*, ¶ 3[v].

[52] One such "severe Calvinist" was John Reading, who dedicated *A faire warning Declaring the comfortable vse both of sicknesse and health* to Bedford in 1621. (Reading was "held in great esteem by the neighbourhood, especially by the puritanical party": Wood, *Ath. Oxon.*, 3: 794, cited in Jason McElligott's *ODNB* entry on Reading. In *A faire warning*, Reading asks for Bedford's patronage which like a "sanctuary secureth from the pursuite of tongues, that which is called yours" (A3[v]).

[53] The full title of Perkins's work is *A golden Chaine: OR, THE DESCRIPTION OF Theologie, containing the order of the causes of Saluation and Damnation, according to Gods word*. The quotation comes from the general dedication "To The Christian Reader," A[v]. All subsequent references to this text will be cited parenthetically within the text.

first opinion on predestination, Perkins tells us, is that of the "Pelagians," "who place the cause of Gods predestination in man," holding "that God did ordaine men either to life or death, according as he did foresee, that they would by their natural *freewill*, either reiect or receiue grace offered" (A^v). The second, "who (of some) are tearmed Lutherans," teach "that God foreseeing, howe all mankinde beeing shutte vp vnder vnbeleefe, would therefore reiect grace offered," did "purpose to choose some to saluation of his meere mercie, without any respect of their faith or good workes, and the rest to reiect." The third, whom he terms "Semipelagian Papists," "ascribe Gods predestination, partly to mercie, and partly to mens foreseene preparations and meritorious workes," and the fourth teach "that the cause of the execution of Gods predestination, is his mercie in Christ, in them which are saued; and in them which perish, the fall and corruption of man." God's decree, accordingly *"hath not any cause beside his will and pleasure"* (A^v, emphasis added). Of the four opinions, Perkins, an orthodox Calvinist, accepts only the last. One of the opinions that he "oppugne[s] as erroneous," however, and which he presumes Bedford would "oppugne" as well, was nonetheless one held by John Donne.[54]

In his *Essays in Divinity*, which he also wrote pre-ordination and during the time of his most direct engagement with Bedford, Donne sounds a great deal like the "Semipelagian Papist" in Perkins's treatise who ascribes predestination "partly to mercie, and partly to mens foreseene preparations and meritorious workes." While Donne asserts that "God is *all-efficient*: that is, hath created the beginning, ordained the way, fore-seen the end of everything; and nothing else is any kind of cause thereof," human "repentances and reconciliations" are nonetheless key.[55] "Though the first grace proceed only from God," he writes, "yet we concur so" (177). "For neither God nor man determine mans will; (for that must either imply a necessitating therof from God, or else *Pelagianisme*) *but they codetermine it*" (177–8, emphasis added). Donne's discussion of what he calls "conficiency" or codetermination is certainly complex, and could indeed "perplex the minds of the fair sex" if they did not so care to be engaged.[56] And yet we know that the Countess of Bedford's mind was engaged with precisely such matters of "Semipelagianism" in her own reading, and that texts with views opposed to Donne's, including on this exact issue of grace and free will, circulated under the "shelter" of her name.

---

[54] In *Pseudo-Martyr* (1610) Donne claims that God "sometimes beginnes at our workes" (88). In one of his letters he also highlights the importance of free will. His muse, he suggests is "but wounded and maimed like Free-will in the Roman Church," not "dead, like Free-will in our Church" (*Letters*, 17, cited in Richard Strier, "John Donne Awry and Squint," 376).

[55] Donne, *Essays in Divinity*, 176–7. Subsequent references will be cited parenthetically in the text.

[56] The latter, much-quoted line about Donne is from Dryden, *Satires of Decimus Junius Juvenalis*, iii.

The tenth article of the Thirty-Nine Articles of the Church of England, "Of Free Will," illustrates the established church's confusion about the issues Perkins and Donne address in their work. "The condition of man after the fall of Adam," it states,

> is such that he cannot turn and prepare himself, by his own natural strength and good works, to faith and calling upon God: Wherefore we have no power to do good works pleasant and acceptable to God, without the grace of God by Christ preventing us, that we may have a good will, and working with us, when we have that good will.[57]

The multiple caveating clauses, provisional "may," and successively dependent "will"s reflect both the accommodation of the English Church's Calvinist compromise and its instability. Calvin, of course, was much clearer about what he too determined to be "the pivotal point of . . . disputation" between Christians: "farewell to the dream of those who think up a righteousness flowing together out of faith and works," he writes in his *Institutes*; "let them try to win God's favour by works!"[58] Indeed this is the basis of the pun Donne makes at the end of "Reason is our Soules left hand" when he asks Bedford to "make" her return home "gracious," a joke I have characterized less as sophistry than as an acknowledgement of and engagement with the key terms of her own reading and beliefs.

Another tract dedicated to Bedford in this same period, Thomas Draxe's *The Worldes Resurrection* (1608), also focuses much of its attention on questions of election and reprobation. (To the question of whether "Gods fore-knowledge doth distinguish the elect from the Reprobate," the reader of the table of contents is relieved of having to wait for the full-text explication by a tidy "*affir*" (A^v). Grace, we learn, is not universal, and cannot be taken away—a doctrine that "checketh the corrupt and presumptuous opinion of the Papists, that teach constancy and saluation to reside in our owne power and potency, wheras it consisteth wholly in the couenant and promises of God" (106). In the text itself, Draxe comes in on the side of double predestination: "*Quest.* Is there then no particular election, or is it only vniuersall? *Ans.* Election is not of all, but of some, for hee that maketh choise of any thing, singleth out some, and leaueth the rest" (110). God does not, Draxe insists, "haue mercy on all," "Christs flocke is but *a little flocke, a remnant, an handfull, a tenth, a gleaning* in comparison of them that perish" (110).

[57] David Cressy and Lori Anne Ferrell (eds), *Religion and Society in Early Modern England: A Sourcebook*, 62.
[58] Calvin, *Institutes*, in *Selections from his Writings*, 441, 459.

In much the same way that he argues against the complete irrelevancy of "works" in salvation, Donne argues against the double predestination expressed by those like Draxe. In his fifth prebend sermon, for example, Donne insists that we must not conceive of God as cruel, either damning us "before we were" or affording us "no assurance that hee is ours, and we his, but let[ting] us live and die in anxiety and torture of conscience, in jealousie and suspition of his good purpose towards us in the salvation of our souls."[59] In another sermon, Donne similarly condemns the "over-pure despisers of others; Men that will abridge and contract the large mercies of God in Christ and elude and frustrate in a great part, the general promises of God."[60] According to Donne, it is men, not God, who deny "that Christ should spread his armes, or shed his bloud in such a compasses, as might fall upon all."[61] While "Reason is our Soules left hand" certainly plays with the conventions of patronage by having grace fall, if not on all, at least on both himself and Bedford, it also takes issue with a doctrine of the "Saints" he considered divisive, and which Bedford herself supported. In querying the restriction of grace to the elect, Donne's verse letter thus revisits the terms and concerns of the reading to which it alludes.

During the same period in which Donne was studying Bedford in what she "read" and "devize[d]," he was also sharing a wide range of texts with her through Henry Goodere. Donne often included letters to Bedford in larger "pacquets" to Goodere, and when he was abroad he frequently asked Goodere to hand-deliver his "poor Letters to her Ladiships hands" (96).[62] Both rhetorically and literally, Donne often presumed that Bedford was present when Goodere was reading his letters. In one letter he expresses his desire that his name pass through Goodere "to that Noble Lady in whose presence you are," and in another he asks Goodere to "kisse her hands, in whose protection I am" (261, 173). He also assumed that Bedford habitually "hear[d]" his letters to Goodere, and that his letters to Goodere would be sent on to Bedford ("That good woman," 149) when he was done with them.[63] This presumed triangulation was so habitual that on one occasion, when Donne expressed his *un*willingness to say anything about Bedford

[59] Donne, "Sermon LXIX: The fifth of my Prebend Sermons upon my five Psalms," in *LXXX Sermons*, 702. Cited in Strier, "Awry and Squint," 362.

[60] Donne, "Sermon XLIV" in *Fifty Sermons*, 416.

[61] Donne, "Sermon XLIV," 417.

[62] He also included letters for Goodere in packages he sent to Bedford: "I writ to you yesterday taking the boldnesse to put a letter into the good Ladies pacquet for you" (*Letters*, 195). In one letter he wonders about the whereabouts of his letters, "which have been many, and large, and too confident to be lost, especially since, (as I remember) they always conveyed others to that good lady" (*Letters*, 148).

[63] In one letter he tells Goodere to "Send this Letter to that good woman, for it is not only mine" (149).

"upon record, that should not testifie to my thankfulnesse for all her graces," he explicitly "importunes" Goodere to burn the letter (218).

Donne also frequently asked Goodere to slip documents of his own execution into Bedford's papers. At one point he asks him to put a translation of French verses "amongst [the Countess's] papers," and on another to add one of his verse letters to her "other papers" (67). In a verse letter to Magdalene Herbert, Donne similarly imagines one of his poems amidst the papers in Herbert's "cabinet." [64] Yet with Bedford he literalizes the conceit, placing his own work in the midst of his patron's working papers. Donne's epistolary exchange with Bedford is at once deferential and honorific, and insistently, even aggressively, intertextual.

Goodere also may have passed on to Bedford some of the many books he exchanged with Donne. In one letter Donne asks Goodere to return the copy of some "Cases of conscience" he loaned to him (226), and in others he alludes to his "problemes" (probably the "Paradoxes and Problems"); a "ragge of [his] verses"; and a wide range of both manuscript and printed books, many of which were theological or doctrinal in nature (88). In one letter, for example, he asks Goodere for a copy of "Baldvinus," a book about the imagined reconciliation of Catholicism and Protestantism, and in another he asks for the "Apology" (Robert Parson's Catholic *Treatise Tending Towards Mitigation,* 1608)—which, he tells Goodere, "by occasion of reading the Deans answer to it, I have sometimes want" (66).[65] (At this point, as R. C. Bald points out, Donne was probably helping Thomas Morton, the "Dean" he alludes to, to compose his own response to Parson.[66]) In still another letter Donne asks Goodere to "send to my lodging my written Books," and to "send that Letter in which I sent you certain heads which I proposed to enlarge, for I have them not in any other paper" (226). Most Donne scholars believe that these "heads," the conventional form in which the key argumentative points in a work of religious polemic were expressed and circulated, were those that Donne would "enlarge" into *Pseudo-Martyr,* his notorious defense of James's Oath of Allegiance. In the "Advertisement to the reader" prefixed to *Pseudo-Martyr,* Donne refers to "these Heads having been caried about, many monethes," "quarrelled

[64] Donne, "To Mrs. M.H." in Grierson, l. 34, p. 216. The letter imagines the fate of his own verses, including Herbert's engagement with them. As he directs his "mad paper" (l. 1, p. 216), "When [Herbert] resolves his papers, marke what show / Of favour, she alone, to them doth make (ll. 39–40, p. 217).

[65] Bald points out that the book was not, in fact, by Baldvinus, but rather Georges Cassandre "and it was an appeal by a moderate Catholic for compromise and reconciliation with the Protestants. The authorship was ascribed to Baldvinus (François Bauduin) because he arranged for the printing of the book in Paris at the time of the opening of the Colloquy of Poissy" (*John Donne: A Life,* 219).

[66] Bald, *John Donne,* 210.

by some, and desired by others."[67] Two days after he first wrote to Goodere asking for these "heads," Donne wrote to ask for them again: "If you have laid my papers and books by," he writes, "I pray let this messenger have them, I have determined upon them" (68). As Bald writes, "all through the summer of 1609 the outline of Donne's argument was available to his friends and acquaintances, and he himself was assiduously extending his reading, collecting facts and opinions to support his case" (219). If Goodere had a copy of the outline for Donne's defense of the Oath of Allegiance at Twickenham in 1609, it is likely that Bedford had access to it as well. It is highly likely, moreover, that she would have been among those who "quarreled" with it.[68]

Donne alludes specifically to Bedford in another letter to Goodere in which he discusses the work of William Barlow, the man who wrote the first and, in his opinion, inadequate, defense of James's Oath.[69] For Donne, Barlow was a mere "advocate," writing as though religion was "a temporall inheritance" determined by men, rather than a matter of truth. In his third satire, one of the first Donne poems that we know the Countess of Bedford read, Donne argues vociferously against precisely this kind of practice, indicting those who "obey / The statecloth where the Prince sate yesterday" in order to determine "true religion" (ll. 48, 43, p. 156). Instead he advises, much like Sidney before him, that it order to "rightly obey power" men ought to "knowe" her "bondes" (l. 100, p. 158). In the letter to Goodere Donne suggests, as he so often does, that "both sides may be in justice, and innocence," and criticizes Barlow's "inconsequent and unscholarlike arguings," "ridiculous triflings," and "extreme flatteries" of the King (*Letters*, 163). (In his satire of a "Courtier's Library," Donne is more explicitly critical, accusing Barlow of being a political time-server,

---

[67] Donne, *Pseudo-Martyr*, ¶1ʳ; see also Bald, *John Donne*, 219.

[68] While the Oath of Allegiance demanded vows of loyalty from all English men and women, especially Catholics, James insisted that he intended "no persecution against them for conscience cause, but onely desired to be secured of them for civill obedience." Yet the Oath itself allowed Catholics to continue practicing their faith in their consciences, and falsely divided the spiritual from the civil, an untenable separation for Protestants like Bedford. If Donne considered uncompromising Jesuits the problem, given their encouragement of other Catholics to reject the Oath of Allegiance, for Bedford, all countenancing with and sympathy for papists—allowing them, as both the Oath and Donne's defense of it did, to maintain their Catholic beliefs provided they swore allegiance to the Protestant King—would have been unacceptable.

[69] William Barlow's bishop-favoring account of the Hampton Court Conference (1604), was notorious for accrediting James I with the line "No Bishop, no King," and for creating (and promoting) the story that the monarchy and the puritans were destined to collide. (He also has James claim that "I shall make [the puritans] conform themselves or have them out of the land, or else do worse": *The svmme and svbstance of the conference*, 82.)

particularly in the way he turned against the Earl of Essex.[70]) Those whose active function it is to guard religion, Donne tells Goodere, "must endevour this unity in Religion: and we at our lay Alters (which are our tables, or bedside, or stools, wheresoever we dare prostrate ourselves to God in prayer)," must not only work for unity ourselves, but "take heed of making misconclusions upon the want of it" (164). For "whether the Maior and Alderman fall out," he offers in a telling analogy, "(as with us and the Puritans; Bishops against Priests) or the Commoners voices differ who is Maior and who is Alderman, or what their Jurisidiction (as with the Bishop of Rome, or whosoever), *yet it is still one Corporation*" (164, emphasis added). This strong statement of universal Christendom concludes with the following injunction to Goodere: "Never leave the remembrance of my poor service unmentioned when you see the good lady" (164). Like his invocation of Bedford at the end of his letter about "over-obedient papists" and "inobedient puritans," Donne's tag line implicitly includes Bedford in the foregoing conversation. By concluding the letter's plea for religious "unity" with a "reminder" of his loyal service to Bedford, Donne seems to have hoped that he might effect a reconciliation between his views and Bedford's. (Many critics, including Bald, have cited Donne's reference to a "fall[ing] out" between "us and the Puritans" in this letter as Donne's first declaration of his new-found loyalty to the Church of England. In context, however, it seems to be a kind of face-to-face with Bedford.) If

---

[70] Donne owned a copy of Barlow's treatise, which he bound with five other tracts. See Geoffrey Keynes, *A Bibliography of Dr. John Donne*. The composite volume is catalogued as UCL (syn. 7.60.26), and seems to be dedicated to the tumultuous years between the Essex rebellion and the early Jacobean religious settlement. In addition to the Barlow, it includes the *Constitutions and Canons* (1604) (which, among other things, condemns "publicke opposition between preachers"); Thomas Roger's critics-accommodating exposition of the 39 Articles (1607); and the polemical work of Matthew Sutcliffe and Gabriel Powell. (Despite being a strict Calvinist and believer in particular election and reprobation, Powell avers the "absolute authority given by God to the church" over ceremonies and rites in his *Consideration of deprived and silenced ministers*, 1606). Bacon's *Declaration of the Practices & Treasons attempted and committed by Robert late Earle of Essex and his accomplices* (1601) was the final book in the volume. (It was Bacon, of course, who tried Essex.) This composite volume does not, however, attest to a clear alliance on Donne's part with the established powers. Indeed his satirical *The Courtier's Library*, a work concerned with the abuse of reading, includes explicit criticism of some of the authors and positions in the volume. It mocks Matthew Sutcliffe's polemical prolixity and arrogance with the mock title "What not? Or a confutation of all errors in Theology as well as in the other sciences, and the mechanical arts, by all men, dead, living, and to be born, put together one night after supper, by Doctor Sutcliffe," and judges Essex's judges even more harshly. Both William Barlow and Francis Bacon, who had been Essex's supporters before his fall, are portrayed as hypocritical and disloyal. (Barlow gave the Paul's Cross sermon defending the execution of Essex, for which he was rewarded with a bishopric.) *The Courtier's Library* includes a treatise called "The Lawyers' Onion, or the Art of weeping during trials," which is credited to Bacon. See Piers Brown, "Hac ex consilio meo," 849, 863.

Donne was concerned about Bedford's co-religionists "making misconclu-sions upon the want of" unity in religion, then this letter, which promotes just such a unity, can be understood as an argument against schism. His "poor service" to the good lady, conducted primarily through the exchange of texts, was a continual process of negotiation, and it was one in which the stakes were very high.

II. "TWICKNAM GARDEN"

While we know a great deal about what Donne wrote to Bedford, both indirectly and directly, there is some evidence than Bedford wrote to him as well. In a letter that he sent to Goodere in 1609, Donne summarizes and includes a copy of a letter that he sent to Bedford asking her "for the verses she shewed [him] in the garden" at Twickenham (64).[71] In the letter itself he writes, with characteristic disingenuity, that he does not remem-ber ever having "seen a petition in verse" before, so he does not want to be "singular" in adding his poem "to [her] other papers" (67). He claims that he is happy, however, to petition her for her *own* verses—those that she did him "the honour to see in Twicknam garden" (67). In "humbly beg[ging] her" for her verses, Donne promises something that he argues would be "threatning" to "any of [her] other compositions": namely that he "will not shew" them to others, and that he "will not beleeve them" (67). Donne not only alludes to other, as yet undiscovered, "compositions," but he acknowledges their normally public and persuasive nature. Habitually, he suggests, Bedford's "compositions" circulated widely and were geared towards convincing readers to "believe" something. Nothing else "that comes from [Bedford's] brain or breast," he argues, should be "so used"; that is, only her verses should be considered private and treated with skep-ticism. (Donne's promise that he will "not believe" her verses is a pun: an acknowledgement of the modesty topos that attends any poetic composi-tion, and a nod towards the typically religiously polemical nature of her "compositions.") With one notable exception, Bedford's verses are now lost, but Donne's allusion to her public and persuasive "compositions" in a letter that both exemplifies and refers to the exchange of "papers" between the two of them, suggests that their exchange went both ways.

---

[71] The letter is particularly neostoic. Donne writes that "if we be frozen, and contracted with lower and dark fortunes, we have within us a torch, a soul, lighter and warmer then any without" (*Letters*, 63). Gosse dates it to 1609 (1: 220). In his letters, Donne frequently alludes to visits to Twickenham, see e.g. 53–4, 117, 139, 143; see also Lewalski, *Writing Women*, p. 360 n. 10.

In another letter to Goodere, much of it focusing on the 1609 truce between the United Provinces and Philip III of Spain, Donne once again alludes to Bedford's verses. He asks Goodere to give an enclosed letter and poem "to the best Lady, who did me the honour to acknowledge the receit of one of mine, by one of hers" (117).[72] This letter was written ten days after the death of one of Bedford's attending gentlewomen, Cecilia Bulstrode, at Twickenham Park, and alludes to a series of elegies exchanged between Donne and Bedford in the subsequent months. Centering, as do the other verse letters, on controversial matters of faith and works, Donne and Bedford's poems on Bulstrode's death serve as the best index of the religiously and politically charged nature of their exchange.

In his first "Elegie on Mris Boulstred," Donne refers to Bulstrode as one of the elect. Writing to a personified "Death," Donne claims that while Death lays many bodies at God's feet, God "Reserve[s] but few, and leaves the most to thee" (ll. 34–5, p. 283). (When Donne writes that Death could have gotten more people if he hadn't taken Bulstrode when she was still so young—the devotion others felt for her might have "stray'd to superstition" (58) and led them astray—he alludes to both saint-worshiping Catholics and to the indeterminate means of salvation.) Claude J. Summers has argued that, despite the fact that Donne's elegy presents Bulstrode as "an exemplar of the regenerate soul," the poem's "universalizing" of death was "insufficiently congruent with the Calvinist principle of predestination to which Bedford subscribed."[73] Regardless, Donne's elegy solicited a poem of her own in response. As Donne writes in his letter to Goodere, Bedford "did me the honour to acknowledge the receit of one of mine, by one of hers."

This poem, credited to the Countess of Bedford in multiple manu-scripts, is a response both to Donne's elegy and to one of the most famous of his Holy Sonnets.[74] "Death be not proud," Bedford's elegy begins, "thy hand gave not this blow" (l. 1, p. 422). Bulstrode's "clearer soule," Bedford asserts, was

> call'd to endlesse rest,
> (Not by the thundering voice, wherewith God threats,
> But, as with crowned Saints in heaven he treats,)
> And, waited on by Angels, home was brought. (ll. 8–11)

---

[72] See also Gosse, 1: 217.

[73] Summers, "Donne's 1609 Sequence of Grief and Comfort," 225.

[74] On two of the manuscripts, RP31 and H40, see Grierson, *The Poems of John Donne*, 2: 209. For Grierson's reading of the poem as "to some extent a rebuke to Donne" for his "too pagan or too Catholic" poems on Death, see 2: 215. Evidence for her authorship is set out in Milgate, *John Donne: Epithalamions, Anniversaries, and Epicedes*, appendix B, 235–7.

Making her faith in double predestination explicitly clear—the parentheses surrounding its expression suggest less the extricability of the doctrine than its taken-for-grantedness—Bedford commands Death to go instead to "people curst before they were," a belief she undoubtedly knew that Donne rejected (l. 21). It is this very formulation he refutes, in almost identical terms, in the fifth prebend sermon when he asserts that we should not believe that God damns us "before we were." The tears her friends cry for Bulstrode, Bedford tells her personified Death, are "The mourning livery given by Grace, not thee, / Which wils our soules in these streams washt should be" (ll. 25–6). Concerning the matter of repentance, Bedford plays up grace as the agent of will—it *"wils* our soules"—implicitly refuting those, like Donne, who value the "work" of repentance itself.

The question of repentance was, in fact, the subject of many of the Holy Sonnets—poems which were not only composed during the same period, but to which Bedford alludes in her own elegy. (In addition to citing it in its opening line, Bedford's poem concludes with a sententious rebuttal of Donne's own aphoristically famous "Death be Not Proud": *"The grave no conquest gets, Death hath no sting"* (l. 42, p. 423).) Richard Strier has suggested that the Holy Sonnets reveal Donne's "difficulties with and occasional successes at imprinting Calvinism on a soul that had, as Donne himself put it in the preface to *Pseudo-Martyr,* 'first to blot out, certaine impressions of the Romane religion.' "[75] Whether we see the struggles in the sonnets as personal or casuistical, repentance is nonetheless one of their central concerns. To take only one example, the clausal conditional that marks the volta in "Of my blacke Soule," "Yet, grace, *if thou repent,* you canst not lack," refocuses attention on repentance as the key to grace, rather than, as Bedford asserts in her poem, the other way around (l. 9, emphasis added).[76] The sonnet's next line, "But who shall give thee that grace to beginne?" (l. 10), seems to reassert the sufficiency of grace, but is followed instead by the speaker's turn to penitential effort ("Oh make thy selfe with holy mourning blacke"), which, in Strier's reading, "supervenes the Calvinism" of the previous line (371). (It also seems to mimic the clausal correctives we see in the tenth of the Thirty-Nine Articles.) Strier suggests that "Oh my black Soule" presents individual repentance and Christ's sacrifice as alternative ways to salvation, but it seems to me that they are, in Donne's terms, "conficient" or codeterminative. The poem,

---

[75] *Pseudo-Martyr,* "Preface," B3r, cited in Strier, "Awry and Squint," 367. See also: "You shall seldome see a Coyne, upon which the stampe were removed, though to imprint it better, but it looks awry and squint" (*Letters,* 101).

[76] See also Strier, "Awry and Squint," 370–1.

like many of the Holy Sonnets, thus treads the same controversial ground that Donne and Bedford take up in the Bulstrode elegies.[77]

In response to Bedford's, Donne wrote another elegy on Bulstrode's death. (This is the poem he asks Goodere to give to her in the letter cited.) Summers sees this third elegy as an "oblique apology," responding to Bedford's objections using her own terms, but "subtly subvert[ing]" them.[78] In a seemingly undermining allusion to Bedford's reference to Bulstrode's elect place among the "crowned saints in heaven" in her own poem, Donne declares that Bulstrode's death could be a "Saint['s]" "holiday" (l. 44, p. 286)—a specifically Catholic practice. Yet rather than "subverting" Bedford's terms in order to mark their religious differences, Donne's allusion seems instead to highlight a matter of *in*difference, the *adiaphora* of intra-Christian debate that he discusses in his earlier letter to Goodere. "[W]hat we turne to *feast*," he writes a few lines later in his elegy, "she turn'd to *pray*" (l. 48). Donne's evocation of these different modes of celebration—Catholic feast and godly prayer—renders them *in*different, presented as they are in metrical and syntactical balance. By chiastically configuring Bulstrode both as a Catholic saint and as a feast-resisting worshiper, Donne creates a kind of similitude between things only falsely considered irreconcilable.[79]

At the end of his second elegy on Bulstrode, Donne characterizes his poem as a form of consolation for her "sad, glad friends," who grieve at losses that "would waste a Stoick's heart" (l. 62).[80] As at the very beginning of "A Valediction: forbidding mourning," when the mourners' feelings of

---

[77] See e.g. "Thou hast made me," in which the speaker claims that "Thy Grace *may* wing me to prevent [Satan's] art" (l. 13). The speaker in "As due by many titles" similarly reckons with faith alone and predestination: "Except thou rise and for thine owne worke fight," he tells God, "Oh I shall soone despaire, when I doe see / That thou lov'st mankind well, yet wilt not chuse me" (ll. 12–14). This final poem expresses what Strier calls "a sense of injured merit" ("Awry and Squint," 370). In "On New-yeares day" Donne expresses a similarly ambivalent take on the role of repentance: "From need of teares he will defend your soule, / Or make a rebaptizing of one teare" (p. 201, ll. 61–2).

[78] Summers, "Donne's 1609 Sequence of Grief and Comfort," 227–8.

[79] Indeed Ben Jonson's own elegy on Bulstrode's death—also an "oblique apology" for an earlier poem—uses a similar configuration to Donne's, identifying Bulstrode as "the Sole Religious house, and Votary / With Rites not bound, but conscience." Jonson's characterization similarly presents Bulstrode in explicitly Catholic terms ("Votary"), and acknowledges the differences between a church "bound" with "Rites" and one bound by "conscience" (Jonson, ll. 10–11, p. 372). Yet the enjambment of the lines—the way in which "Rites" are not "bound" to the "Religious house" of the previous line—suggests continuity, rather than supercession. (Like Donne, Jonson himself had "turned" between Catholic and Protestant (feast and prayer), and thus his presentation of things indifferent can also be seen as a form of accommodation.) See also Robert W. Halli Jr., "Cecilia Bulstrode, 'The Court Pucell.' "

[80] The beginning of "A Valediction: forbidding mourning" features virtuous men who "passe mildly away / And whisper to their soules, to goe," "Whilst some of their sad friends soe say, / The breath goes no, and some say, no" (ll. 1–4, p. 49).

loss signal their belief in, or doubt about, the dying man's salvation (some say "The breath goes now, and some say, no" (l. 4, p. 49)), Bulstrode's "sad, glad friends" embody what remains a dilemma for Donne. This dilemma, moreover, is one with which Bedford dispatches handily in her own poem on Bulstrode's death: the tears Bulstrode's friends cry in her poem are for their *"own* harm" (their loss of their friend), "not for hers" (l. 24). (They are sure, that is, of Bulstrode's election.) Yet when Donne mentions a grief that "would waste a Stoick's heart," he also alludes to the politico-philosophical beliefs that undergirded the community of Bulstrode's "sad, glad friends," and the specific discourse they used for expressing their political and religious discontent. "Would," of course, is a conditional, and the place holder at the end of the poem is the "Stoick's heart," a location not only for managing the passions, but for maintaining a condition associated with aristocratic resistance and critique.[81] Donne had already configured Bedford as a keeper of a "Stoick's heart" in "Reason is our Soules left hand": a "rock" that no "wave" could undermine. Samuel Daniel similarly praised her in a 1603 verse epistle for the neostoic fortitude which he also located in the "Kingdome" of her "Breast": a place not subject, as he rather pointedly puts it, to "others pow'rs" or "royalties."[82] In making use of the neostoicism habitually associated with the Sidney-Essex alliance, Donne thus both acknowledges Bedford's political affiliations and subjects some of her beliefs to scrutiny. Like the other poems Donne exchanged with Bedford, the elegies on Bulstrode's death "represent the voices of an argument," revealing Donne's intimate, first-hand knowledge of the theological, political, and philosophical investments of Lucy Harington Russell and her "friends."

These "friends," moreover, were also invoked in another key textual context for the Bulstrode poems—one in which both Donne and Bulstrode herself were participants. Early in James's reign, Bulstrode and Donne participated in a literary game of wit in which players exchanged politically and religiously topical "news" reports.[83] (The exchanges would eventually

---

[81] A poem in the Dalhousie manuscripts, Sir John Roe's poem to "Mrs Boulstred," which most critics take as proof of their affair, also makes references to these literary tropes and practices. See Sullivan, *Dalhousie Manuscripts*, 79–80. Roe alludes to his work in "despisd Poetry" as something that might "spill" his "fortunes," or "undoe" him, "By having but that dangerous name in court" (80). He thus asks Bulstrode to "keepe" his "lines as secret as [his] love" (80). Rather than testament to an affair, this line is likely an allusion to the political nature of the (anti-)court games to be discussed later; games which took place in Bulstrode's "pit."

[82] Daniel, *Complete Works*, vol. 1, ll. 55, 56, 60, p. 211. Like Donne, Daniel pays particular attention to Bedford's studies, which he calls the "hands and arms of action" (l. 11, p. 209).

[83] See James E. Savage (ed. and commentary), *The "Conceited Newes" of Sir Thomas Overbury and his Friends.* See also Louise Schleiner, *Tudor and Stuart Women Writers,* 109: through these games "moved information, innuendos, reputations, and the makings

be published in 1614 in an appendage to *The Wife. Now the Widow of Sir Thomas Overby* titled "Newes, from Anywence: or Old Truthes under a supposal of Noueltie.") In addition to Donne and Bulstrode, the players included Sir Benjamin Rudyerd, William Herbert's parliamentary spokesman, and the diplomat Sir Thomas Roe—both "Saints" elected to some extent by Bedford.[84] The "Newes" was organized around a "court" and "country" binary; evoked both the ambitions and the religious and political dispositions of its players; and was used as a means of cementing their alliance and rehearsing and thus circulating their views. The politically charged nature of the game is hinted at by the contemporaneous and related circulation of an "outrageous and unchristian" libel attacking the King. When Cecil and Sir Edward Coke attempted to track it down in 1605, a "Mistress Russell" who worked in Bedford's household could only tell them that she did not know who wrote it, nor anybody who had a copy, "*saving only Mrs. Bulstrode*, that waits upon the Countess of Bedford."[85] Bedford's "friends," in other words, were circulating, or at least reading, manuscript attacks on the King. While the published traces we have of the game of "Newes" are less explosively charged than this lost libel, it seems likely that there was some overlap in the kinds of papers "Mrs. Bulstrode, that waits upon the Countess of Bedford" had in her possession. The "Newes" exchanges express the anti-Spanish and militant Protestantism associated with Bedford's circle, and their posture of stoic withdrawal—the participants write either outside the court, or at a critical "country" distance from its machinations—associates them with the alliance's habitual discourse of critique.

One of the most anti-Catholic and anti-Spanish pieces in the volume, the "Newes from the very countrey," is credited to J.D., whom most scholars presume to be John Donne.[86] It includes a joke about Jesuits, which, like apricots, used to be "succoured in a great mans house, and cost dear," but can now

of useful or possibly harmful ties among courtiers." See also Lawson, *Out of the Shadows*, 80: players were given a theme and composed a "sequence of witty sayings which consisted of news appropriate to the location from which they were writing ... Players of the opposing team the attempted an 'answer' in the form of an antithetical response." John Considine argues that the "Newes" exchanges were written by hack writers ("The Invention of the Literary Circle of Sir Thomas Overbury"). In light of the independent corroboration of gaming activities at court, Donald Beecher rejects Considine's "adventurous thesis," and proposes instead that "the Overbury materials were imitations" of actual court practices, and that Lisle hired hack writers "to simulate their activities" (*Characters*, 59, 61). I am grateful to Christina Luckyj for these references.

[84] On Roe's relationship with Bedford, see Lewalski, *Writing Women*, 97, and Michael Strachan, *Sir Thomas Roe*, 12–14 and 170.

[85] HMC Salisbury (Cecil) MS (London: HMSO, 1938), vol. XVII, p. 115, emphasis added, cited in Lawson, *Out of the Shadows*, 78.

[86] The piece was signed "J.D." On Donne as the author, see Savage.

be found "for nothing in every cottage," and it talks about trouble coming in from Spain.[87] Bulstrode's own contribution, a response to B.R.'s (Benjamin Rudyerd's) "News from my Lodging," has a similar tenor: "Honesty in the Court," she writes, "lives in persecution, like Protestants in Spain" (250).[88] The "Foreign News" section in the volume, which the volume's recent editor believes was written by Donne's friend and former Essex ally Sir Henry Wotton, expresses similar opinions; among other things, it identifies the Low Countries as "the grounds of man's libertie." For James I, who honored the pro-monarchical stance of the Habsburgs, the Low Countries represented republicanism and Presbyterianism; for those like Bedford who promoted an internationalist Protestantism, the Low Countries were the grounds of liberty and Spain and the Habsburg empire the implacable enemy.[89] The fact that Donne specifically discusses the 1609 truce between the United Provinces and Philip III of Spain in the letter in which he sends Goodere the Bulstrode elegy suggests a continuum between the concerns expressed in the "Newes" and in Donne's other, routinely triangulated, exchanges with Bedford. The "Newes," then, provides a further context in which to understand both the poems and the networks of literary exchange of which Donne's epistolary dialogue with Bedford was part.

The best known contemporary allusion to the "Newes" occurs in Ben Jonson's "Epigram on the Court Pucell," a poem usually noted for its rather spectacular misogyny. "The Court Pucell," or whore, was none other than Cecilia Bulstrode. In this poem, Jonson explicitly locates the "Newes," a game which makes "State, Religion, Bawdrie, all a theme," in Bulstrode's "Chamber": "the very pit / Where fight the prime Cocks of the game, for wit."[90] Jonson's satirical account of Bulstrode—she "cling[s]" to "Lords" and then leaves them to cling to "Sermoneeres" (ll. 38–9)—also serves as an index of the game's key players and values: the power of the "Lords" and

---

[87] The speaker of the reply, the "Answere to the very Countrey News," also expresses anti-Spanish and anti-Catholic sentiment. She mentions living by the churchyard "where many are buried of the Pest," yet fearing far more an "infection" coming "from *Spaine*," that "will disperse further into the Kingdome" than the plague (234). As Lawson points out, "This witty turn of phrase would have played well to the vehemently anti-Spanish politics of the assembled group" (*Out of the Shadows*, 80).

[88] Another political aphorism: "That vertues favour is better then a Kings favourite" (250).

[89] See S. L. Adams, "Foreign Policy and the Parliaments of 1621 and 1624," 141.

[90] Jonson, "An Epigram on the Court Pucell" in *Works of Ben Jonson*, vol. 8, ll. 12, 3, p. 222–3. Lewalski claims Jonson satirizes Bedford (and Twickenham Park) as "Lady Haughty" in *Epicoene*: "[She will] be a states-woman, know all the newes, what was done at *Salisbury*, what at the *Bath*, what at court, what in progresse; or so shee may censure *poets*, and authors, and stiles [...] be thought cunning in controversies, or the very knots of divinitie; and have, often in her mouth, the state of the question: and then skip to the *Mathematiques*, and demonstration and answere, in religion to one; in state, to another, in baud'ry to a third" (Lewalski, *Writing Women*, 110).

the support of a godly preaching ministry, or "Sermoneeres." "The court is the worst place," Jonson writes towards the end of the poem, "Both for the Mothers and the Babes of Grace" (l. 44). There is certainly a bawdy joke here, but Jonson's use of political-religious terms that appear in contemporary anti-puritan satire—"Sermoneeres" and "Babes of Grace" were pejorative terms for the godly—suggests that he too was aware of the players' values.[91] The "court," moreover, stands in contradistinction to the "pit" where the game was played: Bulstrode's "Chamber" at the Countess of Bedford's Twickenham estate, where she spent much of her time and, as we have just seen, where she died. ("Pit" is a singularly charged term, evoking everything from a trap for wild animals or an enclosure in which they are made to fight (a "cockpit"), to an underground prison and, most tellingly, a "feudal privilege of trial or punishment involving a water-filled pit."[92]) Twickenham Park, in whose "garden" Donne read Bedford's verses, was thus not only seen as a site of literary production and exchange, but also of theo-political opposition and critique—even, as I suggest here, a kind of counter court.

Bedford obtained the lease of Twickenham Park, a 100-acre estate near Hampton Court formerly occupied by Francis Bacon, through Goodere in 1607 and lived there until 1617/18.[93] As the topical notoriety of the "Newes" suggests, contemporaries imagined Twickenham both as retreat or refuge and as a base of (resistant) operations. Donne's "Twicknam Garden" (in some manuscripts, the poem is identified as a verse letter "To the Countess of Bedford. Twitnam Garden") deploys all of the familiar tropes of idealized retreat. The poem is officially about love (the speaker brings the "serpent" of desire to "Paradise," l. 9), but it is told in the conventional language of retreat, complete with the winter of the speaker's own courtly ambitions. "Blasted with sighs, and surrounded with teares," the poem's speaker comes "Hither" (to "Twicknam") to "seeke the spring" (ll. 1–2, p. 28). " 'Twere wholsomer for mee that winter did / Benight the glory of this place," he claims, hoping merely to be "some senslesse peece of this place," a "stone fountaine weeping out [his] yeare" (ll. 10–11,

[91] In Jonson's metaphor, Bulstrode's "Religious House" contrasts with the "Court," where the "Babes of grace" are not welcome.

[92] Among the *OED* definitions are the following: "A hole or excavation made for the storage and protection of roots"; "A hole dug in the ground for a dead body; a grave"; "A covered or concealed hole serving as a trap for a wild animal or an enemy"; "A deep hole or underground chamber for the confinement of a prisoner or prisoners; a dungeon"; "Hell"; "Chiefly *Sc. Law.* A feudal privilege of trial or punishment involving a water-filled pit or waterhole. In later use: the feudal right to imprison criminals"; and "An enclosure in which animals may be set to fight one another for sport; esp. a cockpit."

[93] On Twickenham, see Bald, *John Donne*, 172; and Gosse, 1: 210.

16, 18). The speaker desires refuge in "this place" both to "weepe out his year" of disappointed retreat, and to establish himself as Bedford's most faithful acolyte. Future followers will come with "christal vyalls" to take his tears, "For all are false, that taste not just like mine" (ll. 19, 22). Like the other poems discussed so far, "Twicknam Garden" expresses Donne's desire for ongoing patronage. According to the Petrarchan poetics of mastery and subjection—as well as the realities of patronage—Bedford does, as the poem suggests, have the power to "kill him" (l. 27). Yet the poem also expresses Donne's recognition and promotion of Twickenham Park's stature as a place of retreat from court life—always itself a signal of political ambition.[94]

Another of Donne's verse letters to Bedford, the poem known as "You have refin'd me," also imagines Twickenham Park in opposition to the court. The "Court," he writes, is "not vertues clime," "Where a transcendent height, (as lowness me) / Makes her [Bedford] not be" (ll. 7–9, p. 191). Bedford is not at court, that is, because the court is not virtue's clime, and her "transcendent height" places her both above and outside its machinations. While Donne offers to be Bedford's emissary, "For, as darke texts need notes: there some must bee / To usher virtue, and say, *This is shee*" (ll. 11–12), he also positions Twickenham Garden as a place apart. Simon Adams has argued that, around 1610, the political puritanism with which Bedford was associated suffered a collapse at court and, as he puts it, "retired to the country."[95] Donne's poems about Twickenham date from the same period, and they seem to refer to precisely this kind of retirement.

In "You have refin'd me," the speaker claims that Beauty is "in the country," so he has come "to this place," Twickenham, where Bedford serves both as "the season" and "the day" (ll. 13–14, p. 191). The garden at Twickenham Park was laid out as a pre-Copernican universe, and Bedford, whom Jonson in another poem called "the brightnesse of our spheare," did symbolically reign over her place much as Donne describes.[96] "Since a new world doth rise here from your light," Donne writes, "We your new creatures, by new reckonings go" (ll. 21–2). Now that she has made "the Court the Antipodes"

> And will'd your Delegate, the vulgar Sunne,
> To doe profane autumnall offices,

[94] See e.g. Montrose, "Of Gentlemen and Shepherds."

[95] Adams, "The Protestant Cause," 171.

[96] Mark Girouard, *Robert Smythson and the Architecture of the Elizabethan Era*, 122. Jonson, "Epigram 94" in *Complete Works*, vol. 8, l. 1, pp. 60–1. For a fascinating discussion of Donne's decentering of the traditional cosmic image that linked the monarch with the sun, see William Empson, "Donne the Space Man." *Kenyon Review*, 19/3 (1957): 337–99.

> Whilst here to you we sacrificers run;
> And whether Priests, or Organs, you wee'obey
> We sound your influence, and your Dictates say. (ll. 25–30)

In this conceit, Bedford's "creatures," like Donne, are her "Priests," deploying their literary talents or voices—their "Organs"—in her service. Through her patronage they are able to "sound" (both express, and determine) her influence, and "say" or promote her "Dictates."[97] They are able, in other words, to extend her influence beyond the sphere of Twickenham at the same time as they preserve its integrity.

Yet, Donne argues in a turn away from the initial direction of the conceit, he does not plan to "sacrifice" anything "to that Deity which dwells in" Twickenham (ll. 31–2). Rather than "*Hymns*" of devotion, his poems "are *Petitions*": documents one presents when one wants something (l. 33). "They sue," he writes, "But that I may survey the edifice" (l. 34). The speaker's desire to "survey" the "edifice"—a conflation of Twickenham and Bedford herself—seems to be kind of reconnaissance mission. To "survey" is to "examine and ascertain the condition, situation, or value of (e.g. the boundaries, tenure, value, etc.) of an estate, a building or structure" (*OED* 1). Donne's use of this verb thus alludes not only to Bedford's notoriously difficult financial situation, but also to Twickenham's suitability, and sustainability, as a site of political power.[98]

Donne concludes his "survey" of Bedford's "edifice" by comparing it, in opposition to "all / Bablers of [other] chapels," to "th'Escuriall" (l. 48).[99]

---

[97] On "Dictates," see Joyce S. Beck, "Donne's Scholastic 'Ars Dictaminis,'" 27.

[98] On the Bedford finances, see Margaret M. Byard, "Trade of Courtiership." The Earl's part in the Essex rebellion brought him a fine of £20,000, later reduced by half. The death of her father in 1613 and her brother in 1614 made her heir to two-thirds of the Harington estate, but the estate was encumbered with almost £40,000 in debt.

[99] Donne argues that just

> As all which go to Rome, do not thereby
> Esteem religions, and hold fast the best,
> But serve discourse, and curiosity,
> With that which doth religion but invest,
> And shun th' entangling labyrinths of schools,
> And make it wit, to think the wiser fools:
> So in this pilgrimage I would behold
> You as you are virtue's temple (ll. 37–44)

Via an indictment of both those who "shun th'entangling labyrinths of schools," and those who reject learned theologians ("the wiser"), Donne ultimately claims that, as a result of his "survey," he will "oppose to all / Bablers of chapels, you th'Escuriall" (l. 48). As the allusion to the tower of Babel suggests, intra-religious controversy is likened to an internecine exercise in indifferent babbling. (A "Babler" is a person who "talks foolishly or at great length, esp. to little purpose; a chatterer" (*OED* 1), or one who "talks indiscreetly; a teller of secrets; a gossip, a blabber" (*OED* 2).)

While he was certainly idealizing Bedford's "edifice" by analogizing it to one of the most famous buildings in Renaissance Europe, "th'Escuriall" was also iconistically Catholic, and the headquarters, quite literally, of the Spanish crown and Habsburg dynasty Bedford was known to oppose with such vehemence.[100] Donne's analogy thus both highlights Twickenham's status as a semi-analogous headquarters of religious and political activism, and subtly mocks those very ambitions.[101] Donne backs away from the audacity of his claim by claiming that his evaluation is merely aesthetic: Bedford is "not as consecrate, but merely as fair" as the Escorial (l. 49). He comes to her as others come to Rome, not as a believer, but rather as someone who recognizes, outside of denominational differences, the undeniable "vertues" of the site (l. 10).[102] As in "Reason is our Soules left hand," Donne once again "rests on what the Catholique," or universal, "voice doth teach." And after this subtle promotion of religious unity, Donne then leaves religious references behind to analogize Bedford/Twickenham to "the Commonweale" (l. 69), an often anti-absolutist term for the state.[103] Donne thus configures Twickenham both as an idealized retreat and as an alternative model of governance.

In another verse letter Donne praises Bedford as a model of moral transparency, claiming that her followers can see her "hearts thoughts" in her "through-shine front" ("Honour is so sublime perfection," l. 27, p. 219).

---

[100] On the Escorial, see Guy Lazure, "Possessing the Sacred: Monarchy and Identity in Philip II's Relic Collection at the Escorial," *Renaissance Quarterly*, 60(1) (2007): 58–93.

[101] Donne used politically loaded terms to describe other estates as well. He signs a letter to Sir Henry Wotton "From Sir John Danvers house at Chelsey (of which house and my Lord of Carlils at Hanworth I make up my Tusculum" (Bald, *John Donne*, 474). In likening the houses of these two politically powerful men to Tusculum, first mentioned in Roman history as an independent city state with a constitution and gods of its own, Donne was locating the two houses outside of the Court, and thus as places of (politically orientated) retreat. It was in Tusculum, moreover, that Cicero wrote the *Tusculanae Disputationes*, his attempt to popularize Stoic philosophy.

[102] Donne once again alludes to his poems as religious texts, analogizing them to "nice thin school divinity" which can either "further or repress" heresy (here configured as flattery) (ll. 61–2). Yet, he continues, they "need not" exist "where all hearts one truth profess" (l. 64).

[103] In another verse letter written after 1609, "To have written then, when you writ" (it alludes to Markham and Bulstrode as "new starres" sent "lately to the firmament": l. 68), Donne similarly compares Bedford to a "commonwealth" in which "Vice hath no office, or good worke to doe" (ll. 87–8). He consistently figures her in tension with monarchical prerogative. God alone, he suggests in "On New-yeares day" "will best teach" that "good and bad have not / One latitude in cloysters, and in Court" (ll. 41, p. 200). ("Kings," he writes in a similar formulation in "Honour is so sublime perfection," can certainly "*direct*" our honor towards those they would have honored, but they cannot "bestow" it: ll. 8–9, p. 218.) On the term "Commonwealth," see Norbrook: "Essex had inherited the political alignments built up by Leicester, who had been accused of constructing his own 'commonwealth,' a state within a state made up of followers who were anxious for England to play a decisive part in shifting the balance of European politics away from Hapsbury ascendancy, and who built up their own republic of letters, establishing close contact with republicans and religious radicals on the Continent" ("Monarchy of Wit," 11–12).

This remarkable image may allude to the speech James made in response to the discovery of the Gunpowder Plot, in which he expressed his desire for "a crystal window in my breast wherein all my people might see the secretest thoughts of my heart," a vow of religious and political integrity and transparency.[104] James used this line in a discussion about Catholics, contrasting those "heretical" ones who "maintaine by the grounds of their religion, That it was lawfull, or rather meritorious... to murder Princes or people for quarrell of Religion," to those who are simply deluded about some "Schoole-question" or another. Catholics who "lay their onely trust upon CHRIST and his Merits in tharr last breth," James argued, will be saved; the fire is reserved for those "Puritanes" "that will admit no salvation to any Papist" (153). By transposing this image from James to Bedford, Donne was praising her as an exemplary leader in her own right, and as the bearer of an unalterable "Stoick heart." But he was also suggesting that she might nonetheless moderate some of her positions. While it is unlikely that Donne expected that his allusion to James's speech would encourage Bedford to reconsider her own views on "Papists" and "Puritanes" in light of the King's argument, his poem was nonetheless a kind of challenge to a woman who might herself "admit no salvation to any Papist." Donne's poems that explicitly took Twickenham as their subject alluded to Bedford's stature as a political leader, and to Twickenham's status as a place of politicized retreat from the court and a site of comment on its workings. But they also insisted on her critical engagement with other, often contradictory, texts and ideas.

III. "[A] GREAT MISTRESSE OF THE FACTION"

Critics often claim that the relationship between Donne and Bedford "cooled" sometime after 1613, during which time Bedford had become close with the puritan John Burges, a preacher previously exiled by James I in 1604.[105] Under Burges's influence, Donne suggests in a letter to Goodere, Bedford became "more suspicious of [his] calling" as a Church of England minister (he was ordained in 1615), and possessed of a "better memory

---

[104] James I, "A Speech in the Parliament House," delivered 9 November 1605, four days after the discovery of the Gunpowder Plot. *Political Writings*, 147–58.

[105] The King was "so moved that [Burges] should dogmatise (as he called yt) in his court, that he commaunded the archibishop to look to yt who... injoyned him not to practise within ten miles of London," SP 14 (James I) 74/49, 1 August 1613, cited in Lewalski, *Writing Women*, 116. Burges was reinstated in 1616, largely due to the efforts of Bedford. See also Thompson, "John Donne and the Countess of Bedford," esp. 331–4.

of my past life, then I had thought her nobility should have admitted."[106] Religion, as ever, remained both a subject of contention between them and their bond. Shortly thereafter, while he was actively soliciting the patronage of James's then favorite, Robert Carr, Earl of Somerset, Donne considered publishing a book of poems in Carr's honor. He wrote, accordingly, to Goodere to see if Goodere had made any entrepreneurial use of Donne's verse letters to Bedford and thus whether he might be able to include some of them in the volume (*Letters*, 196–8). Critics have seen this letter as evidence that Donne intended to give this volume a "politically balanced" status.[107] At the same moment that Donne was preparing this volume for Carr, Bedford was working with William Herbert at Baynard's Castle to (successfully) engineer the rise of George Villiers as Carr's replacement.[108] Donne may well have wanted to keep his politically opposed patrons happy, but it seems just as likely that his concern about his verse letters to Bedford—a concern that they *retain their particularity*—was in keeping with the dialogic, even provocative, nature of textual exchanges with Bedford that had been going on for years.

Donne continued to visit with and write to Bedford through the early 1620s, during which time Bedford and her alliance had turned their attention to the cause of the Palatinate in Bohemia (and Donne, as we know, became Dean of St Paul's[109]). The battle in Bohemia, between Protestant subjects who rallied behind James's daughter and son-in-law, the Elector and Electress Palatine, as the rightful holders of the throne of Bohemia, and the Habsburgs, who had appointed their own (Catholic) ruler, provided a new focus for the anti-Spanish and international Protestantism of Bedford and her allies. Seeking peace, and worried as ever about militant Protestantism, James refused to intervene with the force many of his subjects desired. Along with her long-term ally William Herbert, who claimed

[106] "I am afraid," Donne writes, that Bedford's negative opinions on Donne "proceed in her rather from some ill impression taken from D. *Burges* than that they grow in her self" (*Letters*, 218). Thomson wonders if Donne was "trying to set himself up as a spiritual advisor to the Twickenham ladies," in competition with Burges ("John Donne and the Countess of Bedford," 333).

[107] On this dual pursuit, see Bald, *John Donne*, 295–9: Donne "proposed not merely to print a collection of his poems, but also to dedicate the volume to Somerset, and to include a selection of verses addressed to other patrons and patronesses as well as to Lady Bedford herself" (296). "Though he did not offend her by going through with this plan, in the upshot Lady Bedford gave Donne only £30 towards the payment of his debts" (*John Donne*, 296). The letter to Goodere is on pp. 194–8 in Donne's *Letters* and cited in full in Bald, *John Donne*, 297.

[108] On Bedford driving out Carr, see also Lloyd's *State Worthies*, 2: 157; and the Introduction to this volume, p. 14, n. 43.

[109] For letters in which he discusses visiting with Bedford, the Palatinate, and sending her letters via Goodere, see *Letters*, 155, 157, 176, 224–5.

that his "every thought was of Bohemia," Bedford played a key role in pro-moting the cause of the Palatinate both at home and abroad.[110] Sometime in 1620, Elizabeth herself wrote to thank Bedford for addressing her as the "Queen of Bohemia," something James had explicitly prohibited. "I wish that others were of your mind," she wrote, "Then I hope there would be taken a better resolution for us heere [in Bohemia] than yet there is." "I think I can easily guess who it is that doth cheiflie hinder the King in resolving," she continued, "but I am sure that though they have English bodies they have Spanish hartes."[111] Bedford's support of the "Queen of Bohemia" was of a piece with her long-term commitment to a militant (and anti-Spanish) Protestantism.

Despite Donne's career trajectory at the time, he was by no means an apologist for the King. In 1619 he went with Lord Doncaster on his mis-sion to Germany, where he preached before the Elector and Electress.[112] Paul Sellin has recently argued that the sermons Donne preached at The Hague indicated his support for the official Calvinist position recently approved at the Synod of Dort.[113] He took a keen interest in continental Protestantism, and his name is found along with Archbishop Abbot's and a few others in a cipher concerned with international Protestantism, a detail that suggests he was more than a distant observer (Sellin, p. 21). In January 1621, Donne preached a sermon before the Countess of Bedford at Harington House that seems to have acknowledged both her current and ongoing investments.[114] Reasserting his "conficient" take on divine grace (as well as the typically clausally confused nature of the matter), Donne preached that God "will much more assist us with His grace, that we may be able to stand in that state with him, to which he hath brought

---

[110] S. L. Adams, "Foreign Policy and the Parliaments of 1621 and 1624," 143.

[111] HMC, 21, Hamilton MSS Supplementary Report (London: HM Stationery Office, 1932), 9 (undated), cited Lewalski, *Writing Women*, 62. A 1621 letter from the Venetian ambassador suggests the extent to which Elizabeth relied on Bedford. Reporting to the Doge on "a genuine letter of the Queen of Bohemia written to one of the leading countesses here, an intimate of hers," the ambassador notes that the Queen asks "the countess if she heard any talk of her coming to this kingdom" (Girolando Lando to the Doge, 30 April 1621, *Cal. SP Venetian*, XVII (1621–3), 37–8, cited in Lewalski, *Writing Women*, 62).

[112] As Bald writes, "although the ambassador was being sent as an impartial arbitrator, nearly all England and most of those close to him in his entourage were whole-heartedly on the side of the Bohemians" (*John Donne*, 343). At Dover he met Bedford who had come there to meet her mother, and at Calais they found Lady Harington, on her way home from the Palatinate (Bald, *John Donne*, 347). In addition, Donne received friendly wishes from the Earl of Pembroke during his mission. Donne also had some of Pembroke's poems in manuscript; the relationship between them was more intimate than is sometimes presumed (Bald, *John Donne*, 351).

[113] Sellin, *John Donne and 'Calvinist' Views of Grace*, 5–7.

[114] Donne, *Fifty Sermons*, 262–71. All subsequent references will be cited in the text itself.

us" (268). Yet while this sermon returns to a familiar subject of contention between them, it is most notable for its explicitly political tenor. Donne asserts that, while princes and laws are "reverend" and "safe," history shows that laws have been perverted by princes and, in turn, princes subverted by God. There may be some "collaterall and transitory trust in things," he insists, but "the radical, the fundamental trust is only in God" (266). While he is more careful than Burges, whose claim that "the greatest Kings are servants to the great King of Kings" landed him in jail, Donne was nonetheless reminding his listeners that divine mandate supersedes the laws of kings.[115]

Later that year, Bedford herself went to see Elizabeth at The Hague, where she encouraged her to appeal to James I on behalf of the Palatinate.[116] Indeed in the final years of James's reign, Bedford worked in an often semi-diplomatic capacity on behalf of the cause; some scholars believe that Bedford and her allies even hoped that Elizabeth might inherit the English throne. Bedford warned the Queen about rumors of an unauthorized visit on her part to England during Prince Charles's (unpopular) visit to Spain, and after Charles's return reported back on how well he had done in his first Parliament—a sign, as she put it, of the "Divine Majestie's not being yet weary of doing us good."[117] Bedford sent Elizabeth political news through the English ambassador to The Hague, Dudley Carleton, worrying about how the case might be "propounded to the parlament," and interpreting a fight of starlings in the sky as a sign of "victory for the westerne states."[118] She also sent Elizabeth's secretary to Cambridge on some "business" of great "Secrecy," and promoted ministers whose enemies identified them as members "of the puritanical faction."[119] In the months before the death

---

[115] Burges, *A sermon preached before the late King James His Majesty at Greenwich the 19 of Iuly 1604 together with two letters in way of apology for his sermon*, 3.

[116] Green, *Elizabeth, Electress Palatine and Queen of Bohemia*, 186–7.

[117] The letter, identified as the work of "the late Countesse Lucy of Bedford, to the Queen of Bohemia," and as having been "written upon occasion of the Prince, his being in the first Parliament after his coming out of Spain" (1623), is included in *A Collection of Letters Made by Sr. Tobie Matthews Kt*. In it, Bedford reports on how well Charles is doing, and asks the Queen for "leave to wish, that you should in one Letter at least, take notice of what you hear of him, from them, who will neither flatter him, nor dissemble with you" (pp. 60–1).

[118] Quoted in Ariel Franklin-Hudson, "Louing Her Owne Will," 50.

[119] "In a squabble in 1624 over the ministry at St Stephen Coleman Street, London, [John] Davenport, one of the candidates, asked Lady Vere to intervene with Secretary Conway, her brother-in-law. Once again the Countess of Bedford was an important court contact: 'The Countess of Bedford wrote me word this day that my Lord of Canterbury doth interpose for a chaplain of his own one Wilson and pretendeth that the said Wilson hath many friends in the parish as I, and that those who stood for me are but a puritanical faction'" (Peck, *Court Patronage*, 73 n. 147). On Elizabeth's secretary, Nethersole, and his visit to England in 1624, see Lawson, *Out of the Shadows*, 159.

of James I, Bedford asked Carleton to remind the Queen to be careful "whom she used freedom to," and commended William Herbert to the Queen as "the only honest hearted man employed that I know now left to God and his country."[120] In much the same way as Penelope Rich sent her miniature to James in 1586 as a sign of her alliance's loyalty, in 1624 Bedford sent Elizabeth of Bohemia a miniature of William Herbert as a sign of theirs.[121] In Wroth's 1621 romance, *The Countess of Montgomery's Urania*, Bedford appears as Lucenia, whose relationship to William Herbert's cipher Amphilanthus is configured in similar terms: during a scene in Cyprus, he wears her scarf into the day's jousting.[122]

There is some evidence that as early as 1624 godly leaders, in tactical alliance with James's favorite, were developing into something like a "party."[123] According to the French ambassador, James I recognized Elizabeth's capacity to rally English Protestants to the Palatinate cause, claiming that the "King is in the greatest fear that the Electress Palatine his daughter will arrive here [England] and *favour the party of the Puritanes*."[124] A royalist tract of 1647 alleges that, before James died, members of this party, including Robert Rich, 2nd Earl of Warwick (Penelope Rich's son) and John Pym, were meeting at the house of "a great mistresse of the Faction," a woman William Hunt presumes to be the Countess of Bedford.[125] Much as Twickenham had in the second decade of the seventeenth century, Bedford's London estate, Bedford House, assumed a controversial political status in the 1620s. In 1624, the diplomat and James loyalist Sir George Goring warned Buckingham to beware of "the ill counsels of Bedford House."[126] A contemporary satire similarly imagined Bedford House as a site of political machinations: a "puritan shrine" where devotees like the "weake Lord Chamberlain" (William Herbert) and

---

[120] For this March 1624 letter, see *The Private Correspondence of Jane Lady Cornwallis Bacon, 1613–1644*, 129: "my Lord Chamberlain, the last person left of power that I can rely on for the worth of his affection and friendship to me; and, to speak freely to you, the only honest hearted man employed that I know now left to God and his country."

[121] See Franklin-Hudson: "Bedford cannot send military aid to the Palatinate, but she can send a representation of the Lord Chamberlain—the guiding light of the puritan party in England—as a symbol for their hopefull success at home and abroad" ("Louing Her Owne Will," 29).

[122] Wroth, *The First Part of the Countess of Montgomery's Urania*, 164.

[123] William Hunt, *The Puritan Moment*, 180.

[124] Cited in Lawson, *Out of the Shadows*, 157, emphasis added.

[125] Lawson, *Out of the Shadows*, 180. As we have seen, Bedford was the particular friend of Elizabeth of Bohemia; ally of William Herbert and the puritan faction; and holder of her husband's proxy in the House of Lords.

[126] On the "ill counsels of Bedford House," see Hunt, *Puritan Moment*, 18. Bedford House was on the Strand, and had been built for Bedford's husband by his aunt and guardian, Anne Russell Dudley, Countess of Warwick.

"foolish Montgomery" (his brother, Philip Herbert) "counsel" each other to "breake ye Spanish match and ye truce" with Spain, and offer "puritan" sacrifices to "St. Luce" to aid them in their desires.[127] In this satire we see Donne's own terms for Bedford pushed into polemic, his "divinity" rendered a crassly satirical puritan "saint": the key "Factor" in a destructive faction committed to bringing about the fall of the monarchy.

---

[127] According to an anonymous Royalist historian, the Countess of Bedford had claimed that "their party" was "strong enough to pull the king's crown from his head," during his lifetime, "but the Gospel would not suffer them" (Hunt, *Puritan Moment*, 181). Purportedly on James's death there were two lords who did not go with his dead body but rather "to my Lady Bedford's to pass the time and be merry there" (cited in Lawson, *Out of the Shadows*, 159).

4

Wroth's Cabinets

Ladies' cabinets figure prominently in Lady Mary Wroth's 1621 pastoral romance, *The Countess of Montgomery's Urania*.[1] Women are locked in their cabinets by jealous husbands (249); they commit suicide in their cabinets (56–7); write verses in them; store the ashes of their lovers' letters within them (272); even burst open "like a Cabinet so fild with treasure" that "the lock or hinges cannot containe" their stories (253.2–3). The *Urania* also features a number of scenes of violent male intrusion into female spaces, including one in which a jealous husband bursts into his wife's closet and forces her to her desk to write a goodbye letter to her lover "straight before [his] eyes," and another in which a father breaks into his daughter's private cabinets to scour her private letters and papers for evidence of her adultery (12.35, 516). It is uncannily prescient that this final scene, which features the unsolicited male penetration of a female cabinet and the unsolicited male interpretation of private female papers, was to become the most notorious topical allusion in the *Urania*. Lord Edward Denny, who saw himself shadowed in the violent father, accused Mary Wroth of slander and helped to foment publicity for her romance. Much like another invasive male character in the romance, that is, Denny "turnd "downe [the] leaves" of the *Urania* that contained what he deemed to be incriminating evidence, and implicated himself in its pages (534.1).[2] Rather than a regrettable accident, I want to argue that this mode of reading—what

---

[1] Mary Wroth, *The First Part of The Countess of Montgomery's Urania*, ed. Josephine A. Roberts (Binghamton, NY: Medieval & Renaissance Texts & Studies, 1995); and Mary Wroth, *The Second Part of The Countess of Montgomery's Urania*, ed. Josephine A. Roberts, completed by Suzanne Gossett and Janel Mueller (Binghamton, NY: Medieval & Renaissance Texts & Studies, 1999). Subsequent references will be cited parenthetically in the text.

[2] See Mary Wroth, *The Poems of Lady Mary Wroth*, ed. Josephine A. Roberts (Baton Rouge, La., and London: Louisiana State University Press, 1983), 238; and *Urania*, 783, for the controversy. For the incident in which a reader "turn[s] down leaves," see 533–4: "I had set downe some things in an idle Booke I had written, which when hee saw, hee thought touched, or came too neere, or I imagine so, because in some places he had turnd downe leaves, and onely at such as he might if hee would dislike, and were those I thought hee would take notice of, yet he neither did by word nor writing, not honouring me so much, who was his slave, as to finde fault, or to seeme pleasd."

I called in Chapter 1 the deciphering imperative—is a central aspect of Wroth's romance.

The *Urania*'s most insistently topical scenes involving ladies' cabinets often feature the production and circulation of poetry. The romance's main character Pamphilia, a cipher for Mary Wroth herself, notes that "I seldome make any but Sonnets" (460.28), and she stages a number of scenes in which her sonnets are solicited, read aloud, circulated, criticized, praised, and interpreted. She locates many of these scenes in private spaces to which only certain intimates have access. Each of these sonnets-in-cabinets scenes, moreover, is enclosed in another 'case': the pastoral romance, a literary mode known both as a woman's genre and, as we saw in Chapter 1, as a means of indirect commentary on current people and events.[3] While Mary Wroth left no explicit key to the *Urania*, the romance includes many scenes that allude to contemporary political, social, and autobiographical events—including the relationship between Wroth and her first cousin and lover William Herbert, Earl of Pembroke, the figure behind Pamphilia's intermittently unfaithful lover Amphilanthus. Wroth presents a number of scenes involving sonnets and private spaces that, through deploying the recognizable conventions of both sonnet exchange and closet transactions, highlight her relationship with William Herbert and, as I will argue, solicit his attention.

While I agree with Bridget MacCarthy's description of the *Urania* as a form of "financial speculation," I argue that Wroth's speculation relied less on the prospective sales of books *per se* than on the more complex forms of familial and political entrenchment such work solicited.[4] By highlighting scenes in which readers gain access to closets and read private poems, Wroth used the *Urania* to rewrite and control the terms of her own reputation and sociopolitical position. By placing these scenes in a famously topical genre, she made this "private" story a matter of public concern. The *Urania* thus functioned as a literary petition not only to William Herbert, but to the entire alliance of which he and Wroth were part. Throughout the romance Wroth stages scenes in which Amphilanthus solicits and listens to the retelling of his own story, and by it, William Herbert's involvement with her. But she also makes it clear that others, particularly powerful female relatives, are witnesses to these transactions and keepers of their secrets. Since the groundbreaking work of Josephine A. Roberts, most readers of the *Urania* are aware of the ways in which Wroth shadows her

---

[3] Wroth, *Poems*, ed. Roberts, 28; see also David Fleming, "Barclays Satyricon," and Danielle Clarke, *The Politics of Early Modern Women's Writing*, ch. 6, which includes a section on Barclay's *Argenis*, 232–65.

[4] Bridget MacCarthy, *Women Writers*, 55.

own biography in her romance.[5] Yet as I want to argue here, her insistent shadowing of real people in the *Urania* works on a wider scale to encourage and reaffirm the political agenda of the Sidney-Herbert alliance, an agenda both familiar to us from previous chapters, and particular to the moment and place from which Wroth was writing.

I. LADIES' CABINETS

When Pamphilia first meets Amphilanthus she refuses to make her feelings for him public. Instead, she goes to bed alone, "taking a little Cabinet with her, wherein she had many papers, and setting a light by her, began to read them, but few of them pleasing her, she took pen and paper, and being excellent in writing, writ these verses following" (62.28–31). In this scene Wroth seems to allude, sardonically, to Thomas Nashe's comment that Sir Philip Sidney's sonnets had been too long "imprisoned in Ladyes' casks" and needed the "violent enlargement of print," by illustrating that women can produce better poems than those which have been given to them for keeping in those casks.[6] The sonnets that she writes testify to her affection for Amphilanthus, and when Pamphilia recognizes that her verses "bring my owne hands to witnesse against me," she gives them what she calls "a buriall" in the bottom of her cabinet (63.13, 63.16). Rather than serving as an act of erasure, however, this burial marks the sonnets' hidden existence and the possibility for their excavation—an exemplum for the interpretive practices of the romance as a whole.

Wroth made use of many well-known poetic techniques for publicly signaling and encoding private relationships in her romance, including anagrams, acronyms, ciphers, and codes, and the *Urania* illustrates a range of possible readers' responses to these strategies.[7] In an early scene, for example, Pamphilia engraves a sonnet on a tree, and when Antissia, a rival for Amphilanthus's affections, claims that it serves as a "witnese" of Pamphilia's true feelings for Amphilanthus, Pamphilia denies the charge,

---

[5] On the autobiographical elements, see Roberts's introduction, particularly "Personal Contexts"; and Mary Ellen Lamb, "The Biopolitics of Romance." (Lamb insists that the topical allusions and ciphered identifications "Are not just part of the apparatus of Wroth's text; they lie at the core of its narrative act" (110). Rosalind Smith similarly points to the "insistent autobiographical coding" of the *Urania* (*Sonnets and the English Woman Writer*, 110.) See also Josephine A. Roberts, "The Biographical Problem of *Pamphilia to Amphilanthus*."

[6] Preface to the first publication of *Astrophel and Stella, Elizabethan Critical Essays*, 2: 224. See also the discussion in Ch. 1. For commentary on the gender politics of this "violent enlargement," see Wendy Wall, *The Imprint of Gender*, 172.

[7] I am by no means the first person to point out these strategies; my readings throughout this chapter are primarily indebted to the work of Josephine A. Roberts.

claiming that the poem is "no proofe against" her: "many Poets write as well by imitation, as by sence of passion" (94.39–41).[8] In other scenes, Wroth highlights the associations between sonnets and topicality while presenting the readerly penetration of their codes—and the public revelation of this decoding—as a choice.[9]

Yet as I have suggested, Pamphilia's sonnets often do have an intended audience, and his interpretation of their encoded meanings is first delayed in the romance and then replayed again and again. In one scene, after talking together for some time, Pamphilia and Amphilanthus go into the room next to her bedchamber "which was a Cabinet of the Queenes [Pamphilia's], where her bookes and papers lay; so taking some of them, they passed a while in reading of them, and longer they would have done so, but that they heard excellent musick, which cald them to hearken to it" (260.34–7). Suggesting a rueful juxtaposition between the private and public arts, the "excellent musick" from below interrupts this scene's potentially revelatory reading. Yet there are a number of other scenes in the romance that focus on the successful exchange of verses between the two. These scenes allude to the proximity between textual exchange and sexual congress, both spatially, when the lovers read together in the cabinet next to the bedchamber, and symbolically, when Amphilanthus, in an oft-repeated Hamletesque move, lays his head on Pamphilia's lap and asks her to "reveale her secret thoughts" (245.10–15).[10]

This intimacy approaches consummation when, before one of his many departures, Amphilanthus follows Pamphilia into her cabinet, seeking

---

[8] In another scene, Perissus, heir to the Kingdom of Sicily, recognizes Pamphilia's cipher but refuses to discover it publicly to others (490). See also Helen Hackett, "'Yet tell me some such Fiction.'"

[9] While Wroth most clearly plays with her own biography through the figure of Pamphilia, she also presents herself as a series of other ciphers within the romance. In one much-discussed scene, Pamphilia tells the story of Lindamira (an anagram of "Ladi Mari") which she barely conceals as a "faigned" or fictional story that she has rendered in sonnets. Despite Pamphilia's pretence that the sonnets are a record of the fictional Lindamira's disappointment in her own faithless lover, Pamphilia's final claim that the sonnets "conclude *my* rage against him," betrays the sonnets' autobiographical status as a record of Pamphilia's own disappointment in Amphilanthus (502.6–7). (As we saw in the first chapter, Musidorus reveals himself to Pamela in a similar way in the *Arcadia*.) While Pamphilia's female listener knows that there "was some thing more exactly related then a fixion" in the sonnets, however, her "discretion taught her to be no Inquisitor" (505.9–10). *Urania*, ed. Roberts, p. lxx; see also Mary Ellen Lamb, *Gender and Authorship in the Sidney Circle*, 182; Gary F. Waller's chapter, "Some thing more exactly related then a fixion" in *Sidney Family Romance*; and, for the best reading to date by far, Rosalind Smith, "Lindamira's Complaint."

[10] This claim is followed by a bawdy pun on love's "variety." After speaking of many things, "variety of love came among them, I meane the discourses in that kind, every one relating a story" (245.10–15).

"some Verses of hers, which he had heard of" (320.19–20).[11] "When they were there," we are told, Pamphilia "tooke a deske, wherein her papers lay, and kissing them, delivered all she had saved from the fire, being in her owne hand unto him, yet blushing told him, she was ashamed, so much of her folly should present her selfe unto his eyes" (320.22–6). Acquiescing to her ideal reader's solicitation, Pamphilia excavates her verses—those she "buried" in her cabinet earlier—and Amphilanthus praises them as "the best he had seene made by a woman" (320.29).[12] While in her cabinet, Amphilanthus also attempts to extract from Pamphilia's desk her miniature, "curiously drawne by the best hand of that time," which he swears he will "carry with him to the field" (321.2–3, 321.8).[13] Amphilanthus's reading of Pamphilia's poems certainly "enlarges" their meaning, but his thwarted attempt to appropriate her miniature hints that such reading promises neither biographical synthesis nor fidelity. Amphilanthus may wish to carry Pamphilia's miniature into the field of heroic endeavour, but it is in the wider field of the romance that faces and poems are forgotten and infidelity occurs. Pamphilia may be constant, that is, but Amphilanthus, whose name means "lover of many," is not.

In much the same way as Philip Sidney presents Musidorus and Pyrocles in the *Arcadia*, Wroth represents Amphilanthus as a series of ciphers throughout the *Urania*. Among other identities, he appears as the Knight of Love (described, somewhat tongue-in-cheek, as "the honour of his sexe, never enough admired," 76.16), the Knight of the Cipher (339.26), and finally, and perhaps most aptly, the Lost Man (376.10).[14] As the Lost Man, Amphilanthus eagerly listens to the story of "Bellamira," yet another cipher for Mary Wroth (377–8).[15] Bellamira tells the Lost Man yet another thinly concealed account of the intimate relationship between Mary Wroth

---

[11] Right before this scene, Pamphilia had been reading a book about inconstancy which she "threw…away" (317).

[12] On Pamphilia's need to make sure that Amphilanthus sees her poetry as autobiographical, see Clarke, *Politics of Women's Writing*, 244.

[13] On this scene, see Roberts's introduction to the *Urania*, p. lxiii. This scene is much like the scene in the *Arcadia* in which Philisides, Philip Sidney's cipher, sinks "Mira's" "picture into his brest." Both women serve as the symbolic figureheads for the cause.

[14] On William Herbert's fame for his role as a chivalric hero and negotiator of political diplomacy in the tournaments of late Elizabethan and early Jacobean England, see Dick Taylor Jr. "The Masque and the Lance."

[15] Bellamira is married to "a great heire, who was called Treborius," a figure for Wroth's husband Robert Wroth, a man "extreamely favoured by [the king] in outward show, and his house often visited by his Majesty" (176.15). Robert Wroth was known for his love of hunting, not his intellect, and Treborius is described as being fond of "the plaine Jests of his Hunts-men" (389.11). Bellamira's father was Dettareus, "a great Lord in this Country, and Steward of the Kings house," an accurate description, as Roberts points out, of Wroth's father Sir Robert Sidney (379).

and William Herbert—"our loves being so perfectly, and reciprocally embraced: the strong bond of friendship, twixt our fathers... our breeding together"—and the Lost Man concurs that the lovers were "made to be one" (382.31–4, 382.41). As Bellamira continues the story, telling him how both she and her lover were, like Wroth and Herbert (perfidiously) married to others, the Lost Man repeatedly begs to hear more "of the sad story" (390.12, see also 382.21).[16] Eventually, as we might now expect, he asks to hear the verses she wrote as its record. "I have seene some excellent things of [women's] writings," he tells her, "let me so much bound to you, as to heare some of your Verses" (390.34–5). Amphilanthus thus alludes to his previous experience reading Pamphilia's poetry ("the best he had seene made by a woman") at the same time as he solicits that of "Bellamira." Upon hearing her poems, which rather ironically echo those of William Herbert himself, the Lost Man proclaims Bellamira "perfect" in the art of poetry (391.30).[17] It is a "pittie," he claims, that she should "hide, or darken so rare a gift" (391.31).

In this scene, Wroth not only renders Amphilanthus the encouraging voice of female poetic promotion, but by having him both solicit and empathize with Bellamira's ciphered account of Wroth's relationship with Herbert, she hyperbolizes the romance's deciphering imperative. When the Lost Man tells Bellamira not to "hide, or darken" her gift, he suggests that what she has written should be brought into the public light, not kept in the dark of her cabinet. But "hiding" and "darkening" are also synonyms for ciphering, and the "Lost Man" is thus also encouraging "Bellamira" to make her story explicit—to reveal the truth behind its codes. "Dark texts," as Donne put it in one of his verse letters to Bedford, "need notes." The penultimate line of the poem Bellamira reads to the Lost Man, "love is not love, but where truth hath her rights," both alludes to the "truth" behind its fiction and makes a rights-based plea for its acknowledgement (391.28). The line is as good a statement as any of the ways in which poetic love is never simply love, but also a statement about something else.

Some time after Bellamira tells her story, and when she is temporarily gone from the room, the Lost Man takes off his "Helme" (391.36). Upon

---

[16] The "sad story" includes the death of Bellamira's husband and son, as well as her continued disappointments in her lover (380). Wroth's own husband died in 1614, and her son in 1616; her relationship with Herbert certainly continued after their death; she bore two children with him.

[17] Roberts, *Urania*, n. 391.28, p. 765. Alexander notes that "Amphilanthus's appreciation of Pamphilia's poems... can be seen as a wished for attitude of Pembroke to Wroth's writings" (*Writing After Sidney*, 311). In the second part, Pamphilia sings a poem ascribed to William Herbert in contemporary manuscripts. In the romance, she credits it to Amphilanthus, "when hee made a shew of love to Antissia, and had given itt her, thou ment to a higher beauty," meaning, of course, Pamphilia herself (2.30).

reentering, Bellamira recognizes him as Amphilanthus, and he makes her promise "not to disclose him, or to know him to be other then the Lost Man" (392.22–3). Despite his own promotion of unshadowed poetic revelation a few moments earlier, the "Lost Man" chooses to keep his own cipher, and thus Amphilanthus's anonymity, intact. Yet by staging scenes in which Amphilanthus solicits and listens to barely shadowed tales of a wavering man's transactions with a constant woman, Wroth insists not only on Amphilanthus's recognition of his own failings, but on William Herbert's recognition of his. By having his cipher listen to his story, Wroth imagines Herbert, much as Denny did, turning down the leaves of her romance and finding himself implicated in its pages.

In choosing a genre known for "glauncing at greater matters under the vaile of homely persons," and publishing it with a sonnet sequence, Wroth identified her romance as a text with public ambitions. Both the romance and the sonnet sequence were intimately associated with the Sidneys and with the sociopolitical alliance and nexus of power with which Wroth sought to entrench her ties.[18] While Wroth undoubtedly used these two genres to signal continuity with the poets in her family, particularly Philip Sidney and Mary Sidney Herbert, she was also announcing her own ambitions. Like the romance, the sonnet sequence was widely recognized for its efficacy as a vehicle of authorial desires and ambitions—a powerful tool in cementing social relations between the poet and the object of his or her desires.[19] In commenting on contemporary events, including the violent male intrusion into private female spaces and papers, and the secrets kept between lovers, Wroth's topical romance and "private" sonnets sought readers who were not only perspicacious but responsive. By presenting so many of the *Urania*'s cryptically revelatory scenes in closets and other private spaces, Wroth advertised both her own ability to keep secrets, and the fact that the secrets, as is their very nature, await, and even demand, retrieval.

The closet, as Alan Stewart has argued, was "a politically crucial transactive space," one which enabled the retrieval of the content of those transactions by specific people.[20] Wroth used the closets in her romance to signal her desire that her most-evoked reader, William Herbert, retrieve the history of intimate traffic encoded both in the sonnets and their cases. Yet by restaging this private history in a topical romance, Wroth made herself the

---

[18] The *Urania* alludes to Sir Philip Sidney's romance *Arcadia* and sonnet sequence *Astrophel and Stella*, as well as the sonnet sequences of her father Robert Sidney and her cousin and lover, William Herbert.

[19] Wall, *Imprint of Gender*, 330.

[20] Stewart, "The Early Modern Closert Doscovered," 77.

agent of her own revelation, playing with her status as a "lady's cask," rene-gotiating the terms of her notoriety (she had two illegitimate children with Herbert), and, as we will see in the second half of this chapter, announcing her own political voice. It is a fascinating historical fact, and one singularly useful for my argument, that one of the places in which Wroth "pub-lished" her romance was in her private study at Baynard's Castle, when she showed the manuscript of the *Urania* to her cousin, Sir George Manners, Earl of Rutland, and began to explain its topical allusions. (Manners later wrote to her for help completing his key, asking her "to interpret unto me the names as heere I have begunn them."[21]) As the map included in James Howel's *Londinopolis* makes clear, Baynard's Castle was in the center of London's corridors of power (Figures 4.1 and 4.2). It was also, as we saw in the last chapter, the London seat of the Herbert family, and a known location of political machinations; William Herbert and Lucy Harington Russell had planned Buckingham's rise to political prominence within its very walls just a few years earlier.[22] By placing herself in this closet, in full view, as it were, of the Sidney-Herbert family, and the wider London political scene, Wroth announced her presence both in the house and in the alliance. Wroth's cabinet in Herbert's house thus worked in much the same way as the cabinets work in her romance: the "enlargement" of its contents came through specific, often directly solicited, readers' interpre-tations and the acknowledgements they demanded.

Thus while I have argued that William Herbert was in many ways Wroth's most important reader, *The Countess of Montgomery's Urania* is no love let-ter.[23] Nor, for that matter, is it best understood as a dialogue between two people. Among the many witnesses to the cabineted scenes which occur between Pamphilia and Amphilanthus, two stand out in particular: the Queen of Naples, who is the cipher for Mary Sidney Herbert, and Urania, the cipher for Susan de Vere Herbert, Countess of Montgomery, the wife of William Herbert's brother Philip Herbert and the titular dedicatee of the romance.[24] Wroth presents Mary Sidney Herbert's cipher as a poet,

---

[21] Sir George Manners, 7th Earl of Rutland, wrote Wroth a letter on 31 May 1640, "Callinge to remembrance the favor you once did me in the sight of a Manuscrip you shewed me in your study att Banerds Castell And heer meetings with your Urania I make bold to send this enclosed and begg a favor from you that I may read with more delight. If you please to interprete unto me the names as heere I have begunn them, wherein you shall much oblige me" (cited in Wroth, *Poems*, ed. Roberts, 244–5).

[22] Tresham Lever, *The Herberts of Wilton*, 90.

[23] My reading thus contrasts with that of Hannay in her recent biography: "Pembroke's various affairs...may have been for him little more than pleasant diversions from more pressing matters of state. For Wroth that affair defined her life" (Hannay, *Mary Sidney*, 193).

[24] On Susan Herbert, see *Urania*, ed. Roberts, pp. lxxvi–lxxix; and on Mary Herbert, pp. lxxxiv–lxxxvi. See also Margaret P. Hannay, "Your vertuous and learned Aunt," 30.

Figure 4.1 Map of London in Sir James Howell's *Londinopolis* (1657). Reproduced by permission of the Folger Shakespeare Library.

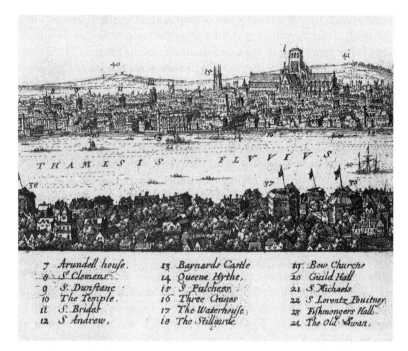

Figure 4.2 Detail of Baynard's Castle in map of London in Sir James Howell's *Londinopolis* (1657). Reproduced by permission of the Folger Shakespeare Library.

champion of women's writing, and keeper of Pamphilia's secrets, identifying her in the second part of the romance as the "true secretary of her thoughts" (364, 368, 371). In many ways Wroth used the *Urania* to identify herself not only as her aunt's literary heir, but as the heir to her literary statecraft.[25] Urania plays an even more important role in the romance. By Pamphilia's "intreaty" she is quite literally sleeping with her in the bedchamber next to the cabinet in which Pamphilia shows Amphilanthus her

[25] Barbara Lewalski points out that in the second part of the *Urania*, Pamphilia takes over the role of her aunt, the Queen of Naples, in offering aid and counsel to the young (*Writing Women*, 292). It is notable that the Queen of Naples discusses political matters with Pamphilia as well as matters of the heart. See e.g. 366.21–2: "Among other speech the Queene of Naples asked Pamphilia what shee hears of the warres in Albania." This line is uncannily similar to the line from Clifford's diary cited in Ch. 1, in which she records Wroth telling her "a great deal of news from beyond sea" (145). On this scene, see also Hannay, *Mary Sidney*, 206. See also Lamb, "Women Readers in Mary Wroth's *Urania*." A secretary, in Angel Day's words, was both "a keeper or conserver of the secrets unto him committed" and "a keeper or conserver" of contents of the "Closet" which housed those secrets (*The English Secretorie*, 108).

poems (260.20).[26] Both the Queen of Naples and Urania, moreover, know the truth about Pamphilia and Amphilanthus's relationship, a fact that is kept secret from most of the other characters in the romance. In the second part of the romance they witness their *de verba praesenti* marriage—a union identified as "the knott never to bee untied" (2.45.184)—and continue to support its primacy through the course of the romance.[27] Both the witnessing of and the bonds between these women are central to the plot of the romance.

Mary Sidney Herbert died in September 1621, just after the first part of the romance appeared in print. Yet the Countess of Montgomery, her daughter-in-law, and the woman under whose "liuerye" the *Urania* circulated, was and continued to be an influential literary and political force until her own death in 1628. The daughter of a man who opined before Elizabeth I's death that "the peers of England should decide the succession," and married to "great *Mongomria* / A mighty Prince in western *Cambria*," Susan de Vere Herbert wielded considerable power.[28] In an early dedication, Nathaniel Baxter configures her in an acrostic poem as the heir of *Cecilia* (Mary Sidney Herbert), a "chast and princely Nymph begot / U Nder *Cecilias* education," and "S Trong in allyed friendes of highest lot" (A3ᵛ). (See Figure 4.3.) (The poem was part of a group of poems dedicated to the Sidney-Herbert family gathered at Baynard's Castle, "mightie Princes and high Potentates, / That with [their] Scepters swaye great Monarchies," Bᵛ.)

Despite the fact that she had the power to "swaye great Monarchies," the *Urania*'s dedication to the Countess of Montgomery was also something of a convention.[29] The romance was frequently characterized as a woman's

---

[26] On Urania's role as advisor, see Cavanagh, *Cherished Torment*: "Urania's talent for perceptive and soothing rhetoric provides a kind of glue to leep these fragile family systems and governments intact" (110).

[27] Pamphilia and Amphilanthus exchange vows in a private ceremony before five witnesses: Urania, Selarina, Antissius, Allimarlus and Polarchos. See Josephine A. Roberts, "The Knott Never to Bee Untide," 117. Urania refers to Pamphilia as Amphilanthus's "truest wife," and recalls that "longe before their harts had binn linked, nay bound together" (II, fol. 51; Roberts, "The Knott," 120). Susan de Vere, the future Countess of Montgomery, had made her own secret marriage. After vowing to her uncle and guardian Sir Robert Cecil in 1601 that "I will never match with any without your consent," she did precisely that, contracting with her husband without permission. The *de praesenti* marriage was followed by a lavish event in 1604, after which James I appeared in their bedroom the next morning (see Edmund Lodge, *Illustrations of British History*, 3 vols, 2nd edn (London: John Chidley, 1838), vol. 2, cited in Roberts, "The Knott," 100).

[28] See the entry on the Countess in the *ODNB*. The cited verse is from Nathaniel Baxter, *Sir Philip Sydneys Ouránia, that is Endimions Song and Tragedie* (1606). Subsequent references will be cited parenthetically. See also her role in advising Anne Clifford in her negotiations with James I. *Diaries of Lady Anne Clifford*, ed. D. J. H. Clifford, 46.

[29] For dedications to both women, see Williams, *Index of Dedications and Commendatory Verses*, 94–5.

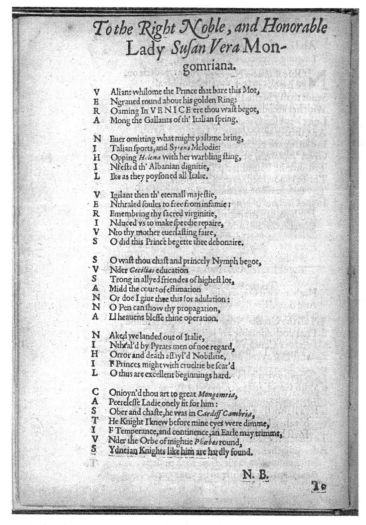

To the Right Noble, and Honorable
Lady *Susan Vera* Mon-
gomriana.

V Aliant whilome the Prince that bare this Mot,
E Ngraued round about his golden Ring:
R Oaming In VENICE ere thou waſt begot,
A Mong the Gallants of th' Italian ſpring.

N Euer omitting what might paſtime bring,
I Talian ſports, and Syrens Melodie:
H Opping *Helena* with her warbling ſting,
I Nſeſted th' Albanian dignitie,
L Ike as they poyſoned all Italie.

V Igilant then th' eternall majeſtie,
E Nthraled ſoules to free from infamie :
R Emembring thy ſacred virginitie,
I Nduced vs to make ſpeedie repaire,
V Nto thy mother euerlaſting faire,
S O did this Prince begette thee debonaire.

S O waſt thou chaſt and princely Nymph begot,
V Nder *Cecilias* education
S Trong in allyed friendes of higheſt lot,
A Midd the court of eſtimation
N Or doe I giue thee this for adulation :
N O Pen can ſhow thy propagation,
A Ll heauens bleſſe thine operation.

N Aked we landed out of Italie,
I Nthral'd by Pyrats men of noe regard,
H Orror and death aſſayl'd Nobilitie,
I F Princes might with crueltie be ſcar'd
L O thus are excellent beginnings hard.

C Onioyn'd thou art to great *Mongomria,*
A Peereleſſe Ladie onely fit for him :
S Ober and chaſte, he was in *Cardiff Cambria,*
T He Knight I knew before mine eyes were dimme,
I F Temperance, and continence, an Earle may trimme,
V Nder the Orbe of mightie *Phœbes* round,
S Ydneian Knights like him are hardly found.

N. B.

Te

Figure 4.3 Acrostic poem on Susan Herbert, Countess of Montgomery, from Nathaniel Baxter's. *Sir Philip Sydneys ouránia* (1606), A3ᵛ. Reproduced by permission of the British Library.

genre; in dedicating his *Euphues* to the "Ladies and Gentlewoemen of England," to give a famous example, John Lyly claimed that his romance "had rather lye shut in a ladyes casket than open in a Schollers studie."[30]

[30] John Lyly, *Euphues* in *Complete Works*, ed. R. Warwick Bond, 3 vols (Oxford: Oxford University Press, 1902), 2: 8–9.

While male writers often imagined the romance as a threat to women's chastity, it was also the genre that most consistently solicited the attention and readerly participation of women readers.[31] Wroth plays with this generic reputation in the *Urania*, which, like the *Arcadia*, makes frequent allusions to women readers, both outside and inside the text. But the *Urania* also suggests that women are more than its privileged readers: their participation is necessary for the full dilation or enlargement of its meanings.

Before she became the titular patron of the *Urania*, Susan de Vere Herbert had been singled out as a supporter of the contemporary romance. In 1619, to take the most pertinent example, Anthony Munday thanked her for providing him with the space and books necessary to complete his translation of the French romance *Amadis de Gaul*—a romance already associated with the Sidney alliance.[32] In identifying her romance as *The Countess of Montgomery's Urania*, Wroth positioned Susan Herbert as the patron of her text, and by presenting her as a character within its narrative, she rendered her a key component of the deciphering imperative. In his famous explanation of poetry's ability to teach through delighting, Philip Sidney claimed to have "known men that even with reading *Amadis de Gaule*...have found their hearts moved to the exercise of courtesy, liberality and especially courage."[33] If Wroth hoped the *Urania* would teach William Herbert to behave with greater courtesy and liberality towards

---

[31] See Helen Hackett, *Women and Romance* (including on the "rhetorical exaggeration of female readership," 26); and Caroline Lucas, *Writing for Women*. See also Ch. 1 of this book; and Tiffany Werth, *The Fabulous Dark Cloister*, esp. ch. 4, on Wroth. See also Das, *Renaissance Romance*, 147.

[32] *The Ancient, Famous, and Honourable History of Amadis de Gaule* (Printed at London by Nicholas Okes, 1619). The dedication "To the Right Honorable Sir Phillip Herbert" acknowledges that "by the helpe of that worthy Lady, I have had such Bookes as were of the best editions, and them (as I have already begun) I intend to follow. In the meane time (Noble Lord) accept of these foure Bookes I beseech you, and defend them from the venomous tongue of foule mouthed detraction, burying all my imperfections herein committed, in the urgent importunitie of that worthy Lady, by whom I have thus boldly presumed, & the rest will beare me blamelesse against your least mislike." Barbara Lewalski has suggested that the Persian Sophia's library in the second part of the *Urania*—"the most sumptuous in the world for a woeman to have and the rarest...all chosen ones, and as choisely chosen, and as truly used, and imployed by ther owner" (fol. 61ᵛ)—is modeled on that of Susan Herbert (Lewalski, *Writing Women*, 293). Hannay points out that the Throne of Love episode in the *Urania*, in which Pamphilia becomes Constancy personified, is adapted from the Arch of Loyal Lovers in *Amadis de Gaul*, and it seems likely that Wroth is alluding to Susan Herbert's known relationship with that romance as well. In the episode, right after Pamphilia takes Constancy "into her breast," she embraces Urania, "and with affection kissing her, told her, the worth which shee knew to bee in her, had long since bound her love to her, and had caus'd that journey of purpose to doe her service" (170.7–9).

[33] *Defence of Poetry*, 40–1.

her, she also knew that her romance's women would provide the larger context and, ideally, encouragement and counsel, for this alteration. Wroth's fantasy alliance is thus not with William Herbert alone, but with the larger alliance of which he is a member. Her romance, moreover, is as concerned with political ends as it is with personal ones. As we will see, the various marital and regional alliances in the *Urania* comment on political matters both by way of political analogy and through the geopolitical bonds they foster.[34] The *Urania* reflects and comments on the Sidney alliance's international concerns, and highlights their power as regional magistrates.

II. WROTH'S POLITICAL CABINETS

In her indispensible introduction to *The First Part of the Countess of Montgomery's Urania* (1621), Josephine A. Roberts points to one of the major political contexts of the *Urania*. At the center of the romance, she writes, "lies one of the most powerful political fantasies of sixteenth and seventeenth-century Europe—the revival of the Holy Roman empire in the West."[35] Roberts suggests that Wroth's romantic imagination of this outcome both flatters her cousin and lover, William Herbert, under the shadow of Amphilanthus, King of Romans and future Holy Roman Emperor, and implicitly supports the cause of international Protestantism in which Herbert and the entire Sidney-Herbert faction were invested. The backdrop to this fantasy was the battle over Bohemia, a cause, as we saw in the last chapter, supported by the pro-Protestant and anti-Spanish faction of the English court headed by William Herbert and Lucy Harington Russell, and alluded to throughout the romance.[36]

[34] The military effort in the romance is collective and interfamilial: "Amphilanthus was to command his Italians, which without comparison were the bravest, and beste order'd, Rosindy the Macedonians, Leandrus the Achaians, Selarinus the Emperians, Antissius his Romanians, Dolorindus those hee brought from his kingdome of Negropont, where hee now raigned King. Other troops there were, whereof the chiefe of their owne Country commanded, but over all, as it was then resolv'd, Steriamus, for whom all these were joyn'd, should have the power, and name of Generall" (315.17–25). While the effect of Wroth's intentions on the outside world is suggested both by the Herberts' later support for the illegitimate children Wroth shared with William Herbert, and by Susan Herbert's active involvement with the alliance, they are borne out even more elaborately in the *Urania*.

[35] *Urania*, ed. Roberts, p. xxxix.

[36] On the Palatinate and the larger political situation, see C. V. Wedgwood, *The Thirty Years War*. On the relationship between the *Urania* and the Palatinate, see *Urania*, ed. Roberts, pp. xl–xli. James was uncomfortable with the open rebellion of Bohemians against their monarch, and initially refused to commit England to "an unjust and needlesse quarrel" (Akrigg, *Jacobean Pageant*, 335; cited in *Urania*, ed. Roberts, p. xli) over its defense. Without English support, Frederick's forces were beaten outside Prague a year later in 1620 and Frederick had to flee to The Hague, creating a radically unsettled state in the region. "At the height of the Bohemian disaster," Roberts writes, "Wroth constructed a countermyth

The loyalty of Pamphilia, future Queen of Pamphilia and the cipher for Wroth, to the oft-unfaithful Amphilanthus has been read as a revalorization of female constancy, a critique of patriarchal marriage, and proto-feminist support for extramarital or supramarital relationships.[37] While others have looked beyond the romantic connotations of Pamphilia's constancy to see it as a sign of self-determination and thus as an enabling logic for the woman author, more recently scholars have considered her in a political light.[38] It is this argument I wish to expand on here. Keeping in mind Arthur Marotti's argument that "love is not love," or, as Maureen Quilligan puts it, that Elizabethan "worldly ambition efficiently wore the livery of [poetic] love," I want to argue that the same was true for women, particularly politicized women writing romance, a genre almost wholly concerned with love and its objects.[39] In particular, Pamphilia's love for Amphilanthus, and her constancy in the face of his inconstancy, affirms Wroth's commitment to the cause most insistently shadowed in the *Urania* and effected—with help from Pamphilia and others—by Amphilanthus: the cause of the Protestant Palatinate and the fate of international Protestantism. In working to buttress Amphilanthus'

within the *Urania* of a young man who brilliantly succeeds in creating an international coalition" (p. xlii). "Implicitly," Roberts adds, "her myth is a critique of the failures of James's original foreign policy of non-involvement" (p. xliv). Bernadette Andrea has pointed to Wroth's implication in a British imperial imaginary (largely through a scene in which Pamphilia and Amphilanthus Christianize Cyprus). Bernadette Andrea, "Pamphilia's Cabinet."

[37] *Urania*, ed. Roberts, p. lxi.
[38] In *Incest and Agency in Elizabeth's England*, Maureen Quilligan argues that Pamphilia's constancy "demonstrates that she has a will of her own, and that she exercises full command over it in order to institute her own active desire as her possession of herself" (*Incest and Agency in Elizabeth's England*, 208). This model of constancy-as-self-possession is also, Quilligan argues, Wroth's own: "she will not be traded out, but remains within the protection of a family that persistently authorized its females' desire to write, thereby increasing its own remarkable status" (p. 212). More recently, Elaine Beilin has illustrated the ways in which the *Urania* comments on the nature of political rule, particularly the mixed government by king, lords, and commons, and limitations on the king's prerogative ("Role of the Political Subject," 5). Wroth, she argues, "invents distinct contractual and absolutist models, but she also creates hybrid systems where a patriarchal ruler must win the people's hearts and their consent, and work within a contract, often represented as a marriage" (p. 7). Picking up on this argument, Melissa Sanchez has argued that the *Urania* is "deeply engaged with questions of rule as it struggles to postulate a viable alternative to the obsession and idolatry inherent in absolutist rhetoric" (*Erotic Subjects*, 124). (In her reading, the masochism in the romance "is a kind of satire on the idea of political submission," or the practice of "subjects so fascinated by the allure of power that they are strangely attracted to his abuse," pp. 118, 134.) While I agree with the general contours of both arguments, I disagree with Sanchez's assertion that Pamphilia is best understood as a "deluded, self-dramatizing mess who willfully embraces her own misery" (*Erotic Subjects*, 135). Rather, I argue that her constancy is the bedrock for the romance's political vision.
[39] Quilligan, "The Constant Subject," 325. See also Marotti, "'Love is not Love.'"

activities in "the field," Pamphilia's constancy signals Wroth's promotion of herself as a new spokesperson for the Sidney-Herbert alliance, an alliance historically committed, through the use of literary texts, both to the cause of international Protestantism and to the affirmation of the English Protestant nobility's role in the political decision-making of England itself.

As we saw in Chapter 1, this same alliance had long made use of the political symbolism of female constancy as part of its metaphorics of discontent. Constant women configured a particular political disposition in relationship to monarchy: simultaneously loyal to legitimate monarchical power and resistant to its abuses. Much like Pamela and Philoclea in the *Arcadia*, Pamphilia functions as the cornerstone of the *Urania*'s political imagination. Her "passions so wisely governed," Pamphilia is both described and speaks in the specifically neostoic language associated with the alliance and its mode of critique. In one scene, to take a particularly emblematic example, a "tempest" forces a group of women to land upon a "Rocke," and while the majority of the victims alternate between "hope" and "the depth of Dispaire," Pamphilia remains constant; she simply climbs "the Rocke till at the top she discover'd a fine Country" (372.24–7).[40] As we saw in Chapter 1, Lipsius's key piece of advice for those seeking to be "truly free" and subject to no king but God was to live "*Nec spe nec metu*" (with neither hope nor fear). Like Philisides in the *Arcadia*, Pamphilia takes this motto as her personal creed. Amphilanthus, by way of contrast, is often overpowered by emotion: "Hee (who governed the world, ore the best part of it)," as Urania puts it in the second part of the romance, is often unable to "overmaster his passion" (2.172).[41]

The union between Pamphilia and Ampilanthus thus functions much like those between the heroes and heroines in the *Arcadia*. In one scene, Amphilanthus tells Pamphilia that he "may be the Knight to adventure with [her]" and she responds that "wee will surely bring an end to [the crisis]; your valour and my loyalty being met together" (168.18, 168.27–8). While Amphilanthus may be martially heroic, Pamphilia is the one with the stable, or constant, commitment to their cause. (Together, among other things, they Christianize the island of Cyprus). In the *Urania*, Wroth thus signals the enduring legacy and triumphant return of constant

---

[40] See also following neostoic description of Pamphilia: "yet she lost not her selfe; for her government continued just and brave, like the Lady she was, wherein she shewed her heart was not to be stirr'd, though her private fortunes shook round about her" (484, cited in Beilin, "Role of the Political Subject," 17). For a discussion of a similar scene in the *Arcadia*, see Ch. 1.

[41] As Margaret P. Hannay points out, these lines echo Mary Sidney Herbert's description of Antonius, who admits to himself that he is "scarce master of thy self, / Late master of so many nations" (Hannay, *Mary Sidney*, 267).

women as the cornerstone of the Sidney alliance's mode of political critique.[42] Beyond combining the names of the *Arcadia*'s heroines into her own, Wroth makes it clear that she is taking over where Philip Sidney and Mary Sidney Herbert left off. At one point when Pamphilia is (literally) in Arcadia, she remembers a better time, when its plains were "in her flourishing time of fortune," and makes what is at once a lament and a vow: "'O Playnes,' cry'd shee, 'how doth constancy protect, and gard you in delicasie?...deere Arcadia I love you yet because my constancy suits with yours, pitty me then that pines in that vertue, and if ever I see you decaying I will waile with you'" (480.1, 481.4–7). Pamphilia's constancy is thus associated not only with the fortunes of "Arcadia," but with its defense as well.

While most scholarship on Wroth has focused on her personal life, she was also invested in, knowledgeable about, and, as I will argue here, actively involved in contemporary politics. Anne Clifford's account of a visit in which Mary Wroth brought the gathered company of powerful Sidney women at Penshurst "news from beyond the seas," offers only one glimpse of her political life.[43] Wroth certainly heard and read about domestic and international politics through her father and brother, but her knowledge was more than second-hand.[44] The Sidney papers give some insight into her political life, recording among other things, her frequent visits to Baynard's Castle, Penshurst, and Elsings (the Montgomery estate in Essex), all locations in which the members of the alliance conducted their business; her involvement in a range of clearly political meetings in London, not least among them a dinner with her father and the Herbert brothers at the Lord Mayor's; and her influence in the English garrison in Flushing, where both her father and brother held military posts.[45] In October 1608, for example, her father's Lieutenant Governor in Flushing,

---

[42] In one scene in the second part of the romance Amphilanthus promises that he will "appeere soe cleerly shining in constancy" that everyone who beholds him "will seeme butt darcke shadows of [his] purest light," and Pamphilia asks to have a place "in the counsell" that will keep him on track (2.28.34–5, 2.29.1–5). Amphilanthus's response is telling. She shall not, he tells her, "beg a place" in his counsel but shall be "Presedent [of it] and governe both thoughts and will in mee" (2.29.7–9). It is shortly after this that they make a "contract" to one another—a "knott never to be untied" that serves as the grounding metaphor for the rest of the romance (2. 44–5).

[43] Clifford, *Memoir of 1603*, 47. For an example of another powerful Stuart woman who maintained political networks, see Daybell, "'Suche newes.'" As with Wroth and Clifford, the women in the *Urania* often share political news: "Among other speech the Queene of Naples asked Pamphilia what shee heard of the warres in Albania" (*Urania*, 366). See also n. 25.

[44] On the Sidneys and the news, see *Report on the Manuscripts of Lord De L'Isle and Dudley*, 4: 280, 284). The personal papers and commonplace books of both Robert Sidneys are also full of political history and news. I discuss these papers in the Epilogue.

[45] *Report on Manuscripts*, 3: 421 and 4: 233.

William Browne, wrote to him recommending a member of his company for promotion on "Lady Wroth's" recommendation.[46] In 1614, she served as a mediatrix for a military dispute.[47] While the many allusions to Wroth's involvement in the day-to-day workings of the garrison are often frustratingly brief, they nonetheless indicate that Wroth's opinions were taken seriously by those active in the administration of English political interests in the Low Countries—the frontline of Britain's commitment to an international Protestant alliance.

Scholars have interpreted the fact that Pamphilia is identified as the heir-designate to her uncle as a sign of Wroth's inheritance of the Sidnean literary genealogy. (In this reading, the uncle who leaves her the kingdom of Pamphilia is a figure for Philip Sidney; the fact that Pamphilia considers the Queen of Naples, Mary Sidney Herbert's cipher, her "deerest mother-Aunte" (2: 278.16), makes it clear that she understood this inheritance as a family affair).[48] Like Pamphilia's Arcadian vow, the title-page of the *Urania* similarly highlights Wroth's family connections, identifying it as "The Countesse of Montgomeries / URANIA. / Written by the right honorable the Lady / MARY WROATH. / Daughter to the right Noble Robert / Earle of Leicester / And Neece to the ever famous, and re- / nowned Sr. Philip Sidney Knight. And to / The most excellent Lady Mary Countesse / of Pembroke late deceased." (See Figure 4.4.) While her literary genealogy is certainly central to her self-presentation, the relationships Wroth chooses to highlight are also those of the highest rank. Wroth is, first and foremost, the "Daughter to" an Earl, the highest title to which she can lay claim, and the one that affords her the most influence.[49] Like her uncle's, Wroth's romance was written not only in the service of a highly

---

[46] The letter was written on 24 October 1608. "May it therefore please you to recommend Mr. Courtney," he wrote, "a gentleman of your company, whom Lady Wroth has heretofore recommended to me." *Report on Manuscripts*, 4: 65. See Browne's letters in the *Calendar of State Papers Foreign and in the HMC Salisbury MSS* (August 1604), XVI, 269).

[47] A 6 May 1614 letter from Flushing mentions an incident in which a man pulled a dagger on a captain there. Shortly thereafter, this same man writes a letter to Robert Sidney in which he mentions the following detail: "I find by a letter from my Lady Wroth and from my wife's letters that my business stands much otherwise than my judgment framed it" (*Report on Manuscripts*, 5: 204). 'I beseech your favour in keeping me in your service,' he writes, "A creature redeemed is better than one created. I understand by my Lady Wroth your honourable 'inclynes' unto me" (5: 204–5). Like my previous example, this letter suggests the extent to which Wroth was involved with the day-to-day political workings of the English garrison in Flushing.

[48] See *Urania*, 145, for Pamphilia's inheritance. On the Sidney genealogy, see *Urania*, ed. Roberts, p. xcvi. See also Joshua Sylvester's claim that Wroth "Her Uncle's noble Veine renewes" (cited in Lewalski, *Writing Women*, 247).

[49] See the introduction for a discussion of women as the "next successors in the dignitie" of an aristocratic title.

Figure 4.4 The title-page of the *Urania*, identifying it as "The Countesse of Montgomeries / URANIA. / Written by the right honorable the Lady / MARY WROATH. / Daughter to the right Noble Robert / Earle of Leicester / And Neece to the ever famous, and re- / nowned Sr. Philip Sidney Knight. And to / The most excellent Lady Mary Countesse / of Pembroke late deceased." Reproduced by permission of the Folger Shakespeare Library.

politicized international Protestant agenda, but in defense of the consiliary rights of the nobility, including herself.

Maureen Quilligan has argued that the title-page of the *Urania* presents an idealized version of the estates of Wilton and Penshurst as the grounds of English Protestant nationalism, a vision of country and customary locality as an alternative to the absolute power of the sovereign.[50] While I, too, see Wilton and Penshurst as providing symbolic blueprints for Wroth's political vision, I want to argue that the windmill on the right side of the frontispiece signals the English alliance with the Low Countries—a Protestant alliance defended in no small part by the Sidney family (Figure 4.5).[51] Indeed the windmill adds an international tenor to the frontispiece's portrait of landed nobility. If Penshurst was their home turf, Flushing was the political arena in which the Sidney family, including Mary Wroth, sought to influence English foreign policy in the direction of an internationalist Protestant militancy. By using an emblem of Dutch ingenuity in her frontispiece, and placing it just over the hill from the Palladian gardens of Wilton, Penshurst, and, as I will suggest, her own estate of Loughton, Wroth hints at the *Urania*'s larger strategy of romanticizing the unions of states of all kinds in the service of the international Protestant cause.

As Roberts's meticulous research shows, the countries and courts in the *Urania* configure or shadow various Sidney-Herbert estates, including Penshurst, the Sidney family home in Kent (the courtly center of the Kingdom of Morea); Wilton, the Herberts' Wiltshire estate (the court of the Kingdom of Naples); and Loughton, the Wroth estate in Essex (the court of the Kingdom of Pamphilia) which Mary Wroth, through her politic pleas to Queen Anne, renovated in 1614 and lived in until her death.[52]

---

[50] See Quilligan, *Incest*, 178–81. Quilligan puts the *Urania*'s frontispiece in dialogue with those of texts like *Poly-Olbion* and *The Surveyer*. According to Richard Helgerson, in chorographical writing, "the emphasis falls on the land itself, in its county and customary locality; in this land is created an authority that may vie with the absolutist authority of the sovereign" (Quilligan, *Incest*, 178). The frontispiece thus offers "an idealized view of a family seat"; "what we see beyond the Palladian frame of the *Urania*'s frontispiece is a picture of the kinship from which Wroth draws her endogamous power" (Quilligan, *Incest*, 181).

[51] While Quilligan suggests that the windmill "is an attempt to call attention to the parodic nature of Wroth's romance" through an allusion to *Don Quixote*'s most famous scene (*Incest*, 187), I see it as part of the land-authority argument, adding an international aspect to a pastoralized domestic resistance. On Robert Sidney's governorship of Flushing (Vlissingen), one of the cautionary towns the Dutch had granted England as security for the large loan Elizabeth had provided, see Robert Shephard's *ODNB* entry. Robert Sidney was governor of Flushing for thirty years until it was returned to the Dutch in 1616. See also Hannay, *Mary Sidney*, 29.

[52] On the families related to the kingdoms, see "Personal Contexts" in Roberts's introduction to the *Urania*. For Penshurst (Morea), see the reference to "a Mount cast up by nature" (133.1–2) and Roberts's note on p. 731: "A piece of high ground on the Sidney estate of Penshurst was known as the Mount. Ben Jonson's poem, "To Penshurst" mentions it: "Thou hast thy walks for health as well as sport: / Thy Mount, to which the dryads do

The Counteſſe
of Mountgomeries
URANIA.

*Written by the right honorable the Lady
MARY WROATH:
Daughter to the right Noble Robert
Earle of Leicester.
And Neece to the ever famous, and re:
nowned Sᵗ Phillips Sidney knight. And to
ẙ moſt exelẜ Lady Mary Counteſſe of
Pembroke late deceaſed.*

Figure 4.5 Detail of windmill from title-page of *The Countess of Montgomery's Urania*. Reproduced by permission of the Folger Shakespeare Library.

As the places in which the interrelated kings and queens of the countries of Morea, Naples, and Pamphilia gather before they set off to Bohemia in order to claim the crown and realign the Holy Roman Empire, Wroth highlights their importance to the larger political vision of an international alliance. Her "countries," in other words, are political puns.

As Martin Elsky has pointed out, "country" was a politically dense, even volatile, term in the period, referring both to the county shires such as those of Kent, Wiltshire, and Essex over which the members of the Sidney-Herbert alliance were lords, and to the nation, or "country" of England itself.[53] In its vision of a cooperative Morea, Naples, and Pamphilia, Wroth's romance thus imagines diverse and cooperative sites of power, rather than one centralized site—a "federation of noble fiefdoms"—and an international coalition whose base is firmly grounded in the sovereign "countries" at home. Indeed both the families and the country court are central to the internationalist plot in the *Urania*. In perhaps the clearest presentation of this connection, Wroth writes of Amphilanthus's arrival in Morea that he "thought Morea was also the Empire of Germany, such a Court he found, and so brave company" (488.35–6). Roberts notes that Amphilanthus's praise of Morea "may be a veiled allusion to a possible alliance between Great Britain and Protestant Germany," but his praise also suggests that a successful Protestant alliance is as dependent on the county nobility and its representatives in Parliament as it is on a king.

In a scene which alludes to, and reimagines, the ill-fated crowning of Frederick as the King of Bohemia, Amphilanthus's ally Ollorandus learns that he is to become King of Bohemia, and he and Amphilanthus organize their troops from Naples (the shadowed Wilton) (260.18–21). Later in the same scene, Amphilanthus walks "into the Woods, and there met Pamphilia, Urania, Rosindy [the figure for Wroth's brother Robert Sidney], Steriamus [the figure for Susan Herbert's husband Philip Herbert] and Selarinus [the

---

resort" (ll. 9–10). The poem on p. 133 is copied in a 17th-cent. manuscript as "Penshurst Mount." See also the description of an estate much like Penshurst on 537.7 (and Roberts's note, p. 784). On Naples as Wilton, see 363.36–7 and Roberts's note on p. 760. See also the reference to the "little Arbour" on p. 135. Roberts relates Wroth's description to the garden that William Herbert created at Wilton in the 1620s (see Roberts, n. 135.40, p. 731). See also Wroth's allusion to a coronet fountain at 424.1, a detail for which Wilton's garden was renowned (see the note on pp. 768–9). The *Urania* also makes a reference to Stonehenge, which was located near Wilton (581.31, see Roberts's note p. 791). For Loughton (Pamphilia), see 344.30 and Roberts's note on p. 758, as well as the allusions to the Forests of Essex, over which the Wroths held sway, through 344.41. See also 630.12, p. 798. Roberts also suggests that Wroth's allusion to "a faire house moated about" in the *Urania* may refer to the moated Wroth estate of Durant's Arbour, located two miles east of Enfield in Middlesex (437.7, p. 770). See also Hannay, *Mary Sidney*, 143.

[53] "Microhistory and Cultural Geography," 519.

figure for Wroth's sister's husband, Sir John Hobart] comming together" (262.1–2). Not only does the family alliance "com[e] together" in this scene, but the meeting takes place in the woods, or countryside, of Naples, symbolically grounding the Bohemian cause in the countryside—in this case, in a shadowed Wiltshire—and the families who govern it. (Among his many titles in 1621, William Herbert was Chief Justice of the royal forests south of the Trent, and the Lord Lieutenant of Wiltshire.[54]) The "political pastoral" of the *Urania* thus insists not only on the central political importance of the country magnates, but on their determinative role in ensuring an international Protestantism. In other words, for Wroth, an internationalist Protestant ascendancy begins at home.

Wroth's vision of governance in the *Urania* is, accordingly, intently consiliary. Regents who lock themselves in secret cabinets with favorites are unfailingly represented as politically corrupt, most notably in the story of the queen who leads her favorite "into a private Cabinet, where she plotted all her wickednes [and] witch-craft" (71.26–9).[55] Wroth goes out of her way to make this queen an example of overweening monarchical prerogative; in the end she is condemned to have her "head struck off" "(for being a subject, shee was under the law)" (74.34–5). (While it is tidily contained in parentheses, Wroth nonetheless includes a defense of constitutionalism in what is essentially a story of tyrannicide.) By contrast, the interconnected protagonist rulers of the key countries in the *Urania* are not only cooperative with one another, but they are consistently solicitous of their subjects' "Councels." On at least two occasions Pamphilia herself leaves the government of her country "with the Councell" (making it clear that she does so "with the consent of [her] people," 168.15–16, 363.41–2).[56] Models for good local government, the kings and queens of Morea, Naples, and Pamphilia frequently insist that rulers need to listen to "counsel," a form of advice not only associated with the nobility, but also, particularly in the 1620s, with their voice in Parliament.[57] In the commonplace book he compiled around the time James last dissolved Parliament, Wroth's father Sir Robert Sidney argued that the King's

---

[54] See Norbrook on the associations between political pastoral and the English countryside. If "political pastoral" used the genre to comment on the corruption of the court, he argues, it also identified the English countryside as the site of Protestant politics, martial arts, and resistance to court corruption (*Poetry and Politics in the English Renaissance*, 208).

[55] See also the activities of the evil Queen of Epirus, 309–10.

[56] See e.g. 168, where Pamphilia leaves her government "for this time with the Councell" when she goes to adventure the Throne of Love, and again when she goes to visit the Queen of Naples and leaves "a grave and good Councell...behind her, to governe in her absence" (363).

[57] Sir Robert Sidney, first Earl of Leicester (1563–1626), was the Queen's chamberlain and sat in the House of Lords. He was present at each Parliament between 1603/4 and his death in 1626 (Hay, *Life of Robert Sidney*, 217). William Herbert was appointed a member of the Privy Council in 1610 and James's Lord Chancellor in 1615, but he often relied on parliamentary support rather than the King's. When he was appointed Lord Lieutenant of

prerogative rested less on divine right than on the "fundamentall Lawes" of the state he governed.[58] In the fractious 1621 Parliament, William Herbert's ally and parliamentary spokesperson Benjamin Rudyerd expressed it in similar ways, insisting that the King listen to the members of the House on matters of parliamentary right, and, with equal vehemence, on the Protestant alliance's desired intervention in Bohemia.[59] The *Urania*'s investment in "counsel" is a mirror for the alliance's investment in Parliament.

While many of the names of the principal characters and kingdoms in the *Urania* are taken from ancient history and, at least on the surface, far removed from contemporary European politics, others are transparently topical.[60] This is particularly true of the romance's myriad references to the battlegrounds of the Thirty Years War. In the course of the romance, to take only a few examples, we meet a gentlewoman from Silesia, a country near Bohemia currently suffering under the Habsburgs (as the gentlewoman says, "in the Country, where the murderer ruled... what could we doe but weepe and wish?" (282.9–11)); travel through Moravia, another country under Habsburg rule (274, 275.32); hear about the evil Princess of Stiria, a province of Austria and home of the Habsburg-appointed Protestant-oppressing Emperor Ferdinand—the man who deposed the Elector Palatine as ruler of Bohemia (296.29); and meet the (favorably represented) Princesses of Swethland (Sweden) and Denmark, countries which played key roles in the militant Protestant alignments of central Europe (657.3; see Wedgwood, *Thirty Years War*, 12).[61] (Amphilanthus rescues said princesses in a "cruel fight at Sea against Pyrates.") Amphilanthus, moreover, is crowned at "Franckford," where the seven electors historically

Wiltshire and Somerset in 1621 he gained further hold over appointments of justices of the peace and Members of Parliament (*ODNB*). See also Waller, *Sidney Family Romance*, 89.

[58] Hay, *Life of Robert Sidney*, 206. On the Sidneys' commonplace books, see Shephard's entry on Sidney in the *ODNB*. For more on the commonplace books, as well as the Sidney library, to which Wroth had access, see Germaine Warkentin, "The World and the Book at Penshurst." By 1671, there were 4,500 titles in the catalogue of the Penshurst Library (Warkentin, "The World and the Book," 330). Between 1618 and 1626, Wroth's brother, Robert Sidney, now Lord Lisle, accumulated over fifty books in England and on the continent ("The World and the Book," 333). These books included a 2-vol. "book of warres," Emanuel van Meteren's anti-Spanish *Historia Belgica* (The Hague, 1618); a Mercator Atlas, which, as Roberts points out, includes almost all the names Wroth uses in the *Urania* its maps of Asia and Greece (Roberts, p. xliv); *The Discovery of Portugal*, Ralegh's *History of the World*; a newsbook; and *The King's Declaration for Parliament* ("The World and the Book," 333–4). See also Warkentin's "Sidney's Authors"; and Shepherd, "Political Commonplace Books of Sir Robert Sidney."

[59] Rudyerd, *Memoirs*, 44, 73.

[60] Roberts found that a 16th-cent. map of the voyages of St Paul provides the best illustration for Wroth's choice of place names (*Urania*, fig. 13).

[61] On Ferdinand, see Wedgwood, *Thirty Years War*, 24, 56. These places were matters of common conversation and news circulation in Wroth's family. Sir William Browne wrote to her father on one occasion: "As to news: In these quarters one sword keeps the other in its

gathered to choose the Holy Roman Emperor.[62] (For Wedgwood's map of the European battleground of the Thirty Years War, see Figure 4.6.)

In what is perhaps the romance's most explicitly allusive scene, the son of the King of Bohemia has a dream in which a woman appears to him saying: "Arise, leave Bohemia, and rescue me from the hands of Rebels" (78.26–7).[63] The woman is a figure for Elizabeth of Bohemia, and the man to whom she appeals, Ollorandus, is the romance's cipher for Benjamin Rudyerd. As we saw in the last chapter, Rudyerd was a long-time member of the alliance (an exchanger of "Newes") and, throughout the 1620s, what one historian describes as "the chief House of Commons Spokesman for Pembroke."[64] Elizabeth's appeal for aid is thus made directly to the representative of the body most invested in her defense: the English Parliament. Unlike James I, moreover, Ollorandus, keeps the princess and her cause "perfect in [his] breast" (78.30).

As he was for the romance's cabineted sonnets, William Herbert was the intended audience for Wroth's vision for Bohemia. As the Earl of Pembroke, Herbert controlled a large voting block in Parliament, and he was also the alliance's representative in the inner circles of power. The Venetian ambassador described him as "the head of the puritans," and a

---

scabbard. The Silesians, those of Austria and those of Moravia still keep up their armies, foot and horse. Our Bohemians have none. They trust in God and in their innocence." *Report on Manuscripts*, 4: 238. Other key figures in the battle over the Palatinate and the Holy Roman Empire are shadowed in the romance: the King of Slavonia, to take one example, is a figure for Christian IV of Denmark, the regent who received Frederick on his flight from Bohemia (388.27–8, note on p. 764; on the historical figures, see Wedgwood, *Thirty Years War*, 29, 136–7). Wroth also presents, as versions of themselves, the princes of Wertenberg and Brunswick who came to England to raise money for the Protestant cause (587; ed. Roberts, p. xlviii).

[62] See Wedgwood, *Thirty Years War*, 95. In one scene, allies in Germany kneel down to Amphilanthus, praising "Ollorandus your worthy friend, having the greatest stroake in the election, making all the assembly remember your right hath chosen you, and triely Sir note onely hee, but all, as soone as you were named gave an equall consent, as if borne and made of one temper to serve you, having justly chose you to it" (441). His election is witnessed by a woman who is clearly a figure for Elizabeth of Bohemia, known as the "Winter Queen": "whose minde knew onely truth, rose likewise to salute him, and with such loyall love as joy of his sight sprang like spring time in her face, before pale and Winter-like in sorrow" (442). As Amphilanthus travels home he "came to the nearest part of Germany, and so pasd without any adventure, carrying the keys as one may say, of all those places to open his passage which way he pleas'd, never so pleasant a journey, all hearts contented, leaving discontent as an unprofitable thing at home; Buda, Prague, Vienna, all places he saw that were of worth." "At Franckford he was crown'd" (463). As Roberts puts it, "At the height of the Bohemian disaster, Wroth constructed a counter-myth within the *Urania* of a young man who brilliantly succeeds in creating an international coalition" (p. xlii).

[63] Ollorandus then goes to Hungary, where he sees picture of her in a gallery (79).

[64] See David L. Smith's entry on Rudyerd in the *ODNB*: "He sometimes answered letters for the third and then the fourth earl, and also acted as a surety for some of their legal transactions such as indentures conveying land. Similarly, his return to Parliament for Portsmouth (1621, 1624, 1625), and then for the Wiltshire constituencies of Old

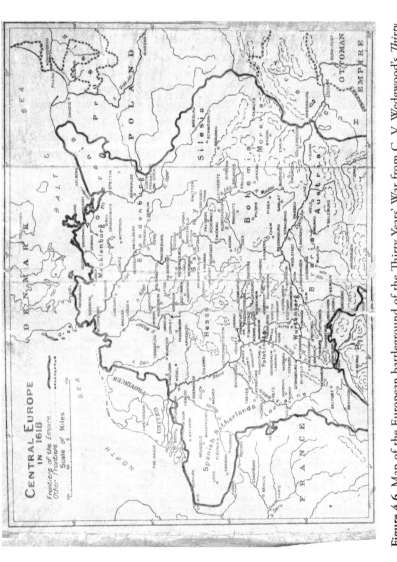

Figure 4.6 Map of the European battleground of the Thirty Years' War from C. V. Wedgwood's *Thirty Years' War*. Reproduced by permission of Yale University Press.

recent historian as the head of a "clandestine opposition" within James's Privy Council.[65] Wroth's romance was thus meant to encourage William Herbert in his role as the leader of the pro-Protestant and anti-Spanish voice in Parliament. In the scene in which Ollorandus vows to save the Queen, it is Herbert's cipher, the "Emperour" Amphilanthus who gives him what he needs to do the job, "honoring him with the gift of an excellent Horse, and furnishing [him] with all conveniencies"—precisely those things that James I refused to provide (78–9). Yet if Herbert saw Parliament both as a legitimate form of political counsel, and as the means by which the country nobility—especially his own alliance—could influence royal policy, he was neither as consistent nor as aggressive in his efforts as some wanted. (One scholar calls him the "Hamlet of English politics" in the 1620s.[66]) Deploying a genre rife with clandestine literary operations to offer advice to the man most associated with a "clandestine opposition" within James's Privy Council, Wroth thus endeavored to ensure that he was acting with sufficient constancy. In ciphering these contexts so explicitly, Wroth identified herself and her romance with the workings of effective oppositional statecraft, and thus with the "political humanism" for which the Sidney-Herbert alliance was known.

The relations between women and between the sovereign families in the *Urania* thus start to look like something far more complex than records of interfamilial friendships, or part of an elaborate attempt to ensure that William Herbert provide for his illegitimate children.[67] Pamphilia herself

---

Sarum (1626), Downton (1628–9), and Wilton (1640–48) was directly due to the earls of Pembroke, whose seat was at Wilton House." "Throughout his parliamentary career Rudyerd co-operated closely with his patrons. During the parliaments of the 1620s he consistently advocated careful collaboration between members of the two houses, and this was reflected in the alignment of his own attitudes with those of the third earl of Pembroke on several key issues. He has been described as 'the chief House of Commons spokesman for Pembroke' (C. Russell, *Parliaments and English Politics, 1621–1629*, 1979, 13) [...] Rudyerd's view of diplomacy was guided primarily by his horror that 'our religion was battered abroad' (Manning, 62)." See also *Urania*, ed. Roberts, p. xci.

[65] On the Venetian ambassador, see Heinemann, *Puritanism and Theatre*, 168. The claim that he maintained a "clandestine opposition" within James's government is Gerald Aylmer's (in *The King's Servants*, 61, cited in Heinemann, *Puritanism and Theatre*, 169). For Herbert's parliamentary power base, see Victor Stater's entry on Herbert in the *ODNB*. "The number of members identified with him varied from parliament to parliament but in the Commons it was never less than a dozen, rising to over thirty at times. Pembroke's extensive properties gave him control over several seats in the Commons, as in Cardiff and Wilton, and his many offices—his lieutenancies, the wardenry of the stannaries, the chancellorship of Oxford—further extended his reach [...] Moreover, he systematically collected proxies in the House of Lords; rarely did he have fewer than five, and at key moments he could deploy as many as ten. This parliamentary faction gave Pembroke an important advantage in his struggle with Buckingham, for though the latter (who had been elevated to duke in 1623) might have the king's heart, Pembroke could, when necessary, defend his position at court through his influence at Westminster."

[66] Derek Hirst, *Authority and Conflict*, 33.

[67] Hannay suggests that when Wroth named her romance "The Countess of Montgomery's Urania" "it was not the usual effort to enlist patronage, but rather an acknowledgement that

is, as we have seen, a symbol for constancy, but she is also consistently presented as a counselor—someone, as she points out on numerous occasions, who will not turn "blabb."[68] In one scene Pamphilia offers advice to her brother Rosindy, a cipher for Wroth's brother Robert Sidney. Rosindy accepts her advice gratefully, if not abjectly: "Binde mee more if you can, sweete Sister, and to make mee happy, enjoy the authoritie over mee and mine" (111.20–1). "What I know," she tells him in turn, "I were a poore weake woman, if I would conceale from you, or reveale of you" (111.13–14). In this scene, and in many others which follow it, Pamphilia is as validated for her reputation as a wise and discreet counselor: someone who will not turn "blabb." Pamphilia explicitly asks the question "Shall I turn blabb?" in the context of revealing her relationship with Amphilanthus. "As none but we doe truly love," she concludes, "so none but our owne hearts shall know we love" (318). She can, in other words, keep counsel. Throughout the romance, numerous characters praise Pamphilia for her "discretion."[69] Urania's claim that Pamphilia "could bee in greatest assemblies as private with her owne thoughts, as if in her Cabinet" (459.26–7) is not, as critics have suggested, a sign of her withdrawal from public circulation, but rather of her ability to be selectively and politically private in the sense William H. Sherman has identified as "privy": privy to information, that is, but discreet about sharing it.[70] The primary connotations of this

the two friends had spent many happy hours talking about that fictional world" (*Mary Sidney*, 138).

[68] In terms of the political implications of this turn of phrase, Elizabeth critically referred to herself "play[ing] the blab" around Mary Queen of Scots (see *Urania*, ed. Roberts, 753). Patricia Parker sees the digressiveness of the romance genre linked to women's garrulity and irrationality. Wroth turns this logic on its head by having a woman who refuses—repeatedly—to "turn blabb." In one of the earliest essays on Wroth, Jeff Masten claims that the sonnets "stage a movement which is relentlessly private, withdrawing into an interiorized space; they foreground a refusal to speak in the public, exhibitionist voice of traditional Petrarchan discourse; in the context of the published portion of *Urania*, they articulate a women's resolute constancy, self-sovereignty, and unwillingness to circulate among men; they gesture toward a subject under self-control" ("'Shall I turne blabb?,'" 68). For Danielle Clarke, "a reluctance to speak or to repeat their narratives in a public context characterizes all Wroth's heroines. This is partly to do with discretion and keeping female desire from public expression, but also with the tensions regarding circulation and interpretation that accrue throughout the *Urania*" (*Politics of Women's Writing*, 247). Pamphilia's silence, in other words, is "related to fears of misinterpretation and application," and a way of guarding against the sexual looseness associated with speech (247). But whereas Clarke sees the end of Pamphilia's refusal to "turn blabb" as the disruption of the sexualization of women's speech and writing, and the accommodation of female subjectivity, I see the end point as political: an advertisement of the political discretion of female counselors.

[69] See e.g. 48, 61.30, "yet was shee generally the most silent and discreetly retir'd of any Princesse" (263.11–12) and "yet her discretion told her, the lesse that were spoken of, the much better it would bee, wherefore she said little of it" (460.13).

[70] Clarke, *Politics of Women's Writing*, 251. Alexander notes that this line echoes Sidney's Astrophel, who seems "most alone in greatest company" (*Astrophel and Stella*, 27.2, cited 310). For "privy," see *John Dee*, 75.

term in early modern England, Sherman points out, "are suggested by its cognates such as 'privileged,' its synonyms such as 'secret' and 'proper' and its use in such institutions as the "Privy Council," the "Privy Chamber" and 'Secret [or Privy] Service'" (75). Rather than a place of female retreat or "female subjectivity," the lady's "Cabinet" in the *Urania* is a place of politic female counsel, and it is presented in precisely the language of stoic fortitude associated with the alliance.[71] Like Pamela and Philoclea before her, Pamphilia "lost not her self...though her private fortunes shook roundabout her," and when she is temporarily side-tracked, she has plenty of back-up in Urania (1: 484).

From the very beginning of the romance, Urania is represented as a counselor of singular importance; the *Urania* opens with her giving "some counsel" to a prince wavering in his political righteousness (4.41–2). This prince, Perissus, is in love with a woman who is subject to a tyrant, and Urania counsels him to rescue her from his clutches. (The tyrant, Philargus, has promised Limena that if she "consent not to [his] will," he will kill her.) "[W]hy make you not the Phoenix of your deeds live again," Urania asks Perissus, "Philargus's house is not in all places" (10.8).[72] As we saw in the *Arcadia*, a rapacious tyrant often serves as a political metaphor for overweening monarchical privilege, the would-be rapist's threats of sexual violation and misogyny analogous to the tyrant's abuse of his subjects.[73] Resisting such abuse thus also signifies a political commitment to a mixed rather than an absolute monarchy, and reciprocal love the model for what a mixed monarchy might look like. (Philargus's house, after all, is not in all places.) As the merry Marquise reminds Pamphilia in the second part of the romance, "Love" may be "Emperiall and all soveraily governing," but just as "a Monarchy hath many lawes to be governed by," so too does Love (2:282.6–7).[74] Stories that feature the correction of "Love"'s

---

[71] In one particularly interesting scene, Rosindy asks Pamphilia for military advice, which he accepts gratefully. As the rulers of Achaia, Morea, and Romania agree to send men to free Macedon, Pamphilia ensures that Rosindy is made General of the Morean forces (123.5–15). This act exemplifies both her trustworthy, even Elizabethan, circumspection as well as her political efficacy. (Indeed, the De L'Isle and Dudley papers suggest that female members of the Sidney-Herbert families played key roles in ensuring that Rosindy's real-life counterpart, Robert Sidney, was made a captain of forces in Flushing.) See *Report on the Manuscripts of Lord De L'Isle and Dudley*, 4: 240, 241. On the political presence of the Sidney and Herbert women, see also 4: 245 and 276.

[72] Quilligan argues that Urania urges Perissus to heroic action just as Britomart does to Scudamore in book 2 of the *Faerie Queen* (*Incest*, 194–5).

[73] See e.g. the story of Perselina who did not want to "grow subject to a Husband," and of Lisia who "suffered like a Martyre under [her husband's] churlishness" but "resolved to alter him" (527, 559).

[74] She advises Pamphilia to "obay your husband with discresion and noe farder, and that will make him so discreete as nott to tiranise. Which else they will doe fiercely (when they

overweening monarchical prerogative, Wroth tells us, are "profitable for Princes," and as in the *Arcadia*, these stories frequently rely on female constancy and counsel.[75]

The nature of the as-yet unidentified Urania's advice to Perissus at the beginning of the *Urania* is familiar to any reader of Lipsius or the *Arcadia*: she advises reason ("discretion and judgement") over passion, and the commitment to virtue in the face of outside accidents.[76] Utterly convinced by "that reason which abounds in" his interlocutor and vowing that "the glory of his attempt" will be hers, Perissus begs Urania, whom he explicitly calls his "Counsellor," to tell him who she is (15.40–1, 16.1). Thus while the tyrant-resister Limena plays one part of the role Pamela plays in the *Arcadia*—admitting that her body is in his hands "to dispose of to death if [he] will," she nonetheless asserts that Philargus cannot "purchase" her "consent" (13.3–6)—the real hero of the story is Urania. In much the same way as Pamela and Philoclea (repeatedly) turn Musidorus and Pyrocles from despair to heroic action, Urania turns Perissus from considering himself "a castaway of fortune" ("Despair having left [him] no more ground for hope"), into a Phoenix for the cause. "[L]et it never be said," she states by way of encouragement, that Perissus "ended unrevenged of Philargus, and concluded his dayes like a Fly in a corner" (15.36–7).

Much as Sidney does in the *Arcadia*, Wroth stops her account of monarchical correction short of tyrannicide; Philargus repents and insists on a contractual marriage between Perissus, the true sovereign, and his beloved. And it is Urania's counsel that brings it all about.[77]

have the raines, like horses get the bitt betweene their teeth and runn the full race or course) of their owne humour, and the wives slaverye. Love itt selfe is nott to bee commaunded; hee is Emperiall and all soverainly governing. Butt as a Monarchy hath many lawes to be governed by, so is this a part" (2.281). See also Melissa Sanchez's discussion of the ways in which "feminine counsel restrain[s] masculine will" in such scenes (*Erotic Subjects*, 143).

[75] The Cecropia figure in the *Urania* is Nereana, described as "absolute Lady of [her] Iland [Stalamina]" whose people "permitted her to have her fond desires without limiting her power" (192). Her story, as Elaine Beilin has argued, "moves towards delivering the people from subjugation and requiring their consent, even their hearts, in the establishment of a stable government" ("Role of the Political Subject," 13). Imprisoned in Tower, the "punishment justly allotted for such excessive over-weening" (*Urania*, 338.7–8), she is eventually released because a nobleman becomes her advocate: "he sway'd much, and so far proceeded, as hee with the rest of the Counsel, fetched Nereana forth, solemnly againe establish'd her" (496.16–17). She reforms herself, becoming an "excellent Governesse" of her passions, and the narrator designates her story as "most profitable to Princes" (496.27–8, 30).

[76] When Perissus tells her that Limena has asked him to "revenge not my death on my murderer who, how unworthy soever he was or is, yet he is my husband," Urania advises a different route. How can so "brave a prince" she asks, "by will without reason willfully lose himself?" (14.34–5).

[77] Urania's marriage to Steriamus is a model of marital reciprocity: "Love," Steriamus tells a misogynist interlocutor, "is only to be gained by love equally bestowed, the giver and receiver reciprocally liberall, else it is no love" (194). Like Pyrocles, he also offers a defense of

Urania goes on to serve as Pamphilia's counselor throughout the romance, urging Pamphilia to "governe" her passions (else what can the people "hope of your government?"), and defending her constancy to Amphilanthus when he doubts it.[78] "[A]bove all worldly motions," she tells him, Pamphilia is "fixt, and onely fixt to you" (2:139.19–20). In the oft-used pun on Wroth's name, Urania declares that Pamphilia is an exemplar of "worthe and Constancie," a "magasine," in an equally loaded metaphor, "of spottles love" (2:140.24). When Pamphilia herself is threatened by a tyrant and vows to resist him—like Limena, she is "resolutely resolved to dy rather then consent" to be his wife (2:155.8–9)—Steriamus (the cipher for Philip Herbert) and Urania are "in the highest ranck of [the] hoped-for freinds" who come to her aid (2:155.16–17). Praising Pamphilia's "knowledge and judiciall counsell" Steriamus vows not only his own help, but also the "forces" of his "wyfe," a woman whose counsel he describes as "more Judiciall, more exquisite then the whole great counsels of the greatest Monarckies" (2:157.24, 2:153). (It is no coincidence that Steriamus and Urania's marriage is a model of reciprocity.)

As we have seen, Urania is with Pamphilia and Amphilanthus in many of their crucial moments. In one emblematic scene, "the two incomparable Princesses" Urania and Pamphilia lay down on Amphilanthus's "Mantle," and "the king casting himselfe at their feete," speaks to them with "his head in Urania's lap, and holding Pamphilia by the hand" (192.4–9). In another, Pamphilia visits Urania and Amphilanthus at Naples and claims to be "never so happy as when in this company" (256.23–4).[79] Rather than merely buttressing Wroth's personal claims to Herbert's attention,

women: "your mother was a woman," he tells the same misogynist, "and you must be favor'd by an other, to be blessed with brave posterity" (189.18–20).

[78] "Where is your judgement and discreet govern'd' spirt," Urania asks (468.6). Her advice that Pamphilia use her constancy to "hate" her inconstant lover, to "let him goe and rejoice" is tempered by her caveat that Pamphilia must bee sure that she "mistake him not, or unmeritingly condemn him" (469.13–14). But much like Euarchus in the *Arcadia*, who is willing to condemn his own son to death for breaking the law, Urania vows that she would give Pamphilia the same advice, "though I knew it were mine owne brother had caused this mischief" (469.16–18). While Pamphilia responds with characteristic irony, "Your brother might yet challenge more care from you, and testimonie of love, who ought as a sister rather to hide or cover his imperfections," Urania insists that "[h]e is not such a Deity as your Idolatry makes him" (469.19–21, 42). In the end, Pamphilia stays her constant course ("Pamphilia must be of a new composition before she can let such thoughts fall into her constant breast") and Urania vows to support her (470.24–6).

[79] Robert Sidney frequently writes to his wife from London about occasions in which he saw members of the Sidney/Herbert family together: "Your daughter I thank God is very well and so is your son also" (8 November 1610, *Report on Manuscripts*, 4: 245); "My Lady of Montgomery and your daughter have been here and are returned very well" (4: 276); and, on 14 October 1607, "I am going that day to Loughton [Hall in Essex] to see your daughter and to meet my Lord of Pembroke there" (3: 414).

such triangulations, or more accurately *alliances*, provide the real structure for the romance. Pamphilia and Amphilathus may be at its apex, but the members of the romance's interrelated counties are nonetheless crucial to the *Urania's* plot.

Ollorandus and Amphilanthus are crowned King of Bohemia and of Romans respectively about halfway through the first part of the romance (275.1–2).[80] After the Princess of Stiria attempts to seduce him (Ferdinand of Styria, as I have mentioned, was the ruthless monarch of Bohemia deposed by the people in favor of Frederick), Amphilanthus sets out for home, vowing that "the dainty Pamphilia will be the kingdome he'le first visit" (296, 303.41–2). When he arrives home in Naples he is made the King of Naples as well, a scene that not only shadows William Herbert's accession at the death of his father to the Earldom of Pembroke, and, in 1621, to the Lord Lieutenancy of the entire county of Wiltshire, but of non-absolutist sovereignty more generally. When he arrives in Naples "the Lords and Commons all with one consent (and that consent accompanied with gladnesse in their good) received Amphilanthus for their King."[81] When Amphilanthus does finally visit Pamphilia, he finds her outdoors "in her owne Country[side]," privately attesting, in a now familiar refrain, to her loyalty and discretion: "'Soft,' said she, 'shall I turne blabb?'" (317.13, 318.5–9). Her beloved, she reflects, may be "in the field performing famous acts" or "on the Sea passing to fetch more fame," but his thoughts, as hers are with him, may well be with her at home: "one love still governs him and me, are wee not most properly one?" (318.22–3, 319.10–11). If, as Maureen Quilligan has argued, endogamy served to keep power within the family, in the *Urania* it also serves as a symbol of political loyalty and alliance.[82] It is immediately after this vow—"are wee not most properly one?"—that Pamphilia shows Amphilanthus her poems in her cabinet (320), and then engraves his "sypher, which contained the letters, or rather the Anagram of his name she most and only lov'd" into an

---

[80] When Ollorandus's wife Melasinda finds out that he has become King of Bohemia she calls it "Happie newes" "but most happie that hee crownes himself with constancy, the perfect lawrell for lovers" (272).

[81] See Roberts's note on p. 752. There was "a Coronation" in which the Embassadours of Morea, France, Great Brittany, Bohemia, Romania, and "the sweet and delicate Pamphilia" participate. Amphilanthus then settles "all his estate in good or quiet government, to which end he did appoint the Prince his brother to be Regent, and setled such a grave and honest Councell, as he was secure (though absent) of his Kingdomes good" (304.21–4). Both brothers were in the political ascendancy when Wroth wrote her romance. James I paid another summer visit to Wilton in 1620, and in 1621 appointed Pembroke Lord Lieutenant of Somerset and Wiltshire, further consolidating his already significant power in the west (see the *ODNB*).

[82] On endogamy, see also Zurcher, who argues that endogamy is a kind of "metaphorical chastity," a form of "consolidation from which [Wroth] can defy contingency" (11, 43).

oak tree on her estate—a symbol not only of their union, but of the union between their "countries" (325.40–2). In these carefully orchestrated scenes, Wroth writes herself, and her estate, into the Sidney-Herbert alliance of "counties," rendering the shadowed Loughton a site of power and privilege equal to those of—even "one" with—Wilton and Penshurst.[83]

When Amphilanthus next goes abroad he travels as "the Knight of Cipher": Pamphilia's chivalric servant. His cipher, made "of all the letters of his Mistrisses name, delicately composed within the compasse of one," alludes explicitly to Wroth herself (339.25–6). "[A]lthough a Cipher were nothing in it selfe," he notes, "yet joyned to the figures of her *worth*, whose name was therein, it was made above the valew of her selfe or Country," 339.35–7, emphasis added).[84] When he returns home from being crowned Holy Roman Emperor, moreover, the climax of the romance's political fantasy, he is greeted by "Queene Pamphilia with her counsell, and Noble men" (565.32). The Emperor, the narrator tells us, "marking her, had inwardly new power and might given him by her constancy" (566.5–6). When the Emperor mounts his horse for his battle against the King of Celicia who "came with such an Army against [Pamphilia], to have her by force" (571.5–6), he again affirms her centrality, meeting his opponent with "the State and Counsell of Pamphilia wayting on him" and "his face towards [Pamphilia's] Castle" (566.14–15, 17).

During the fight itself, Amphilanthus's entourage is made up of precisely the international forces deemed necessary for a successful international Protestant coalition: "the Prince of Transilvania carried his Crowne, the Duke of Brunswicke, Bavaria, Lorraine, Savoy, Sax, Millan, the Prince of Venice, and the rest carried the Armour, Launce, and led the spare horse" (566.21–3).[85] By placing Pamphilia in the middle of this heavily symbolic scene, and by identifying her "constancy" as the source of the Emperor's power, Wroth highlights the key roles that the home countries and their sovereign families played in the international effort. When the battle is

[83] The De L'Isle papers also give tantalizing evidence of meetings at Loughton. On 14 October 1607 e.g. Robert Sidney wrote to Barbara Gamage Sidney to tell her that he was "going that day to Loughton [Hall in Essex] to see your daughter and to meet my Lord of Pembroke there" (3: 414).

[84] In the second part of the romance, Amphilanthus meets a youth who tells him "I have a sipher on my hart, which is sayd to bee her name whom I must by many hard adventures att last gaine, and knowe her by having a sipher likewise, which shall discover my name, and then I shall be knowne. I am furder tolde I must have my knighthood from your most Royall hands" (2.297). Roberts points out that this youth, who is identified as "Fair Design," is a cipher for Wroth's son with William Herbert.

[85] In this period, Transylvania was ruled by the fierce Calvinist Gabriel Blethen and sought independence from Emperor Rudolph II who conquered it in 1604 (*Urania*, 478, n. 21.15–16).

over, "the Councell standing all before [Pamphilia and Amphilanthus], and his Princes with her Nobility, they two sate downe under a cloath of estate" (568.3–5).[86] While Amphilanthus is "Master of the greatest part of the Westerne World" (568.18–19), he is also intimately allied with and loyal to his neighboring country of Pamphilia, surrounded by both countries' nobility, and faced, both dialogically and emblematically, with their "Councell." When Pamphilia takes Amphilanthus "into her Castle" (567.41) after he beats the Cecilian King, and he gazes into "her affectionately requiting eyes" (568.9), we have an emblem of the marriage of sovereignty and counsel located firmly in an alliance between sovereign counties and their chief "Castle[s]."

In the scene that follows this reunion, Pamphilia broods over the love and loyalty of Amphilanthus while the pair is out hunting, and they run into a local shepherd. Without knowing who he is speaking to, the shepherd praises Pamphilia's local sovereignty, telling them that she is

> a Lady loved and well thought on by all that ever I heard speake of her, curteous, affable, no pride dwells in her, to the meanest she will speake; yet the greatest feare her, which is her judgement and goodnesse that breedes that respect to her; shee is upright and just, in her government mild, and loving to her subjects, shee loves all good exercises as well abroad as at home; shee hath indeed they say, a brave and manlike spirit, and wonderous wise shee is (570.36–42)

In this "shepherd's" account, Pamphilia is described as the ideal country magnate and magistrate, her "government mild, and loving to her subjects."[87] To use the term Jonson uses to flatter Sir Robert Sidney in "To Penshurst," Pamphilia "dwells" in her country, maintaining its governorship with politic care. This good governorship, as we have seen, is also directly implicated in the internationalist vision of the romance as a whole. During this scene, moreover, Amphilanthus himself goes missing (577).

Following these events, in which Pamphilia's resistance to a tyrant is enabled both by the cooperation of sovereign counties and her own effective local governance, Wroth includes a seemingly gratuitous account of the fall of a noble family. The story, recounted to Pamphilia by a shepherdess named "Mirasilva" she meets while searching for Amphilanthus, is a barely shadowed account of the fall of John Dudley, Duke of Northumberland, a Sidney ancestor executed for rebelling against the monarchy in an attempt

---

[86] In an earlier scene, again before they sit down under the "cloath of State," Pamphilia offers Amphilanthus her life, and he tells her that there is "not in the world, next her selfe that hee respected more, or in any degree of comparison with her liberty, and pleasure, therefore she might assure her selfe, that her honor, and safety, should command his life, which could never be so well imployed as in serving her" (508.34–6).

[87] She fishes, hawks, and hunts as well (575).

to put Lady Jane Grey on the throne.[88] (The unnamed "Earl" is the grand-father of Mirasilva's beloved, Sildurino; Roberts suggests that Sildurino is a cipher for Philip Sidney, and Mirasilva for Penelope Rich.) At first, the account seems like a rather flat-footed attempt to rehabilitate the family's reputation: "There is no reason to use them with the lesse respect," Mirasilva asserts, "who suffer for others offences, not their own" (577.7–9). Yet the story she tells turns out to be an account of baronial righteousness. Living under "a mighty Tyrant" who ruled (in a classic neostoic formulation) "like a Tree in the midst of a plaine" with "his branches cut off" and shaken by every "storme," Sildurino's family suffers but "would not consent to thinke of ill courses" (577.20, 39, 40, 16–17). Eventually, however, "most of the remayning Nobility, and especially all the auncient Lords by desent" "agreed together" to an unnamed plan.[89] When the King calls them to an "assembly of all his Lords," as if to "rectifie some things that were amisse, and to give satisfaction to his people, if any thing troubled them," these ancient Lords came, hoping to air their grievances (578.17–19). (They remained, as Mirasilva points out, "earnest" for their Country, and "too honest," for the most part, "to be called conspirators" (578.23–4, 20–1).) Yet when the King "cross'd and cut [them] short," she recounts, "they flew out" rather than suffer dishonor, and "many of the Commons, tooke part with them" (578.24–6). Mirasilva's account of a Parliament "cut...short," or dissolved, by a manipulative king, suggests not only that such an act is an abuse of monarchical prerogative, but that it can lead to rebellion: "to fly out" in the seventeenth century meant to "come out suddenly, or to explode," "to burst out into extravagant conduct, language, or temper" (*OED* 8e).[90] More than a strict account of the fortunes of the Dudleys, then, Mirasilva's story is a kind of mash-up of aristocratic rebellion, bear-ing traces of stories ranging from Northumberland's in 1553 to the Earl of Essex's in 1601. The story serves in this place, deep in the romance, not only as a defense of Wroth's Sidney ancestors, but as an argument for tak-ing Parliament, particularly the consiliary rights of the "auncient Lords by desent," seriously.

---

[88] See Roberts, n. 577.5–6, p. 791.

[89] Intuiting that there is something afoot, the King "thrust[s]" his "instruments," or favourites, into the "counsells, and companyes" of his ancient nobility (578.1–4, 9). His "instruments" are classic favorites, "content to sweare and forsweare any thing, nay theire owne soules to winne his favour, such a Tyrant is ambition over man to get the grace of Kings, who being king is enough, and no matter what Kings they are" (578.10–13). Mirasilva makes it clear that it is these men who lead the nobility into a "snare" (578.15).

[90] Mirasilva recounts that Sildurino's grandfather was executed and his sons, "[n]ot being of the confederacy," were "degraded, their houses razed, and their name utterly forgotten." "Many other noble families fell also" (578.30–1, 578.36).

Immediately following this scene, Pamphilia comes to a place "made round like a Crowne of mighty stones" that is clearly a figure for Stonehenge, the national landmark near the Herberts' Wilton estate (581.31). There she finds Amphilanthus's bloody armour and his sword stuck in one of the stones, and, fearing the worst, panics. "What account can I give the world of his losse, whom all the world admired and loved?" she asks herself. "What will Germany, Italy, and all say of me? what curses lay upon me, and my Country, when they shall know that with me, and in this place they have lost him?" (582.14–17). In this scene, Pamphilia reveals that she is as devoted to the House of Naples (the shadowed Herberts) as she is to the Moreans (or Sidneys), and that together they are responsible for providing the resolution to a political crisis.[91]

In the final scene of *The First Part of the Countess of Montgomery's Urania*, when the recovered Amphilanthus is once again on his way to Germany with the Duke of Saxony (historically one of the other Electors of the German Liberties), he insists that he must stop and visit Pamphilia, "enjoyning [the party] to saile on for Germany, giving the Duke of Saxony letters to Ollorandus, and the rest of the Counsell, with all instructions fit for such imployment" (659.5–7).[92] Having established his dual loyalty to home and abroad, and stepping nimbly on the "Pamphilian shore," Amphilanthus finds Pamphilia once again alone in a wooded forest (659.5). In a whirlwind imitation of the relationship between the powerful county magnates and the court, Pamphilia and Amphilanthus "returned to the Cittie, and the next day to the wood againe," a London–country progress made frequently by both Herbert and Wroth during the contentious final years of James's reign (660.34–5).[93] In this final scene, Pamphilia and Amphilanthus's movements between the country and the court allegorize the relationship Wroth sought to idealize: an exchange not between center and periphery, but between interrelated and mutually dependent sites of power and political influence. From the "Pamphilian shore" and "allied" with his neighbors, Amphilanthus is able to communicate with and maintain order in Germany through diplomatic and Parliamentarian means, entrusting the matter "to Ollorandus, and the rest of the Counsell." Amphilanthus "now recovered his Sword, and brought home his Armour, resolving nothing should remaine as witnesses of his former

---

[91] In a similarly heavy-handed scene in the second part of the romance, Pamphilia is visiting Steriamus and Urania and a lion, a symbol of royal and martial power and part of the Herbert arms, comes to court and latches onto Pamphilia "att night lying at her chamber doore; in the day time waiting on her" (2.308).

[92] For the Duke of Saxony, see Wedgwood, *Thirty Years War*, 40.

[93] During the years 1619–21, Wroth frequently traveled between London, and the country estates of Penshurst, Wilton, Loughton, and Durant's Arbour; see also n. 80.

fickleness" (661.1–2).[94] Due to Pamphilia's constancy, Amphilanthus's is firmly and finally entrenched, and the "Sword" and "Armour" of militant Protestantism are brought resolutely "home."

On 23 December 1620 James I made an official proclamation "against excesse of Lavish and Licentious Speech of matters of State," ordering English men and women to cease meddling in "causes of State, and secrets of Empire."[95] In June 1621, a month before Wroth registered the *Urania* in the Stationers' Register, a supplementary proclamation sought to buttress the first: "wee are given to understand, that notwithstanding the strictnesse of Our commandement, the inordinate libertie of unreverent speech, touching matters of high nature, unfit for vulgar discourse, doth daily more and more increase."[96] A month before this second proclamation, Parliament had met, and many members saw the proclamation for what it was: an attempt to halt their criticism of royal policy, particularly in the matter of the Palatinate. The proclamations, moreover, sought to silence the polemical efficacy of "political pastoral," literary texts that were frequently critical not only of the court, but of the ways in which it was handling both domestic and foreign policy.[97] As Philip Sidney put it, pastoral romance was a tool of critique deemed necessary when sovereign princes "put off publique action," and in the 1620s many pastoral texts were working—and were perceived to be working—in the service of a parliamentary opposition.[98]

---

[94] There is an interesting moment in the *Urania* when Amphilanthus is praised for his talent in writing poetry, "a quallitie among the best much prized and esteemed, Princes brought up in that, next to the use of Armes" (136.12–14). Like militancy, in other words, poetry serves political ends.

[95] The proclamation is cited in F. J. Levy, "Staging the News," 252 and n. 1. See also *Stuart Royal Proclamations*, 1: 495–6.

[96] *Stuart Royal Proclamations*, 1: 519–21 (26 July 1621), cited in Levy, "Staging the News," 253.

[97] As Norbrook argues, not long after James took the throne, poets "used the traditional symbolism of Protestant pastoral to voice their discontent. They could almost be described as constituting a poetic 'opposition.'" *Poetry and Politics*, 198. Much attention has been devoted to the role that news and newspapers and topical drama played in the shift in power between court and Parliament and court and country in the 1620s, but pastoral played an equally significant role. On news, see Richard Cust, "News and Politics in Early Seventeenth Century England"; and F. J. Levy, "How Information Spread among the Gentry."

[98] Cited in Paul Salzman, "The Strang[e] Constructions of Mary Wroth's 'Urania,'" 116. Wroth has a sense of humour about the specifically political stakes of the way in which her romance glances at greater matters. Shortly after reminding her readers that people use the "Sheapardesse names" in "pretty Pastorall" "to cover [their] owne ill fortune the better" (613.40–1), she tells the story of a "Sheperdess" of "the fair Rocks of Britany, anciently called Albion" (627.9–10). Armed with "strong resolution" and "defended by [her] own virtue," this English shepherdess receives overtures from the Prince of Venice—always a synecdoche for republican rule—and, after only a brief flirtation, sends him away from "these parts." For Wroth, England may not have been ready for republicanism, but it was ready for Parliament.

In the same month as James's second proclamation "Against excess of lavish and licentious speech of matters of state," the poet George Wither was arrested for publishing one of these texts, and imprisoned, pointedly, until the end of the 1621 parliamentary session.[99] On 4 June 1621, Wither's printer, Augustine Mathewes, and publishers, John Marriot and John Grismond, were fined for their role in publishing his work.[100] One month later, the same team published Mary Wroth's *Urania*. Rather than an unfortunate choice on Wroth's part, I want to suggest instead that Wroth chose these publishers precisely *because* of their association with politically critical texts.[101] Like Wither and the other authors whom David Norbrook has identified with "political pastoral," Wroth saw her work, which she published in the middle of one of the most contentious parliamentary sessions in English history, as a form of advice for Parliament and, as I have argued throughout this chapter, in support of the alliance's cause.[102]

We know that those active in the political arena considered reading immediately relevant to contemporary affairs of state, and there is some evidence that her contemporaries read Wroth's romance in such a way. William Davenport, an assiduous reader and commonplace book-transcriber of contemporary political newsletters and newsbooks,

---

[99] The book was *Withers Motto* (1621). On Wither's arrests and imprisonments, see Norbrook, *Poetry and Politics*, 209–19, and Michelle O'Callaghan's entry on Wither in the *ODNB*: "Wither was not freed until 15 March 1622, and he later thanked both Prince Charles and William Herbert, earl of Pembroke, for their intervention on his behalf."

[100] *Urania*, ed. Robert, p. cviii. See also the *ODNB*: "There was a great deal of co-operation between Wither and his publishers, John Marriot and John Grismond, in evading licensing restrictions. Senior members of the Stationers' Company also sought to profit from its unlicensed printing: Lownes, a warden of the company who had actually prosecuted Marriot, Grismond, and their printer, Augustine Mathews, daily bought copies from Grismond to sell at his shop. *Wither's Motto* proved highly popular, going into at least eight editions in 1621—he later claimed that 30,000 copies were printed within a few months (*Ecchoes from the Sixth Trumpet*, 1666, 47)." On Marriott and Grismond, see also Brennan, *Sidneys of Penshurst*, 135; and Smith, *Sonnets*: "*Urania* might itself be read as a Spenserian text" (101). In his *Motto* Wither praises Pembroke, Robert Sidney, and Wroth, making the "worth/Wroth" pun (Hannay, *Mary Sidney*, 232–3).

[101] The *Urania* is thus an excellent example of a text whose "polyvocal thickness" is built not only through the imaginative resources of the author, but through "the textual presence and activities of many non-authorial agents." See Jerome McGann, "The Socialization of Texts," 42.

[102] The authors Norbrook associates with political pastoral are Drayton, Wither, William Browne, Fulke Greville and Samuel Daniel. He does not include Wroth, the author of the longest, and, arguably, most notorious, pastoral romance of the era. Similarly, Paul Salzman does not include Wroth in his section on "The Political Allegorical Romance," in *English Prose Fiction, 1558–1700*. He finds what he calls Wroth's "verisimilarity" to be her most original contribution to the development of prose fiction; it offered "a new engagement with the minutiae of contemporary life, which makes it possible for later political romances to encompass events of the Civil War in detail" (141).

also owned a copy of the *Urania*.[103] His notations bear out contemporary perceptions of some of the "personal" topicality of the romance; he twice wrote "cozens" opposite "lovers" in his copy of the romance.[104] But he also carefully took notes on a passage in which a man vows that a subject ought not "upon any termes to weare armes against his rightfull King," and one in which the text describes the "doings, and lyffe of a Tyraunt" (445.11–12, 791). These notes suggest that Davenport understood the *Urania* not only as a *roman à clef* about the Sidney-Herbert family, but as a political pastoral intended to reflect on the political actions of men, including the taking of military action.[105] Another contemporary, the historian Edmund Bolton, placed the *Urania* in the company of the *Arcadia* and *Argenis* as texts which "shadowe out some persons, or matter, which it were not otherwise safe, or convenient to discover directly."[106] All three romances, he suggests, made their "arguments" much more deeply than they could have

---

[103] See Morrill, "William Davenport and the 'Silent Majority' of Early Stuart England." On his ownership of the *Urania*, see *Urania*, ed. Roberts, 663. Roberts identifies Davenport only as a "book collector." According to Morrill, Davenport was the member of one of the leading families of his county, his interests were "overwhelmingly local," and his reading and annotating suggest that he was a member of the country gentry who were alienated from the court (117, 118). Until 1641, most of the material he read was "consistently anti-government and particularly anti-Court" (119). He was particularly concerned with "hard political scandal[s]" like the murder of Overbury, and made "careful copies of parliamentary speeches by the leading oppositionists," especially about the Spanish match (119). Davenport's concern about bad courtiers and bad marriages may well have resonated with the way he read Wroth's topical romance.

[104] See *Urania*, ed. Roberts, n. 33, p. lxvii. Davenport made his notes at 417.11 and 418.34). See also 416.29–30, p. 767, where Roberts notes that Davenport heavily annotated a story inserting "her kinsman" above Wroth's text "was also married."

[105] William Davenport called attention to this first passage in his copy by underlining and marking it with a flower in the margin (see Roberts's note on p. 771). For the second example, see Roberts's note on p. 791. While Morrill argues that the other documents Davenport keeps "reflect a conventional Protestant nationalism," and that he was not attached to any organized opposition party or interest, he was nonetheless attuned to the ways in which the *Urania* reflects on such controversial matters as the role of kings and the nature of tyranny (120). See also Orgis, "'[A] story very well woorth reading,'" who points out that Davenport calls Urania's counsel "good perswation," and frequently notes female constancy (95–6). Lois Potter discusses similar marginal notes made in a 1625 edition of Barclay's *Argenis*, which highlight its concern with "tribute and impositions of kings upon their subjects" (*Secret Rites and Secret Writing*, 75).

[106] Cited in Thomas H. Blackburn, "Edmund Bolton's *The Cabanet Royal*," 169. Bolton's text (BM Ms. Royal 18A. LXXI) was written in 1627 as a plea to get Charles I interested in the Academy Royal, which Bolton first introduced in the reign of James I. Such stories as *Argenis* and the *Arcadia* "may greatly profit the reader," Bolton writes, "and not delight him only" (Blackburn, "Edmund Bolton's *The Cabanet Royal*," 169). "None of them, nor ye like, can enter so deeply if their arguments had the opinion of realitie." "Finallie," he continues, "if there bee but a conceipt, or fame, that they shadowe out some persons, or matter, which it were not otherwise safe, or convenient to discover directly, this only phansye of a secret truthe makes the keyes of those mysteries pretious, and the book passeth away much ye more roundly. The Countess of MONTGOMERIES late volume, as well as SIDNEYS,

done if they "had the opinion of realitie." Each text, moreover, benefited from the "conceipt, or fame" that it shadowed important matters, making the "keyes of those mysteries pretious" and, whether readers understood the "realitie" shadowed or not, increasing its circulation and renown. Contemporary readers of the *Urania*, in other words, were often obedient to its deciphering imperative.

After Denny accused her of slandering him in her romance, Wroth famously complained of the "strang constructions which are made of my book contrary to my imagination," and swore that it was in "no way meant to give cause of offence."[107] In December 1621 she told the Duke of Buckingham that she had caused the sale of the *Urania* to be forbidden and the books "left to bee shut up."[108] There is, however, no evidence that Wroth ever tried to halt its circulation, and considerable evidence that she did all she could to promote it. Wroth named the *Urania* after an influential noblewoman; alluded to multiple contemporary literary, social, and political events within its pages; gave a presentation copy to the Duke of Buckingham, the King's favorite and chief advisor; partially deciphered its codes for the Earl of Rutland at Baynard's Castle; and showed some of what she called her "rude lines" to Sir Dudley Carleton, the English ambassador to The Hague and perhaps the biggest gossip in seventeenth-century English letters.[109] While Denny expressed fear of

and BARCLAYES, felt the benefit of this supposal, much life and quickness being inspirited into the Sale, and perusal by that occasion, whither it were rightly understood or noe."

[107] On 15 December 1621, apparently in response to public outrage, Mary Wroth requested the duke of Buckingham to procure a warrant from the King to enable her to gather in any books that had already been sold because of the "strang constructions which are made of my booke," that were "as farr from my meaning as is possible" (Bodl. Oxf., MS Add. D.111, fol. 173[r-v], cited in Wroth, *Poems*, ed. Roberts, 236).

[108] The complete letter reads as follows: "Understanding some of the strang constructions which are made of my booke contrary to my imagination, and as farr from my meaning as is possible for truth to bee from conjecture, my purpose noe way bent to give the least cause of offence, my thoughts free from soe much as thinking of any such thing as I ame censurd for, I have with all care caused the sale of them to bee forbidden, and the books left to bee shut up, for those that are abroad, I will likewise doe my best to gett them in, if itt will please your Lordship to procure mee the kings warrant to that effect, without which non will deliver them to mee, besids that your Lordship wilbe pleased to lett mee have that which I sent you, the example of which will without question make others the willinger to obay; For mine own part I ame extreamely grieved that I ame thus much mistaken, butt yet comforted with this that itt is an injury dun to me undeservedly, although to bee accus'd in this nature is a great wrong unto me; I beeseech your Lordship therfor thus far to right mee as to beeleeve this for truthe, and what I ame able to doe for the getting in of books (which from the first were solde against my minde I never purposing to have had them published) I will with all care and diligence parforme." *Poems*, ed. Roberts, 236.

[109] On the circulation and promotion of her romance, see Wroth, *Poems*, ed. Roberts, 35; and Lewalski, *Writing Women*, 249. See also Smith, *Sonnets*, 91. On her allusions to the poetry of Mary Sidney Herbert and William Herbert, see Wroth, *Poems*, ed. Roberts, 44. (See also 490.6 in the *Urania*; and Roberts's note on p. 776). John Chamberlain reported that "many others" besides Lord Denny believed themselves implicated in the *Urania*

Wroth's "noble allies," it seems that Wroth wanted those same "allies" to see themselves and their circumstances in her romance.[110] As the ambassador to The Hague, Carleton had considerable influence in the Low Countries and, as we saw with the Countess of Bedford, was frequently solicited by members of the alliance on behalf of international Protestant concerns. (Wroth herself planned to visit The Hague in 1619, writing to Carleton about the "crosses" that prevented her from doing so," and the "constancy" of her commitment to Elizabeth of Bohemia.[111])

As James's favorite, Buckingham was perpetually caught between warring interests, including those supporting and those opposing English intervention in the Palatinate. By circulating the *Urania* to these men, a text ciphering a more ideal political vision than that being enacted by either court or Parliament in 1621, Wroth was practicing the "practically active" humanism associated with the alliance. In keeping with Sidney's belief that "under the prettie tales of Woolves and sheepe, [a poet] can enclude the whole considerations of wrong doing and patience," Wroth's romance put forth the idea that only a strong nobility could safeguard political and religious liberty.[112] And as for Sidney before her, that strong nobility included women.

("Many others she makes bold with, and they say she takes great libertie or rather licence to traduce whom she place, and thinckes she daunces in a net" (*Letters*, 2: 427; *Urania*, ed. Roberts, p. lxxi; Lamb, *Gender and Authorship*, 183). The romance was widely recognized for its controversial topicality. In his poem "A Remedy of Love," Sir Aston Cokayne asserted that "The Lady Wrothe's Urania is repleat / With elegancies, but too full of heat" (1662; cited by Roberts, "An Unpublished Literary Quarrel," 534. On the presentation copies annotated by Wroth, see *Urania*, ed. Roberts, pp. cxii–cxviii. On 25 April 1619 Wroth wrote a letter to Sir Dudley Carleton from Baynard's Castle in which she mentions a visit she made to her at Loughton during which she "took the boldnes to present some rude lines" to him which she hopes she "shall receave pardon for: the truth they carried with them." In the same letter, she mentions "the constant respect" she has for Carleton (cited in full in Wroth, *Poems*, ed. Roberts, 235).

[110] For the Denny letter, see Wroth, *Poems*, ed. Roberts, 241. Denny wrote to Wroth: "Madam, I saie, you are a noble Ladie, And for those noble allies of yours, I will ever honor and serve them" (241). And Wroth to Denny: "Feare not to saie what you please, for beleeve it my noble allies will not thank you for forbearing mee; nor [when] <iff> the tyme shall serve spare you for what you have done" (240).

[111] She wrote the letter on 19 April 1619, ending it by vowing that her "crosses" "shall they not have power to make me other than constant in my respect to my noble friend[s] which number I presume to hold you" (cited in Hannay, *Mary Sidney*, 202).

[112] *Defence of Poetry*, 22. On the tradition of literary advice to princes (and Sidney's appearance in the *Arcadia* as the political commentator Philisides), see Victor Skretkowicz, "'A More Lively Monument.'" Norbrook argues that Philisides's Ister Bank eclogue "reflects the view of these aristocratic radicals that only a strong nobility could safeguard liberty. It is possible to trace a clear line of succession, both in intellectual and familial kinship, from Sidney and his circle down to the classical republicans of the Commonwealth in the 1650s—down to Sir Philip's great nephew Algernon Sidney (*Poetry and Politics*, 98). One of my goals in this chapter is to place the missing Wroth in this genealogy.

Wroth's resistance to the "strang constructions" made of her romance should thus be considered in light of George Wither's similarly defensive claim that he had not "taxt (directly) any one by name" in his own work.[113] Both authors' claims signal their texts' pertinent topicality even as they remind censors of their deniability. Neither author, that is, "taxt" anyone "directly." It thus seems likely that the "scandal" Wroth's romance caused was as political as it was personal. John Chamberlain's observation that Wroth "takes great libertie or rather licence to traduce whom she please, and thincks she daunces in a net" is often read as an indictment of her mode of purportedly *ad hominem* attack. Yet the phrase to "dance in a net" meant to act with "practically no disguise while expecting to escape detection."[114] In explaining his actions, George Wither wrote that he erred in his pastoral by "speaking so much in his own person rather than adopting a conventional persona."[115] Despite Pamphilia's claim that one could write "aswell by imitation, as by sence of passion" (94.39–41), Chamberlain might have felt that as the insistently self-referential "Pamphilia," Wroth nonetheless signaled her own person, and views, with too much "license" in her romance, flouting the 1621 injunction against speaking about matters of state, and "traducing" those with the power to silence her. The fact that Wroth's text was considered "too full of heat" then, may have been less about personal gossip than political opposition: the persons indicted in the shadowed Denny case were, after all, members of the pro-Spanish and pro-Catholic Howard faction with whom the Sidney-Herbert alliance was in constant contention.[116] The editors of the second volume of the *Urania* suggest that the manuscript came to be in the hands of the Morgans of Tredega because they too were invested in local baronial rights and allied with the Herbert faction in opposition to the same pro-Spanish interests.[117]

---

[113] Cited in Norbrook, *Poetry and Politics*, 219.

[114] Roberts cites this definition in her notes to the *Urania*, n. 409.4, p. 767. In her biography of Wroth, Hannay notes that the phrase had been in circulation for some time: "On 22 March 1572/3, for example, the Earl of Pembroke wrote to the Earl of Leicester about some who had been plotting against him: 'But good my Lord they dance in a net that thinks to throw stones and hide their hands'" (HMC Longleat, 5: 194, cited in Hannay, *Mary Sidney*, 242 n. 5.

[115] Postscript to *The Shepherds Hunting*, cited in Norbrook, *Poetry and Politics*, 212.

[116] The line is from Sir Aston Cokayne, and is cited in Roberts, "An Unpublished Literary Quarrel," 534. Lord Edward Denny's daughter Honora married James Hay, viscount of Doncaster, later first Earl of Carlisle, one of James's favorites and an ally of the Catholic Howards. Pembroke did not participate in Campion's masque for Twelfth Night 1607, which was written to celebrate this marriage; it was an all-Howard affair (Taylor, "The Masque ansd the Lance," 43). (The *Urania* also includes negative allusions to the Carr-Howard affair: see 563 and Roberts's notes on p. 789). In addition to the general factional enmity between the Howards and the Herberts, Lord Hay also fought with Wroth's younger brother Robert in 1620 (see Ian Atherton's entry on Sidney in the new *ODNB*).

[117] Though not yet advanced to the nobility, the Morgans of Tredega held important offices in Wales in the early 17th cent. Thomas Morgan (d. 1664) was arrested at the King's

Early in the *Urania*, Pamphilia cites Elizabeth I's 1559 speech avowing her marriage to England when she herself swears loyalty to her own country of Pamphilia. She was already married, she tells her would-be suitor, "to the Kingdom of Pamphilia, from which Husband shee could not bee divorced" (262.32–3). "[M]y people" she continues, "looke for me, and I must needs be with them" (262.35–6; see also 264.26–30).[118] As Margaret P. Hannay has shown, Wroth did in many ways "govern" in her kingdom in much the way that Pamphilia herself and the shepherd in the hunting scene just discussed suggest that Pamphilia governed in hers. Wroth lived at Loughton until 1630 and, in the words of her father, effectively "governed her own by herself."[119] The Penshurst accounts bear traces of this governance: at one point she sends her gamekeeper to her parents; her nieces and nephews stayed with her at Loughton for extended periods of time; we know that she hosted at least one politically charged wedding at Loughton; and that Wroth held a high social rank in the county.[120]

If Mary Wroth effected a magisterial level of governance at the ground level in Loughton, she did so through her status as a Sidney as much as a Wroth. Like her aunt, she signed her letters with the S fermé, and used the Sidney phaeon in her official correspondence. In his 1622 *The Compleate Gentleman*, Henry Peacham includes a discussion of a lozenge (or rhomb) as the shape of arms "proper to women never married, or to such in courtesy who are born Ladies; who though they be married to Knights, yet are they commonly styled and called after the Surname of their fathers, if he be an Earl; for the greater Honor must ever extinguish the lesse."[121] By way

order as a hinderer of the royal cause in 1645 and "It has been suggested that the causes of this disaffection were the adherence of some of the Monmouthshire gentry to the house of Pembroke and their consequent opposition to the increasing influence of the rival house of Somerset" (*Urania*, part 2, ed. Roberts, Gossett, and Mueller, p. xxv).

[118] Roberts cites Camden's account of Elizabeth's speech in her notes to the *Urania*, pp. 747–8: "Yea, to satisfie you, I have already joined myself in Marriage to an Husband, namely the Kingdom of England." See Beilin, "Role of the Political Subject," 228, for the parallel with Elizabeth: "Certainly the image of Elizabeth shadowing Pamphilia through the romance reinforces the significance of Pamphilia's constancy beyond her devotion to Ampilanthus."

[119] His letter is cited in Hannay, *Mary Sidney*, 249.

[120] On her nieces and nephews, see Hannay, *Mary Sidney*, 255. On the gamekeeper, *Mary Sidney*, 254. Wroth also supplied her family with venison from hunts at Loughton (254). Thomas Wentworth, Earl of Strafford's sister Elizabeth Wentworth, was married at Loughton (277). Hannay also notes that Wroth was listed as the person with the second highest rank in the Woodford parish records (she had inherited a small copyhold four miles from Loughton in Woodford) (305).

[121] Peacham, Y1ʳ⁻ᵛ. On "lozenge," see the *OED*: 1a. A plane rectilineal figure, having four equal sides and two acute and two obtuse angles; a rhomb, 'diamond.' In *Heraldry*, such a figure used as a bearing, less elongated than the fusil *n.1*, and placed with its longer axis vertical. The *OED* suggests that, by 1696, a lozenge had become "b. A lozenge-shaped shield upon which the arms of a spinster or widow are emblazoned."

of illustration, he features Wroth's own coat of arms: the Sidney phaeon (or dart) inside a lozenge (Figure 4.7). "[F]or example, the bearer hereof," Peacham notes, is "the Lady *Mary Sidney*, the late wife of Sir *Robert Wroth*, Knight, and daughter of the [...] Earle of *Leicester*."[122] In much the same way as Wroth had done a year earlier on the title-page of the *Urania*, Peacham privileges her highest rank—"the Lady *Mary Sidney*" is the daughter of an Earl—and endows her with the accompanying honors and status. (Though she was married to a Knight, she was "stiled and called after the Sirname" of her father, "for the greater Honor must euer extinguish the lesse.") Indeed Wroth is the only woman identified by name in this famous book on the "most necessary & commendable qualities concerning minde or bodie that may be required in a noble gentleman."

When "the Lady *Mary Sidney*"'s husband, Robert, died in 1614, leaving her with the debt mentioned in the introduction, he also left her with some moveables, most notably the "books and furniture of her closet."[123] While this bequest was, perhaps, less a recognition of her skill in poetry than a sign of her larger dispossession (the bulk of his unmoveable property was entailed to male heirs), the tools Robert Wroth left her, and the closets she used them in, provided Wroth not only with the means to write her romance, but to signal her entrenchments in a family alliance much more powerful and influential than his. The *Urania* announced the right of "Lady *Mary Sidney*," and her ability, to offer advice both to and on behalf of that alliance.

At the end of the second part of the *Urania*, after the next generation has been called in to reaffirm the continued political efficacy of the shadowed Sidney-Herbert alliance, Amphilanthus and Pamphilia end up back in Cyprus, the country they helped to Christianize in the first part of the romance.[124] There we learn that Cyprus is being governed by a "Counsell of state." "[B]utt" (the qualifier is Wroth's), the counsell "is wholly of men.

---

[122] Peacham, Y1.

[123] Wroth, *Poems*, ed. Roberts, 23; see also Waller, *Sidney Family Romance*, 120–1. See also Hannay, *Mary Sidney*, 171.

[124] The next generation is refered to as the "new, brave come-abroade-and-tride youths" (2.401.39). On the Christianization of Cyprus, see 170. As Andrea points out, the idealized Holy Roman Empire that becomes the field of action in Wroth's *Urania* was in fact ruled by the Ottoman Empire from the middle of the 15th century to the end of the 17th. "Wroth's political fantasy of a revived Holy Roman Empire effaces the historical specificity of Cyprus as a stronghold of the Ottoman Empire" (349). Margaret P. Hannay offers the following summary of the second part of the romance: "The complex political plot of Part Two involves a world torn by the Thirty Years' War, depicted as armed rebellions in Austria, Hungary, Denmark, and Bohemia [...]. The central plot stems from the desire of the usurping Sophy, or ruler, of Persia to kill his niece Lindafilla the true Sophy. He captures Lindafilla and he also demands that Pamphilia marry him. The Morean princes band together to kill the usurping Sophy and rescue Lindafilla, who is loved by Fair Design" (Mary Sidney, 268). The second part thereby shifts to the next generation, "the prospect of the conjugal union of

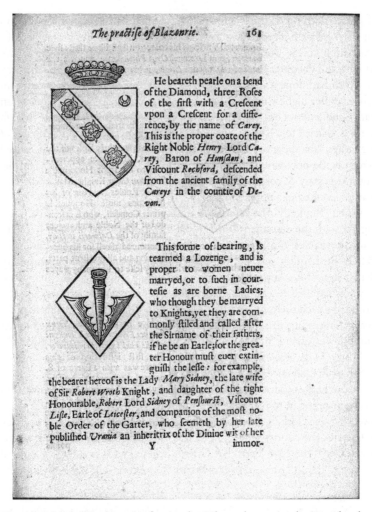

The practise of Blazonrie.   161

He beareth pearle on a bend of the Diamond, three Roſes of the firſt with a Creſcent vpon a Creſcent for a difference, by the name of *Carey.* This is the proper coate of the Right Noble *Henry* Lord *Carey,* Baron of *Hunſdon,* and Viſcount *Rochford,* deſcended from the ancient family of the *Careys* in the countie of *Devon.*

This forme of bearing, Is tearmed a Lozenge, and is proper to women neuer marryed, or to ſuch in courteſie as are borne Ladies; who though they be marryed to Knights, yet they are commonly ſtiled and called after the Sirname of their fathers, if he be an Earle; for the greater Honour muſt euer extinguiſh the leſſe : for example, the bearer hereof is the Lady *Mary Sidney,* the late wife of Sir *Robert Wroth* Knight ; and daughter of the right Honourable, *Robert* Lord *Sidney* of *Penſhurſt,* Viſcount *Liſle,* Earle of *Leiceſter,* and companion of the moſt noble Order of the Garter, who ſeemeth by her late publiſhed *Vrania* an inheritrix of the Diuine wit of her
Y   immor-

Figure 4.7 Mary Wroth's coat of arms: the Sidney phaeon (or dart) inside a lozenge, from Henry Peacham, *The Compleat Gentleman* (1622), Y1. Reproduced by permission of the Folger Shakespeare Library.

East and West adumbrated in Part One" (*Urania*, part 2, p. xxx). While space prevents me from addressing the entirety of the second part of the romance in this chapter, I do want to suggest that Wroth's choice to circulate the second volume of her romance in manuscript is neither self-evidently a sign of her depoliticization nor of her "retreat back" into a private realm (Hannay, *Mary Sidney*, 225). In many ways, manuscript circulation heightened both the deciphering imperative and the political purchase of a text's content.

And where woemen had little Joye of a Court to com to, hath made all great ones butt the Counsell to stay and keepe att home" (2:411). Wroth thus ends her romance with what is at once a fantasy of a consiliary state, and one in which women play little part. The editors of the volume suggest that these comments allude both to the dissolution of Queen Anna's (largely female) court after her 1619 death and James's attempt to send the nobility back home to their country estates as a way of limiting their political opposition. Yet as the *Urania* as a whole seems to suggest, while the English court may have sent many of its most powerful mediatrixes "back home" in the years between 1619 and 1621, their best work might well have been done from there anyway.

Epilogue

The Sidney papers in the Kent History and Library Centre include a wide range of documents related to the political career of Mary Wroth's father, Robert Sidney, first Earl of Leicester (1587–1626). These documents include a letter about his sister, the Countess of Pembroke, being in Antwerp, and the dissolution of the 1614 Parliament; a letter expressing concern that James I is "unaware of the true state of Dutch feeling, especially in religious matters"; and news about the politics surrounding the 1613 election of the King of the Romans.[1] Most notable, however, are his four commonplace books, which are largely concerned with world history, particularly with the ruling families of Europe and the divisions of empires. These books feature such commonplace headings and entries as: "The Kings of Hungary and Bohemia up to 1619," "Of the Families of the Electors Palatine of the Rhine" (which culminates in the birth of Frederick and Elizabeth's children in 1620), "The German Emperor (Or Roman as hee stileth himself) is chosen by seven Electors," "Kingdom of Cyprus," "Kingdome of Morea," and "Kings of Naples without Sicilia."[2] Sidney was particularly interested in independent states, and Naples, the first city in Europe to convert to Christianity, seems to have been a particular subject of interest.[3] (Robert Shephard notes that Pandolfo Collenuccio's *Compendio de le istorie del Regno di Napoli* (1498)—a book prompted by the French invasions and the loss of kingdom's independent monarchy—is one of the books Sidney cites most frequently.[4])

---

[1] U1500, C10/101 (Countess of Pembroke and the dissolution of parliament); C9/360 (Dutch feeling, 10 September 1614, HMC X 188); C79/13 (election of the King of the Romans, March 1613, HMC VII 95). See also C1/15, for a letter from the Earl to his wife about the King's movements and lack of news of the crowning of the King of Bohemia (20 October 1619). Other references to the Sidney papers will be cited parenthetically within the text itself.

[2] In order, these entries appear in: U1475, Z1/3, 147 (Kings of Hungary and Bohemia); Z1/2, 295 (Families of the Elector), 297 (Elizabeth and Frederick's children); Z1/1, 19 (German Emperor); Z1/2, 25 (Cyprus); Z1/3, 228 (Morea and Naples).

[3] The "Kings of Naples," he tells us in one entry, "styled themselves Kings of Jerusalem," and in another that Naples and Sicily "have never bin one body," but rather had "kings of their owne," a detail he takes from "Colennuccio" (Z1/2, 177; 6). See also: "Naples continued to have Kings of their Own until the time of K: Frederick of the hows of Arragon who was dispossessed by Lewis 12 King of France and Ferdinand the Catholick King of Arragon" (Z1/1, 6).

[4] Shephard, "The Political Commonplace Books of Sir Robert Sidney," 5.

Presented in this way, Sidney's commonplace entries read like a primer for Wroth's *Urania*, a romance centered, as we saw in the last chapter, on the ruling families of Morea and Naples, the election of the King of the Romans, and the political and religious reclamation of Bohemia and Cyprus. Indeed the connections between the histories and genealogies in Sidney's commonplace books and those in Wroth's romance are both myriad and revelatory: Sidney's commonplace book entry on the "Government of Weomen," for example, begins with the Queen of Naples, who is also one of the main characters in his daughter's romance (Z1/10, 283); the King of Sicily in Wroth's romance is related to the Queen of Naples, but, much as Robert Sidney notes in his commonplace book, he is also the ruler of a kingdom in his own right; when the *Urania*'s Amphilanthus is crowned King of the Romans, it is done, as Robert Sidney similarly notes in his commonplace book, by the electors at "Franckford" (*Urania*, 463.36). The list is nearly endless, and it is remarkable that it has never been compiled before.

Yet while the resonances between the books are certainly notable, the *Urania* is more than a series of vivid illustrations of the political histories that captured Sidney's attention—it is a casebook for the political ideas that animated the alliance of which both writers were part. As I argued in the last chapter, the *Urania*'s sovereign countries, like Morea and Naples, map onto English counties, like Kent and Wiltshire, in order to promote the role of the landed nobility in both the government of England and the future of Protestant Christendom. Sidney's papers and commonplace books reveal a similarly strong sense of the analogy between independent countries and English counties. The commonplace book concerned with the genealogies of the ruling families of Europe, for example, also features an entry on the "Lords of Kent according to Sir Henry Savile."[5] Another entry on the "Kings of Kent, Northumberland and Sussex" appears under the list of "Empires and Kingdoms" in another commonplace book, a juxtaposition that indicates Sidney's interest in the governing power of the county magnates, or "Kings" (Z1/1, 2). (In this analogy, Sidney would be the "King" of Kent in much the same way as he is ciphered as the "King of Morea" in Wroth's romance.) On the other hand, the entries under the heading "Kings of England" in the same commonplace book are curiously unmonarchical, featuring details about Prince Henry's death—an event Wroth registers in the *Urania* as well—the marriage of Elizabeth

---

[5] U1475 Z1/3, 191. In 1598 Savile published a collection of chronicles and histories of England under the title *Rerum Anglicarum scriptores*. Savile was a translator of Tacitus and ally of the Earl of Essex. The catalogue of books at Penshurst reveals that Sidney also owned a copy of Henry Wotton's *Elements*, the text responsible for the claim about England as a series of "fiefdoms" ruled over by local magnates in their "Princedoms" (U1474, Z/45/2, 214).

and Frederick, and the role of the peers in Parliament (Z1/2, 378–).[6]
Sidney also blazons his own official ascendancy into the peerage under the
same heading: "In 1618," he records, "Leycester and others Made Earles"
(Z1/2, 398).

As I have argued throughout this book, the interest Sidney expressed
in the genealogies, history, and power of the English nobility is less a sign
of vainglory than of an investment in the political rights of the nobility.
Sidney's papers bear the traces of this commitment as well: the Penshurst
library included a manuscript identified in its inventory as "Priviledge of
speciall rights belonging to Baronage in England"; his copy of William
Segar's *Honor Military and Civil* (1602) includes a marginal marker in
the chapter on "An Earl" where it discusses certain earls ruling "as absolute Princes in their provinces"; and he had a manuscript copy of Walter
Ralegh's notorious defense of the "charter," or Magna Carta, a document first forced on the King of England by the feudal barons in order
to defend their rights and limit his prerogative.[7] As Ralegh points out to
Robert Cecil and the other "reserved counselors" of whom he is so critical, those who are "bound to adventure" their lives for their master—the
great barons or nobility—are also "bound," or entitled, to adventure their
"advise," or counsel. The Magna Carta "hath been confirmed by sixteen
acts of Parliament," he insists, and should not be "treade...under foote,
as a forme of parchment or waste paper" by the King's "prerogative" (28ᵛ).
Such conviction about the rights of the nobility is also a motivating force
in Wroth's *Urania*, a work dedicated not only to promoting the rights of
the nobility to serve as counselors and co-magistrates, but of the exemplary role of women—particularly Sidney women—in this regard.

Like the *Arcadia* before it, the *Urania* promotes monarchy as "the
Sweetest, Noblest, and gentlest of all" forms of government, and avers that
"a subject ought not upon any termes to weare armes against his rightfull King" (2:244.31, 445.11–12).[8] Yet it also features multiple forms of
non-absolutist monarchical rule: alternative modes of appointing rulers
(in a number of scenes princes are "made" or "chosen"); examples of governance in the absence of rightful rulers (princes away on international

---

[6] During a description of the king Museteria's son ("all the parfections of his fathers
Noble parts and the addition of such an excellent and warlike spirit"), Amphilanthus asks
for his name, and Wroth leaves an ellipses in the text that highlights the name's topical
relevance: "His name is [ ] and a finer, sweeter, nay braver disposed prince the Earthe never
bore nor the Sun shined on" (2:194.20–1, 25–6).

[7] For the baronage text, U1474, Z/45/2, 151; Catalogue of books at Penshurst, 151; for
Segar, Z27; and for Ralegh, Z7 (HMC 1112).

[8] Rebels are described as a headless body: "for having noe Commaunder in Chiefe with
them, they were butt a rotten body without a head" (2:301.12–14). See also the *Arcadia*'s
description of the rebellion as a "many-headed multitude" (*OA* 115).

business habitually leave "the government of all [they] governed to the Counsell and president," 2:158.2–3); and, most notably, the defense and establishment of rightful sovereigns by outside forces.[9] Unsurprisingly, each of these scenarios also illustrates an entry in Robert Sidney's commonplace book: "Principalities by election"; "gouvernment of the kingdome in absence of the King"; and "Absolute princes who have put themselves in other princes dominions" (Z1/1, 10, 92, and 701–11).[10] In many ways, this last entry serves as the motivating logic for the action in both parts of the romance. In much the same way as the Sidneys and their allies believed that England should come to the aid of the Palatinate, so do the ruling families of Morea and Naples in the *Urania* come to the aid of Bohemia, Cyprus, and, in the second half of the romance, Persia.[11] In a crucial scene in the second part of the *Urania*, for example, the daughter of the Sultan of Persia—and the country's rightful heir—vows that the "Court of Morea" will "rescue [her] out of... tiranny" and "settle [her] in [her] right againe" (2:170.23–4). As "absolute [or sovereign] princes" themselves, the leaders of the romance's sovereign countries "put themselves in other princes dominions" in the service of (their own vision of) political justice.[12]

In the second part of the *Urania*, Rosindy, who has "longe binn shutt up in idleness," is respurred to chivalric action and offers the daughter of the Sultan of Persia a speech about his suitableness for action (2:166.11). He is, he tells her, unused to "tounge-labour," favoring "onely the bare, sincere phrace of impliset truth, leaving all other speaking businesses to Courtiers and studiers of phrases" (2:170.41–2). "I ame a meere soldier

---

[9] For examples of rulers made and chosen, see 2:402, and 2:249. Pamphilia herself chosen heir by her uncle on the basis of popular pressure. After having long delivered their country from tyrants, he grew old and "his subjects had 'gain'd of him' his consent to welcome his niece as their new and younger ruler (145.33–4).

[10] See also "sovereign princes have bin requested by the states of other countries to com to governe them" (Z1/1, 703), "Princes driven owt of theyr states restored by helpe of forein princes" (cited in Shephard, "Political Commonplace Books," 24), and "some are driven out (as now the K of Bohemia into the low contryes)" (Z1/1/, 702). A later book includes the commonplace heading "Armes taken for breach of priviledges, grievances by impositions, etc," and its sole entry has to do with King John and the rebellion against him after his repudiation of Magna Carta, which Sidney considers relevant to James's dismissal of parliament in 1614 (Shephard, "Political Commonplace Books," 24).

[11] For a description of the geopolitical terrain of Part Two, see Mueller and Gossett: "Wroth pointedly shifts aspects of her active narrative terrain eastward in Part Two, bring in the realms and ruling houses of Persia and Babylon (present day Iran and Iraq, respectively) which in her day were sultanates exercising some measure of autonomy within the Ottoman Empire" (p. xxx). Persia itself was on Robert Sidney's mind. See a letter dated 8 July 1611 (C9/104) in which he discusses the arrival of Sir Robert Basset and Sir Robert Shirley, ambassadors from the emperor of Persia.

[12] Absolute in this sense does not mean absolutist, but rather sovereign, "Free from dependency, autonomous; not relative" (*OED* A. I).

and scoller," he says in what sounds a lot like a commonplace, "yett know how to winn and keepe kingdomes" (2:170–1). Like many others in the *Urania*, this scene is a fantasy of wish fulfillment; Wroth imagines Rosindy, the cipher for her brother, Robert Sidney, recommitting himself to the political humanism practiced by their alliance—a combination of soldiery and scholarship that can "winn and keep kingdoms."[13] Later on in the romance, Rosindy does in fact inherit the Kingdom of Morea, becoming a "mighty Monarck in Greece," and serving as both the savior and interim governor of Persia (2:406.30, 2:354). On the death of his father, Robert Sidney became a "mighty Monarck" as well, inheriting his father's title and serving as both an MP and the Lord Lieutenant for Kent, as well as as a foreign ambassador.[14] And like his father and sister, he was also a "scoller," keeping commonplace books and papers on such matters as the royal prerogative that he compiled, as he put it more than once, "partly out of a paper of [his] fathers."[15]

[13] "Algernon Sidney argued that absolute monarchs of the seventeenth century…had gained absolute power from the previously balanced constitutions by breaking the independent power and 'interest' of the nobility in the state. Whereas the ancient nobility had received political honour for 'the number of men thy could bring into the field' for voluntarily putting their private interest at the service of the public, the modern 'titular nobility' have neither the interest nor the estates required for such work…Those who have estates at rack-rent have [money but] no dependents" (*Discourses*, cited in Jonathan Scott, *Algernon Sidney and the English Republic*, 40).

[14] On Robert Sidney, see Ian Atherton's entry in the *ODNB*: Sidney became Viscount L'Isle in 1618 when his father became an Earl. In the 1621 Parliament he was MP for Kent and in those of 1624 and 1625 for Monmouthshire. On his father's death on 13 July 1626 he succeeded as second Earl of Leicester. In his career he went as ambassador-extraordinary to Christian IV of Denmark and ambassador-extraordinary to France (where he agitated for an Anglo-French alliance against the Habsburgs). "Laud blocked Sidney's further preferment, representing him to the King as a puritan, and as Lord Lieutenant of Ireland from 1641, Sidney was caught between King and Parliament as they argued over who should control the army sent to crush the Irish rebels. Leicester retained the confidence of the Lords until the summer of 1642, acting as temporary speaker of the House in May and June, and appointed Parliament's Lord Lieutenant for Kent. As England drifted into civil war, he was unable to choose between the two sides and irresolutely sought to satisfy both. Penshurst was briefly sequestered by the Kent county committee on the grounds that Leicester had flown to an enemy garrison, but the Countess, probably with the help of Northumberland, one of the most influential Parliamentarian peers, persuaded the Parliament to lift the sequestration. In November 1643 the King induced Leicester to resign the lord lieutenancy so that he could appoint Ormond in his place. Leicester remained in Oxford, expecting that he would be appointed governor to Prince Charles. His refusal in January 1644 to sign the letter from the English peers at Oxford to the Scottish Privy Council urging them not to support the covenanters' invasion of England, however, lost him all hope of preferment, and in June 1644 he left Oxford to make his peace with Parliament before retiring to Penshurst, where he attempted to sit out the war quietly, declining to seek readmission to the House of Lords. Leicester was a broken man and spent almost all of his remaining three decades in retirement at Penshurst, occasionally visiting his London residence, Leicester House, and concerning himself with his estates and scholarly pursuits." See also Warkentin, "Humanism," 247–8.

[15] Like his father, Sidney was largely concerned with limits to the King's prerogative— "the King used not the style of supreme head in his Charters etc. till 22 H:8," he notes in

In the first part of the romance, Pamphilia serves as Rosindy's chief advisor, wielding "the authoritie," as he puts it, "over mee and mine."[16] But in the second half of the *Urania*, Rosindy's wife serves in this capacity. Shortly before the scene in which Rosindy presents himself as a "soldier and scoller" to the Sophy of Persia, he vows his loyalty to his wife Meriana.[17] Though he admired the Sophy—possessor of "skinn" that "would make a thousand Jasons madd on travaile butt to see"—"his good starrs ever blessed himm with som present apprehentions to keepe him safe with. For did hee love, as in love, butt once" (2:168.29–30, 34–5). As is so often the case in the *Urania*, a woman provides the buttressing for a man's commitment to a cause, their union—what Rosindy calls a "Crowne of hapines"—a symbol for political justice and integrity. Thus while the Sophy offers "the soldier and scoller" Rosindy access to a sumptuous library full of "the rarest of bookes" in support of his efforts, it is Meriana who ensures his political passage to save Persia from tyranny (2:171.14, 2:277).[18]

"Meriana" is the romance's cipher for Robert Sidney's wife, Dorothy Percy Sidney, the daughter of Henry Percy, ninth Earl of Northumberland, and Dorothy Devereux Perrot Percy, Sir Philip Sidney's Pamela. Wroth notes more than once in the course of the romance that Rosindy was "King of Macedon" (another of his titles) "by his wyfe," and frequently refers to Meriana herself as "Queen of Macedon" (2:170.29).[19] Robert Sidney did gain access to the considerable Percy lands and political influence through his wife, and his papers reveal the extent to which he was interested in the property rights and political entitlements of noble women. At one point, he

one entry—and the rights of the nobility (Z/9, 15). His loose papers include a list of the "Nobility with Titles, Precedence, Reception of Princes, etc. Ceremonies" c.1641 (Z/9, 10); the "Charters of creation of Nobility" (Z/9, 14), "Of the antient manner of creating Earles and calling of them, and Barons by writ to Parlement" from Sir Edward Coke (Z9, 17), and a document on the history of "county rule from custos rotularum to the March laws" (Z/9, 265).

[16] Rosindy accepts her advice gratefully, if not abjectly: "Binde mee more if you can, sweete Sister, and to make mee happy, enjoy the authoritie over mee and mine" (111.20–1). "What I know," she tells him in turn, "I were a poore weake woman, if I would conceale from you, or reveale of you" (111.13–14). I discuss Pamphilia's refusal to turn "blabb" in Ch. 4.

[17] Rosindy gives an account of how he was governed by passion, and subject to "loves tiranny" before he met Meriana. This subjection became a "Crowne of hapines" when they were married (2:32–3).

[18] The Sophy leads Rosindy into "her librearie...the most sumptious in the world for a woeman to have" and gives him "a key into the studdy and galery," trusting him to spend time in her "scoole" (2:171.13, 23–4, 27).

[19] Wroth notes this the second time when the first King of Morea points out that his son Rosindy "is nott under my commaund furder then his dutifull love to mee bindes him, butt freely his owne, except tide in the bands of mutuall love to his wife by whom hee hath that Crowne [of Macedon]" (2:273.37–9).

invokes the "Countesse of Derby in Elizabeth's time" (who, in John Milton's words, ruled as a "rural Queen" in Hertfordshire) as an example of noble women's ongoing property and political rights *after* marriage.[20] At another he discovers that he cannot "endow [his] wife with Penshurst because it is *caput Baroniae*, the house of my Barony" (Z1/9, 22), an indication that he had nonetheless considered doing exactly such a thing.[21] (Sidney himself inherited Penshurst in 1626.) It should come as no surprise that Dorothy Percy Sidney was also a singularly influential mediatrix in the period, particularly as a gatherer of what she called "intelligence" during the years between the contentious parliaments of the 1620s and her death in 1659.[22]

Dorothy Sidney's recently published correspondence offers a wealth of information about her political life.[23] At one point her son Algernon Sidney, already well on his way to a storied political career, wrote that he awaited his "Ladyship['s] command" for what to do next in a sensitive political matter. She characterized herself as one of the "saints" at court: "it shall be part of my litany," she wrote in 1636, "to deliver all my friends

---

[20] The reference to the Countess of Derby occurs in Z1/9, 87. See also the comment "I know not what nobility [the author he is citing] means that may so be lost by a woman if she marry" (91). See Peacham's discussion of "born Ladies; who though they be marryed to Knights, yet are they commonly stiled and called after the Sirname of their fathers, if he be an Earle; for the greater Honour must euer extinguish the lesse" (Y1r) in Ch. 4.

[21] On Penshurst, see Z1/9, 22. As multiple commonplace entries suggest, Sidney was particularly interested in the "Government of Woeman"—see e.g. the entries gathered under "Emperesses and Queens that have gouverned either in theyre own right or absence of theyre husbands either by appointment of theyre husbands or by election of the state or their own usurpation" (Z1/1, 281–30)—as well as in women's consiliary roles. One entry, for example, "Of the power that wives mothers and mistresses have had with princes and great men. What their humours are in general and how they are to bee handled. How women have been involved in matters of state" (Z1/10, 315) suggests a range of ways in which women wielded political influence. As we saw in the last chapter, Wroth was also interested in the ways in which women were "involved in matters of state." The *Urania* situates counsel in a central political metaphor—"sovereignty," in Bacon's words, "should be married to Counsel"—but it also grounds it in women, particularly, "the brave and discreet Queene of Naples" (2:22.15), the "Judiciall" counselor Urania, and Pamphilia, whom Amphilanthus identifies in the second part of the romance as the "Presedent" of his counsel and the "govern[or]" of his "thoughts and will" (2:29.8–9).

[22] Sidney's correspondence frequently refers to her use of "intelligence." For example, at one point her sister, Lucy, the Countess of Carlisle, wrote to tell Dorothy that "The Queen was very glad of your letter and liked your intelligence, which was very good and well told" (*Correspondence*, 164). For a discussion of her role as an "intellegencer," see the "Introduction" to her correspondence (32). All subsequent references to this book will be cited parenthetically within the text.

[23] Others characterized her this way as well. In February 1638/9 Sir John Temple wrote that he was "almost ready to mutiny that I yet hear nothing of your Ladyship's coming up. I want my oracle whereunto I should repair, and without your Ladyship's advice I know not how further to govern myself in these two particulars that concern your service here" (142). From August 1637 Leicester had been scheming to be recalled to England and to be made secretary in place of Coke. Two years later Northumberland suggested an alternative, namely that he should succeed Thomas Wentworth, Viscount Wentworth, as Lord Deputy of Ireland. Dorothy Sidney spent many years trying to obtain these and other offices for her husband.

from embassies till Secretary Coke be laid down in peace" (174, 72).[24] Her correspondence also reveals the evolution of her political views. Most notably, in the 1630s she asked her husband for a cipher, "for I think I could understand it, and then I should venture to say many things to you which by this plain way I dare not express."[25] In the years leading up to the civil war she became increasingly critical of the King, particularly in his treatment of the Sidneys' property and political rights.

In December 1644, Dorothy Sidney wrote to her agent and solicitor William Hawkins about a "cabinet which I am content they should see it opened at Leicester House," the Sidneys' London seat (181). She was particularly concerned that it not be opened "at the custome house," which would "much endanger the spoiling of it." To avoid such an eventuality, she advised Hawkins that her "son" might assist him in getting the cabinet "home without search or payment, which I think was never refused to any person of condition." "If his power be not sufficient," she added, "I am confident my brother will also give you his help if you please to call for it" (181). This account of a mysterious cabinet entrusted to the "power" of politically-sympathetic family members is in many ways a microcosm of Sidney family loyalties during the English civil wars. Both the "son" in this account (probably Philip, who eventually succeeded his father as third Earl, or Algernon, who would eventually become famous as a monarchomach), and the "brother" (Algernon Percy, tenth Earl of Northumberland and Lord Lieutenant of Cumberland, Northumberland, and Westmorland) eventually became supporters of Parliament. (In June 1642, Percy wrote to the attorney general defending the "laws, liberties, and privileges" of the aristocracy and parliaments as the king's "greatest and most supreme Councils.")[27] Lost in what he called a "labyrinth" of competing Parliamentarian and monarchical commands, Robert Sidney himself "withdrew" to Penshurst and his books later that year, essentially avoiding making a firm political commitment either way.[26] For her part, Dorothy Sidney Percy resolved to support the Parliamentarian cause.

[24] Brennan, Kinnamon, and Hannay note that Sidney considered Coke her husband's competitor. In January 1642/3, the Countess of Leicester wrote to her husband: "Since your letter was read to the House of Commons I have not heard anything said from them to your prejudice, but I believe they will shortly send to press your speedy dispatch, or if the King have any dislike to you, then will they desire him to choose another" (168). Her sons often wrote to her expressing concern about their father's "usage at Court." See e.g. Philip, Lord Lisle's letter dated 21 June 1643 (175).

[25] She asked for the cipher on 17 November 1636, *Correspondence*, 32. She then wrote to him frequently in cipher. See e.g. "I am glad that you wish a friendship betwixt 85 [Earl of Leicester] and 93 [Thomas Wentworth], for I am confident it would be an easy work and if 116 [Countess of Carlisle] be not much deceived for the service of 85 [Leicester], which above all things at this present I think of, 82 [Earl of Northumberland] is better with 93 [Wentworth] than she has been" (19 December 1639, cited p. 35).

[26] In September 1643 Parliament ordered the sequestration of Penshurst and other family estates, on the dubious grounds that Leicester had been neglecting his Irish duties, and replaced him (with his enemy) as Lord Deputy of Ireland. The editors of Dorothy Percy

In February 1657/8 Robert Sidney wrote an angst-filled letter to Algernon Percy about a rumour that "I had broken open your sister's cabinets and taken away her letters and her jewels" (43–4). While he vehemently denied the accusations ("if there were one syllable of truth, let me suffer death"), he nonetheless informed Percy that he was "thinking of a retreat for myself that your sister may live somewhere being secure from my passion and all disturbances by me more to her contentment" (44).[27] If the *Urania*'s Rosindy finds his source of constancy in Meriana, in real life it seems that Robert Sidney's "passion" got the better of him. There may well be no connection between the two cabinets featured in these letters, one secured from prying eyes in 1644 and the other (allegedly) broken into by a politically and maritally conflicted man over a decade later, but the resonances are nonetheless remarkable. It seems that "ladies' cabinets" continued to serve as a kind of synecdoche for Sidney women and their political commitments through the most trying years of the English civil wars, their contents simultaneously demanding and refusing retrieval, even all these years later.

In November 1659, a few months before the restoration of the monarchy, Algernon Sidney wrote his father a singularly moving letter about his mother's death the previous August. People mortally ill, he wrote, "are most fit to die, but they are also most wanted here; and we, that for a while are left in the

---

Sidney's correspondence suggest that the Sidneys considered themselves abandoned by the King by 1644, and while Robert Sidney "withdrew," his son Algernon and wife Dorothy, along with her brother Northumberland, "were now resolved in their own minds to support the parliamentary cause" (41). Their son Robert went into exile with the King. Clarendon later wrote that Leicester "was a man of honour and fidelity to the king, and his greatest misfortunes proceeded from the staggering and irresolution in his nature" (cited in Warkentin, "Humanism," 234).

[27] On Algernon Percy, see George A. Drake's entry in the new *ODNB*. "The Percy tradition of rebellion also had its effect. The sixth through to the eighth Earls died violently in rebellion against the crown, and the ninth Earl suffered a long imprisonment at the hands of James I. Furthermore, Northumberland was the nephew of the rebellious Earl of Essex. Writing to his friend, the attorney-general John Bankes in June 1642, Northumberland said: 'we believe that those persons who are most powerful with the King do endeavour to bring Parliaments to such condition that they shall be instruments to execute the commands of the King, who were established for his greatest and most supreme council ... but let us have our laws and liberties and privileges secured to us' (G. Bankes, *Story of Corfe Castle* (1853), 122–3). Towards the end of the protectorate Northumberland declined the invitations of both Oliver and Richard Cromwell to sit in the Upper House of their Parliaments. Expressing once again his cherished constitutional views, he told Richard that, 'till the government was such as his predecessors have served under, he could not in honour do it' (*Clarendon State Papers*, 2: 432). Clarendon called him 'the proudest man alive,' continuing 'If he had thought the King as much above him as he thought himself above other considerable men, he would have been a good subject ... He was in all his deportment a very great man'—a person who behaved with dignity and independence more characteristic of a feudal baron than a 17th-cent. lord (Clarendon, *Hist. rebellion*, 3: 495; 2: 538)."

world, are most apt, and perhaps with reason, to regret most the loss of those we most want" (48). "It may be," he continued, that "light and human passions are most suitably employed upon human and worldly things, wherein we have some sensible concernment: Thoughts, absolutely abstracted from ourselves, are more suitable unto that steadiness of mind that is much spoken of, little sought, and never found, than that which is seen amongst men" (48). Even in death, it seems, the specter of neostoic constancy hovered over Dorothy Sidney, her son's testimony eloquently evoking the "steadiness of mind" so rare among men, but nonetheless evinced by his mother.

A frequently told story about early modern English politics draws a line of political genealogy between the first Earl of Leicester, Philip Sidney's uncle Robert Dudley, through Sidney's great-nephew Algernon Sidney, tracing a line of nascent republicanism through the lives and work of these famous Sidney men.[28] Arguing for the place of women in this story is, of course, one of the primary goals of this book—a desire to recharacterize the "constancy" with which women like Dorothy Percy Sidney signed their letters less as a sign of wifely devotion than as a political vow, and to see their lives and work as central rather than peripheral to English political history.[29] (It remains shocking to me that Wroth's *Urania*, one of the most radical examples of "politically active humanism" produced in the seventeenth century, appears in none of the standard political histories of the Sidney family, let alone in discussions of "political pastoral.") The other goal of this book is to tell this refined political history as an integral part of literary history as well. Once again, Dorothy Sidney has something to contribute to this history as well.

In addition to having access to the Penshurst library and its 4,000 books, Dorothy Sidney also had a library of her own, eighty books in total, which she kept in her "closet" at Penshurst.[30] The recent editors of her correspondence characterize this library as "primarily devotional," but, as was the case with Margaret Hoby, it tells a far more complicated story (209).

---

[28] Such narratives are presented in Worden, *Sound of Virtue*; Jonathan Scott, *Algernon Sidney*; Warkentin, "Humanism"; Skretkowicz, "Algernon Sidney and Philip Sidney"; and Shephard, "Political Commonplace Books." For example, Shephard argues that Sidney's commonplace books "comprise a missing link in the family's political tradition, between his older brother Philip and later generations of the Sidney family, including Robert's grandson, Algernon" ("Political Commonplace Books," 3). Mary Wroth appears in none of these accounts.

[29] Dorothy Percy Sidney is mentioned exactly four times in Scott's book on Algernon Sidney. (We are told e.g. that her "principle object in life was to marry off her daughters to noblemen," 63.) While the editors of her correspondence similarly focus on her role as a "loving and supportive spouse" (1), they nonetheless point out that "hardly any attention has been paid to the role of [Algernon Sidney's] mother in forming his earliest political perspectives" (48).

[30] The inventory of her books was compiled after her death in August 1659, and is included in its entirety in appendix 2 in *The Correspondence of Dorothy Percy Sidney*, 209–13.

The collection included books by religious conformists and royalists like Launcelot Andrews and Henry Hammond (Penshurst's own chaplain from 1633 until 1643, when he left to follow the exiled King to Oxford), but most were the work of separatists, independents, Nonconformists, and Parliamentarians. (The list includes Henry Ainsworth, Richard Baxter, Jeremiah Burroughs, William Greenhill, Nicholas Lockyer, Richard Sibbes, William Strong—whose body would be disinterred in 1661 and thrown into a pit—Joseph Symonds, and Ralph Venning.) At least two of the books were also explicitly political: the Parliamentarian Henry Vane's *The retired mans mediations* (1655), a response to the political fragmentation of 1653 and defense of earthly magistracy, and a book by the tyrannomach and republican Arrigo Caterino Davila, *The Historie of the Civil Warres of France* (tr. 1647).[31] Political historians have long noted that Algernon Sidney worked with Vane throughout the commonwealth period, and that he cited Davila's *Historie* extensively in the explicitly anti-monarchical papers that would be used as part of his trial for treason. Dorothy Sidney Percy's personal copies of these books have not yet made their way into this history. While we cannot know who gave Algernon Sidney his copy of Davila, knowing that his mother read it as well, keeping it in her "closet" at Penshurst during some of the most tumultuous years in English history, offers one of many glimpses into the as-yet-unconsidered political and literary lives of women.

---

[31] Algernon Sidney was beheaded for attempting to assassinate Charles II in 1683. Algernon and Vane worked together throughout the commonwealth period. As Ruth Mayers points out in her *ODNB* entry on Vane, "a fascinating chapter contends that magistracy has a vital place in God's design, that it is rightly instituted by man's 'rational and voluntary' subjection to gain justice in external matters, and that it will share in the ultimate redemption of creation (Vane, *Meditations*, 385). Godly and 'good men' might then by 'free debate and common consent' (ibid., 394, 395) attempt to create a government repudiating self-interest and matching God's 'original pattern' as closely as possible (ibid., 395)." On Algernon Sidney's use of the French monarchomachs, including Mornay, Hotman, Davila, and de Comines, see Scott, *Algernon Sidney*, 52.

Bibliography

PRIMARY

Maidstone, Kent History and Library Centre, De L'Isle Mss. U1474, U1475, U1500.

Aldrich-Watson, Deborah, ed. *The Verse Miscellany of Constance Aston Fowler: A Diplomatic Edition*. Tempe, Ariz.: RETS 7th ser. 25, 2000.

Arthington, Henry. *The Seduction of Arthington by Hacket*. London: Printed by R.B. for Thomas Man, [1592].

Bacon, Francis. *Francis Bacon*. Ed. Brian Vickers. Oxford and New York: Oxford University Press, 1996.

—— *A Declaration of the Practises & Treasons Attempted and Committed by Robert Late Earle of Essex and his Complices, against her Maiestie and her Kingdoms*. London: By Robert Barker, printer to the Queenes most excellent Maiestie, Anno 1601.

—— *The Essayes or Counsels, Civill and Morall*. Ed. Michael Kiernan. Cambridge, Mass.: Harvard University Press, 1985.

Bacon, Jane Cornwallis. *The Private Correspondence of Jane Lady Cornwallis Bacon, 1613–1644*. Ed. Joanna Moody. Madison, Teaneck: Fairleigh Dickinson University Press, 2003.

Barlow, William. *The svmme and svbstance of the conference which, it pleased his excellent Maiestie to haue with the lords, bishops, and other of his clergie, (at vvhich the most of the lordes of the councell were present) in his Maiesties priuy-chamber, at Hampton Court. Ianuary 14. 1603*. London: Imprinted by Iohn Windet [and T. Creed] for Mathew Law, 1604.

Batho, G. R., ed. *The Household Papers of Henry Percy, Ninth Earl of Northumberland (1564–1632)*. London: Offices of the Royal Historical Society, 1962.

Baxter, Nathaniel. *Sir Philip Sydneys ouránia that is, Endimions song and tragedie, containing all philosophie*. London: Printed by Ed. Allde, for Edward White, and are to be solde at the little north doore of Saint Paules Church, at the signe of the Gun, 1606.

Beilin, Elaine V., ed. *Protestant Translators: Anne Lock Prowse and Elizabeth Russell*. Early Modern English Woman: A Facsmile Library of Essential Works, 2. Aldershot and Burlington, Vt.: Ashgate, 2001.

Blok, P. J., ed. *Correspondence inédite de Robert Dudley, Comte de Leycester, et de François et Jean Hotman*. Archives du Musée Teyler, 2/12, 2nd part. Haarlem: Loosjes, 1911.

Breton, Nicholas, *Religions Love in Wisedomes Worth, the Truest Beauty, Best Sets Forth*. [London]: Are to be sould in Popes head Ally by Ioh. Sudbury & Geo. Humble, [1615].

—— *The Pilgrimage to Paradise, Ioyned with the Countesse of Penbrookes Loue*. [London, by Toby Cooke], at the signe of the Tygres head, 1592.

Breton, Nicholas, *The Works in Verse and Prose of Nicholas Breton:* for the first time collected and edited: with memorial-introduction, notes and illustrations, glossarial index, facsimiles, etc. / by the Rev. Alexander B. Grosart. [Edinburgh]: Printed for private circulation [by T. and A. Constable], 1879. 2 vols.

Burges, John. *A sermon preached before the late King James His Majesty at Greenwich the 19 of Iuly 1604 together with two letters in way of apology for his sermon.* London: Printed by Thomas Brudenell, 1642.

Byfield, Nicholas. *An Exposition upon the Epistle to Colossians.* London: Printed by T. S. for NATHANIEL BVTTER, and are to be sould at his Shop at the signe of the Pide-Bull in Pauls Church-yard, neare to S. Austins Gate, 1615.

—— *The Marrow of the Oracles of God. The seuenth Edition.* London: Printed by Iohn Legatt, and are to bee sold by P. Stephens, and C. Meredith. at the golden Lyon in Pauls Church-yard, 1630.

—— *A Commentary upon the Three First Chapters of the First Epistle Generall of St. Peter.* London: Printed by Miles Flesher and Robert Young, [1637].

Calendar of the Manuscripts of the Most Honourable, the Marquess of Salisbury Preserved at Hatfield House, Hertfordshire (The "Cecil Papers"). Part X. London: His Majesty's Stationery Office, 1904.

Calendar of the Manuscripts of the Most Honourable Marquess of Salisbury, Preserved at Hatfield House, Hertfordshire. Part X. Ed. M. S. Giuseppe. London: His Majesty's Stationery Office, 1938.

Calvin, John. *John Calvin: Selections from his Writings.* Ed. John Dillenberger. Missoula, Mont.: Published by Scholars Press for the American Academy of Religion, 1975.

—— *The Institution of Christian Religion, Written in Latine by M. Iohn Caluine, Translated into English According to the Authors Last Edition... by Thomas Norton.* London [by Eliot's Court Press] for Iohn Norton, 1611.

Cavendish, Margaret. *Poems and Fancies: Written by the Right Honourable, the Lady Margaret Marchioness Newcastle.* London: Printed by T.R. for J. Martin and J. Allestrye, 1653.

Chamberlain, John. *The Letters of John Chamberlain.* Ed. N. E. McClure. 2 vols. Philadelphia: American Philosophical Society, 1939.

Chapman, George. *The Iliads of Homer Prince of Poets.* London: Printed [by Richard Field] for Nathaniell Butter, [1611?].

[Clark, William.] *Repertorium Bibliographicum; or, Some Account of the Most Celebrated British Libraries.* Vol. 1. London: William Clarke, New Bond Street, 1819.

Clarke, Samuel. *The Lives of Two and Twenty English Divines Eminent in their Generations for Learning, Piety, and Painfulnesse in the Work of the Ministry, and for their Sufferings in the Cause of Christ.* London: Printed by A.M. for Thomas Vnderhill and John Rothwell, 1660.

Cleaver, Robert. *A Godly Forme of Household Government for the Ordering of Priuate Families, According to the Direction of Gods Word.* London: Printed by Thomas Creede, for Thomas Man, 1603.

Clifford, Anne. *The Diaries of Lady Anne Clifford*. Ed. D. J. H. Clifford. Wolfeboro Falls, NH: Alan Sutton, 1991.

—— *The Memoir of 1603 and The Diary of 1616–1619*. Ed. Katherine Acheson. Peterborough, ON: Broadview editions, 2007.

Collinges, John. *Par Nobile. Two Treatises, the One Concerning the Excellent Woman, Evincing a person Fearing the Lord, to be the Most Excellent Person: Discourses More Privately upon Occasion of the Death of the Right Honourable, the Lady Frances Hobart, Late of Norwich . . . the Other . . . the Lady Katharine Courten*. London: [s.n.], 1669.

Constable, Henry. *The Poems of Henry Constable*. Ed. Joan Grundy. Liverpool: Liverpool University Press, 1960.

Cooper, Thomas. *The Christians Daily Sacrifice Containing a Daily Direction for a Setled Course of Sanctification*. London: Imprinted by N.O. for Walter Bvrre and are to bee sold in Paules Church yard at the signe of the Crane, 1615.

"Danby v. Syndenham: A Restoration Chancery Suit," *Yorkshire Archaeological Journal* 17 (1903): 72–93.

Daniel, Samuel. *The Vision of the 12 Goddesses Presented in a Maske the 8 of Ianuary, at Hampton Court: By the Queenes Most Excellent Maiestie, and her Ladies*. London: Printed by T[homas] C[reede] for Simon Waterson, and are to be sold at his sop [sic] in Pauls Church-yard, at the signe of the Crowne, 1604.

—— *The Complete Works in Verse and Prose of Samuel Daniel*. Ed. A. B. Grosart. 5 vols. London, 1885–96. Reprinted 1963.

—— *A panegyrike congratulatorie to the Kings Maiestie Also certaine epistles, by Samuel Daniel*. London: Printed by Valentine Simmes for Edward Blount, 1603.

—— *Delia and Rosamond augmented Cleopatra*. London: [By James Roberts and Edward Allde] for Simon Waterson, and are to be sold in Paules Church-yarde at the signe of the Crowne, [1594].

Davies, John. *The Muses Sacrifice*. London: Printed by T.S. for George Norton, 1612.

Day, Angel. *The English secretorie, or, Plaine and Direct Method, for the Enditing of All Manner of Epistles or Letters . . . Finally, the Partes and Office of a Secretorie, in Like Maner, Amplie Discoursed, All which to the Best and Easiest Direction that may be, for Young Learners and Practizers*. London: By Richard Iones, dwelling at the Rose and Crowne neere Holborne Bridge, 1592.

Devereux, Robert, Earl of Essex. *Essex to Stella: Two Letters from the Earl of Essex to Penelope Rich*. Ed. Arthur Freeman. Boston: Godine, 1971.

—— *[An apologie of the Earle of Essex]*. [London?: For J. Smethwick?, 1600?]. STC 6787.7.

Donne, John. *Satires, Epigrams and Verse Letters. By John Donne*. Ed. with introd. and commentary by W. Milgate. Oxford: Clarendon Press, 1967.

—— *John Donne's Poetry: Authoritative Texts, Criticism*. Ed. Donald R. Dickson. New York: W. W. Norton & Co., 2007.

—— *Essays in Divinity*. Ed. Evelyn M. Simpson. Oxford: Clarendon, 1952.

—— *Essayes in Divinity; by the Late Dr Donne, Dean of St Paul's*. London: Printed by T.M. for Richard Marriot, and are to be sold at his shop in St Dunstan's Church-yard Fleet-street, 1651.

—— *Letters to Several Persons of Honor*. London: J. Flesher, 1651.

Donne, John. *The Life and Letters of John Donne, Dean of St. Pauls.* Ed. Edmund Gosse. 2 vol. Gloucester, Mass.: Peter Smith, 1959.

—— *Letters to Severall Persons of Honour.* Delmar, NY: Scholars' Facsimiles and Reprints, 1977.

—— *Pseudo-Martyr.* Ed. Anthony Raspa. Montreal and Buffalo, NY: McGill-Queen's University Press, 1993.

—— *Pseudo-martyr. Wherein out of Certaine Propositions and Gradations, this Conclusion is Euicted. That those which are of the Romane Religion in this Kingdome, May and Ought to take the Oath of Allegiance.* London: printed by W. Stansby for Walter Burre, 1610.

—— *Selected Prose.* Chosen by Evelyn Simpson. Ed. Helen Gardner and Timothy Healey. Oxford: Clarendon, 1967.

—— *Sermons.* Ed. George R. Potter and Evelyn M. Simpson. 10 vols. Berkeley and Los Angeles: University of California Press, 1953–62.

—— "Sermon Preached to the Countesse of Bedford, then at Harrington house. January 7. 1620." *Fifty Sermons. Preached by that Learned and Reverend Divine, John Donne.* London: Printed by Ja. Flesher for M.F., J. Marriot, and R. Royston, 1649. Wing/D1862.

—— *The Major Works.* Ed. John Carey. Oxford: Oxford University Press, 1990.

—— *Devotions upon Emergent Occasions.* Ed. Anthony Raspa. Montreal: McGill Queens University Press, 1975.

—— *LXXX Sermons Preached by that Learned and Reverend Divine, Iohn Donne, Dr in Divinity.* London: Printed by Miles Flesher for Richard Royston, in Ivie-lane, and Richard Marriot in S. Dunstans Church-yard in Fleetstreet, 1640.

Drayton, Michael. *The Works of Michael Drayton.* Ed. J. William Hebel. 5 vols. Vol. 2. Oxford: Basil Blackwell, 1932.

—— *Mortimeriados. The Lamentable Ciuell Warres of Edward the Second and the Barrons.* London: Printed by I[ames] R[oberts] for Humfry Lownes, and are to be solde at his shop at the west end of Paules Church, [1596].

—— *Matilda. The Faire and Chaste Daughter of the Lord Robert Fitzwater. The true glorie of the noble house of Sussex.* London: Printed by Iames Roberts, for N[icholas] L[ing] and Iohn Busby, 1594.

—— *Idea. The Shepheards Garland Fashioned in Nine Eglogs.* London: [By T. Orwin] for Thomas Woodcocke, dwelling in Pauls Churchyarde, at the signe of the black Beare, 1593.

Draxe, Thomas. *The Worldes Resurrection, or The Generall Calling of the Iewes.* London: Printed by G. Eld, for Iohn Wright, and are to be sold at his shop neere Christ Church gate, 1608.

Dryden, John. *The Satires of Decimus Junius Juvenalis Translated into English Verse by Mr. Dryden and Several Other Eminent Hands.* London: Printed for Iacob Tonson at the Iudge's-Head in Chancery-Lane, near Fleetstreet, 1693.

Dyke, Daniel. *The Mystery of Selfe-Deceiuing.* London: Printed by Edvvard Griffin for Ralph Mab, at the signe of the Grayhound in Pauls Church yarde, 1614.

Foxe, John. *Actes and Monuments of Matters Most Speciall and Memorable, Happening in the Church* [7th edn]. London, for the Company of Stationers, 1610.

Franklin, Julian H., ed. *Constitutionalism and Resistance in the Sixteenth Century: Three Treatises by Hotman, Beza, & Mornay*. Tr. and ed. Julian H. Franklin. New York: Pegasus, 1969.

Fraunce, Abraham. *The Countesse of Pembrokes Yuychurch*. London: Printed by Thomas Orwyn for William Ponsonby, dwelling in Paules Churchyard, at the signe of the Bishops head, 1591.

—— *The Third Part of the Countesse of Pembrokes Yuychurch*. London: Printed [by Thomas Orwyn], for Thomas Woodcocke, dwelling in Paules Church-yeard, at the signe of the blacke Beare, 1592.

Fuller, Thomas. *The History of the Worthies of England who for Parts and Learning Have Been Eminent in the Several Counties: Together with an Historical Narrative of the Native Commodities and Rarities in Each County*. London: Printed by J.G.W.L. and W.G. for Thomas Williams, 1662.

Gardiner, Samuel Rawson, ed. *The Fortescue Papers; Consisting Chiefly of Letters Relating to State Affairs, Collected by John Packer, Secretary to George Villiers, Duke of Buckingham*. London: Printed for the Camden Society, 1871.

Glover, Robert. *The Visitation of Yorkshire, Made in the Years 1584/5, by Robert Glover, Somerset herald*. Ed. Joseph Foster. London, 1875.

Greenham, Richard. *The Workes of the Reuerend and Faithfull Seruant of Iesus Christ M. Richard Greenham*. London: Imprinted by Felix Kingston [and Richard Bradock] for Robert Dexter, and are to be solde at his shop in Paules Churchyard at the signe of the brasen Serpent, 1599.

Greville, Fulke. *The Prose Works of Fulke Greville, Lord Brooke*. Ed. John Gouws Oxford: Clarendon, 1986.

Harington, John. *The Letters and Epigrams of Sir John Harington*. Ed. Norman Egbert McClure. Philadelphia: University of Pennsylvania Press, 1930.

Herbert, Mary Sidney. *Collected Works of Mary Sidney Herbert, Countess of Pembroke*. Ed. Margaret P. Hannay, Noel J. Kinnamon, and Michael G. Brennan. Oxford: Clarendon Press, 1998.

Herrick, Robert. *The Poetical Works of Robert Herrick*. Vol. 1. Ed. George Saintsbury. London: George Bell & Sons, 1893.

Hobbs, Mary, ed. *Stoughton Manuscript: A Manuscript Miscellany of Poems by Henry King and his Circle, circa 1636*. Aldershot and Brookfield, Vt.: Scolar, 1990.

Hoby, Sir Edward. *A Letter to Mr. T.H. Late Minister: Now Fugitiue: From Sir Edvvard Hoby Knight. In Answere of his First Motiue*. London: Printed by F[elix] K[ingston] for Ed. Blount and W. Barret, 1609.

—— *A Curry-combe for a Coxe-combe*. London: Printed by William Stansby for Nathaniel Butter, and are to be sold at his shop neere S. Austins gate at the signe of the Pied Bull, 1615.

Hoby, Margaret. *Diary of Lady Margaret Hoby, 1599–1605*. Ed. Dorothy M. Meads. Boston and New York, Houghton Mifflin, 1930.

—— *Private Life of an Elizabethan Lady: The Diary of Lady Margaret Hoby 1599–1605*. Ed. Joanna Moody. Phoenix Mill: Sutton, 1998.

Hutton, Matthew. *The Correspondence of Dr. Matthew Hutton, Archbishop of York.* Surtees Soc. Vol. 17. London: J. B. Nichols & Son, 1843.

James VI and I. *Political Writings.* Ed. Johann P. Sommerville. Cambridge and New York: Cambridge University Press, 1994.

Jonson, Ben. *The Works of Ben Jonson.* Ed. C. H. Herford, P. Simpson, and E. M. Simpson. 11 vols. Oxford: Clarendon Press, 1925–52, vol. 8.

—— *The Poems of Ben Jonson.* Ed. Bernard H. Newdigate. Oxford: Basil Blackwell, 1938.

Klene, Jean, ed. *The Southwell-Sibthorpe Commonplace Book: Folger MS V.b.198.* Tempe, Ariz.: Medieval & Renaissance Texts & Studies, 1997.

Lanyer, Aemilia. *The Poems of Aemilia Lanyer. Salve Deus Rex Judaeorum.* Ed. Susanne Woods. New York: Oxford University Press, 1993.

Lipsius, Justus. *Justus Lipsius' Concerning Constancy.* Ed. and tr. R. V. Young. Tempe, Ariz.: Arizona Center for Medieval and Renaissance Studies, 2011.

—— *Two Bookes of Constancie, written in Latine by Iustus Lipsius; Englished by Sir John Stradling.* Ed. with an introduction by Rudolf Kirk; notes by Clayton Morris Hall. New Brunswick, NJ: Rutgers University Press, 1939.

Lucan. *Lucans Pharsalia Containing the Ciuill Warres betweene Caesar and Pompey.* Tr. Sir Arthur Gorges Knight. London: Printed [by Nicholas Okes] for Edward Blount, 1614.

Lyly, John. *Ephues* in *Complete Works.* Ed. R. Warwick Bond. 3 vols. Oxford: Clarendon Press, 1902, vol. 2.

Matthew, Tobie. *A Collection of Letters Made by Sr. Tobie Mathews, Knight.* London: Printed for Henry Herringman, and are to be sold at his shop, at the sign of the Anchor in the lower walk in the New Exchange, 1660 [i.e. 1659].

Meres, Francis. *Palladis Tamia* (1598). In *Elizabethan Critical Essays*, ed. with an introduction by G. Gregory Smith. London and Oxford: Clarendon Press, 1904.

Millman, Jill Seal, and Gillian Wright, eds. *Early Modern Women's Manuscript Poetry.* Victoria E. Burke and Marie-Louise Coolahan, contributing eds. New York: Manchester University Press, 2005.

Moffet, Thomas. *The Silkewormes and their Flies* (1599), Facsimile. Ed. Victor Houliston. Binghampton, NY: Medieval and Renaissance Texts and Studies, 1989.

—— *NOBILIS or A View of the Life and Death of a Sidney.* With introd., tr., and notes by Virgil B. Heltzel and Hoyt H. Hudson. San Marino, Calif.: Huntington Library, 1940.

Montaigne, Michel de. *The Essayes or Morall, Politike and Millitarie.* Tr. John Florio. London: Val. Sims for Edward Blount dwelling in Paules churchyard, 1603.

Mornay, Philippe de, seigneur du Plessis-Marly. *Fowre Bookes, of the Institution, Use and Doctrine of the Holy Sacrament of the Eucharist in the Old Church.* 2nd edn reviewed by the author. London by John Windet, for I.B[inge], T.M[an] & W. [Ponsonby], 1600.

—— *A Treatise of the Church. Wherein are Handled the Principall Questions Mooued in Our Time Concerning that Matter.* London: L. S[nowden] for George Potter, 1606.

Nashe, Thomas. "Preface to *Astrophil and Stella.*" *Elizabethan Critical Essays*, ed. G. Gregory Smith. 2 vols. Oxford: Clarendon Press, 1904. Vol. 2.

Overbury, Thomas, Sir (and others). *Characters: Together with Poems, News, Edicts, and Paradoxes Based on the Eleventh Edition of a Wife now the Widow of Sir Thomas Overbury.* Ed. Donald Beecher. Ottawa: Dovehouse Editions, 2003.

Ortúñez de Calahorra, Diego. *The Mirroir of Princely deedes and Knighthood.* Tr. Margaret Tyler. London: Thomas East, 1578.

Ostovich, Helen, and Elizabeth Sauer, eds. *Reading Early Modern Women: An Anthology of Texts in Manuscript and Print, 1550–1700.* Assisted by Melissa Smith. New York: Routledge, 2004.

Morton, Thomas, Bp. of Durham. *A Catholike Appeale for Protestants, Out of the Confessions of the Romane Doctors.* Londini, [by R. Field?] impensis Georg. Bishop & Ioh. Norton, 1610.

—— *Two Treatises Concerning Regeneration.* London: Printed by Thomas Creede for Robert Jackson and Raph Iackson, 1597.

Perkins, William. *A Golden Chaine: or The Description of Theologie Containing the Order of the Causes of Saluation and Damnation.* [Cambridge]: Printed by Iohn Legat, printer to the Vniuersitie of Cambridge, 1600.

—— *A Salve for a Sicke Man. or, A Treatise Containing the Nature, Differences, and Kindes of Death as also the Right Manner of Dying Well.* London: By Iohn Legat, printer to the Vniuersitie of Cambridge 1611.

Perry, Sir Erskine, ed. *The Van den Bempde Papers.* The Philobiblion Society Miscellany, 12. London, 1868–9.

Puttenham, George. *The Arte of English Poesie.* A facsimile reproduction, with an introd. by Baxter Hathaway. Kent, Ohio: Kent State University Press, 1970.

Pyott, Lazarus. *The Ancient, Famous, and Honourable History of Amadis de Gaule.* Printed at London by Nicholas Okes, 1619.

Quarles, Francis. *Argalus and Parthenia: The Argument of ye History.* London: Printed for Iohn Marriott in St. Dunstons Churchyard fleetstreet, 1629.

Rainbow, Edward, Lord Bishop of Carlisle, *A Sermon Preached at the Funeral of the Right Honorable Anne Countess of Pembroke, Dorset and Montgomery, Who Died March 22, 1675/6.* London: Printed for R. Royston, Bookseller to his most Excellent Majesty, and H. Broom at the Gun at the West-end of St. Paul's, 1677.

Reading, John. *A Faire Warning Declaring the Comfortable Use Both of Sicknesse and Health.* London: Printed by Bernard Alsop, for Iohn Hodgets, 1621.

Register of the Parish of Hackness, 1557–1783. Transcribed by Charles Johnstone and Emily J. Hart. Leeds: Knight & Forster, 1906.

Report on the Manuscripts of Lord De L'Isle and Dudley Preserved at Penshurst Place, Kent. Vol. 4. *Sidney Papers, 1608–1611.* Ed. William A. Shaw. London: His Majesty's Stationery Office, 1942.

Rudyerd, Benjamin. *Memoirs of Sir Benjamin Rudyerd*. Ed. James Alexander Manning. London: T. & W. Boone, 1841.

Saul, Arthur. *The famous game of chesse-play truely discouered, and all doubts resolued*. London: [By Thomas Snodham] for Roger Iackson, and are to be sould at his shop neere Fleetstreet-Conduit, 1614.

Savage, James. E, ed. and commentary. *The "Conceited Newes" of Sir Thomas Overbury and His Friends*. A facsimile reproduction of the 9th impression of 1616 of *Sir Thomas Overbury His Wife*. Gainesville, Fla.: Scholars' Facsimiles & Reprints, 1968.

Segar, William. *Honor military, and ciuill contained in foure bookes*. London: Robert Barker, printer to the Queenes most Excellent Maiestie, 1602.

Shaw, William A., ed. *Report on the Manuscripts of Lord De L'Isle and Dudley Preserved at Penshurst Place, Kent*. Vol. 4. *Sidney Papers, 1608–1611*. London: His Majesty's Stationer's Office, 1942.

Shutte, Christopher. *A verie godlie and necessary sermon preached before the yong countesse of Cumberland*. London: By [H. Middleton? for] Christopher Barker, printer to the Queenes Maiestie, 1578.

Sidney, Dorothy Percy. *The Correspondence (c. 1626–1659) of Dorothy Percy Sidney, Countess of Leicester*. Ed. Michael G. Brennan, Noel J. Kinnamon, and Margaret P. Hannay. Aldershot: Ashgate, 2010.

Sidney, Philip. *The Miscellaneous Works of Sir Philip Sidney*. Ed. William Gray. AMBS Press, 1966.

—— *The Poems of Sir Philip Sidney*. Ed. William A. Ringler, Jr. Oxford: Clarendon Press, 1962.

—— "A Discourse of Syr Ph. S. to the Queenes Majesty Touching Hir Marriage with Monsieur." In *The Complete Works of Sir Philip Sidney*. Ed. Albert Feuillerat. Cambridge: Cambridge: Cambridge University Press, 1923. Vol. 3.

—— *Miscellaneous Prose of Sir Philip Sidney*. Ed. Katherine Duncan-Jones and Jan Van Dorsten. Oxford: Clarendon Press, 1973.

—— *The Countess of Pembroke's Arcadia (The Old Arcadia)*. Ed. Katherine Duncan-Jones. Oxford and New York: Oxford University Press, 1985.

—— *Countess of Pembroke's Arcadia: The New Arcadia*. Ed. Victor Skretkowicz. Oxford: Clarendon Press; New York: Oxford University Press, 1987.

—— *The Countess of Pembroke's Arcadia*. Ed. Maurice Evans. London: Penguin, 1977.

—— *A Defence of Poetry*. Ed. Jan Van Dorsten. Oxford: Oxford University Press, 1966.

—— *Sir P.S. his Astrophel and Stella*. London: Printed [by J. Danter] for Thomas Newman, 1591.

—— *The Countesse of Pembrokes Arcadia*. London: Printed by Iohn Windet for william Ponsonbie, 1590.

Sidney, Robert. *The Poems of Robert Sidney*. Ed. from the poet's autograph notebook, with introd. and commentary, by P. J. Croft. Oxford and New York: Oxford University Press, 1984.

—— and Barbara Gamage Sidney. *Domestic Politics and Family Absence: The Correspondence of Robert Sidney, First Earl of Leicester, and Barbara Gamage Sidney*. Ed. Margaret P. Hannay, Noel J. Kinnamon, and Michael G. Brennan. Aldershot: Ashgate, 2005.

Smith, Sir Thomas. *DE REPVBLICA ANGLORVM. The maner of Gouernement or policie of the Realme of England, compiled by the Honorable man Thomas Smyth, Doctor of the ciuil lawes, Knight and principall Secretarie vnto the two most worthie Princes, King Edwarde the sixt, and Queene Elizabeth. Seene and allowed.* London: Printed by Henrie Midleton for Gregorie Seton, 1583.

—— *De Republica Anglorum.* Ed. Mary Dewar. Cambridge: Cambridge University Press, 1982.

Stock, Richard. *The Churches Lamentation for the losse of the Godly.* London: John Beale, 1614.

Stuart Royal Proclamations. Vol. I. *Royal Proclamations of King James I, 1603–1625.* Ed. James F. Larkin and Paul L. Hughes. Oxford: Clarendon Press, 1973.

Sullivan Ernest W., ed. *The First and Second Dalhousie Manuscripts Poems and Prose by John Donne and Others.* A Facsimile Edition. Columbia, Mo.: University of Missouri Press, 1988.

Travitsky, Betty, ed. *The Paradise of Women: Writings by Englishwomen of the Renaissance.* Westport, Conn.: Greenwood, 1981.

Udall, John. *A Parte of a register contayninge sundrie memorable matters, written by diuers godly and learned in our time, which stande for, and desire the reformation of our Church, in discipline and ceremonies, according to the pure worde of God, and the lawe of our lande.* Middelburg: Printed by Richard Schilders, 1593.

Walton, Izaak. *The Life of Dr. John Donne.* Project Canterbury. Available at: <http://anglicanhistory.org>.

Whitgift, John, Archbishop of Canterbury. *The Defense of the Aunswere to the Admonition, against the Replie of T. C[artwright].* London: Henry Binneman for Humfrey Toye, 1574. STC 2–25430.

Wotton, Henry. *Life and Letters of Sir Henry Wotton.* Ed. Logan Pearsall Smith. 2 vols. Oxford: Clarendon Press, 1907.

Wroth, Mary. *The First Part of the Countess of Montgomery's Urania.* Ed. Josephine A. Roberts. Binghamton, NY: Medieval & Renaissance Texts & Studies, 1995.

—— *The Second Part of the Countess of Montgomery's Urania.* Ed. Josephine A. Roberts, completed by Suzanne Gossett and Janel Mueller. Binghamton, NY: Medieval & Renaissance Texts & Studies, 1999.

—— *The Poems of Lady Mary Wroth.* Ed. Josephine A. Roberts. Baton Rouge, La., and London: Louisiana State University Press, 1983.

Yorkshire Archaeological Society. *Yorkshire Probate Inventories 1542–1689.* Ed. Peter C. D. Brears. Record Series 134. [Kendal, UK: Yorkshire Archaeological Society, 1972].

Yorkshire Parish Register Society. *The Register of the Parish of Hackness, Co. York, 1557–1783.* Transcribed Charles Johnstone and Emily J. Hart. Leeds: Knight & Forster, Publications of the Yorkshire Parish Register Society, 25.

SECONDARY

Adams, S. L. "Favourites and Factions at the Elizabethan Court." In Ronald G. Asch and Adolf M. Birke (eds), *Princes, Patronage, and the Nobility: The Court at the Beginning of the Modern Age, 1450–1650.* London: German Historical Institute and Oxford University Press, 1991, 265–88.

Adams, S. L. "Foreign Policy and the Parliaments of 1621 and 1624." In Kevin Sharpe (ed.), *Faction and Parliament: Essays on Early Stuart History.* Oxford: Clarendon, 1978, 139–72.

—— *Leicester and the Court: Essays on Elizabethan Politics.* Manchester and New York: Manchester University Press, 2002.

—— "Spain or the Netherlands? The Dilemmas of Early Stuart Foreign." In Howard Tomlinson (ed.), *Before the English Civil War: Essays on Early Stuart Politics and Government.* London: Macmillan, 1983, 79–102.

—— "The Protestant Cause: Religious Alliance with the Western European Calvinist Communities as a Political Issue in England, 1585–1630." Diss., Oxford University, 1973.

Adamson, J. S. A. "Chivalry and Political Culture in Caroline England." In Kevin Sharpe and Peter Lake (eds), *Culture and Politics in Early Stuart England.* Stanford, Calif.: Stanford University Press, 1993, 161–97.

—— "The Baronial Context of the English Civil War." *Transactions of the Royal Historical Society,* 5th ser. 40 (1990): 93–120.

Aers, David, and Gunther Kress. "'Darke texts need notes': Versions of Self in Donne's Verse Epistles." In Arthur Marotti (ed.), *Critical Essays on John Donne.* New York: G. K. Hall; Toronto: Maxwell Macmillan Canada, 1994, 102–22.

Alexander, Gavin. *Writing After Sidney: The Literary Response to Sir Philip Sidney, 1586–1640.* Oxford: Oxford University Press, 2006.

Andrea, Bernadette. "Pamphilia's Cabinet: Gendered Authorship and Empire in Lady Mary Wroth's *Urania.*" *English Literary History,* 68/2 (2001): 335–58.

Aveling, Hugh. *Northern Catholics: The Catholic Recusants of the North Riding of Yorkshire, 1558–1790.* London: Geoffrey Chapman, 1966.

Baker-Smith, Dominic. "John Donne's Critique of True Religion." In A. J. Smith (ed.), *John Donne: Essays in Celebration.* London: Methuen, 1972, 404–32.

Barnard, John, and Maureen Bell, *The Early 17th Century York Book Trade and John Foster's Inventory of 1616.* Leeds: Leeds Philosophical and Literary Society, 1994.

Barnes, Geraldine. *Counsel and Strategy in Middle English Romance.* Cambridge: D. S. Brewer, 1993.

Barroll, Leeds. *Anna of Denmark, Queen of England: A Cultural Biography.* Philadelphia: University of Pennsylvania Press, 2001.

Bald, R. C. *John Donne: A Life.* Oxford: Oxford University Press, 1970.

Bastow, Sarah L. "'Worth Nothing, But Very Wilful': Catholic Recusant Women of Yorkshire, 1536–1642." *Recusant History,* 25/4 (2001): 591–603.

Beal, P. *In Praise of Scribes: Manuscripts and their Makers in Seventeenth-Century England.* Oxford: Clarendon Press, 1998.

—— "John Donne." *Index of English Literary Manuscripts.* Ed P. J. Croft et al. London: Mansell, 1980.

—— "John Donne and the Circulation of Manuscripts." In John Barnard et al. (eds), *Cambridge History of the Book in Britain,* vol. 4. *1557–1695.* Cambridge: Cambridge University Press, 1999, 122–6.

Beal, P., and Margaret J. M. Ezell, eds. *English Manuscript Studies 1100–1700,* vol. 9. *Writings by Early Modern Women.* London: The British Library, 2000.

Beck, Joyce S. "Donne's Scholastic 'Ars Dictaminis' in a Verse Epistle to the Countess of Bedford." *Explorations in Renaissance Culture,* 8/9 (1982/3): 22–32.

Beilin, Elaine V. *Redeeming Eve: Women Writers of the English Renaissance.* Princeton: Princeton University Press, 1987.

—— "Winning 'the harts of the people': The Role of the Political Subject in the *Urania*." In Sigrid King (ed.), *Pilgrimage for Love: Essays in Early Modern Literature in Honor of Josephine A. Roberts.* Tempe, Ariz.: Arizona Center for Medieval and Renaissance Studies, 1999, 1–18.

Bell, Ilona. *Elizabethan Women and the Poetry of Courtship.* Cambridge: Cambridge University Press, 1998.

Bellany, Alastair. *Politics of Court Scandal in Early Modern England: News Culture and the Overbury Affair, 1603–1666.* Cambridge and New York: Cambridge University Press, 2002.

Bergbusch, M. "Rebellion in the New Arcadia." *Philological Quarterly,* 53 (1974): 29–41.

Bernard, G. W. *Power and Politics in Tudor England.* Aldershot and Burlington, Vt.: Ashgate, 2000.

Berry, Philippa. *Of Chastity and Power: Elizabethan Literature and the Unmarried Queen.* London: Routledge, 1989.

Betcherman, Lita-Rose. *Court Lady and Country Wife: Two Noble Sisters in Seventeenth-Century England.* New York: William Morrow, 2005.

Blackburn, Thomas H. "Edmund Bolton's *The Cabanet Royal*: A Belated Reply to Sidney's *Apology for Poetry*." *Studies in the Renaissance,* 14 (1967): 159–71.

Blakiston, Georgiana. *Woburn and the Russells.* London: Constable, 1980.

Bourdieu, Pierre. *The Field of Cultural Production: Essays on Art and Literature.* Cambridge: Polity Press, 1993.

Boutcher, Warren Vincent, "Florio's Montaigne: Translation and Pragmatic Humanism in the Sixteenth Century." Ph.D. Diss. Queen's College, 1991.

Bowden, Caroline. "Women as Intermediaries: An Example of the Use of Literacy in the Late Sixteenth and Early Seventeenth Centuries." *History of Education,* 22/3 (1993): 215–23.

Braden, Gordon. *Renaissance Tragedy and the Senecan Tradition: Anger's Privilege.* New Haven: Yale University Press, 1985.

Bradford, Alan T. "Stuart Absolutism and the 'Utility' of Tacitus." *Huntington Library Quarterly,* 46/2 (1983): 127–55.

Brennan, Michael G. *Literary Patronage in the English Renaissance: The Pembroke Family.* London and New York: Routledge, 1988.

—— *The Sidneys of Penshurst and the Monarchy, 1500–1700.* Aldershot: Ashgate, 2006.

Brennan, Michael G., and Noel J. Kinnamon, *A Sidney Chronology 1554–1654*. New York: Palgrave, 2003.

Briggs, W. D. "Political Ideas in Sidney's *Arcadia*." *Studies in Philology*, 28 (1931): 137–61.

Brown, Cedric C. "Presence, Obligation and Memory in John Donne's Texts for the Countess of Bedford." *Renaissance Studies*, 22/1 (2008): 63–85.

Brown, Elizabeth. "'Companion me with my Mistress': Cleopatra, Elizabeth I, and their Waiting Women." In Susan Frye and Karen Robertson (eds), *Maids and Mistresses, Cousins and Queens: Women's Alliances in Early Modern England*. New York and Oxford: Oxford University Press, 1999, 131–45.

Brown, Piers. "'Hac ex consilio meo via progredieris': Courtly Reading and Secretarial Mediation in Donne's *The Courtier's Library*." *Renaissance Quarterly*, 61 (2008): 833–66.

Bruce, Yvonne. "'That which Marreth All': Constancy and Gender in *The Virtuous Octavia*." *Medieval and Renaissance Drama in England*, 22 (2009): 42–59.

Brumbaugh, Barbara. "Cecropia and the Church of Antichrist in Sir Philip Sidney's *New Arcadia*." *Studies in English Literature*, 38/1 (Winter 1998): 19–43.

Burgess, Glenn. *The Politics of the Ancient Constitution: An Introduction to English Political Thought 1603–42*. University Park, Pa.: Penn State University, 1993.

Burke, Mary E., Jane Donawerth, Linda L. Dove, and Karen Nelson, eds. *Women, Writing and the Reproduction of Culture in Tudor and Stuart Britain*. Syracuse, NY: Syracuse University Press, 2000.

Burke, Peter. "Tacitism, Scepticism, and Reason of State." In J. H. Burns and Mark Goldie (eds), *The Cambridge History of Political Thought*. Cambridge: Cambridge University Press, 1991, 479–98.

Burke, Victoria E., and Jonathan Gibson, eds. *Early Modern Women's Manuscript Writing: Selected Papers from the Trinity/Trent Colloquium*. Aldershot and Burlington, Vt.: Ashgate, 2004.

Burner, Sandra A. *James Shirley: A Study of Literary Coteries and Patronage in Seventeenth Century England*. Lanham, Md.: University Press of America, 1988.

Bushnell, Rebecca W. *Tragedies of Tyrants: Political Thought and Theater in the English Renaissance*. Ithaca, NY: Cornell University Press, 1990.

Buxton, John. *Elizabethan Taste*. London: Macmillan, 1963.

—— *Sir Philip Sidney and the English Renaissance*. London: Macmillan, 1954.

Byard, Margaret M. "The Trade of Courtship: The Countess of Bedford and the Bedford Memorials: A Family History from 1585 to 1607." *History Today*, 29/1 (1979): 20–8.

Byrne, M. St. Clare, and Gladys Scott Thomson. "'My Lord's Books': The Library of Francis, Second Earl of Bedford, in 1584." *Review of English Studies*, 7/28 (1931): 385–405.

Cambers, Andrew. "Readers' Marks and Religious Practice: Margaret Hoby's Marginalia." In John N. King (ed.), *Tudor Books and Readers: Materiality and the Construction of Meaning*. Cambridge: Cambridge University Press, 2010, 211–31.

—— "Reading, the Godly and Self-Writing in England, Circa 1580–1720." *Journal of British Studies*, 46 (2007): 769–825.

—— "'The Partial Customes of these Frozen Parts': Religious Riot and Reconciliation in the North of England." *Studies in Church History*, 40 (2004): 169–79.

Carlson, David. *English Humanist Books*. Toronto: University of Toronto Press, 1993.

Cavanagh, Sheila T. *Cherished Torment: The Emotional Geography of Lady Mary Wroth's Urania*. Pittsburgh, Pa.: Duquesne University Press, 2001.

—— "The Politics of Private Discourse: Familial Relations in Lady Mary Wroth's *Urania*." In Naomi J. Miller and Naomi Yavneh (eds), *Sibling Relations and Gender in the Early Modern World*. Aldershot: Ashgate, 2006, 104–15.

Charles, Amy. *A Life of George Herbert*. Ithaca, NY, and London: Cornell University Press, 1977.

Charlton, Kenneth. *Women, Religion and Education in Early Modern England*. London and New York: Routledge, 1999.

Chartier, Roger. "Leisure and Sociability: Reading Aloud in Early Modern Europe." In Susan Zimmerman and Ronald Weissman (eds), *Urban Life in the Renaissance*. Newark: University of Delaware Press, 1989, 103–20.

—— "Texts, Printing and Readings." In Lynn Hunt (ed.), *The New Cultural History*. Berkeley: University of California Press, 1989, 154–75,

—— *The Order of Books: Readers, Authors and Libraries in Europe between the Fourteenth and Eighteenth Centuries*. Tr. Lydia G. Cochrane. Stanford, Calif.: Stanford University Press, 1994.

Chaytor, Miranda. "Household and Kinship: Ryton in the Late 16th and Early 17th Centuries." *History Workshop Journal*, 10 (1980): 25–60.

Clarke, Danielle. *The Politics of Early Modern Women's Writing*. Harlow, Essex: Pearson Education Ltd, 2001.

Clarke, Elizabeth. "Beyond Microhistory: The Use of Women's Manuscripts in a Widening Political Arena." In James Daybell (ed.), *Women and Politics in Early Modern England, 1450–1700*. Aldershot and Burlington, Vt.: Ashgate, 2004, 211–27.

—— "Elizabeth Jekyll's Spiritual Diary: Private Manuscript or Political Document?" In Peter Beal and Margaret J. Ezell (eds), *English Manuscript Studies, 1100–1700*, vol. 9. *Writings by Early Modern Women*. London: Blackwell, 2000, 218–37.

Clay, J. W. "The Clifford Family." *Yorkshire Archaeological Journal*, 18 (1905): 355–411.

Clegg, Cyndia Susan. *Press Censorship in Jacobean England*. Cambridge and New York: Cambridge University Press, 2001.

Cliffe, J. T. *The Puritan Gentry: The Great Puritan Families of Early Stuart England*. London: Routledge, 1984.

Cloclough, David, ed. *John Donne's Professional Lives*. Cambridge: D. S. Brewer, 2003.

Clucas, Stephen, and Rosalind Davies, eds. *The Crisis of 1614 and the Addled Parliament: Literary and Historical Perspectives*. Aldershot and Burlington, Vt.: Ashgate, 2003.

Cogswel, Thomas. "The Path to Elizium 'Lately Discovered': Drayton and the Early Stuart Court." *Huntington Library Quarterly*, 54/3 (Summer 1991): 207–33.

Collinson, Patrick. *De republica anglorum, or, History with the Politics Put Back*. Cambridge and New York: Cambridge University Press, 1990.

—— "'Not Sexual in the Ordinary Sense': Women, Men and Religious Transactions." In *Elizabethan Essays*. London and Rio Grande: Hambledon Press, 1994, 119–50.

—— *The Elizabethan Puritan Movement*. London: Cape, 1967.

—— "The Monarchical Republic of Queen Elizabeth I." *Bulletin of the John Rylands University Library of Manchester*, 69 (1987): 394–424.

—— "The Monarchical Republic of Queen Elizabeth I." In *Elizabethans*. London: Hambledon Press, 2003, 31–58.

Considine, John. "The Invention of the Literary Circle of Sir Thomas Overbury," in Claude J. Summers and Ted-Larry Pebworth (eds), *Literary Circles and Cultural Communities in Renaissance England*. Columbia, Mo., and London: University of Missouri Press, 2000, 59–74.

Corthell, Ronald J. "'Friendships Sacraments': John Donne's Familiar Letters." *Studies in Philology*, 78 (1981): 409–25.

Crane, Susan. *Insular Romance: Politics, Faith, and Culture in Anglo-Norman and Middle English Literature*. Berkeley, Calif.: University of California Press, 1986.

Craft, William. "Remaking the Heroic Self in the *New Arcadia*." *Studies in English Literature*, 25/1 (Winter 1985): 45–67.

Crawford, Julie. "Lady Anne Clifford and the Uses of Christian Warfare." In Micheline White (ed.), *English Women, Religion, and Textual Production, 1500– 1625*. Aldershot and Burlington, Vt.: Ashgate, 2011, 101–23.

—— "Literary Circles and Communities." In Caroline Bicks and Jennifer Summit (eds), *The History of British Women's Writing, 1500–1610*. Basingstoke and New York: Palgrave Macmillan, 2010, 34–59.

—— "Preachers, Pleaders, and Players: Margaret Cavendish and the Dramatic Petition." In Pamela Brown and Peter Parolin (eds), *Beyond the 'All-Male' Stage in Early Modern England: Women Players, 1500–1660*. London: Ashgate, 2005, 241–60.

—— "Reconsidering Early Modern Women's Reading, or How Margaret Hoby Read Her De Mornay." *Huntington Library Quarterly*, 73/2 (2010): 193–223.

—— "Sidney's Sapphics and the Role of Interpretive Communities." *English Literary History*, 69/4 (Winter 2002): 979–1007.

—— "The Case of Lady Anne Clifford; Or, Did Women Have a Mixed Monarchy?" *PMLA* 121/4 (October 2006): 1682–9.

Cressy, David. "Kinship and Kin Interaction in Early Modern England." *Past and Present*, 113 (1983): 38–69.

—— *Literacy and the Social Order: Reading and Writing in Tudor and Stuart England*. Cambridge: Cambridge University Press, 1980.

—— and Lori Anne Ferrell, eds. *Religion and Society in Early Modern England: A Sourcebook*. London and New York: Routledge, 1996.

Crewe, Jonathan. *Hidden Designs: The Critical Profession and Renaissance Literature*. New York and London: Methuen, 1986.

Croft, Pauline. "Capital Life: Members of Parliament outside the House." In Thomas Cogswell, Richard Cust, and Peter Lake (eds), *Politics, Religion and Popularity in Early Stuart Britain: Essays in Honour of Conrad Russell*. Cambridge and New York: Cambridge University Press, 2002, 65–83.

Cross, Claire. *Church and People: England, 1450–1660*. Oxford and Malden, Mass.: Blackwell Publishers, 1999.

—— *The Puritan Earl: The Life of Henry Hastings Third Earl of Huntingdon, 1536–1595*. London: Macmillan; New York: St Martin's Press, 1966.

Cust, Richard. "News and Politics in Early Seventeenth Century England." *Past and Present*, 112 (1986): 60–90.

Das, Nandini. *Renaissance Romance: The Transformation of English Prose Fiction, 1570–1620*. Farnham, Surrey; Burlington, Vt.: Ashgate, 2011.

Davies, Godfrey. "English Political Sermons, 1603–1640." *Huntington Library Quarterly*, 1 (October 1939): 1–22.

Davis, Joel B. "Multiple Arcadias and the Literary Quarrel between Fulke Greville and the Countess of Pembroke." *Studies in Philology*, 101/4 (Fall 2004): 401–30.

—— *The Countesse of Pembrokes Arcadia and the Invention of English Literature*. Basingstoke and New York: Palgrave Macmillan, 2011

Davis, Walter R. "A Map of *Arcadia*," in *Sidney's Arcadia*. New Haven: Yale University Press, 1965, 59–83.

Daybell, James. "'I wold wyshe my doings myght be...secret': Privacy and the Social Practices of Reading Women's Letters in Sixteenth-Century England." In Jane Couchman and Ann Crabb (eds), *Women's Letters across Europe, 1400–1700: Form and Persuasion*. Aldershot and Burlington, Vt.: Ashgate, 2005, 143–61.

—— "'Suche newes as on the Quenes hye wayes we have mett': The News and Intelligence Networks of Elizabeth Talbot, Countess of Shrewsbury (c.1527–1608)." In James Daybell (ed.), *Women and Politics in Early Modern England, 1450–1700*. Aldershot and Burlington, Vt.: Ashgate, 2004, 114–28.

—— ed. *Women and Politics in Early Modern England, 1450–1700*. Aldershot and Burlington, Vt.: Ashgate, 2004.

—— *Women Letter Writers in Tudor England*. Oxford: Oxford University Press, 2006.

—— "Women, Politics and Domesticity: The Scribal Publication of Lady Rich's Letter to Elizabeth I." In Anne Lawrence-Mathers and Phillipa Hardman (eds), *Women and Writing, 1340–1650: The Domestication of Print Culture*. Woodbridge: York Medieval, 2010, 111–30.

—— "Women's Letters of Recommendation and the Rhetoric of Friendship in Sixteenth-Century England." In Jennifer Richards and Alison Thorne (eds), *Rhetoric, Women and Politics in Early Modern England*. London and New York: Routledge, 2007, 172–90.

Dean, William. "Henry Oxinden's Key (1628) to *The Countess of Pembroke's Arcadia*: Some Facts and Conjectures." *Sidney Newsletter and Journal*, 12/2 (1993): 14–21.

De Bom, Erik, ed. (*Un)masking the Realities of Power: Justus Lipsius and the Dynamics of Political Writing in Early Modern Europe*. Leiden and Boston: Brill, 2011.

DeZur, Kathryn. *Gender, Interpretation and Political Rule in Sidney's Arcadia*. Newark: University of Delaware Press, 2013.

Dickens, A. G. "The Writers of Tudor Yorkshire." *Transactions of the Royal Historical Society*, 5th ser. 13 (1963): 49–76.

Drennan, W. R. "'Or Know Your Strengths': Sidney's Attitude toward Rebellion in 'Ister Banke.'" *Notes and Queries*, 231 (1986): 339–40.

Dobell, Bertram. "New Light Upon Sir Philip Sidney's *Arcadia*." *Quarterly Review*, 211 (1909): 74–100.

Dobranski, Stephen. *Readers and Authorship in Early Modern England*. Cambridge and New York: Cambridge University Press, 2005.

Donnelly, M. L. "Saving the King's Friend and Redeeming Appearances: Dr. Donne Constructs a Scriptural Model for Patronage." In Cedric C. Brown (ed.), *Patronage, Politics and Literary Traditions in England, 1558–1658*. Detroit: Wayne State University Press, 1991, 79–92.

Duncan-Jones, Katherine. "Notable Accessions: Western Manuscripts." *Bodleian Library Record*, 15 (1996): 308–14.

—— *Philip Sidney: Courtier Poet*. New Haven: Yale University Press, 1991.

—— "Sidney in Samothea: A Forgotten National Myth." *Review of English Studies*, NS 25/98 (May 1974): 174–7.

—— "Sidney's Personal Imprese." *Journal of the Warburg and Courtauld Institutes*, 33 (1970): 321–4.

Dutton, Richard. *Licensing, Censorship and Authorship in Early Modern England*. Basingstoke and New York: Palgrave Macmillan, 2000.

Eckhardt, Joshua. *Manuscript Verse Collectors and the Politics of Anti-Courtly Love Poetry*. Oxford and New York: Oxford University Press, 2009.

Elsky, Martin. "Microhistory and Cultural Geography: Ben Jonson's 'To Sir Robert Wroth' and the Absorption of Local Community in the Commonwealth." *Renaissance Quarterly*, 53/2 (Summer 2000): 500–28.

Elton, G. R. "Tudor Government: The Points of Contact: III. The Court." *Transactions of the Royal Historical Society*, 5th ser. 26 (1976): 211–28.

Empson, William. "Donne the Space Man." *Kenyon Review* 19.3 (1957): 337–399.

Erickson, Amy Louise. *Women and Property in Early Modern England*. London and New York: Routledge, 1993.

Evans, Robert C. *Ben Jonson and the Poetics of Patronage*. Lewisburg, Pa.: Bucknell University Press; London: Associated University Presses, 1989.

Ezell, Margaret J. M. "Reading Pseudonyms in Seventeenth-Century English Coterie Literature." *Essays in Literature*, 21/1 (1994): 14–25.

—— *Social Authorship and the Advent of Print*. Baltimore and London: Johns Hopkins University Press, 1999.

—— " 'To Be Your Daughter in Your Pen': The Social Functions of Literature in the Writings of Lady Elizabeth Brackley and Lady Jane Cavendish." In S. P. Cerasano and Marion Wynne-Davies (eds), *Readings in Renaissance Women's Drama*. New York and London: Routledge, 1998, 246–58.

Farber, Elizabeth. "The Letters of Lady Elizabeth Russell (1540–1609)." Ph.D. diss. Columbia University, 1977.

Ferguson, Arthur B. *The Articulate Citizen and the English Renaissance*. Durham, NC: Duke University Press, 1965.

Ferguson, Moira. *First Feminists: British Women Writers 1578–1799*. Bloomington, Ind.: Indiana University Press, 1985.

Fish, Stanley. "Is There a Text in This Class?" Reproduced in *The Stanley Fish Reader*, ed. H. Aram Veeser. Malden, MA, and Oxford: Blackwell, 1999, 38–54.

Fleming, David. "Barclays Satyricon: The First Satirical Roman à Clef." *Modern Philology*, 65 (1967): 95–102.

Fleming, Juliet. "The Ladies' Man and the Age of Elizabeth." In James Grantham Turner (ed.), *Sexuality and Gender in Early Modern Europe: Institutions, Texts, Images*. Cambridge: Cambridge University Press, 1993, 158–81.

Flynn, Dennis. *John Donne and the Ancient Catholic Nobility*. Bloomington, Ind., and Indianapolis: Indiana University Press, 1995.

Fogel, Ephim G. "The Personal References in the Fiction and Poetry of Sir Philip Sidney." Diss. Ohio State University, 1958.

Forster, G. C. F. "Faction and County Government in Early Stuart Yorkshire." *Northern History*, 11 (1976): 70–86.

—— "The North Riding Justices and their Sessions, 1603–1635." *Northern History*, 10 (1975): 102–25.

Fox Bourne, H. R. *Life of Sir Philip Sidney: Type of English Chivalry in the Elizabethan Age*. New York and London: G.P. Putnam & Sons, 1914 (first publ. 1891).

Franklin-Hudson, Ariel. " 'Louing Her Owne Will': The Countess of Bedford to Dudley Carleton." M.Res. Queen Mary, University of London, 2009.

Freedman, S. *Poor Penelope: Lady Penelope Rich, an Elizabethan Woman*. Abbotsbrook, Bourne End, Bucks.: Kensal Press, 1983.

Friedrich, Walter G. "The Stella of Astrophel." *English Literary History*, 3/2 (1936): 114–39.

Fumerton, Patricia. *Cultural Aesthetics: Renaissance Literature and the Practice of Social Ornament*. Chicago: University of Chicago Press, 1991.

Gallagher, Catherine. "Embracing the Absolute: The Politics of the Female Subject in Seventeenth-Century England." *Genders*, 1 (1988): 24–39.

Gardner, Helen L. "Notes on Donne's Verse Letters." *Modern Language Review*, 41/3 (1946): 318–21.

Garrett, Martin, ed. *Sidney: The Critical Heritage*. London and New York: Routledge, 1996.

Girouard, Mark. *Robert Smythson and the Architecture of the Elizabethan Era*. London: Country Life, 1966.

Goldberg, Jonathan. *Desiring Women Writing: English Renaissance Examples.* Stanford, Calif.: Stanford University Press, 1997.

—— *Sodometries: Renaissance Texts, Modern Sexualities.* Stanford, Calif.: Stanford University Press, 1992.

—— *Writing Matter: From the Hands of the English Renaissance.* Stanford, Calif.: Stanford University Press, 1990.

Goldie, Mark. "The Unacknowledged Republic: Officeholding in Early Modern England." In T. Harris (ed.), *The Politics of the Excluded, c.1500–1850.* Basingstoke: Palgrave, 2001, 153–94.

Goldman, Marcus S. *Sir Philip Sidney and the* Arcadia. Urbana, Ill.: University of Illinois, 1934.

Goldsmith, J. B. Greenbaum. "All the Queen's Women: The Changing Place and Perception of Aristocratic Women in Elizabethan England, 1558–1620." Ph.D. diss., Northwestern University, 1987.

Grafton, Anthony, and Lisa Jardine. *From Humanism to the Humanities: Education and the Liberal Arts in Fifteenth- and Sixteenth-Century Europe.* Cambridge, Mass.: Harvard University Press, 1986.

Green, Mary Anne Everett. *Elizabeth Electress Palatine and Queen of Bohemia.* London: Methuen, 1855.

Greenfield, Thelma N. *The Eye of Judgment: Reading the "New Arcadia."* Lewisburg, Pa.: Bucknell University Press, 1983.

Greenlaw, E. A. "Sidney's *Arcadia* as an Example of Elizabethan Allegory." *Anniversary Papers by Colleagues and Pupils of George Lyman Kittredge.* New York, 1913; repr. 1967, 327–37.

—— "The Captivity Episode in Sidney's *Arcadia.*" *The Manly Anniversary Studies in Language and Literature.* Chicago: University of Chicago Press, 1923, 54–63.

Grimble, Ian. *The Harington Family.* London: Jonathan Cape, 1957.

Guibbory, Achsah. " 'Oh, Let Mee Not Serve So': The Politics of Love in Donne's Elegies." *English Literary History,* 57/4 (Winter 1990): 811–33.

Guy, John. "The Rhetoric of Counsel in Early Modern England." In Dale Hoak (ed.), *Tudor Political Culture.* Cambridge: Cambridge University Press, 1995, 292–310.

Hackel, Heidi Brayman. " 'Boasting of Silence': Women Readers in a Patriarchal State." In Kevin Sharpe and Steven N. Zwicker (eds), *Reading, Society and Politics in Early Modern England.* Cambridge and New York: Cambridge University Press, 2003, 101–21.

—— *Reading Material in Early Modern England: Print, Gender, and Literacy.* Cambridge: Cambridge University Press, 2005.

Hackett, Helen. *Women and Romance Fiction in the English Renaissance.* Cambridge: Cambridge University Press, 2000.

—— " 'Yet tell me some such Fiction': Lady Mary Wroth's *Urania* and the 'Femininity' of Romance." In Clare Brant and Diane Purkiss (eds), *Women, Texts, and Histories 1575–1760.* New York: Routledge, 1992, 39–68.

Halewood, William H. *The Poetry of Grace: Reformation Themes and Structures in English Seventeenth Century Poetry*. New Haven: Yale University Press, 1970.

Halli, Jr., Robert W. "Cecilia Bulstrode, 'The Court Pucell.'" In David G. Allen and Robert A. White (eds), *Subjects on the World's Stage*. Newark: University of Delaware Press, 1995, 295–312.

Hamilton, A. C. *Sir Philip Sidney: His Life and Works*. Cambridge: Cambridge University Press, 1977.

Hamlin, Hannibal. "Psalm Culture in the English Renaissance: Readings of Psalm 137 by Shakespeare, Spenser, Milton, and Others." *Renaissance Quarterly*, 55/1 (Spring 2002): 224–57.

Hammer, Paul E. J. *Polarisation of Elizabethan Politics: The Political Career of Robert Devereux, 2nd Earl of Essex, 1585–1597*. Cambridge and New York: Cambridge University Press, 1999.

Hanford, James Holly, and Sara Ruth Watson, "Personal Allegory in the *Arcadia*: Philisides and Lelius." *Modern Philology*, 32/1 (August 1934): 1–10.

Hannay, Margaret P. "'Bearing the livery of your name': The Countess of Pembroke's Agency in Print and Scribal Publication." *Sidney Journal*, 18/1 (2000): 7–42.

—— "'Doo What Men May Sing': Mary Sidney and the Tradition of Admonitory Dedication." In Hannay (ed.), *Silent But for the Word*. Kent, Ohio: Kent State University Press, 1985, 149–65.

—— *Mary Sidney, Lady Wroth*. Aldershot and Burlington, Vt.: Ashgate, 2010.

—— *Philip's Phoenix: Mary Sidney, Countess of Pembroke*. New York: Oxford University Press, 1990.

—— "'Princes you as men must dy': Genevan Advice to Monarchs in the Psalms of Mary Sidney." *English Literary Renaissance*, 19 (1989): 22–41.

—— ed. *Silent But for the Word: Tudor Women as Patrons, Translators, and Writers of Religious Works*. Kent, Ohio: Kent State University Press, 1985.

—— "'This Moses and This Miriam': The Countess of Pembroke's Role in the Legend of Sir Philip Sidney." In M. J. B. Allen, Dominic Baker-Smith, Arthur F. Kinney, and Margaret Sullivan (eds), *Sir Philip Sidney's Achievements*. New York: AMS, 1990, 217–26.

—— "'Your vertuous and learned Aunt': The Countess of Pembroke as a Mentor to Mary Wroth." In Naomi Miller and Gary Waller (eds), *Reading Mary Wroth: Representing Alternatives in Early Modern England*. Knoxville, Tenn.: University of Tennessee Press, 1991, 15–34.

Harris, Barbara J. "Women and Politics in Early Tudor England." *Historical Journal*, 33/2 (1990): 259–81.

Haselkorn, Anne M., and Betty S. Travitsky, eds. *The Renaissance Englishwoman in Print: Counterbalancing the Canon*. Amherst, Mass.: University of Massachusetts Press, 1990.

Hay, Millicent V. *The Life of Robert Sidney, Earl of Leicester (1563–1626)*. Washington, DC: Folger Shakespeare Library, 1984.

Heal, Felicity. "Reputation and Honour in Court and Country: Lady Elizabeth Russell and Sir Thomas Hoby." *Transactions of the Royal Historical Society*, 6/6 (1996): 161–78.

Heinemann, Margot. *Puritanism and Theatre: Thomas Middleton and Opposition Drama Under the Early Stuarts*. Cambridge and New York: Cambridge University Press, 1980.

Helgerson, Richard. *Forms of Nationhood: The Elizabethan Writing of England*. Chicago: University of Chicago Press, 1992.

—— *Self-Crowned Laureates: Spenser, Jonson, Milton and the Literary System*. Berkeley: University of California Press, 1983.

Herbert, Anne. L. "Oakham Parish Library." *Library History*, 6 (1982–4): 1–11.

Herman, Peter C. " 'Bastard Children of Tyranny': The Ancient Constitution and Fulke Greville's "A Dedication to Sir Philip Sidney." *Renaissance Quarterly*, 55/3 (2002): 969–1004.

Herz, Judith Scherer. "Of Circles, Friendship, and the Imperatives of Literary History." In Claude J. Summers and Ted-Larry Pebworth (eds), *Literary Circles and Cultural Communities in Renaissance England*. Columbia, Mo., and London: University of Missouri Press, 2000, 10–23.

Hiller, Geoffrey. " 'Where Thou Doost Live, There Let All Graces Be': Images of the Renaissance Woman Patron in her House and Rural Domain." *Cahiers Elisabethains*, 40 (1991): 37–51.

Hirst, Derek. *Authority and Conflict: England, 1603–1658*. Cambridge, Mass.: Harvard University Press, 1986.

—— "Court, Country, and Politics Before 1629." In Kevin Sharpe (ed.), *Faction and Parliament: Essays on Early Stuart History*. Oxford: Clarendon, 1978, 105–37.

Howell, Roger. *Sir Philip Sidney. The Shepherd Knight*. London: Hutchinson, 1968.

—— "The Sidney Circle and the Protestant Cause." *Renaissance and Modern Studies*, 19 (1975): 31–46.

Hudson, Hoyt H. "Penelope Devereux as Sidney's Stella." *Huntington Library Bulletin*, 7 (April 1935): 89–129.

Hunt, Arnold. "The Books, Manuscripts and Literary Patronage of Mrs. Anne Sadleir (1585–1670)." In Victoria E. Burke and Jonathan Gibson (eds), *Early Modern Women's Manuscript Writing: Selected Papers from the Trinity/Trent Colloquium*. Burlington, Vt.: Ashgate, 2004, 205–36.

Hunt, William. *The Puritan Moment. The Coming of Revolution in an English County*. Cambridge, Mass.: Harvard University Press, 1983.

Hutson, Lorna. *The Usurer's Daughter: Male Friendship and Fictions of Women in Sixteenth-Century England*. London and New York: Routledge, 1994.

Ioppolo, Grace. " 'I desire to be held in your memory': Reading Penelope Rich through her Letters." In Dympna Callaghan (ed.), *The Impact of Feminism in English Renaissance Studies*. Basingstoke and New York: Palgrave Macmillan, 2007, 299–325.

Isler, Alan D. "Moral Philosophy and the Family in Sidney's *Arcadia*." *Huntington Library Quarterly*, 31/4 (1968): 359–71.

James Mervyn. *Society, Politics, and Culture: Studies in Early Modern England*. Cambridge and New York: Cambridge University Press, 1986.

Jardine, Lisa, and Anthony Grafton. "'Studied for Action': How Gabriel Harvey Read his Livy." *Past and Present*, 129 (1990): 30–78.

Jardine, Lisa, and William H. Sherman. "Pragmatic Readers: Knowledge Transactions and Scholarly Services in Late Elizabethan England." In Anthony Fletcher and Peter Roberts (eds), *Religion, Culture and Society in Early Modern Britain: Essays in Honour of Patrick Collinson*. Cambridge and New York: Cambridge University Press, 1994, 102–24.

Johnson, S. "Sir Henry Goodere and Donne's Letters." *Modern Language Notes*, 63/1 (1948): 38–43.

Justice, George, and Nathan Tinker, eds. *Women's Writing and the Circulation of Ideas: Manuscript Publication in England, 1550–1800*. Cambridge and New York: Cambridge University Press, 2002.

Kahn, Victoria. "Margaret Cavendish and the Romance of Contract." *Renaissance Quarterly*, 50/2 (1997): 526–66.

—— *Wayward Contracts: The Crisis of Political Obligation in England, 1640–1674*. Princeton: Princeton University Press, 2004.

Kettering, Sharon. "The Household Service of Early Modern French Noblewomen." *French Historical Studies*, 20/1 (1997): 55–85.

Keynes, Geoffrey. *A Bibliography of Dr. John Donne, Dean of Saint Paul's*. 4th edn. Oxford: Clarendon, 1973.

Klawitter, George. "John Donne and Salvation through Grace." In William P. Shaw (ed.), *Praise Disjoined: Changing Patterns of Salvation in Seventeenth-Century English Literature*. New York: Peter Lang, 1991, 137–49.

Knafla, Louis A. "Mr. Secretary Donne: The Years with Sir Thomas Egerton." In David Cloclough (ed.), *John Donne's Professional Lives*. Cambridge: D. S. Brewer, 2003, 37–71.

Krontiris, Tina. *Oppositional Voices: Women as Writers and Translators of Literature in the English Renaissance*. London and New York: Routledge, 1992.

Kunin, Aaron. "From the Desk of Anne Clifford." *English Literary History*, 71/3 (2004): 587–608.

Lake, Peter. "Matthew Hutton: A Puritan Bishop?" *History*, 64/211 (1979): 182–204.

—— "Feminine Piety and Personal Potency: The 'Emancipation' of Mrs. Jane Ratcliffe." *Seventeenth Century*, 2/2 (1987): 143–65.

Lamb, Mary Ellen. "Constructions of Women Readers." In Susanne Woods and Margaret P. Hannay (eds), *Teaching Tudor and Stuart Women Writers*. New York: Modern Language Association, 2000, 23–34.

—— *Gender and Authorship in the Sidney Circle*. Madison, Wis.: University of Wisconsin Press, 1990.

—— "Margaret Hoby's Diary: Women's Reading Practices and the Gendering of the Reformation Subject." In Sigrid King (ed.), *Pilgrimmage for Love: Essays in Early Modern Literature in Honour of Josephine A. Roberts*. Tempe, Ariz.: Center for Medieval and Renaissance Studies, 1999, 63–94.

—— "The Biopolitics of Romance in Mary Wroth's *The Countess of Montgomery's Urania*." *English Literary Renaissance*, 31/1 (2001): 107–30.

Lamb, Mary Ellen. "The Myth of the Countess of Pembroke: The Dramatic Circle." *Yearbook of English Studies*, 11 (1981): 194–202.

—— "The Sociality of Margaret Hoby's Reading Practices and the Representation of Reformation Interiority." *Critical Survey*, 12/2 (2000): 17–32.

——. "Women Readers in Mary Wroth's *Urania*." In Naomi Miller and Gary Waller (eds), *Reading Mary Wroth: Representing Alternatives in Early Modern England*. Knoxville, Tenn.: University of Tennessee Press, 1991, 210–27.

Lander, Jesse. *Inventing Polemic: Religion, Print, and Literary Culture in Early Modern England*. Cambridge: Cambridge University Press, 2006.

Lawry, Jon S. *Sidney's Two "Arcadias": Pattern and Proceeding*. Ithaca, NY, and London: Cornell University Press, 1972.

Lawson, Lesley. *Out of the Shadows: The Life of Lucy, Countess of Bedford*. Hambledon: Continuum, 2007.

Lee, Jongsook. "Who Is Cecilia, What Was She? Cecilia Bulstrode and Jonson's Epideictics." *Journal of English and Germanic Philology*, 85/1 (1986): 20–34.

Leishman, J. B. *The Monarch of Wit: An Analytical and Comparative Study of the Poetry of John Donne*. London: Hutchinson, 1962.

Lewalski, Barbara. "Lucy, Countess of Bedford: Images of a Jacobean Courtier and Patroness." In Kevin Sharpe and Steven N. Zwicker (eds), *Politics of Discourse: The Literature and History of Seventeenth-Century England*. Berkeley and Los Angeles: University of California Press, 1987, 52–77.

—— *Writing Women in Jacobean England*. Cambridge, Mass.: Harvard University Press, 1993.

Lever, Tresham. *The Herberts of Wilton*. London: John Murray, 1967.

Levy, F. J. "Francis Bacon and the Style of Politics." In Arthur F. Kinney and Dan S. Collins (eds), *Renaissance Historicism: Selections from English Literary Renaissance*. Amherst, Mass.: University of Massachusetts Press, 1987.

—— "How Information Spread among the Gentry, 1550–1640." *Journal of British Studies*, 21 (1982): 11–34.

—— "Staging the News." In Arthur F. Marotti and Michael D. Bristol (eds), *Print, Manuscript, Performance: The Changing Relations of the Media in Early Modern England*. Columbus: Ohio State University Press, 2000, 252–78.

Lindheim, Nancy. *Structures of Sidney's Arcadia*. Toronto and Buffalo, NY: University of Toronto Press, 1982.

Lloyd, David. *State-Worthies: Or, the statesmen and favourites of England from the Reformation to the Revolution. Their Prudence and Policies, Successes and Miscarriages, Advancements and Falls*. 2 vols. London: printed for J. Robson, Bookseller to her Royal Highness the Princess Dowager of Wales, in New Bond-Street, 1766.

Lockey, Brian C. *Law and Empire in English Renaissance Literature*. Cambridge and New York: Cambridge University Press, 2006.

Lockyer, Roger. *Buckingham, the Life and Political Career of George Villiers, First Duke of Buckingham, 1592–1628*. London and New York: Longman, 1981.

Logan, George M. "Daniel's Civil Wars and Lucan's *Pharsalia*." *Studies in English Literature*, 11/1 (Winter 1971): 53–68.

Longley, Katharine M. "Blessed George Errington and Companions: Fresh Evidence." *Recusant History*, 19/1 (1988): 39–46.

Love, Harold. *Scribal Publication in Seventeenth-Century England*. Oxford: Clarendon Press, 1993.

Lucas, Caroline. *Writing for Women: The Example of Women as Readers in Elizabethan Romance*. Milton Keynes: Open University Press, 1989.

Luckyj, Christina. "*A Mouzell for Melastomus* in Context: Rereading the Swetnam–Speght Debate." *English Literary Renaissance*, 40/1 (2010): 113–31.

—— "The Politics of Genre in Early Women's Writing: The Case of Lady Mary Wroth." *English Studies in Canada*, 27/3 (2001): 253–82.

Lynch, Katherine A. *Individuals, Families and Communities in Europe, 1200–1800*. Cambridge: Cambridge University Press, 2003.

MacCaffrey, Wallace. "Place and Patronage in Elizabethan Politics." In S.T. Brudoff, J. Hurstfield, and C. H. Williams (eds), *Elizabethan Government and Society: Essays Presented to Sir John Neale*. London: Athlone Press, 1961, 95–126.

MacCarthy, Bridget. *Women Writers: Their Contribution to the English Novel, 1621–1744*. Dublin: Cork University Press, 1964.

McCoy, Richard. *Sir Philip Sidney: Rebellion in Arcadia*. New Brunswick, NJ: Rutgers University Press, 1979.

—— *The Rites of Knighthood: The Literature and Politics of Elizabethan Chivalry*. Berkeley: University of California Press, 1989.

McCrea, Adriana. *Constant Minds: Political Virtue and the Lipsian Paradigm in England, 1584–1650*. Toronto: University of Toronto Press, 1997.

Macfarlane, Alan. *Reconstructing Historical Communities*. Cambridge: Cambridge University Press, 1977.

McGann, Jerome. "The Socialization of Texts." Reprinted in David Finkelstein and Alistair McCleery (eds), *The Book History Reader*. London and New York: Routledge, 2002, 39–46.

McKitterick, David. *Print, Manuscript and the Search for Order, 1450–1830*. Cambridge; New York: Cambridge University Press, 2003.

McKitterick, David. "Women and their Books in Seventeenth-Century England: The Case of Elizabeth Puckering." *The Library*, 7th ser. 1 (December 2000): 359–80.

Marchant, Ronald A. *The Puritans and the Church Courts in the Diocese of York 1560–1642*. London: Longman's, 1960.

Marcus, Leah. "Politics and Pastoral: Writing the Court on the Countryside." In Kevin Sharpe and Peter Lake (eds), *Culture and Politics in Early Stuart England*. Stanford, Calif.: Stanford University Press, 1993, 139–59.

Margetts, Michele. "Lady Penelope Rich: Hilliard's Lost Miniatures and a Surviving Portrait." *Burlington Magazine*, 130/1027 (1988): 758–61.

—— "Stella Britanna: The Early Life (1563–1592) of Lady Penelope Devereux, Lady Rich (d. 1607)." Ph.D. diss., Yale University, 1993.

—— "'The wayes of mine owne hart': The Dating and Mind Frame of Essex's 'fantasticall' letter." *Bodleian Library Record*, 16 (1997): 101–10.

Marotti, Arthur F. *John Donne: Coterie Poet*. Madison, Wis.: University of Wisconsin Press, 1986.

—— "'Love is not Love': Elizabethan Sonnet Sequences and the Social Order." *English Literary History*, 49/2 (1982): 396–428.

Marotti, Arthur F. *Manuscript, Print and the English Renaissance Lyric.* Ithaca, NY: Cornell University Press, 1995.

—— "The Social Context and Nature of Donne's Writing: Occasional Verse and Letters." In Achsah Guibbory (ed.), *The Cambridge Companion to John Donne.* Cambridge: Cambridge University Press, 2006, 35–48.

Marshall, Peter. *The Face of the Pastoral Ministry in the East Riding, 1525–1595.* [York]: Borthwick Institute of Historical Research, University of York, 1995.

Masten, Jeffrey. "'Shall I turne blabb?' Circulation, Gender and Subjectivity in Mary Wroth's Sonnets." In Naomi Miller and Gary Waller (eds), *Reading Mary Wroth: Representing Alternatives in Early Modern England.* Knoxville, Tenn.: University of Tennessee Press, 1991, 67–87.

Maurer, Margaret. "John Donne's Verse Letters." *Modern Language Quarterly,* 37 (1976): 234–59.

—— "Samuel Daniel's Poetical Epistles, Especially those to Sir Thomas Egerton and Lucy, Countess of Bedford." *Studies in Philology,* 74 (1977): 418–44.

—— "The Real Presence of Lucy Russell, Countess of Bedford, and the Terms of John Donne's 'Honour is so sublime perfection.'" *English Literary History,* 47/2 (1980): 205–34.

May, Steven W. *The Elizabethan Courtier Poets: The Poems and their Contexts.* Columbia, Mo., and London: University of Missouri Press, 1991.

Mears, Natalie. "Politics in the Elizabethan Privy Chamber: Lady Mary Sidney and Kat Ashley." In James Daybell (ed.), *Women and Politics in Early Modern England, 1450–1700.* Aldershot and Burlington, Vt.: Ashgate, 2004, 67–82.

—— *Queenship and Political Discourse in the Elizabethan Realms.* Cambridge and New York: Cambridge University Press, 2005.

Mendelson, Sara Heller. "Stuart Women's Diaries and Occasional Memoirs." In Mary Prior (ed.), *Women in English Society, 1500–1800.* London and New York: Methuen, 1985, 181–210.

Merton, Charlotte. "The Women Who Served Queen Mary and Queen Elizabeth: Ladies, Gentlewomen and Maids of the Privy Chamber, 1553–1603." Ph.D. diss., Cambridge University, 1992.

Miner, Earl. *The Cavalier Mode from Jonson to Cotton.* Princeton: Princeton University Press, 1971.

Mohr, Mary Hull. "Lucy Harington and John Donne: Reinterpreting a Relationship." In Dennis M. Jones (ed.), *A Humanist's Legacy: Essays in Honor of John Christian Bale.* Decorah, Iowa: Luther College Press, 1990, 49–62.

Monsarrat, Gilles D. *Light from the Porch: Stoicism and English Renaissance Literature.* Paris: Didier-Erudition, 1984.

Montrose, Louis. "Celebration and Insinuation: Sir Philip Sidney and the Motives of Elizabethan Courtship." *Renaissance Drama,* ns 8 (1977): 3–35.

—— "Of Gentlemen and Shepherds: The Politics of Elizabethan Pastoral Form." *English Literary History,* 50/3 (1983): 415–59.

Moore, Dennis. "Philisides and Mira: Autobiographical Allegory in the *Old Arcadia.*" *Spenser Studies,* 3 (1982): 125–37.

Morgan, Florence Humphrey. "A Biography of Lucy Countess of Bedford, The Last Great Literary Patroness." Ph.D. diss., University of Southern California, 1956.

Morgan, Paul. "Frances Wolfreston and 'Hor Bouks': A Seventeenth Century Woman Book-Collector." *The Library*, 6th ser. 11 (September 1989): 197–219.

Milward, Peter. *Religious Controversies of the Elizabethan Age: A Survey of Printed Sources*. With a Foreword by G. R. Elton. London: Scolar Press, 1977.

Morrill, J. S. "William Davenport and the 'Silent Majority' of Early Stuart England." *Journal of the Chester Archaeological Society*, 58 (1975): 115–29.

Mueller, Janel. "Women among the Metaphysicals: A Case, Mostly, of Being Donne for." In Arthur F. Marotti (ed.), *Critical Essays on John Donne*. New York: G. K. Hall, 1994, 37–48.

Mueller, William R. *John Donne: Preacher*. New York: Octagon Books, 1977.

Munden, R. C. "James I and 'the growth of mutual distrust': King, Commons, and Reform, 1603–1604." In Kevin Sharpe (ed.), *Faction and Parliament: Essays on Early Stuart History*. Oxford: Clarendon, 1978, 43–72.

Newdigate, Bernard H. *Michael Drayton and his Circle*. Oxford: Shakespeare Head Press, 1941.

Newman, Christine M. "'An Honourable and Elect Lady': The Faith of Isabel, Lady Bowes." In Diana Wood (ed), *Life and Thought in the Northern Church*. 1100–1700. Studies in Church History. Subsidia 12. Woodbridge, Suffolk, 1999, 407–19.

Norbrook, David. "The Monarchy of Wit and the Republic of Letters: Donne's Politics." In Elizabeth D. Harvey and Katharine Eisaman Maus (eds), *Soliciting Interpretation: Literary Theory and Seventeenth-Century English Poetry*. Chicago: University of Chicago Press, 1990, 3–36.

—— *Poetry and Politics in the English Renaissance*. Oxford: Oxford University Press, 2002.

—— "Lucan, Thomas May, and the Creation of a Republican Literary Culture." In Kevin Sharpe and Peter Lake (eds), *Culture and Politics in Early Stuart England*. Stanford, Calif.: Stanford University Press, 1993, 45–66.

—— "The Masque of Truth:" Court Entertainments and International Protestant Politics in the Early Stuart Period." *Seventeenth Century*, 1 (1986): 81–110.

O'Callaghan, Michelle, *The 'Shepheard's Nation': Jacobean Spenserians and Early Stuart Political Culture 1612–1625*. Oxford: Clarendon; New York: Oxford University Press, 2000.

O'Connor, Marion. "Godly Patronage: Lucy Harington Russell, Countess of Bedford." In Johanna Harris and Elizabeth Scott-Baumann (eds), *The Intellectual Culture of Puritan Women, 1558–1680*. Basingstoke and New York: Palgrave Macmillan, 2011, 71–83.

Oestreich, Gerhard. *Neostoicism and the Early Modern State*, ed. Brigitta Oestreich and H. G. Koenigsberger; tr. David McLintock. Cambridge and New York: Cambridge University Press, 1982.

Oh, Elisa. "'[T]he art to desifer the true Caracter of Constancy': Female Silence in Wroth's *Urania*." *Early Modern Women: An Interdisciplinary Journal*, 5 (2010): 45–75.

Oliver, P. M. *Donne's Religious Writing: A Discourse of Feigned Devotion*. New York: Longman, 1997.

Orgis, Rachel. "'[A] story very well woorth readinge': Why Early Modern Readers Valued Lady Mary Wroth's *Urania*." *Sidney Journal*, 31/1 (2013): 81–100.

Orlin, Lena. "Gertrude's Closet." *Shakespeare-Jahrbuch*, 134 (1998): 44–67.

Parry, Graham. *The Golden Age Restor'd: The Culture of the Stuart Court, 1603-42*. New York: St Martin's Press, 1981.

Patterson, Annabel. "All Donne." In Elizabeth D. Harvey and Katharine Eisaman Maus (eds), *Soliciting Interpretation: Literary Theory and Seventeenth-Century English Poetry*. Chicago: University of Chicago Press, 1990, 37–67.

—— *Censorship and Interpretation: The Conditions of Writing and Reading in Early Modern England*. Madison, Wis.: University of Wisconsin Press, 1984.

—— "John Donne, Kingsman?" In Linda Levy Peck (ed.), *The Mental World of the Jacobean Court*. Cambridge and New York: Cambridge University Press, 1991, 251–72.

—— "'Under…Pretty Tales': Intention in Sidney's Arcadia." *Studies in the Literary Imagination*, 15/1 (Spring 1982): 5–21.

Parker, Patricia. *Inescapable Romance: Studies in the Poetics of a Mode*. Princeton: Princeton University Press, 1979.

—— *Literary Fat Ladies: Rhetoric, Gender, Property*. London: Methuen, 1987.

Payne, Helen. "Aristocratic Women, Power, Patronage and Family Networks at the Jacobean Court, 1603–1635." In James Daybell (ed.), *Women and Politics in Early Modern England, 1450–1700*. Aldershot and Burlington, Vt.: Ashgate, 2004, 164–80.

Pearson, A. F. Scott, *Thomas Cartwright and Elizabethan Puritanism, 1535–1603*. Cambridge: Cambridge University Press, 1925.

Pebworth, Ted-Larry. "'Let Me Here Use That Freedom': Subversive Representation in John Donne's 'Obsequies to the Lord Harington.'" *Journal of English and Germanic Philology*, 91/1 (1992): 17–42.

Pebworth, Ted-Larry, and Claude J. Summers. "'Thus Friends Absent Speake': The Exchange of Verse Letters between John Donne and Henry Wotton." *Modern Philology*, 81/4 (1984): 361–77.

Peck, Linda Levy. "Benefits, Brokers and Beneficiaries: The Culture of Exchange in Seventeenth-Century England." In Bonnelyn Young Kunze and Dwight D. Brautigam (eds), *Court, Country, and Culture: Essays on Early Modern British History in Honor of Perez Zagorin*. Rochester, NY: University of Rochester Press, 1992, 109–27.

—— *Court Patronage and Court Corruption in Early Stuart England*. London: Unwin Hyman, 1990.

Peltonen, Markku. *Classical Humanism and Republicanism in English Political Thought, 1570–1640*. Cambridge and New York: Cambridge University Press, 1995.

Perry, Curtis. "The Uneasy Republicanism of Thomas Kyd's *Cornelia*." *Criticism*, 48/4 (September 2006): 535–55.

—— *Literature and Favoritism in Early Modern England.* Cambridge and New York: Cambridge University Press, 2006.

Peters, Belinda Roberts. *Marriage in Seventeenth-Century Political Thought.* Houndmills and New York: Palgrave Macmillan, 2004.

Pitcher, John. *Samuel Daniel: The Brotherton Manuscript: A Study in Authorship.* Leeds Texts and Monographs, 7. Leeds: University of Leeds School of English, 1982.

Pocock, J. G. A. *Ancient Constitution and the Feudal Law: A Study of English Historical Thought in the Seventeenth Century: A Reissue with a Retrospect.* Cambridge and New York: Cambridge University Press, 1987.

Potter, Lois. *Secret Rites and Secret Writing: Royalist Literature, 1641–1660.* Cambridge and New York: Cambridge University Press, 1989.

Purvis, J. S., ed. *Tudor Parish Documents of the Diocese of York.* Cambridge and New York: Cambridge University Press, 1948.

Quilligan, Maureen. *Incest and Agency in Elizabeth's England.* Philadelphia: University of Pennsylvania Press, 2005.

—— "The Constant Subject: Instability and Authority in Wroth's *Urania* Poems." In Elizabeth Harvey and Katharine Maus (eds), *Soliciting Interpretation: Literary Theory and Seventeenth-Century English Poetry.* Chicago: University of Chicago Press, 1990, 307–35.

Quint, David. *Epic and Empire: Politics and Generic Form from Virgil to Milton.* Princeton: Princeton University Press, 1993.

Rackin, Phyllis. "Misogyny is Everywhere." In Dympna Callaghan (ed.), *A Feminist Companion to Shakespeare.* Oxford: Blackwell, 2000, 42–56.

Raitiere, Martin N. *Faire Bitts: Sir Philip Sidney and Renaissance Political Theory.* Pittsburgh, Pa.: Duquesne University Press, 1984.

Rawson, Maud Stepney. *Penelope Rich and her Circle.* London: Hutchinson, 1911.

Raymond, Joad. "Irrational, Impractical and Unprofitable: Reading the News in Seventeenth-Century Britain." In Kevin Sharpe and Steven N. Zwicker (eds), *Reading, Society and Politics in Early Modern England.* Cambridge and New York: Cambridge University Press, 2003, 185–212.

Rebholz, Ronald A. *The Life of Fulke Greville, Lord Brooke.* Oxford: Clarendon Press, 1971.

Reid, R. R. (Rachel Robertson). *The King's Council in the North.* London: Longmans, Green & Co., 1921.

Ribeiro, Alvaro. "Sir John Roe: Ben Jonson's Friend." *Review of English Studies,* ns 24/94 (May 1973): 153–64.

Ribner, I. "Sir Philip Sidney on Civil Insurrection." *Journal of the History of Ideas,* 13 (1952): 257–65.

Riggs, David. *Ben Jonson: A Life.* Cambridge, Mass.: Harvard University Press, 1989.

Roberts, Josephine A. "An Unpublished Literary Quarrel Concerning the Suppression of Mary Wroth's *Urania* (1621)." *Notes and Queries,* NS 24 (1977): 532–5.

—— "The Biographical Problem of *Pamphilia to Amphilanthus.*" *Tulsa Studies in Women's Literature,* 1/1 (Spring 1982): 43–53.

Roberts, Josephine A. "The Imaginary Epistles of Sir Philip Sidney and Lady Penelope Rich (with Texts)." *English Literary Renaissance*, 15/1 (1985): 59–77.

—— " 'The Knott Never to Bee Untide': The Controversy Regarding Marriage in Mary Wroth's Urania." In Naomi J. Miller and Gary Waller (eds), *Reading Mary Wroth: Representing Alternatives in Early Modern England*. Knoxville, Tenn.: University of Tennessee Press, 1991, 109–32.

Roberts, Sasha. "Shakespeare 'Creepes into the Womens Closets about Bedtime': Women Reading in a Room of their Own." In Gordon McMullan (ed.), *Renaissance Configurations: Voices/Bodies/ Spaces, 1580–1690*. New York: Palgrave Macmillan, 1998, 30–63.

Robertson, Karen. "Tracing Women's Connections from a Letter by Elizabeth Ralegh." In Susan Frye and Karen Robertson (eds), *Maids and Mistresses, Cousins and Queens: Women's Alliances in Early Modern England*. New York: Oxford University Press, 1999, 149–64.

Rose, Mark. *Heroic Love: Studies in Sidney and Spenser*. Cambridge, Mass.: Harvard University Press, 1968.

Rose, Mary Beth. *Gender and Heroism in Early Modern English Literature*. Chicago: Chicago University Press, 2002.

Rowe, Kenneth Thorpe. "The Countess of Pembroke's Editorship of the *Arcadia*." *PMLA*, 54/1 (1939): 122–38.

—— "The Love of Sir Philip Sidney for the Countess of Pembroke." *Papers of the Michigan Academy of Science, Arts, and Letters*, 25 (1939): 579–95.

Rowlands, Marie B. "Recusant Women, 1560–1640." In Mary Prior (ed.), *Women in English Society, 1500–1800*. London: Methuen, 1985, 149–80.

Ruff, Lillian M., and D. Arnold Wilson, "The Madrigal, The Lute Song, and Elizabethan Politics." *Past and Present*, 44 (August 1969): 3–51.

Salmon, J. H. M. "Stoicism and Roman Example: Seneca and Tacitus in Jacobean England." *Journal of the History of Ideas*, 50/2 (1989): 199–225.

Salzman, Paul. "Contemporary References in Mary Wroth's *Urania*." *Review of English Studies*, 29 (1978): 178–81.

—— *English Prose Fiction, 1558–1700: A Critical History*. Oxford: Clarendon Press, 1985.

—— "The Strang[e] Constructions of Mary Wroth's 'Urania': Arcadian Romance and the Public Realm." In Neil Rhodes (ed.), *English Renaissance Prose: History, Language and Politics*. Tempe, Ariz.: Medieval and Renaissance Texts and Studies, 1997, 110–24.

Sanchez, Melissa A. *Erotic Subjects: The Sexuality of Politics in Early Modern English Literature*. Oxford and New York: Oxford University Press, 2011.

Sandy, Amelia Zurcher. "Pastoral, Temperance, and the Unitary Self in Wroth's *Urania*." *Studies in English Literature*, 42/1 (2002): 103–19.

Saunders, J. W. "The Stigma of Print: A Note on the Social Bases of Tudor Poetry." *Essays in Criticism*, 1 (1951): 139–64.

Schleiner, Louise. *Tudor and Stuart Women Writers*. Bloomington, Ind.: Indiana University Press, 1994.

Schurink, Fred. "'Like a hand in the Margine of a Booke': William Blount's Marginalia and the Politics of Sidney's *Arcadia*." *Review of English Studies*, 59/238 (February 2008): 1–24.

Scodel, Joshua. "The Medium is the Message: Donne's Satire 3, "To Sir W' (Sir More than Kisses) and the Ideologies of the Mean." *Modern Philology*, 90/4 (1993): 479–511.

Scott, Alison V. *Selfish Gifts: The Politics of Exchange and English Courtly Literature, 1580–1628*. Madison, NJ: Fairleigh Dickinson University Press, 2006.

Scott, Jonathan. *Algernon Sidney and the English Republic,1623–1677*. Cambridge and New York: Cambridge University Press, 1988.

Scott-Warren, Jason. "News, Sociability, and Bookbuying in Early Modern England: The Letters of Sir Thomas Cornwallis." *The Library*, 7th ser. 1 (December 2000): 381–402.

—— "Reconstructing Manuscript Networks: The Textual Transactions of Sir Stephen Powle." In Alexandra Shepard and Phil Whithington (eds), *Communities in Early Modern England: Networks, Place, Rhetoric*. Manchester and New York: Manchester University Press, 2000, 18–37.

—— *Sir John Harrington and the Book as Gift*. Oxford and New York: Oxford University Press, 2001.

Scribner, Bob. "Communities and the Nature of Power." In Bob Scribner (ed.), *Germany: A New Social and Economic History 1450–1630*. London: Arnold, 1996, vol. 1, 291–325.

Seaver, Paul S. *The Puritan Lectureships: The Politics of Religious Dissent, 1560–1662*. Stanford, Calif.: Stanford University Press, 1970.

Sedinger, Tracey. "Sidney's *New Arcadia* and the Decay of Protestant Republicanism." *SEL*, 47/1 (2007): 57–77.

Sellin, Paul R. *So Doth, So Is Religion: John Donne and Diplomatic Contexts in the Reformed Netherlands, 1619–1620*. Columbia, Mo.: University of Missouri Press, 1988.

—— "'Soldiers of One Army': John Donne and the Army of the States General as an International Protestant Crossroads." In Mary A. Papazian (ed.), *John Donne and the Protestant Reformation: New Perspectives*. Detroit: Wayne State University Press, 2003, 143–92.

Shackford, Martha Hale. "Samuel Daniel's Poetical 'Epistles,' Especially That to the Countess of Cumberland." *Studies in Philology*, 45/2 (April 1948): 180–95.

Shami, Jeanne. "Donne on Discretion." *English Literary History*, 47/1 (1980): 47–66.

Shannon, Laurie. *Sovereign Amity: Figures of Friendship in Shakespearean Contexts*. Chicago: University of Chicago Press, 2002.

Sharpe, Kevin, ed. *Faction and Parliament: Essays on Early Stuart History*. Oxford: Clarendon, 1978.

—— *Reading Revolutions: The Politics of Reading in Early Modern England*. New Haven: Yale University Press, 2000.

Sharpe, Kevin, and Peter Lake, eds. *Culture and Politics in Early Stuart England*. Stanford, Calif.: Stanford University Press, 1993.

Sharpe, Kevin and Steven N. Zwicker, eds. *Reading, Society and Politics in Early Modern England*. Cambridge and New York: Cambridge University Press, 2003.

Shephard, Robert. "The Political Commonplace Books of Sir Robert Sidney." *Sidney Journal*, 21 (2003): 1–30.

Sherman, William H. *John Dee: The Politics of Reading and Writing in the English Renaissance*. Amherst, Mass.: University of Massachusetts Press, 1995.

—— *Used Books: Marking Readers in Renaissance England*. Philadelphia: University of Pennsylvania Press, 2008.

Shifflett, Andrew. *Stoicism, Politics and Literature in the Age of Milton: War and Peace Reconciled*. Cambridge and New York: Cambridge University Press, 1998.

Shuger, Deborah. "Castigating Livy: The Rape of Lucretia and the *Old Arcadia*." *Renaissance Quarterly*, 51/2 (Summer 1998): 526–48.

Sinfield, Alan. "Power and Ideology: An Outline Theory and Sidney's *Arcadia*." *English Literary History*, 52 (1985): 259–78.

Skretkowicz, Victor. "Algernon Sidney and Philip Sidney: A Continuity of Rebellion." *Sidney Journal*, 17 (1999): 3–18.

—— "'A More Lively Monument': *Philisides in Arcadia*." In M. J. B Allen, Dominic Baker-Smith, Arthur Kinney, and Margaret Sullivan (eds), *Sir Philip Sidney's Achievements*. New York: AMS, 1990, 194–200.

—— *European Erotic Romance: Philhellene Protestantism, Renaissance Translation and English Literary Politics*. Manchester: Manchester University Press, 2009.

—— "Mary Sidney Herbert's *Antonius*, English Philhellenism and the Protestant Cause." *Women's Writing*, 6 (1999): 7–25.

Smith, Barbara. *The Women of Ben Jonson's Poetry*. Aldershot: Scolar Press, 1995.

Smith, Charlotte Fell. *Mary Rich, Countess of Warwick (1625–78): Her Family and Friends*. London and New York: Longmans, Green, & Co., 1901.

Smith, J. L. "Music and Late Elizabethan Politics: The Identities of Oriana and Diana." *Journal of the American Musicological Society*, 58/3 (2005): 507–58.

Smith, Rosalind. "'I thus goe arm'd to field': Lindamira's Complaint." In Jo Wallwork and Paul Salzman (eds), *Women' Writing 1550–1750*. Melbourne: Meridian, 2001, 73–85.

—— *Sonnets and the English Woman Writer, 1560–1621: The Politics of Absence*. New York: Palgrave, 2005.

Smuts, Malcom. "Court Centered Politics and the Uses of Roman Historians." In Kevin Sharpe and Peter Lake (eds), *Culture and Politics in Early Stuart England*. London: Macmillan; Stanford, Calif.: Stanford University Press, 1993, 21–44.

Snow, Vernon F. "Essex and the Aristocratic Opposition to the Early Stuarts." *Journal of Modern History*, 32/3 (September 1960): 224–33.

Sommerville, J. P. "Absolutism and Royalism." In J. H. Burns and Mark Goldie (eds), *Cambridge History of Political Thought, 1450–1700*. Cambridge and New York: Cambridge University Press, 1996, 347–73.

Sprunger, Keith L. *The Learned Doctor William Ames: Dutch Backgrounds of English and American Puritanism*. Urbana, Ill.: University of Illinois Press, 1972.

Stachniewski, John. "John Donne: the Despair of the Holy Sonnets." *English Literary History*, 48/4 (1981): 677–705.

Stagen, Ruth M. "Lucy, Countess of Bedford." MA thesis, Columbia University, 1937.

Stevenson, Jane. "Mildred Cecil, Lady Burleigh: Poetry, Politics, and Protestantism." In Victoria E. Burke and Jonathan Gibson (eds), *Early Modern Women's Manuscript Writing: Selected Papers from the Trinity/Trent Colloquium*. Burlington, Vt.: Ashgate, 2004, 51–73.

Stewart, Alan. "The Early Modern Closet Discovered." *Representations*, 50 (1995): 76–100.

Stillman, Robert. "The Politics of Sidney's Pastoral: Mystification and Mythology in the *Old Arcadia*." *English Literary History*, 52/4 (1985): 795–814.

Stone, Lawrence. *Crisis of the Aristocracy, 1558–1641*. Oxford: Clarendon, 1965.

Strachan, Michael. *Sir Thomas Roe, 1581–1644*. Wilby, Norwich: Michael Russell, 1989.

Strier, Richard. "John Donne Awry and Squint: The Holy Sonnets, 1608–1610." *Modern Philology*, 86/4 (1989): 357–84.

—— "Radical Donne: 'Satire III.'" *English Literary History*, 60/2 (1993): 283–322.

Summers, Claude J. "Donne's 1609 Sequence of Grief and Comfort." *Studies in Philology*, 89 (1992): 211–31.

Summers, Claude J., and Ted-Larry Pebworth. "Donne's Correspondence with Wotton." *John Donne Journal*, 10 (1991): 1–36.

Summers, Claude J., and Ted-Larry Pebworth, eds. *Literary Circles and Cultural Communities in Renaissance England*. Columbia, Mo., and London: University of Missouri Press, 2000.

Tadmore, Naomi. "'In the even my wife read to me': Women, Reading and Household Life in the Eighteenth Century." In James Raven and Helen Small (eds), *The Practice and Representation of Reading in England*. Cambridge and New York: Cambridge University Press, 1996, 162–74.

Taylor Jr., Dick. "The Masque and the Lance: The Earl of Pembroke in Jacobean Court Entertainments." *Tulane Studies in English*, 8 (1958): 21–53.

Thomas, Keith. "Cases of Conscience in Seventeenth-Century England." In John Morrill, Paul Slack, and Daniel Woolf (eds), *Public Duty and Private Conscience in Seventeenth-Century England: Essays Presented to G. E. Aylmer*. Oxford, Clarendon, 1993, 29–56.

Thomson, Gladys Scott. *Life in a Noble Household, 1641–1700*. London: J. Cape, 1937.

—— *Two Centuries of Family History: A Study in Social Development*. London: Longmans, Green & Co., 1930.

Thomson, Patricia. "Donne and the Poetry of Patronage: The Verse Letters." In A. J. Smith (ed.), *John Donne: Essays in Celebration*. London: Methuen, 1972, 308–23.

Thomson, Patricia. "John Donne and the Countess of Bedford." *Modern Language Review*, 44 (1949): 329–40.

—— "The Literature of Patronage, 1580–1630." *Essays in Criticism*, 2/3 (1952): 267–84.

Tillyard, E. M. W. *The English Epic and its Background*. London: Chatto & Windus, 1954.

Tomlinson, Howard, ed. *Before the English Civil War: Essays on Early Stuart Politics and Government*. London: Macmillan Press, 1983.

Trafton, Dain A. "Politics and the Praise of Women: Political Doctrine in the Courtier's Third Book." In Robert Hanning and David Rosand (eds), *Castiglione: The Ideal and the Real in Renaissance Culture*. New Haven: Yale University Press, 1983, 29–44.

Tricomi, Albert. *Anticourt Drama in England, 1603–1642*. Charlottesville, Va.: University Press of Virginia, 1989.

—— "Philip, Earl of Pembroke, and the Analogical Way of Reading Political Tragedy." *Journal of English and Germanic Philology*, 85 (1986): 332–45.

Tuck, Richard. *Philosophy and Government 1572–1651*. Cambridge: Cambridge University Press, 1991.

Turner, Myron. "The Heroic Ideal in Sydney's Revised *Arcadia*." *Studies in English Literature*, 10/1 (Winter 1970), 63–82.

Van Dorsten, J. A. *Poets, Patrons and Professors: Sir Philip Sidney, Daniel Rogers and the Leiden Humanists*. Leiden: Published for the Sir Thomas Browne Institute at the University Press, 1962.

Varlow, Sally. *The Lady Penelope: The Lost Tale of Love and Politics in the Court of Elizabeth I*. London: André Deutsch, 2007.

Venn, J., and J. A. Venn, *Alumni Cantabrigienses, Part I: From the Earliest Times to 1751*. 4 vols. Cambridge: Cambridge University Press, 1922–7.

Wade, Mara R. "The Queen's Courts: Anna of Denmark and her Royal Sisters— Cultural Agency at Four Northern European Court in the Sixteenth and Seventeenth Centuries." In Clare McManus (ed.), *Women and Culture at the Courts of the Stuart Queens*. Houndmills and New York: Palgrave Macmillan, 2003, 49–80.

Wall, Wendy. "Circulating Texts in Early Modern England." In Susanne Woods and Margaret P. Hannay (eds), *Teaching Tudor and Stuart Women Writers*. New York: Modern Language Association, 2000, 35–51.

—— *The Imprint of Gender: Authorship and Publication in the English Renaissance*. Ithaca, NY: Cornell University Press, 1993.

Waller, Gary. *The Sidney Family Romance: Mary Worth, William Herbert, and the Early Modern Construction of Gender*. Detroit: Wayne State University Press, 1993.

Waller, Gary, and Michael D. Moore, eds. *Sir Philip Sidney and the Interpretation of Renaissance Culture: The Poet in his Time and in ours: A Collection of Critical and Scholarly Essays*. London: Croom Helm; Totowa, NJ: Barnes & Noble, 1984.

Walzer, Michael. *The Revolution of the Saints: A Study in the Origins of Radical Politics*. Cambridge, Mass.: Harvard University Press, 1965.

Warkentin, Germaine. "Humanism in Hard Times: The Second Earl of Leicester (1595–1677) and his Commonplace Books, 1630–60." In Ton Hoenselaars and Arthur F. Kinney (eds), *Challenging Humanism: Essays in Honor of Dominic Baker-Smith*. Newark: University of Delaware Press, 2005, 229–53.

—— "Sidney's Authors." In M. J. B. Allen, Dominic Baker-Smith, Arthur F. Kinney, and Margaret M. Sullivan (eds), *Sir Philip Sidney's Achievements*. New York: AMS, 1990, 68–90.

—— "The World and the Book at Penshurst: The Second Earl of Leicester and his Library." *The Library*, 20/4 (1998): 325–46.

Wedgwood, C. V. *The Thirty Years War*. New Haven: Yale University Press, 1949.

Werth, Tiffany Jo. *The Fabulous Dark Cloister Romance in England After the Reformation*. Baltimore: Johns Hopkins University Press, 2011.

Wheale, Nigel. *Writing and Society: Literacy, Print and Politics in Britain, 1590–1660*. London and New York: Routledge, 1999.

Whigham, Frank. *Ambition and Privilege: The Social Tropes of Elizabethan Courtesy Theory*. Berkeley: University of California Press, 1984.

White, Micheline, ed. *English Women, Religion, and Textual Production, 1500–1625*. Aldershot and Burlington, Vt.: Ashgate Press, 2010.

Wiffen, J. H., ed. *Historical Memoirs of the House of Russell*. 2 vols. London: Longman, Rees, Orme, Brown, Green, & Longman, 1833.

Williams, Franklin B. *Index of Dedications and Commendatory Verses in English Books before 1641*. London: Bibliographical Society, 1962.

Williams, Raymond. *Keywords: A Vocabulary of Culture and Society*. London: Fontana, 1976.

Williamson, George C. *Lady Anne Clifford, Countess of Dorset, Pembroke, and Montgomery, 1590–1676: Her Life, Letters, and Work*. Kendal: Titus Wilson & Son, 1922.

Willen, Diane. "Godly Women in Early Modern England: Puritanism and Gender." *Journal of Ecclesiastical History*, 43/4 (October 1992): 561–80.

Winship, Michael. "Bridget Cooke and the Art of Godly Female Self-Advancement." *Sixteenth Century Journal*, 32/4 (2002): 1045–59.

Wiseman, Susan. *Conspiracy and Virtue: Women, Writing, and Politics in Seventeenth Century England*. New York: Oxford University Press, 2006.

Withington, Phil, and Alexandra Shepard, eds. *Communities in Early Modern England: Networks, Place, Rhetoric*. Manchester: Manchester University Press, 2000.

Worden, Blair. "Republicanism, Regicide and Republic: The English Experience," In Martin van Gelderen and Quentin Skinner (eds), *Republicanism: A Shared European Heritage*, vol. 1. *Republicanism and Constitutionalism in Early Modern Europe*. Cambridge: Cambridge University Press, 2002.

—— *The Sound of Virtue: Philip Sidney's 'Arcadia' and Elizabethan Politics*. New Haven: Yale University Press, 1996.

Woudhuysen, H. R. *Sir Philip Sidney and the Circulation of Manuscripts, 1558–1640*. Oxford: Clarendon Press; New York: Oxford University Press, 1996.

Wright, Pam. "A Change in Direction: The Ramifications of Female Household, 1558–1603." In David Starkey (ed.), *The English Court: From the War of the Roses to the Civil War*. New York: Longman, 1987, 147–72.

Wynn-Davies, Marion. "'For Worth, Not Weakness, Makes in Use but One': Literary Dialogues in an English Renaissance Family." In Danielle Clarke and Elizabeth Clarke (eds), *"This Double Voice": Gendered Writing in Early Modern England*. New York: Macmillan Press, 2000, 164–84.

—— "'So much Worth as lives in you': Veiled Portraits of the Sidney Women." *Sidney Journal*, 14/1 (1996): 45–56.

Young, R. V. "Donne's Holy Sonnets and the Theology of Grace." In *John Donne's Poetry: A Norton Critical Edition*, ed. Donald R. Dickson. New York: Norton, 2007, 311–24.

Ziegler, Georgiana. "'More Than Feminine Boldness': The Gift Books of Esther Inglis." In Mary E. Burke, Jane Donawerth, Linda L. Dove, and Karen Nelson (eds), *Women, Writing and the Reproduction of Culture in Tudor and Stuart Britain*. Syracuse: Syracuse University Press, 2000, 24–5.

Zwicker, Steven N. "Reading the Margins: Politics and the Habits of Appropriation." In Kevin Sharpe and Steven N. Zwicker (eds), *Refiguring Revolutions: Aesthetics and Politics from the English Revolution to the Romantic Revolution*. Berkeley: University of California Press, 1998, 101–15.

Index